ISBN 978-0-282-98565-3
PIBN 10875731

1 MONTH OF
FREE
READING

at
www.ForgottenBooks.com

By purchasing this book you are eligible for one month membership to ForgottenBooks.com, giving you unlimited access to our entire collection of over 1,000,000 titles via our web site and mobile apps.

To claim your free month visit:

www.forgottenbooks.com/free875731

NERVOUS AND MENTAL DISEASE MONOGRAPH SERIES No. 58

WHO SHALL SURVIVE?

A New Approach to the Problem of Human Interrelations

by

J. L. MORENO, M.D.

Nervous and Mental Disease Publishing Co.

Washington, D. C.

1934

Dedicated
to
FANNIE FRENCH MORSE
Educator and Liberator
of Youth

The materials and illustrations in the book are drawn from institutions and schools. These institutions and schools are not responsible for the interpretations of the findings.

CONTENTS

PART IV

CONSTRUCTION AND RECONSTRUCTION OF GROUPS

INDEX TO CHARTS

FOREWORD

A CRUDE concept of structure thinks of it as composed of parts after the fashion of a mosaic. Such a construct could be expanded to any size because each of its parts is separate and distinct from the others and has nothing to do, no function to perform, with respect to them. Even biological structures have been thought of in this way, but the affairs of men are not so constituted. They are not static. They do not remain in any particular state but are ever changing, ever responding to the bombardment of forces which alter them in some way. One of the ways in which these affairs can be considered is after the analogy of the heart beat, ever-recurring diastoles and systoles. We might take as an example the function of administration. A small institution, say a hospital of one hundred or two hundred beds, is building. From the time it begins to function it begins to add here and there to its undertakings, and perhaps increases somewhat in size. It is a very simple matter to begin with to concentrate all these functions in a central office. We have the well known administrative unit centrally organized. But let this process of complexity and differentiation proceed a bit further. Let the extent of the increase, its operations, extend spatially further and further from the central office. It soon comes to be seen that an exclusively centralized administration has self-imposed limitations. The whole structure becomes so complicated that instant response to needs is no longer possible. These needs develop at some distance from the functional center of the institution, and unless there is someone at the point where these needs develop to respond to them adequately a disintegration of the administrative scheme begins. If this does not take place the needs are met by a beginning decentralization of administration, the locating of individuals at critical points throughout the institution with power to act when the necessity demands, the transferring to these subordinate centers of an increasing amount of responsibility as the institution begins to grow, and the building up of each one according to the same general principles involved in the building up of the original central office. Then this process continues until it limits itself in the same way as did the original process and a still further differentiation begins, and so the diastole and the systole of administrative development is represented by the repeated replacement of the functions of centralization and decentralization by each other in accordance with the needs as they develop.

I have given the above illustration because it seems that it might be within the experience of almost every reader to have observed something closely similar, and to warn the reader that in approaching the contents of this book he must not expect to find society or social groups considered as if they consisted of the sum of the individuals composing them. Wherever two or more people are functioning as a social group that group not only consists of those individuals, but, more important perhaps, if that is possible, than the individuals themselves and without which their functioning as a social group could not be expressed, are the relations which maintain between them. It is these intangible, imponderable and invisible aspects of the situation which enable the mathematical sum of a certain number of individuals to function as a social group. Dr. Moreno's book might be described briefly as a study of these relations between individuals. To qualify this description still further, it might be added that it is a study of the emotional relations between individuals who are functioning as a social group, or, as I have often chosen to call them, the cross-currents of emotion as they play back and forth between individuals.

The statement of the material studied as I have expressed it above is a very simple statement, but, like a small hospital unit which starts with a very simple administrative set-up, as we begin to investigate it and to study it it becomes increasingly complex, more and more highly differentiated in accordance with the growth, development and evolution of the social group studied.

All of us, not only in our work but in our daily life, are constantly classifying individuals after some principle or other but usually largely on the basis of our likes or dislikes, upon our feelings of their trustworthiness and dependability or the contrary. In our institutions our classifications are crude. They are based upon behavioristic principles and the trial and error method, putting patients together who seem to belong together on the basis of their general outward appearances and conduct manifestations and separating those who seem to introduce discord into the situation. Dr. Moreno develops a technique for a process of classification which is calculated, among other things, to bring individuals together who are capable of harmonious inter-personal relationships, and so creating a social group which can function at the maximum efficiency and with the minimum of disruptive tendencies and processes. I will not undertake to explain this technique, which he has described so well in his book—in fact that is what the book is about—but will only make certain comments which strike me as pertinent to the entire problem which he sets himself.

In the first place, one can think advantageously of the whole problem of the emotional cross-currents of plus and minus sign which flow between individuals in terms of energy distribution. Complex patterns of social structure are built from simpler ones by increasing the number of individuals, increasing the qualities of interest which each has for the other, and so increasing in the final analysis the capacity for bringing about results of a social nature. These emotional cross-currents, as has already been indicated, may be attractive in their function or they may be repellent, so that every individual in the group feels the pull of the emotional interests of his fellows and the pressure of their repulsion. These currents not only flow as between individuals who are differently located and thus have a spatial pattern of distribution, but they also flow as between individuals of different degrees of development and thus have a temporal pattern of distribution. The quality of the interest differs in each instance. There may be a definite love attraction or an attraction based upon an emotional factor which is perhaps less positive, certainly is so in its description; for example, a likeness, which may be very mild and may refer to any one of many things. The same thing may be said of

the repellent currents. They may run the gamut from hate to
the simplest sorts of dislike, while, in addition, certain individuals may find themselves isolated because no currents of
any sort move in their direction. There is an indifference of
their associates to them. We therefore can vision an infinite
series of possibilities: people who are held in high esteem
and are much beloved by a large number of people, on the
other hand individuals who are hated or feared or both, and,
finally, a group who are isolated either by a preponderance of
repellent emotions or by a general attitude of indifference.

Without pursuing this matter further it is interesting, and
to my mind significant, that in the analysis of social groups
Dr. Moreno has discovered again many homely truths which
have been recognized by others but he has rediscovered them
by a different method and a method which permits of their
development to a more highly differentiated degree and also
their utilization for the benefit of the individual. For example, he refers to the so-called volume of " emotional expansiveness " of an individual, upon which depends the number of
those with whom he may at any one time be acquainted, the
" acquaintance volume," or, when expressed in number of
individuals, the " social expansion." This at any particular
time for any particular individual seems to be rather definitely limited. On the other hand, experimentation indicates
that the volume of acquaintance may be enlarged by stimulating the individual's interest along certain lines that include
types of other individuals not previously encompassed within
the limits of his acquaintance. Similarly, within a given
more or less homogeneous group members of an alien group
may be introduced, but it will be found that there is a fairly
definite saturation point for such aliens. The group can
assimilate, as it were, a certain number, but beyond that point
assimilation is rendered difficult or impossible and the group
tends to break up along the lines of cleavage created by the
alien group forming a minority group within the majority
group. The preserving and conserving tendencies of group
traditions, the development of cultural patterns, the adding
by the individual of his mite to the traditions or the patterns
as he passes through,—all of these things are discovered anew

by Dr. Moreno's methods, and discovered in a way which makes them available for constructive purposes, which means, in many instances at least, for therapeutic ends.

Just a word about the therapeutic ends mentioned above. Certain individuals with certain patterns of personality find themselves merely by the accident of circumstances in a certain group which operates in a specially disadvantageous way with respect to their particular personality patterns. For example, an exceedingly timid person may find himself in a gang dominated by a cruel bully and be so completely frustrated as to find no avenues of adequate self-expression. Generally speaking, the same principle is involved in any situation where an individual has a personality pattern which requires certain kinds of individuals through which his emotions can find some sort of adequate outlet, and when placed in a social group where these possibilities are reduced to a minimum the type of personality he presents, finding no possibilities of expression and growth, is stunted in its development, retarded in its growth, rendered frequently regressive in the directions in which it seeks satisfactions, and the individual to whom it belongs becomes an increasing social liability. If, now, the problem can be appreciated in all its ramifications, if the individual can be sufficiently understood on the basis of his needs of expression, and the qualities of other individuals who, so to speak, are needed to supplement him can be derived from this understanding, then it is theoretically possible to place such an individual in a human environment where he would, as it were, blossom and grow and be not only a socially acceptable and useful, but a relatively happy person. These are some of the possibilities which not only suggest themselves but which have been definitely intimated in the discussion of the formulations and the theory, and examples of which are here and there given.

To revert to my remarks at the beginning of this introduction, that man's affairs proceeded by alternating processes of diastole and systole, it is interesting in reading Dr. Moreno's book to bear in mind what has been happening during the present century with respect to certain particular therapeutic problems. In the early part of the century our therapeutic devices which were available for handling problem children were confined almost entirely to changing their environment. It was generally felt that whatever the symptoms of the child might be, whether they expressed themselves in cruelty, lying and stealing, sex offenses, or what not, that in some way or other they were the expressions of disharmonies existing within the household, more especially as between the parents, and that if the child could be removed to another family group he had a fair chance of straightening out his emotional difficulties. And thus among other things arose the frequent utilization of the foster home as a therapeutic agent. As time went on, however, and under the constantly increasing influence of the psychoanalytic school, more attention was paid to the purely subjective aspects of the problem, and child analysis began to develop. The attack on the problem, therefore, was shifted somewhat by this new growth from the environment to the individual child. Now it is very interesting that Dr. Moreno comes back, apparently, to the position in which the environment seems to have the greater significance, but he comes back to that aspect of the problem not on the same level as it existed originally but at a higher level; and the interesting thing is that while he does come back to a consideration of the environment, that consideration includes the subjective aspect which has been almost exclusively emphasized in the development of child analysis. So we have here one of those typical advances which swings from one point of view to another but in doing so includes that other. At the same time Dr. Moreno emphasizes the fact that he differs from the psychoanalytic approach in another very significant way, namely, that the analyst works backward to an explanation for the individual's conduct while he takes the individual's conduct as the starting point and works forward. All of these various points of view, methods, techniques, seem to me to be of very great significance. Take, for example, if this technique works out with the possibilities that it has, what a valuable aid it would be in choosing a foster home, in relating the individuals of this home to the child and the child to these individuals. Think of how much may be added to our capacity for dealing with our mentally ill patients in institutions by a more intelligent classification, a classification which shall not be just a simple matter of practically conducting the wards as administrative units but a classification which would go deeply into the individual problems of each patient and relate them one to another, and more particularly perhaps to the nurses, upon a basis which has definite therapeutic objectives. And think, further, if you have no objections to flights of the imagination, of what possibly it may offer to an understanding of the problems of democracy as they occur in a country like the United States made up of races from all the four quarters of the globe.

WILLIAM A. WHITE

Washington, D. C.

PART I:
PRESENTATION OF THE PROBLEM

ered the individual *in* the collective, we entered into the group to call all the subject-centers within the group to aid. And as we studied the development of the collective from within the collective we became able to estimate its inner organization.

A fourth line of thought originated by Comte in his Positive Philosophy was brought to fresh advance by Le Play and his disciples. His study of the nature occupations, hunting, mining, agriculture, fishing, herding, woodcraft, gave the general concepts of Comte a concrete anchorage. His observational method elaborated by his disciples disclosed man in interaction with nature, conditioned by environment. But the further they moved away from their original objective of investigation, man's inter-dependence with nature, the more they attempted to study in civic surveys more complex conditions than the rural district, for instance, urban populations, the more their methods began to look stale and their results unconvincing. Man is not only conditioned by nature's environment but also by man's society, by its social structure. The economic side is only one phase of this structure, covering up the psychological structure of society which is beneath the surface and most difficult to ascertain. To produce an advance here a changed methodology was necessary. Instead of developing a survey from the geographical set-up in its relation to men and their occupations, we have developed a survey from within society. The channels and structures as they are erected by man, families, schools, factories, etc., had to be presented in their inner unfoldment. A picture was thus gained which was geographic and psychological at the same time, the *psychological geography* of a community.

A fifth line of thought was represented by economic planning based on an analysis of society as an economic-materialistic process (Marx). Economic planning was a real advance. But the tacit basis of this planning was the collective, the collective of *symbolic* membership. It attempted to function in disregard of the individual as a psychological energy and of society as a growing complex continuously pressed by psychological currents and the networks they form. Or better said, it had so little regard for the psychological factor that it thought to suppress or denaturalize without expecting any particularly harmful consequences.[8] As the planning progressed and began to manage the nature of man and society according to the economic criterion curious disturbances appeared the cause of which was a puzzle.

Finally a sixth line of thought developed, the idea to improve man as a kind through eugenic measures (Galton).[9] But is it meant to improve what is worth improving or to improve what just happens to survive in the battle of existence? Who shall survive?

It is through a synthesis of these six lines of development that gradually the preliminary ground was laid for an experiment in the psychological planning of society.

III. DEFINITION AND METHOD

1. SOCIONOMY

Socionomy is a science which is concerned with the psychological properties of populations and with the communal problems which these properties produce. Its principal concern is with the intricate interrelations of various groups and their activities and the way in which these activities affect the welfare of the community. The attention which socionomy gives to the social aspects of the interplay of these activities is born of its interest in the measures which governments take or which they might take with a view to guiding them through regulated channels. Like every science socionomy proceeds upon the premise that there is some sort of order in the phenomena with which it deals. The psychological activities of groups are not altogether aimless or directed wholly by chance. The psychological situation of a community viewed as a whole has a discernible ordered pattern. It presents itself in laws and tendencies which are discoverable by means of experiment and analysis.

2. SOCIOMETRY

That part of socionomy which deals with the mathematical study of psychological properties of populations, the experimental technique of and the results obtained by application of quantitative methods is called *sociometry*. This is undertaken through methods which inquire into the evolution and organization of groups and the position of individuals within them. One of its special concerns is to ascertain the quantity and expansion of psychological currents as they pervade population.

3. SOCIOMETRIC TEST

An instrument to measure the amount of organization shown by social groups is called *sociometric test*. The sociometric test requires an individual to choose his associates for any group of which he is or might become a member. He is expected to make his choices without restraint and whether the individuals chosen are members of the present group or outsiders.

This test has been made in respect to home groups, work groups, and school groups. It determined the position of each individual in a group in which he has a function, for instance, in which he lives or works. It revealed that the underlying psychological structure of a group differs widely from its social manifestations; that group structures vary directly in relation to the age level of the members; that different criteria may produce different groupings of the same persons or they may produce the same groupings; that groups of different function, as, for instance, home groups and work groups, tend towards diverse structures; that people would group themselves differently if they could; that these spontaneous groups and the function that individuals act or intend to act within them have a definite bearing upon the conduct of each individual and upon the group as a whole; and that spontaneous groupings and forms of groupings which are superimposed upon the former by some authority provide a potential source of conflict. It was found that chosen relations and actual relations often differ and that the position of an individual cannot be fully realized if not all the individuals and groups to which he is emotionally related are included. It disclosed that the organization of a group cannot be fully studied if all related groups or individuals are not included, that individuals and groups are often to such an extent interlocked that the whole community to which they belong has to become the scope of the sociometric test.

4. METHOD

We have studied group formation in three ways. The first way may be called observational and interpretative. We watched the children as, free of supervision, they ran out of school to the playgrounds, the manner in which they grouped themselves spontaneously. We noted a regularity in their spontaneous groupings,—one particular girl followed by a bunch of others, many who paired themselves off and two or three, often more, walking alone. Similar patterns were formed when they played about the grounds undirected. A rough classification of the position of the individuals in the groups was possible,—the isolates, the pairs, and the bunch that clung to the leader,—but this did not reach beyond surface judgments in understanding the organization of the groups.

We then approached the task from a different angle. Instead of observing the formation of groups from without we entered *into* the group, became a part of it, and registered its intimate developments. We ourselves experienced the polarity of relations among members, the development of gangs within the group, the pressure upon one individual or another. However, the larger the group under study was the more we ourselves became victim of such pressure, the more attached we found ourselves to some of its sections and the more blindfolded to other parts. Through this method of " partnership " we arrived at a somewhat finer classification of each individual than we were able to through observation. Or we selected a member of the group who is in the position to know its underlying relations,—for instance, in a family group we consulted the mother; in a school class, the teacher; in a cottage group of an institution, the housemother; in a work unit, the foreman, etc. The selected informer due to the mechanism of partnership had often an inaccurate insight into the workings of the group.

But we cannot adequately comprehend the central direction of an individual in his development neither through observation, for instance, a child, through watching its most spontaneous expression, its play life, nor through partnership. We must make him an experimenter. Considering group formation, we must make the members of the prospective groups themselves the authors of the groups to which they belong. To reach a more accurate knowledge of group organization the sociometric test is used. It consists in an individual choosing his associates for any group of which he is or might become a member. As these choices are initiated by the persons themselves, each individual taken into partnership and not only for himself but each individual towards each other individual who has a relationship to him, we win an insight how group structures of their own look compared with group structures imposed upon them from without. This method is experimental and synthetic.

In school groups the test had the following form. The tester entered the classroom and addressed the pupils:

" You are seated now according to directions your teacher has given you. The neighbor who sits beside you is not chosen by you. You are now given the opportunity to choose the boy or girl whom you would like to have sit on either side of you. Write down whom you would like first best; then, whom you would like second best. Look around and make up your mind. Remember that next term your friends you choose now may sit beside you."

One minute was allowed for deciding upon choices before the pupils were to write. The tester tried to get into rapport with the pupils and to transfer clearly the particular significance of the decisions.

For home groups the test had to be varied. The tester called the whole population of a given community together and addressed them:

" You live now in a certain house with certain other persons according to the directions the administration has given you. The persons who live with you in the same house are not ones chosen by you and you are not one chosen by them. You are now given the opportunity to choose the persons whom you would like to live with in the same house. You can choose without restraint any individuals of this community whether they happen to live in the same house with you or not. Write down whom you would like first best, second best, third best, fourth best, and fifth best. Look around and make up your mind. Remember that the ones you choose will probably be assigned to live with you in the same house."

Three points are of methodological significance. First, every individual is included as a center of emotional response. Second, this is not an academic reaction. The individual is caught by an emotional interest for a certain practical end *he* wishes to realize and upon his knowledge that the tester has the authority to put this into practice. Third, the choice is always related to a definite criterion. In the first instance, the criterion is of *studying in proximity*, actually sitting beside the pupils chosen. In the second, the criterion is of *living in proximity*, actually within the same house. When this test was applied to work groups, the criterion was working in proximity, actually within the same work unit and collaborating in the function to be performed. Other criteria must be used according to the special function of any group under study.

The test has been carried out in three phases: 1, spontaneous choice; 2, motivation of these choices; and 3, causation of these choices. Spontaneous choice reveals how many members of his own group, whatever the criterion of the group, are desired by an individual as associates in the activity of this group. The motivations, as they are secured through interview of each individual, reveal further the number of attractions and repulsions to which an individual is exposed in a group activity. The underlying causations for these attractions and repulsions are studied through the Spontaneity Test adapted to sociometric aims. The Spontaneity Test places an individual in a standard life situation which calls for definite fundamental emotional reactions, called Impromptu states, as fear, anger, etc. The range of mimic and verbal expression during this test is recorded and offers characteristic clues to the makeup of the personality acting, to his relation to the life situation acted, and to the person or persons who act opposite him in the test.

5. CONSTRUCTION OF THE TEST

The problem was to construct the test in such manner that it is itself a motive, an incentive, a purpose, primarily for the *subject* instead of for the tester. If the test procedure is identical with a life-goal of the subject he can never feel himself to have been victimized or abused. Yet the same series of acts performed of the subject's own volition may be a " test " in the mind of the tester. We have developed two tests in which the subject is in action for his own ends. One is the sociometric test. From the point of view of the subject this is not a test at all and this is as it should be. It is merely an opportunity for him to become an active agent in matters concerning his life situation. But to the sociometric tester it reveals his actual position in the community in relation to the actual position of others. The second test meeting this demand is the Spontaneity Test. Here in a standard life situation the subject improvises to his own satisfaction. But to the tester it releases a source of information in respect to the character, intelligence, conduct, and psychological position of the subject.

Psychometric tests and psychoanalysis of the child and of the adolescent, however contrasting in procedure, have one thing in common. They throw the subject into a passive state, the subject being in a rôle of submission. The situation is not motivated for him. This tends to produce an attitude of suspicion and tension on the part of the subject towards the tester and to attribute to him ulterior motives in inducing the subject to submit to the test. This *situational* fact has to be considered irrelevant to how valuable and significant the revelations may be which come from psychometric testing and from psychoanalysis. This aspect of the testing becomes especially conspicuous if the findings are used for the purpose of determining some change in the life situation of the subject, as, for instance, his transfer to an institution for the feeble-minded. Through the sociometric test and Spontaneity Test the artificial setting of the psychoanalytic situation and of the Binet intelligence tests can be substituted by natural or life settings.

6. DIRECTIONS FOR THE TEST

A point which deserves emphasis is the *accurate giving* of the sociometric test. Only such a test can be correctly called *sociometric* which attempts to determine the *feelings* of individuals towards each other and, second, to determine these in respect to the *same criterion*. For instance, if we demand from the inhabitants of a given community to choose the individuals with whom they want to live together in the same house and to motivate these choices, this is a sociometric procedure. Or, if we determine through such procedure to whom the individuals are sexually attracted or with whom they want to study together in the same classroom. In each of these cases a definite criterion is given, living in proximity, working in proximity, or sexual proximity. Further, a sociometric test to be accurate has *not* to gain the necessary information through observation of these individuals only, how they appear to behave in their home groups, work groups, or whatever, to one another and to construct, through these observations, the position they possibly have in their groups. But it is necessary that the subjects themselves be taken into partnership, that they become sufficiently interested in the test, that they transfer to the tester their spontaneous attitudes, thoughts, and motivations in respect to the individuals concerned in the same criterion. Whatever additional material is gained by other methods to support the essential information, this is not able to substitute the two requirements mentioned above. If, therefore, the inhabitants of a community are asked whom they like or dislike in their community irrespective of any criterion this should not be called sociometric. These likes and dislikes being unrelated to a criterion are not analytically differentiated. They may relate to sexual liking, to the liking of working together, or whatever. Secondly, the individuals have no interest to express their likes and dislikes truthfully as no practical consequences for themselves are derivable from these. Similarly if children in a classroom are asked whom they like or dislike among their classmates irrespective of any criterion and without immediate purpose for them. Even if such a form of inquiry may at some age level produce similar results as the results gained through our procedure, it should not be called sociometric testing. It does not provide a systematic basis for sociometric research.

7. PLACES OF RESEARCH

The research as presented in this book was carried out in several phases:

A. Study of the evolution of group distinctions. Places: Public School 181, Brooklyn, N. Y.; Riverdale Country School, Riverdale, N. Y.

B. Sociometric study of a whole community and the application of the findings to this community. Place: New York State Training School for Girls, Hudson, N. Y.

C. Development of the Spontaneity Test and of Spontaneity Training. Places: Grosvenor Neighborhood House, New York City; New York State Training School for Girls, Hudson, N. Y.

D. Report on the question of principles in relation to the psychological planning of communities prepared at the request of the Subsistence Homestead Commission, Department of Interior, Washington, D. C.

The planning of population assignment has been first studied by us between 1915 and 1918. The place of study was an Italian colony with a population of more than ten thousand. It was during the World War when great numbers of peasants, Austrian citizens of Italian extraction, fleeing from their homes in southern Tyrol before the oncoming Italian army, were transplanted by the Austrian government to a place near Mittendorf in close proximity to Vienna. The community consisted of cottage dwellings each holding several families and at the head of each cottage was a capo di baracka, a man who was responsible for the welfare of that group. The cost of minimum maintenance was supplied by the Austrian government and, in addition, a shoe factory was established employing at times one to two thousand workers. The government was concerned with three problems and reflected them into the planning: safety from the enemy, sanitation, and subsistence. However, social and psychological planning was not considered, not even conceived of. A staff of which we were a member was appointed by the government to supervise the problem of sanitation in the new community. In this position and later as superintendent of the children's hospital established within it, we had the opportunity to study this community from its earliest beginning to its final dissolution three years later when at the end of the war the colonists returned to their homes in Tyrol.   During this period a whole community life developed.   Step by step, hospitals, schools, church, theater, department stores, shops, industry, social clubs, newspaper, came into function.   Yet in the face of an attempt of the government to meet the emergency and not-withstanding the establishment of practically all the outward signs of a community life, there was great unhappiness and friction among the population.   Whole villages of wine grow-ers were transplanted into a suburban industrial district, mountaineers from Tyrol into a flat spot of country near Vienna.   They were thrown together unselected, unaccus-tomed to the environment, unadjusted within themselves. We studied the psychological currents they developed upon varying sorts of criteria,—the criterion of nationality, of poli-tics, of sex, of staff versus colonists, and so on,—and considered them as the chief contributory source of the flagrant malad-justments and disturbances.   It was through this experience that the idea of a psychologically planned community began to occupy us.

Our first move in the direction of sociometric planning was begun with small spontaneously formed groups of individuals in which the factors involved in their organization could be readily studied.   This early research was carried out in Vienna, 1921–1925, and later in New York (see p. 169).   We became able to select one group of individuals to function with a second group of individuals to the mutual satisfaction of both groups and to the better performance of each.   After this laboratory study of groups was fairly far advanced, we re-turned to the community proper looking for groups appearing to have a simple structure.   The pattern of a public school community first presented itself.   We sought for a school which should offer a composite picture of many of the nation-alities represented in the fabric of the American population, in which all social classes were mixed, and which at the same time should offer an unselected sampling of the public school population. Public School 181, Brooklyn, N. Y., was chosen. The affinities and disaffinities among the children in the groups set up by the school's administration were studied chiefly from the point of view of the criterion which had made them members of this collective,—the criterion of studying in proximity. But the more varied criteria of human interrelations were here untouched,—such criteria as living in proximity (in the home), working in proximity (in the factory), etc. In the community at large the different collectives as they are conditioned by these criteria are intimately interlocked. Therefore the school groups analyzed apart from the community had still a touch of the artificiality of the laboratory phase through which we had passed. For a fuller inquiry we should have had to follow the leads from the school community into the neighborhoods and into the families from which the children came. But here we found ourselves faced with a problem beyond the present possibility of scientific integration. The complex loomed too large and too intricate. We needed an intermediate stage.

It was at this point that we thought of approaching first a miniature community instead of an urban population whose networks would lead us into endless avenues and in the course of which the single individual might be " forgotten " as he so frequently is in sociological surveys. We looked for a small community within whose boundaries all collectives flourish,— home, school, work, cultural,—interlocked one with another and at the same time which as a whole is cut off to a great extent from the population at large so that the currents which might flow from without into it could be discounted without too great an error, a community which is " closed." The pattern of an institutional community presented itself, the New York State Training School for Girls at Hudson, New York, whose superintendent is Fannie French Morse.

We met in Hudson with a unique form of administration which radiated from the superintendent into all directions: to release, to restrain, and to rule through asthetic principles projected into the community. Aesthetic principles entering into every detail of living are a powerful device of an invisible government. Here we found exemplified the effects of education when it is not limited to a specific locality, the school alone, but is the very atmosphere itself of the whole community.

The findings and techniques secured in the various phases of the research opened up finally the possibility to apply them to the community at large. We were well aware that to attempt the psychological reorganization of any community which had already established patterns and traditions would meet with resistance. The next logical step could be the construction of a *new* community. At this point the Subsistence Homestead Projects under the Department of Interior offered a road for experimentation in the open community. The government was interested to select the proper locality and a population best adjustable to it. The opportunity to interject into the homestead project, besides agricultural and economic, also psychological planning was given.

of organization persists which had been found characteristic for this class in the first test. It appears that although one or the other pupil's position changes the general trend of organization persists. After a period of almost two years (twenty-two months) the population of the same public school was retested. Tables 3–5 accompanying indicate the findings.

The findings of the second test corroborate the findings of the first test in every main aspect. This appears of great significance as it can be said that we met the second time a practically different population due to the turnover within two

PUBLIC SCHOOL, SECOND TEST

TABLE 3

QUANTITATIVE ANALYSIS OF CHOICES BETWEEN THE SEXES IN THE GRADES OF A PUBLIC SCHOOL

Of All Choices Made	Boys Chose Girls	Girls Chose Boys	Both Sexes
Kindergarten	15.0%	12.0%	27.0%
1st Grade	13.0%	8.6%	21.6%
2nd Grade	16.0%	9.8%	25.8%
3rd Grade	9.2%	10.6%	19.8%
4th Grade	4.2%	4.7%	8.9%
5th Grade	2.4%	1.5%	3.9%
6th Grade	.5%	.6%	1.1%
7th Grade	1.5%	1.9%	3.4%
8th Grade	1.2%	.4%	1.6%
Ungraded Classes	1.2%	.0%	1.2%
Physically Handicapped Class..	5.1%	2.2%	7.3%

TABLE 4

STRUCTURAL ANALYSIS OF SCHOOL GROUPS

	Isolated	Mutual Pairs	Triangles	Chains
Kindergarten	27%	6%	0	0
1st Grade	32%	5%	0	0
2nd Grade	29%	12%	0	0
3rd Grade	29%	10%	0	0
4th Grade	25%	16%	2	1
5th Grade	21%	18%	1	2
6th Grade	16%	16%	6	1
7th Grade	21%	17%	3	3
8th Grade	20%	20%	3	2
Ungraded Classes	27%	17%	0	0
Physically Handicapped..	29%	17%	3	2

years and the changed distribution of the classes. It can be expected that future sociometric testing of similar public school populations will further corroborate our findings.

However, the following variations between the findings of the first and of the second test can be noted. The number of intersexual attractions was found to decline more gradually and the number of mutual pairs to increase more gradually from the 1st grade on. Complex structures appear a year

TABLE 5

Degree of Accuracy of Teachers' Judgments in Respect to
Most Popular Pupils and Isolated Pupils

Classes	Percentage of Accuracy
Kindergarten	62.5%
1st Grade	64.5%
2nd Grade	50%
3rd Grade	50%
4th Grade	37.5%
5th Grade	30%
6th Grade	30%
7th Grade	25%
8th Grade	40%

later. Other variations are very slight. The degree of accuracy of teachers' judgments in respect to most popular and to most isolated pupils has the highest point in the kindergarten and 1st grade, declines from then on, and shows the lowest point in the 7th grade.

TABLE 6

A PRIVATE PREPARATORY SCHOOL

Analysis of Choices

Unchosen

After 1st Choice	After 2nd Choice	After 3rd Choice	After 4th Choice
45%	22%	16%	9%

Chosen

5 or more times chosen including 2 or more mutual choices	53% of population
2 or more times chosen including 1 mutual choice	32% of population
Chosen once and with no mutual choice	6% of population

Revision of choices taken three months after the first choosing showed adjusted boys usually maintain or improve their position and unadjusted boys maintain generally the same position or else regress. Of the unadjusted boys, only 15% improved their position as against 44% of the adjusted boys who improved their position.

On the basis of the 1st choice, 10% of the new boys (that is, boys who had not attended the school the year before) remained unchosen. It will be noted that this is practically the same proportion as that for the school population generally. New boys received 2.8 choices per boy as against 3.75 choices per boy for the whole school.

It is of interest to compare the two divisions in the population: the dormitory boys and the day school boys. Considering the dormitory boys exclusively, 82% of this population formed mutual pairs; considering the day school boys exclusively, only 68% formed mutual pairs. The former class of students comprised 25% of the school population; the latter class, 75% of the population. It is at once evident that the psychological position of the two groups is vastly different. The boys living in the more intimate situation and having more frequent and more constant social contact with one another become better adjusted than the day school boys whose opportunities for close contact are more casual. It appears also that the dormitory students are a greater attraction for the day school boys than their fellow students who are similarly " outsiders." The average number of choices received by the dormintory student is 4.85 while for the day student it is 3.32. This is the more striking when we consider the disproportion in numbers of members of the two groups.

The first sociometric test of the Riverdale school population was given two months after the school was in session in the fall. After an interval of three months, the test was again given. The findings in respect to changing of choices were as follows: 8% of the 1st choices were changed, 18% of the 2nd choices. Thus the 1st and 2nd choices appear to have a high degree of validity,—92% of the 1st choices made remaining unchanged and 82% of the 2nd choices remaining unchanged after this period.

		BOY
ATTRACTION	**GIRL**	
MUTUAL ATTRACTION	**GIRL IN DIFFERENT GROUP**	**BOY IN DIFFERENT GROUP**

		COLORED BOY
REPULSION	**COLORED GIRL**	
MUTUAL REPULSION	**COLORED GIRL IN DIFFERENT GROUP**	**COLORED BOY IN DIFFERENT GROUP**

	HOUSEMOTHER OR INSTRUCTOR	MALE INSTRUCTOR
INDIFFERENCE		
MUTUAL INDIFFERENCE	**HOUSEMOTHER OR INSTRUCTOR IN DIFFERENT GROUP**	**MALE INSTRUCTOR IN DIFFERENT GROUP**

A circle represents a girl.

A triangle represents a boy.

A large circle represents a woman.

A large triangle represents a man.

A double circle or double triangle signifies that the respective individual is a member of a different group from the charted one.

A line drawn from one individual to another individual represents the emotional reaction of the one individual to the other.

In one-color charts (Nos. 31–44) each line represents an attraction.

In multi-colored charts each different color represents a different emotional reaction:

A red line represents attraction;

A dotted line represents indifference;

A black line represents repulsion.

An arrowed line indicates one-sided reaction.

A crossed line represents two-sided reactions.

In charts (Nos. 155–7) representing specific emotional reactions of one individual towards another, a red line represents sympathy; a green line represents fear; a thin line represents anger; a heavy black line represents dominance.

1. Stage of Organic Isolation

A group of 9 babies of the same age level were placed in the same room and in close proximity throughout the first year of life. The emphasis of observation was not placed upon the development of the different responses, as crying, sucking, clucking, sulking, and whether these are or are not truly social responses, and so on, but upon the early beginnings of interrelation and group formation. No sign of such beginning could be traced during the first 26 weeks in infant-to-infant relation. Each baby lives in isolation from the other. Within this period of isolation and close to the 2-months level, the voice of a crying baby may arouse the attention of his neighbor—marking the subdivision of this period between full isolation and the beginning of the recognition of others.

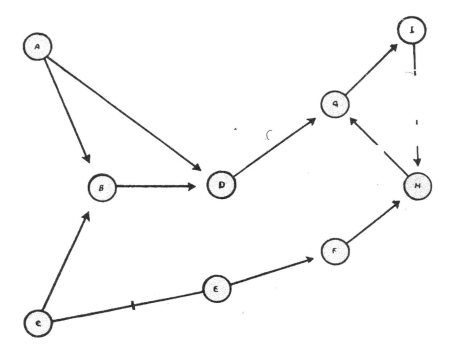

2. Stage of Horizontal Differentiation

The true beginning of group development is illustrated above. One baby, C, recognizes its neighbor, E, who recognizes it in return. One baby, D, is recognized by two neighbors, A and B, and recognizes one neighbor, G. One baby, A, recognizes two babies, B and D, but remains unrecognized. B is attracted to D, C is attracted to B; by indirection through C, baby B may become influenced by E,—we see here the forerunner of a " chain." On this level interrelations are aroused by physical proximity and are based upon physical distance or nearness. Physical distance produces psychological distance. At this level emotions travel through physical proximity in space horizontally and in consequence there follows the development of group structures through *horizontal* differentiation.

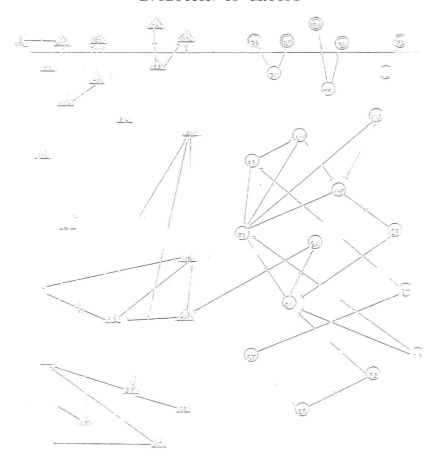

CLASS STRUCTURE, 5TH GRADE

19 boys and 18 girls. *Unchosen,* 10, HN, ES, TR, SL, RS, HR, RF, MR, JN, FS; *Pairs,* 19, ST-HN, ST-NI, NI-HN, MR-ES, ES-FS, TR-PN, ML-MR, AD-VR, DA-LV, AD-RE, RE-VR, JL-KR, RT-ER, ER-SS, RT-BT, DM-GA, MR-CR, DM-FI, FI-MR; *Stars,* 2, FI, DM; *Chains,* 2, GA-DM-FI-MR-CR, SS-ER-RF-BT-SR; *Triangles,* 2, AD-VR-RE, HN-NI-ST; *Inter-sexual Attractions,* 1.

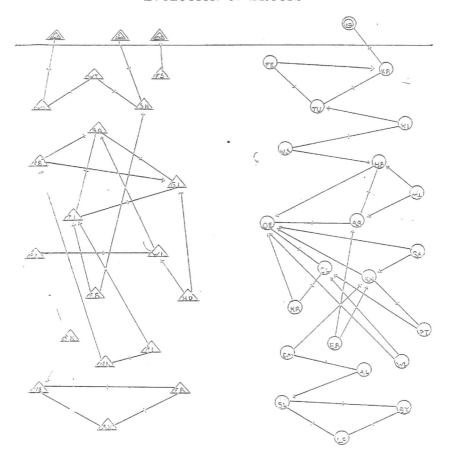

CLASS STRUCTURE, 6TH GRADE

18 boys and 21 girls. *Unchosen,* 6, FS, HD, ML, GA, BR, WL; *Pairs,* 26, WL-WT, WT-SH, GO-TI, GO-GI, TI-GI, PI-WI, PI-SH, NL-PI, YG-FR, YG-SH, SH-FR, DM-AL, SL-BY, SL-LP, LP-BY, FE-TU, TU-KR, NS-HI, HR-AR, OE-AR, OE-CL, CL-KR, KN-PT, WL-LY, CA-SH, KR-HD; *Stars,* 1, OE; *Chains,* 2, LY-WL-WT-SH-CA, HR-AR-OE-SL-KR; *Triangles,* 3, YG-FR-SH, GO-TI-GI, SL-LP-BL; *Inter-sexual Attractions,* 0.

EVOLUTION OF GROUPS

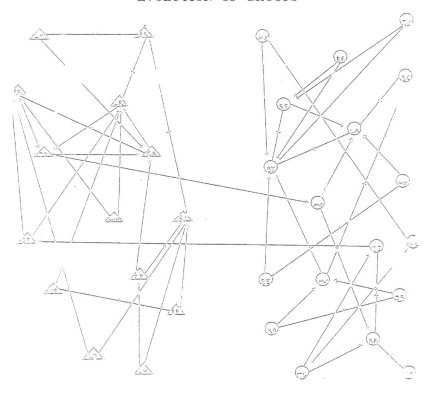

CLASS STRUCTURE, 7TH GRADE

14 boys and 18 girls. *Unchosen,* 5, WN, CH, LB, JH, BR; *Pairs,* 15, LN-SR, SR-LR, SR-RI, FR-BA, RI-TP, MR-EB, KR-HE, KR-JR, KR-KE, BB-MY, WL-MN, MN-BC, BY-LA, LA-BC, BY-SP; *Stars,* 5, LR, RI, BY, LA, MR; *Chains,* 2, SP-BY-LA-BC-MN-BY, LN-SR-RI-TP-BA; *Triangles,* 0; *Inter-sexual Attractions,* 2.

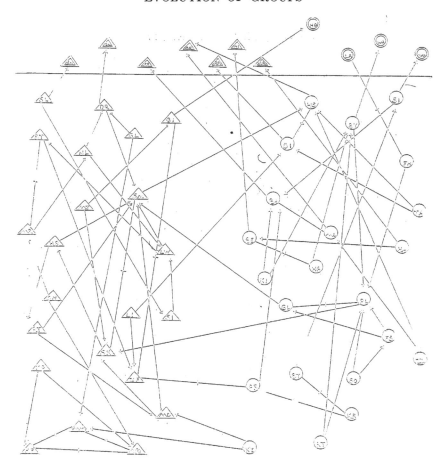

CLASS STRUCTURE, 8TH GRADE

22 boys and 22 girls. *Unchosen,* 12, KP, GL, SN, LI, SL, MT, KE, SO, ZL, KI, HA, RA; *Pairs,* 13, BT-MR, SM-SK, GI-ZF, HF-MM, MM-YD, HF-YD ZF-PR, BT-KR, GL-PL, SE-HR, HS-OI, BA-ML, FN-LR, *Stars,* 2, SM, PL; *Chains,* 0; *Triangle,* 1, HF-MM-YD; *Inter-sexual Attractions,* 8.

FIG. 2

CLASS STRUCTURES, UNGRADED CLASSES

Fig. 1. Ungraded Class 1. 14 boys and 6 girls. *Unchosen*, 4, J, LS. MN, VL; *Pairs*, 7, PA-TT, TT-SF, CC-LO, BR-VC, FT-JT, JT-CT, CT-ES; *Stars*, 0; *Chains*, 0; *Triangles*, 0; *Inter-sexual Attractions*, 1.

Fig. 2. Ungraded Class 2. 9 boys and 8 girls. *Unchosen*, JS, WJ, CV, EH, N, FL; *Pairs*, 5, PD-PA, PA-TP, CM-CC, CC-RL, RL-CM; *Stars*, CM; *Chains*, 0; *Triangles*, 1; *Inter-sexual Attractions*, 0.

43

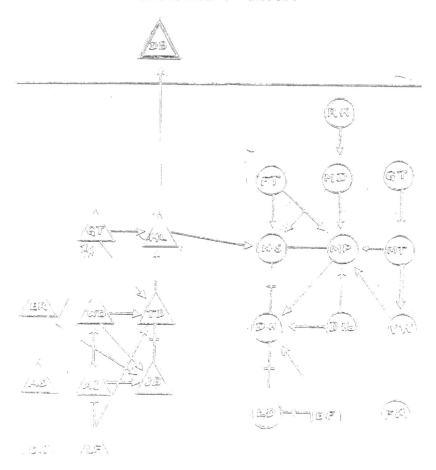

CLASS STRUCTURE, CRIPPLE CLASS

10 boys and 13 girls. *Unchosen,* 7, EK, AS, ER, DHa, FT, RK, GT; *Pairs,* 5, JB-TD, EF-LD, LD-DH, DH-NS, NS-MP; *Stars,* 3, MP, NS, DH; *Chains,* 1, EF-LD-DH-NS-MP; *Triangles,* 0; *Inter-sexual Attractions,* 1.

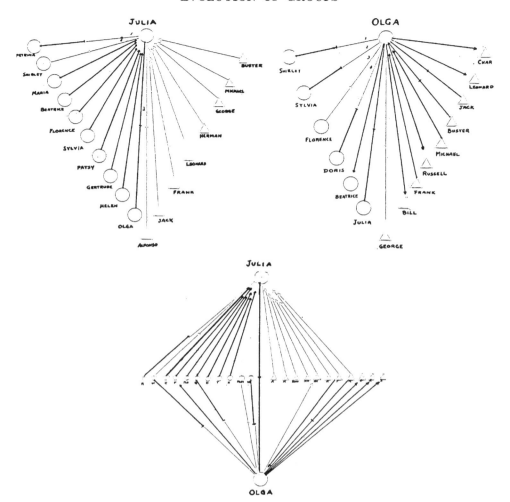

Fig. 1. Psychological organization around a pupil Julia; criterion, studying in proximit social atom of the subject has developed after eight months in class group 8B1 in P 181, Brooklyn, N. Y. Julia is the first choice of eight boys, Buster, Michael, Geor Herman, Leonard, Frank, Jack, and Alfonso, who all want to sit beside her in t classroom. Alfonso is the boy who receives her third choice. She is at the same ti rejected by nine girls, Olga, Helen, Gertrude, Patsy, Sylvia, Florence, Beatrice, Mai and her first choice, Petrina, who do not want to sit near her. She is the first choice Shirley whom she chooses second.

Fig. 2. Psychological organization around a pupil Olga; criterion, studying in proximit social atom of the subject has developed after eight months in class group 8B1 in P 181, Brooklyn, N. Y. Olga rejects six boys whom she does not want to sit near h Charles, Leonard, Bill, Frank, Buster, and Jack; the latter three reject her as de also Michael. She is attracted to one boy, George, who does not respond. S chooses four girls, Shirley, Sylvia, Florence, and Doris, whom she wants to sit ne her, and with one of them, Florence, she forms a mutual pair. She is rejected by t other three girls and in addition by Julia with whom she forms a mutual rejecti The sixth girl shown in the chart, Beatrice, is rejected by her.

Fig. 3. The psychological organization around Julia, shown in Fig. 1, and that arou Olga, shown in Fig. 2, are presented together in this chart to indicate how the t girls are interlocked directly and by indirection.

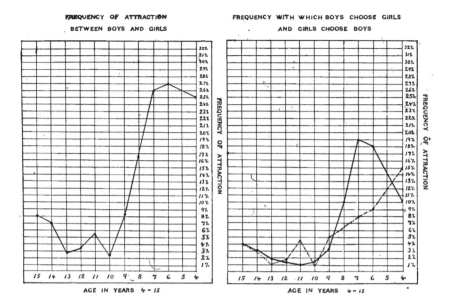

FREQUENCY HISTOGRAM

PUBLIC SCHOOL 181, BROOKLYN, N. Y., POP. 1853 BOYS AND GIRLS

Fig. 1. Attraction between the sexes, boys attracted to girls and girls attracted to boys, is represented. This attraction is indicated as highest in the kindergarten and 1st grade: 25% and 27% respectively. The ages of these pupils range between 4 and 7 years. In the 2nd grade, the attractions fell to 16½%; in the 3rd grade, to 8½%; in the 4th grade, to 2½%, its lowest level; in the 5th, 6th, and 7th grades there is shown a slight increase to 4%, 3½% and 3%, respectively. In the 8th grade, where the ages of the pupils range between 13 and 15 years, the attractions rose decidedly to 8%.

Fig. 2. Initiative on the part of each sex in choosing the other is indicated. From the 1st grade up to the 5th, the initiative of the boys in choosing girls is about twice as great as that of girls in choosing boys. In the 5th grade the tables are reversed: girls show an initiative greater than that of boys. In the 6th, 7th, and 8th grades (age range 11-15 years), the initiative of boys and of girls are about equal. (The dot-dash line indicates girls and the plain line indicates boys.)

The chart shows a school fraternity—Forces of Repulsion are naturally not given by the students frankly, because of feelings of loyalty, but significant situations may be seen in the fact that two seniors, 6/13, 6/14, are not desired by anyone in the fraternity in spite of the fact that they have been formally elected. The individual 5/11 is the center of forces of attraction, and is in fact the president of the fraternity.

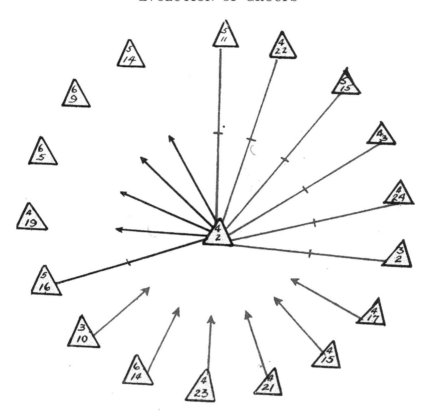

The chart shows the position occupied by a typical leader in the school. Note that 4/2 has six reciprocal attractions; six additional attractions toward him by individuals to whom he is indifferent; one mutual dislike and four additional dislikes, each of whom feels neutral toward him. This is a high "batting average." The total number of individuals (17) toward whom relations have been expressed in the course of the survey, distributed over four forms, indicates that 4/2 takes an active attitude toward his fellow students and to life and is not on the "side lines."

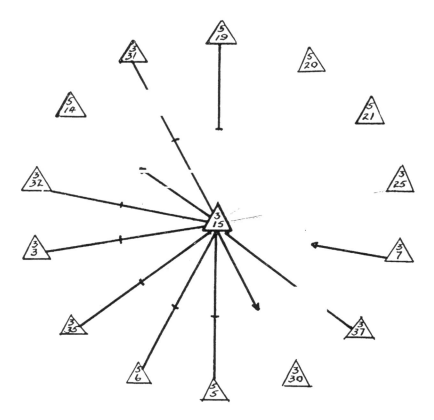

The chart depicts an isolated individual. The student 3/15 arouses active feelings—he is the focus of a great deal of antipathy; he likes 3/25, and is accepted by him; he also likes two others, 5/20 and 5/21 who, significantly are new boys and who are indifferent to him, and he also likes 5/19, who, however, dislikes him. This shows that 3/15 has formed only one satisfactory contact in the whole school, while there are seven mutual dislikes, two dislikes for persons who are indifferent to him, and one dislike toward him from a person toward whom he is indifferent.

3. INTERPRETATION

The three directions or tendencies of structure we have
described for baby groups, organic isolation, horizontal differentiation, and vertical differentiation, are fundamental
features in the development of groups. We find them appearing again and again however extensive and complex the
groups become. But the earliest developmental points at
which sex, nationality, or other specific factors begin to affect
group organization is in need of further investigation.

In the groups from 4 years on (through 15) the attraction
of the sexes for each other appears highest in the kindergarten,
1st and 2nd grades, declines sharply after the 3rd grade, not to
show any appreciably marked increase again until the 8th
grade. This indicates the restraint of both sexes up to the
age of puberty and the significance of the restraint upon group
organization. The lowest number of mutual pairs and the
highest number of isolated children in the public school are
found in the kindergarten, 1st and 2nd grades, indicating that
children of this age are seldom sufficiently certain whom to
choose. This suggests the need of more protection for them
then than is needed in later years. The high increase, on the
other hand, of mutual pairs and more complex structures from
the 4th grade on suggests that children of this age exchange
emotions readily and freely form partnerships and secret associations. It suggests that the organization which young children and adolescents form among themselves comes more and
more to compete in influence with organizations which adolescents form in relationship to adults. Proportionately, the
influence of adults upon children, compared to the influence
of children upon children, may be beginning to wane. This
may account for the fact that the teacher's ability to recognize
the position of the most desired and of the least desired boy
or girl in her class is to a large extent inaccurate. The teacher-
judgments concerned only the extremes in position. The
average positions of individuals are, it is evident, far more
difficult to estimate accurately. The intricacies of the children's own associations prevent the teacher from having a true

insight. This fact appears as one of the great handicaps in the development of teacher-child relationships.

The further increase in pairs and more complex structures for the age levels 14 to 18 years compared with the findings of the grammar school group indicates a still growing differentiation of group organization with increase in chronological age. But parallel is also an increase in the number of the isolated. This is still greater than the highest number found in the first grades of grammar school. At the 4–7 year level the unchosen child appears to be " left out," forgotten. It does not appear, in general, left out because of being disliked or rejected by the members of the group. The unchosen children as they are found at later age levels, particularly after 13 years, appear so not only because they are left out by the others but in numerous cases due to the attitudes members have formed in respect to each other.

The periodical recurrence of heterosexual and homosexual tendencies among the members of a group produces an effect upon group organization. The heterosexual cycle between the ages of 4 and 8 is displaced by a homosexual cycle between the ages of 8 and 13. Then a new heterosexual cycle begins apparently overlapping a second homosexual cycle. The homosexual tendency which can be deducted from the high number of mutual pairs among the boys of ages 14 to 18 would probably appear to be curtailed and sharply displaced by a high number of pairs between boys and girls if they would have been participants in mixed groups. Among adult groups a further greatly increased complexity is probable and that these structures break down into simpler ones in the period of senescence.

The organization of a class group in the early school grades presents the initial beginnings of structures which become increasingly numerous in the next succeeding grades and, *vice versa,* an organization of a higher grade still retains scant remnants of structures which have been numerous in the lower grades. For instance, 30 pupils of kindergarten 2 formed 3 pairs. In the 2nd grade B1, the same number of pupils formed 15 pairs. Structures of attraction between the sexes were formed by 25% of the pupils in this kindergarten. In

4th grade B1 only 2% took part in such structures. This interdevelopmental growth of group distinctions can also be observed through the study of the development of the same group from year to year.

The organization of groups in which mentally retarded prevail reveals numerous unreciprocated choices, a low number of mutual pairs, and many isolates. It resembles the organization produced by children of pre-school ages and in the early grades of grammar school.

The evolution of social groups opens the way to a classification of individuals according to their development within them which in turn makes possible the construction of social groups. We have demonstrated that chronological age or mental age does not point out to what social group an individual belongs or should belong. A sociometric test is necessary to determine his position in this respect. Our public school classes are at present formed according to chronological age, mental age, scholastic progress, or, occasionally, according to a combination of these. The sociometric position of the pupil within the school and within the groups in which he moves is neglected. A grouping of individuals may not become desirable as a social grouping although the members have studied or worked or lived together for a time, or although they appear to have a similar intelligence level, are of the same religious or nationality affiliations, and so on. The subjects themselves, in this case, the pupils, have attitudes towards one another which are crucial for them and for the social grouping. Their own feelings have to be considered in the forming of social groupings to which they must belong. And this leads, when systematically carried out, to sociometric testing.

If the sociometric test is performed on a large scale and the findings studied in relation to behavior, our knowledge of the more desirable organization for children at various age levels will become more accurate. At the end of the school term the sociometric test can reveal what organization the pupils within the classes have developed. Certain patterns of organization discovered through continuous sociometric testing may indicate undesirable prognosis for the future development of a group or of certain individuals within it notwithstanding that

of a goal, one or two children are found who are older and who act as their leaders.

2. FIRST SOCIALIZED PERIOD

From about 7–8 years on children become able to form groups themselves which are independent of adults and which show coöperative action and the pursuit of a common goal. From this age level on throughout adolescence the desire to have a function in association with individuals of the same level of differentiation can be detected and, if this is not satisfied openly, the individual may join secretly a group found available. In the first socialized period children form independent social groups among themselves. Older individuals may be present but they are not necessary. The organization of children groups in this period indicates that interrelationships of the members are sufficiently differentiated to understand certain codes and to pursue a common aim.[13]

The sex attitude characteristic for this age level is suggested in the organization of the groups developing in this period, the homosexual tendency beginning to be more marked at about 8 years of age and commencing to decline after the age of 13. The homosexual tendency in group organization continues although in lesser degree throughout the whole period of adolescence. Besides these homosexual or uni-sexed gangs, there are found mixed groups of boys and girls with a definite interest in sex. It is reported that the majority of the members are usually of ages from 12 up. This coincides with the showing of group structures which indicates the gradual increase of inter-sexual choice from 13 years of age up. In this sense, one or another partner in the group may be several years younger than 13 if there are boys or girls of the mentioned age level present who initiate the younger. In other words, children between 6 and 12 years do not develop a gang for sexual purposes spontaneously. From about 7 to 8 years on they are able to form a non-sexual gang; from 12–13 years on the sexual factor can enter into it and differentiate it further. Even children of the pre-socialized level can be led by older leaders into belonging to a gang, but there is no genuine spontaneous participation on their part before their socialized growth begins at 7 to 8 years of age or their social sexual period begins at 13 years. The effect which the maturing sexual function of individuals has upon the structure of groups led us therefore to distinguish the following stages:

Up to 6–8 years:	First Inter-Sexual Stage
8 years to 13 years:	First Homosexual Stage
13–15 years on:	Second Inter-Sexual Stage
13–15 years on:	Second Homosexual Stage

Our experience with children societies consisting of many hundreds of members may throw a further light upon the problem. We found that children, boys and girls, who had reached the 8 years age level or were near to it were able to run a society of their own without the aid of any older individuals. Usually they formed societies with one leader as the head. If growth had been stopped at this age level and if no more highly differentiated societies would exist these children societies would persist and develop an orderly organization as they attain the minimum of constancy and differentiation necessary for common pursuits. These tests could not be developed beyond a certain limit as in actuality the adolescent and adult groups press upon children groups when they are in spontaneous formation and they have no chance to overcome this pressure and to develop beyond neighborhood gangs and local groups.

3. CLEAVAGES IN GROUPS

Gradually from the 1st grade on the group develops a more differentiated organization; the number of unchosen decreases, the number of pairs increases, from about the 3rd grade on chains and triangles appear. The organization becomes more and more ready and mature to function for the group. Cooperative group action which begins to flourish from the 3rd and 4th grades on is potentially inherent in the organization of this age level before the functioning in this direction may become apparent to outsiders. The increased differentiation of groups formed by the children from about the 2nd grade on and the declining insight of adults into the rôle and the position a particular child in the group mark the begining of *a social cleavage, a cleavage between adult groups and children groups.*

From the 4th grade on the percentage of heterosexual attractions drops very low. There is indicated the beginning of a *sexual cleavage* which characterizes the organization from then on up to the 8th grade. Parallel with this the number of pairs and of other social structures increases rapidly. It appears as if the sexual cleavage is accelerating the process of socialization, deepening the emotional bonds between the members of the fraternity and sisterhood into which the class is now broken up.

From about the 5th grade another phenomenon can be observed in the sociograms. A greater number of Italian children begin to choose Italian neighbors; a greater number of Jewish children begin to choose Jewish neighbors; a greater number of German children begin to choose German neighbors, etc.; and a larger number of Italian children reject Jewish children, of Jewish children reject Italian, of German children reject Jewish, and of white children reject colored children, and so on, than before. This phenomenon could not be observed in the pre-school groups nor in the 1st, 2nd and 3rd grades although the percentage of members of the different nationalities was about the same. It indicates the beginning of a *racial cleavage.* The organization which was already broken up into two homosexual groups, into two halves, tends to break up further into a number of sub-groups, more or less distinct, each consisting of boys or girls of the same or similar nationality. Whether this is characteristic only for the particular sample of children population studied or is a general phenomenon will become clear as soon as a great variety of children populations in urban and rural sections is studied. However, it is evident that children have no *spontaneous* aversion in respect to nationality differences. Where a cleavage appears it is largely the projection of adult influence.

The three phenomena just mentioned are related to several factors. One is the physical and mental difference between adults and children. Children are becoming aware of the differences between themselves and the adults and of the similarities between themselves and other children. The psychological distance between adults and children increases, the psychological nearness between children and children increases. This is one basis for the development of children associations independent of adult associations. As the networks among the children having become finer and stronger the collaborative activities of children which up to this point were relatively an open vista are now difficult for the adults to detect. However, the children associations inherent in the social structure never actually develop beyond an embryonic stage. Up to a certain age this is due to their insufficiency in the forming of groups. But from the 2nd and 3rd grades on this failure is largely due to the 'pressure coming from adult groups which bear down upon them and do not permit of their full expression.

Soon after the difference between adults and children begin to affect group organization there follows the effect of the differences between the sexes. The distinction between boy and girl occupies the mind of children long before this period but up to this point it rather enhances their curiosity for each other and drives towards attraction rather than towards separation. Yet once the period of the free mixing of the sexes is over, the distance between the two sexes increase and leads to a new cleavage. The break-up of the group into fraternal homosexual associations and homosexual sister associations begins. This sexual cleavage may be said to have a counterpart in certain imageries of primitive societies. In an African legend related by Frobenius men and women lived apart in different villages. Each village was governed by the one sex alone which comprised it and Frobenius describes periodic hostilities occurring between the two communities. The ground for this real or imagined outcome may, symbolically, lay in the first stage in which the warfare between the sexes is able to assume group form. This cleavage, although it does not develop beyond an embryonic stage, is never entirely overcome. The oncoming increase of heterosexual gravitation itself is not able to repair completely the rift in which all future tendencies towards homosexual groupings are inherent.

When the homosexual tendency in group formation becomes an impelling force it aids to knit the individuals into a group which is more finely integrated than before and through emotional bondage gives an impetus for achievement. It may appear more economical and more secure to look for identity or similarity in fellowships, a lesser risk in a period in which the development of collective feeling is in an experimental stage. Aims are more easily achieved if resistances within the group are abolished. Slight differences in color of the skin, size, figure, facial expression, or mental traits, gain in significance as they appear resistances for transference. The effect of the suggestion coming from parents or from other older individuals whose opinion is respected by the child is immense. But why such suggestion does not leave a lasting impression upon the child before this age level can be perhaps explained. It may be that the emotional bondage in children groups during the phase of sexual cleavage prepared the soil so that such suggestion may be comprehended, found useful, and so take root more easily. But these factors alone would not suffice to intrench these feelings, to transform them from individual into collective expression. A retaining and conserving factor is needed. This is supplied by the networks whose significance we describe elsewhere and which begin to develop at this age level. It is through these networks that verbal and non-verbal opinion can travel.

There appears clearly to be a parallel between intersexual and interracial attraction. Curiosity in respect to the other sex and curiosity in respect to another race both presuppose an expansive mood. When heterosexual attraction gives way to homosexual attraction, just as curiosity for the other sex fatigues and indifference or antagonism towards it develops, also the curiosity for members of another race fatigues and indifference or antagonism towards it develops. When children are intelligent enough to form more finely integrated interrelations they feel out for the first time the two great hindrances in the pursuit of closed and aggressive group action: the other sex and the other race. In the first schemes to conquer the world it seems so much easier and safer for boy groups to leave out girls and to leave out nationalities contrasting to their own.

While sexual cleavage was found in all the nationalities among the groups studied, what appears to be a longer duration of this phenomenon in certain nationality groups may be related to the later coming-on of puberty. It may also be that in nationality groups in which homosexual groupings are more emphatic and have a longer duration it provides a better soil for male groups to develop as cohesive units later and with hostile, aggressive attitudes towards the rest of society from which they deviate to a greater or slighter degree. On the other hand, the very long duration of the sexual cleavage in girl groups and the emotional bondage resulting from it may, when this takes place, facilitate an increased sense for independence. The situation in the sexual cleavage has a tendency towards recapitulation. · It will probably be found that with the rising to power of homosexual aggressive male groups there goes hand in hand their suppression of cohesive female groups and their claims for equal opportunity.

4. CONCEPT OF AGE

The fundamental mark in the process of socialization appears to be reached at 7–9 years. This does not mean that this process is finished at that age but that children reach at that age the point when they can form and direct a society. The next mark in the process of socialization is the age of 13–15 years, when the sexual development begins to reflect upon it. A third mark is 16–17 years, when the limit of mental development begins to reflect upon it.

An individual appears to reach the different marks in his general devolopment at different times. An individual whose mental development may appear average normal may appear socially retarded and emotionally advanced. These differences in the growth of mental, emotional, and social characteristics of an individual suggest that the hypothesis of *age* be either discarded or redefined. Instead of using different tests for the different aspects of personality development, for the abstract level of intelligence, intelligence tests, for the performance level of intelligence, performance tests, for the emotional level of the individual, psychoanalytic inquiry, there is need of a test of the individual which evaluates all these factors in their interrelations and when they appear in conjunction, that is, when the individual is acting. The Spontaneity Test is devised to accomplish this objective and it demonstrates that the unity of personality organization is the primary fact to be considered. It appears that this unity functions as an active principle in the evolution of personality. We cannot well differentiate one part of this unity, for instance, the intellectual development, and say it is "retarded" and differentiate another part of this unity, the emotional development, and say it is "accelerated." We need to consider the organization of personality above any of its various aspects, as a unity which, just like the physical organism, cannot escape from functioning as a unity all the time. As a unity it moves forward from year to year. It is interesting to note here that the sociometric test of groups has demonstrated a similar principle operating in group evolution. In groups of children and adolescents with the increasing age of the members— whatever the position of individual members may be—the group organization as a whole moves forward from year to year.

VI. SOCIOGENETIC LAW

The finding that with the maturing of the intelligence and the emotions also the sociability of an individual matures was to be expected. But it is unexpected to find that a group of individuals "grows," that the organization of their interrelations crystallizes, that the clashes between the different intelligences, emotionabilities and sociabilities of the individuals within the group do not destroy the process of maturation nor prohibit the existence and recurrence of regular tendencies within it. The criss-cross currents in a group come to a synthesis, they produce organizations which have a "sense" and invite interpretation.

Our survey of the development of spontaneous group organizations from year to year of age among children and adolescents appears to indicate the presence of a fundamental "sociogenetic" law which may well be said to supplement the biogenetic law. Just as the higher animals have evolved from the simplest forms of life, so, it seems, the highest forms of group organization have evolved from the simple ones. If children were given the freedom to use their spontaneous groups as permanent associations, as children-societies, then similarities in structure and conduct with primitive human societies become apparent.

It is well known that primitive family association regulated more functions than does the modern family. Within its organization the function of education and labor as well as numerous other objectives were executed. Children societies might give us an indication how primitive societies would develop if we could recapitulate them today. The girls in Hudson, when given the opportunity to choose associates for home, work, etc., chose frequently, and more often at the younger age levels, the *same* persons for all the different functions,—with whom they wanted to live, to work, to play, etc. Whenever it was put into practice it led to an overlapping of functions within the same organization of individuals. This is an expression of society similar to that found in certain primitive family associations. The fact that other girls made distinct choices for different functional groups suggests that within the same community different patterns of society organization are desired by different individuals. The fact that all these individuals have been brought up in a similar industrial environment and still have tendencies towards producing contrasting society organizations may argue that the machine is not the sole factor in producing specialization of function and social differentiation.

Our findings suggest the notion that group organization is in its ontogenetic development to a great extent an epitome of the form-modifications which successive ancestral societies of the species underwent in the course of their historic evolution. This view is supported by:

(a) Spontaneous organizations of grouping among children and adolescents develop year by year from simple to more complex stages of integration.

(b) These groups reveal that a remainder of lower organization can always be traced in the next higher stage and that indicators of a beginning towards higher organization can be traced in the next lower stage.

(c) Similarities have been noted between spontaneous group organizations among classes of children in the early grades and spontaneous group organizations among mentally retarded adolescents...

(d) Similarities of tendencies in social organization are suggested between children societies and those of primitives.

PART III:
SOCIOMETRY OF GROUPS

VII. SOCIOMETRIC CLASSIFICATION

1. ORGANIZATION OF A COMMUNITY

The project to determine the psychological process comprising a whole community seems like an unsurmountable task. A duplicate of this process to be accurate has to take into account more than the trends in the population. The process is broken up in numerous individual processes, each of whom contributes something to the total picture. The detailed combination of these individual processes again are very numerous. All the lights and shades need to be integrated in the presentation or else a form of fiction will take the place of scientific truth. The first task, therefore, which we set ourselves was to analyze all individuals of a given community in their interrelations. We were encouraged in the difficult undertaking by the experiences in other sciences—a few carefully thought out breeding-experiments led to the foundation of biogenetics—from the careful psychological study of few individuals a good knowledge of men in general resulted. So we counted that from the careful study of *one* community a better knowledge of the structure of *any* community may develop also. Finally, we thought, however unique a certain concrete sample of population may be, the methods and techniques gained in the course of investigation will be universal.

The community in which the study was made is near Hudson, New York; it has the size of a small village, between 500 and 600 persons; it is a closed community; it has a unisexed population; the girls are still in their formative age and remain in Hudson for several years until their training has been completed; they are sent in from every part of New York state by the courts; they are a cross-section of the nationality and social groups of New York.

The organization is dual, consisting of two groups, staff members and inmates. There are 16 cottages for housing purposes, a chapel, a school, a hospital, an industrial building, a steam laundry, a store, an administration building, etc., and a farm. The housemother has the function of the parent; all meals are cooked in the house under the direction of a kitchen officer; the girls participate in the household in different functions, as waitresses, kitchen helpers, cooks, laundresses, corridor girls, etc.

The colored population is housed in cottages separate from the white. But in educational and social activities white and colored mix freely. These and similar aspects can be termed the " social organization of the community." And whatever the " social structure " of a particular cottage may be it is necessary to ascertain the psychological function of each of its members and the " psychological organization " of the cottage group. The social function of a girl, for instance, may be that of supervising the dormitory, but her psychological function may be that of a housemother pet who is rejected by the members of her group and isolated in it. These emotional reactions and responses among the girls of the group must result in a dynamic situation, its " psychological organization."

The social organization of the total community has beneath its outer appearance another aspect. Although separately housed, there are attractions and repulsions between white and colored girls which gravely affect the social conduct in this community. The " emotional currents " radiating from the white and colored girls, and *vice versa,* have to be ascertained in detail, their causes determined, and their effects estimated. Similarly emotional currents radiate among the white population irrespective of their housing and other distinctions from one cottage to another. Such psychological currents flow finally between officers and inmates and within the group of officers themselves in its sum total affecting and shaping the character and the conduct of each person and of each group in the community.

2. Sociometric Test of Home Groups

The cell of the social organization in the community at large is missing in Hudson: the natural family. These girls are separated from their parents; instead of to the latter they are assigned to a housemother; they are also separated from their siblings and are placed into groups of girls who are unrelated to them and to each other. The opinion is held by many that it is the parental instinct and affinity of blood relation that makes the association of parents with their own children desirable. But here in Hudson the natural affinities are missing. For the natural parent a " social " parent has been substituted, for the natural child, a " social " child. A device, therefore, has been invented to determine the " drawing power " one girl has for another, one girl has for a housemother, and in return one housemother has for a girl. Through such device we may find out to whom each girl is attracted and by whom each girl is repelled. The study of the sum total of these attractions and repulsions may give us an insight into the distribution of emotions in this community and the position of each individual and group in relation to its currents.

The sociometric test provides such a device. The *criterion* towards which the attention of the children has been directed is their liking or dislikes for the individuals in a given community in respect to living together in the same home with them. The size of the population from which the child could select her home associates was five hundred and five. It was estimated by us on the basis of similar try-outs that it would be sufficient if five choices were allowed to every girl. The test was then given to the whole population at the same time in the manner described on page 13. We were then able to classify each girl according to the choices she had made and the choices she had received. An illustration of a typical choice slip follows:

```
WL Cottage 5
Choices made
1. ML, C14     2. KT, C5     3. GE, C5     4. CN, C14     5. SV, C4
Choices received
1. ML, C14     2. .......     3. PR, C5     4. SV, C4     5. EH, C8
(C designates cottage)
```

The choice findings indicate the amount of interest WL in C5 has for the 35 girls with whom she lives compared with the amount of interest she has for girls outside her cottage; it indicates also the amount of interest girls of her own cottage have for her compared with the amount of interest girls of other cottages have for her. It shows her interlocked with members of four cottages. The first choice of WL was ML from another cottage, C14, who also chose her first. Altogether she chooses 2 (KT and GE) from her own cottage and 3 (ML, CN, and SV) from other cottages. She is chosen by 1 (PR) from her cottage and by 3 (ML, SV, and EH) from other cottages. See sociogram of WL, p. 86.

When, then, each girl of cottage 5 is classified as above illustrated in the case of WL, the actual composition of cottage 5 can be compared with the composition desired by its members, whom they would like to have in and whom out of the cottage. See sociogram of C5, p. 122. Looking within the cottage we discover girls who, like stars, capture most of the choices, others forming mutual pairs, sometimes linked into long mutual chains or into triangles, squares, or circles, and then an unlooked-for number of unchosen children. Looking over the total community, we observe that the choices run criss-cross throughout, uncovering the invisible dynamic organization which actually exists below the official one. Suddenly what has seemed blank or impenetrable opens up as a great vista. We see the choices running in streams to one or to another cottage. And we see other cottages practically isolated. We see cottages concentrating their choices within their own groups and then we see another sending so many choices to other cottages that seemingly its own group desires to disband.

3. LIMITS OF EMOTIONAL INTEREST

Instead of the 2,525 choices expected, only 2,285 choices were actually made. Two hundred and forty choices, *i.e.*, $9\frac{1}{2}\%$, remained unused. Nine and one-half per cent indicates to what extent the emotional interest of the whole Hudson population is limited when five choices are allowed in respect to the criterion of living in proximity.

If we analyze one group from this aspect, cottage 1, we find that it left 26 choices unused. Two individuals from C1, we find, made no choices during the stage of the first choice; 4, during the second; 4, during the third; 5, during the fourth; 11, during the fifth. Obviously the girls were fresh at the start, only 2 made no choice then. But from choice to choice the amplitude of their interest declined. During the last phase, when the fifth choice was made, the number of unused choices rises from 8% (1st choice) to 16% (2nd choice) to 16% (3rd choice) to 20% (4th choice) to 44% (5th choice). The following table presents the percentage of unused choices from 1st to 5th choice for each cottage group:

TABLE 7

PERCENTAGE OF UNUSED CHOICES FROM 1ST TO 5TH CHOICE

	First Choice	Second Choice	Third Choice	Fourth Choice	Fifth Choice
Cottage B	0%	0%	0%	0%	0%
Cottage 9.........	0%	0%	0%	0%	8%
Cottage A	0%	0%	0%	5%	25%
Cottage 12........	0%	0%	4%	4%	28%
Cottage 5.........	3%	6%	6%	9%	12%
Cottage 14........	3%	3%	3%	7%	27%
Cottage 8.........	4%	8%	8%	12%	12%
Cottage 13........	3%	3%	9%	9%	35%
Cottage 4.........	4%	4%	4%	8%	44%
Cottage 10........	12%	12%	12%	15%	15%
Cottage 11........	11%	9%	9%	20%	24%
Cottage 6.........	3%	3%	12%	27%	48%
Cottage 1.........	8%	16%	16%	20%	44%
Cottage 7.........	20%	20%	20%	24%	36%
Cottage 2.........	12%	15%	20%	35%	60%

With almost the regularity of a clock the interest declines. It is interesting how rapidly their interest started to weaken. Usually after the 3rd choice a crisis is evident. Only three cottages, C*A*, C*B*, and C9, passed through the first three choices without losing one, and only cottage B reached the final 5th choice still unbeaten. Cottage 2 left 60% unused in the 5th choice and three other cottages left little less than 50% unused in that choice. One choice more, perhaps, or two, and the girls of most of the groups would have reached the limit of their interest.

The gradual decline of *emotional expansiveness* can be illustrated in still another way. From the 505 girls, 500 participate in the 1st choice; 460 are still marching in the 2nd choice; 420 girls, in the 3rd choice; 375, in the 4th choice. To make the 5th choice only 300 girls have a sufficient amount of interest left. A 6th, 7th, or 8th choice may have furnished us with a picture exemplifying a slow approximation to the freezing point.

This demonstrates what we may call the process of slowing down of interest, the cooling off of emotional expansiveness, the *sociodynamic decline* of interest. After a certain number of efforts the interest grows fatigued. It reaches extinction of interest in respect to a certain criterion, the sociodynamic limit of a person's expansion, its social entropy.

4. SOCIODYNAMIC EFFECT

Another process was observed to recur with a peculiar regularity. The number of choices was not equally divided among the girls. Some attracted more attention, they received more choices; some attracted less attention, they received fewer choices or remained unchosen. Some girls accumulated more choices the further we progressed from the 1st to the 5th choice. There were cases where a girl received more than 40 choices, contributed from girls from all parts of the community. On the other hand, many of the girls seemed to be entirely cut off from the circuit of attention. The number of unchosen after the 1st choice oscillated between 35% and 15% of the members of the cottages.

We had good reasons to hope that with the progressing choices everyone would catch something for herself. The number of the unchosen became smaller in the second and still smaller in the third choice. But after the 3rd choice the progress started to slacken. The number of the unchosen did not fall as rapidly as before the 3rd choice: the figures tended to stand still. The number of the unchosen in cottage 1 after the 1st choice was 13 girls; it fell down to 6 girls in the 3rd choice, but from then on the number of the unchosen did not change. It was still 6 in the last choice. Cottage 13 started with 11 unchosen and finished with 3. Cottage 14 started with 18 unchosen girls and reduced them to 6 in the end. Cottage 6 started with 22 unchosen girls and had 6 at the end. Of course the surplus of choices went somewhere. It went to the girls who attracted more attention from the start. Their greater attraction seemed to be responsible for the fact that 75 girls from 505 (15%) remained unchosen, isolated in the community after all the choices were counted.

It might be speculated that if the girls had chosen each other at a rate of more than 5 choices per person that finally every girl of the population would have received a choice. But all indications in our research support the conclusion that a higher rate than 5 choices would have increased the number of choices for those who have been " stars " under 5 choice conditions and would have continued to leave stubbornly out the unchosen ones. We call this process of persistently leaving out a number of persons of a group the *sociodynamic effect*.

TABLE 8

NUMBER OF UNCHOSEN FROM 1ST TO 5TH CHOICE

Cottages:	1st Choice	2nd Choice	3rd Choice	4th Choice	5th Choice
C1...............	13	8	6	6	6
C2...............	13	10	6	5	4
C4...............	12	9	7	6	6
C5...............	10	8	5	4	3
C6...............	22	15	9	7	6
C7...............	18	11	7	7	6
C8...............	12	8	7	6	5
C9...............	11	5	2	2	2
C10.............	14	9	7	6	5
C11.............	12	7	6	5	4
C12.............	16	7	6	6	6
C13.............	11	7	3	3	3
C14.............	18	12	8	7	6
CA	13	9	6	4	2
CB.............	9	4	2	2	2
Totals.......	201	129	87	74	66

5. LOCATION OF CHOICES

The location of the choices, whether inside or outside the group and as their distribution changes from the 1st to the 5th choice, has a definite effect upon the organization of the group. The following three samples illustrate the most characteristic patterns of organization resulting from this factor:

COTTAGE 7, LOCATION OF CHOICES

	Inside	Outside
1st choice......................	14	7
2nd choice......................	15	3
3rd choice......................	14	7
4th choice......................	13	7
5th choice......................	10	7

The same trend is repeated through all the phases from 1st to 5th choice: the majority of choices go inside, the minority of choices go outside the group. It is a sample of an *introverted* organization.

COTTAGE 8, LOCATION OF CHOICES

	Inside	Outside
1st choice.....................	10	15
2nd choice.....................	9	16
3rd choice.....................	6	18
4th choice.....................	8	15
5th choice.....................	9	14

Cottage 8 gives a sample of an *extroverted* organization. The majority of choices go persistently in each phase outside, the minority in each phase inside.

COTTAGE 5, LOCATION OF CHOICES

	Inside	Outside
1st choice.....................	13	17
2nd choice.....................	16	14
3rd choice.....................	17	12
4th choice.....................	11	17
5th choice.....................	16	11

Cottage 5 is a sample in which the majority of choices swings between inside and outside the group without any decided trend. Two phases, 1st and 4th choice, the majority goes outside; in the remaining three phases, 2nd, 3rd, and 5th choice, it goes inside. It can be called a *balanced* organization.

6. ATTRACTIONS AND REPULSIONS

The emotions going out from persons are only half of the problem. Human relations are a stick with two ends. The emotions coming back are the other half. Here were 505 girls who at the rate of 5 choices each had the opportunity to make 2,525 choices. To secure the other half meant to ascertain the responses to these choices. As every girl was in the center of a varying number of reciprocated or unreciprocated choices, every girl belonging to such an atomic structure, a form of interrogation had to be applied in which all the individuals related to each other in respect to the criterion of wanting to live in proximity could participate. In each case all the girls revolving around each girl and she herself had to be interviewed separately and still in relation to each other. This was accomplished by a group of interviewers who attempted through coöperative action, each from another individual's angle, to secure the structure existing in relation to any individual in this community. In the case of WL before mentioned, 8 persons were interviewed, including WL. WL was asked: 1, " How do you feel about living with ML, KT, GE, CN, SV, PR, or EH in the same cottage? Say ' Yes, No, or Indifferent '; " 2, " What motives have you for accepting or rejecting her? " And then ML, KT, GE, CN, SV, PR, and EH were asked in return: " How do you feel about living in the same cottage with WL? Say ' Yes, No, or Indifferent.' What motives have you for accepting or rejecting her? "

The findings reveal WL is attracted to 5, 2 of whom are in her own cottage and the other 3 in other cottages. She rejects 2, one from her own cottage and one from another. She attracts 7, 3 of whom are in her own cottage and 4 outside in other cottages. She is rejected by none. Attractions are mutual in 5 instances. The most intensive mutual attraction as shown by first choice and motivations is towards a girl in another cottage. See sociogram of WL, second phase. See also Motivations Table of WL, p. 78. This inquiry ascertained in the same manner for each individual of the population the number of attractions or repulsions going out from her towards other members and the attractions and repulsions going back to her from them.

The seven individuals interlocked with WL delineates the border-lines of what may be called a *social atom* with WL as its nucleus. In relation to every other individual another group of persons were found interlocked in respect to the same criterion. It can be said that the sociometric test in its first phase (spontaneous choice) attempted to detect these atoms. In its second phase it will attempt to penetrate beneath their surface, as it were, to crush the social atom.

Through the study of the 505 atomic structures it was found that they oftentimes differed widely from the position of the respective individuals in their actual home groups, that these atomic structures frequently overlap one another, many individuals being parts of diverse structures at the same time with, however, a varying degree of interest. First we classified, as expressed from the 1st to the 5th choice, the Yes attitude, attraction, in respect to living in proximity, the No attitude, repulsion, and the Neutral attitude, indifference, irrespective of the motivations expressed for these attitudes. Then we secured from the individuals themselves what motivations they considered as underlying their attractions and repulsions. It was found that rarely did one emotion but usually a complex of emotions seem to motivate them. And these emotions appeared like a " current " centering in and moving two or more persons at the same time. The study of the motivations (see Motivation Table, p. 164) gave, if pieced together and weighed for each individual of the same group, a deeper insight into the forces regulating or disturbing group organization.

MOTIVATIONS OF WL

1st Choice, ML, C14:

We seem to understand each other although we are very different. I am excitable and moody and she is always calm and cheerful. We are both going to do the same kind of work in the future, stenography and office work. She has a calming effect upon me and I always wanted to live with her.

2nd Choice, KT, C5:

KT is just the opposite of ML. She is Hungarian and sometimes teaches me a few words. She is wonderful in sports and the star in baseball. I am not such a good player but a fast runner and KT makes the others have patience with me. She is determined she will make a star out of me too. She is slow about some things, like sewing, and so I often help her with it. It's good to be around her. I like her next after ML.

3rd Choice, GE, C5:

GE I want in my cottage because I feel towards her like she was my little sister. I never had any and I

1st Choice, ML, C14:

WL is so interesting. She seems to feel things so deeply. The slightest happening and she is tearful or else ecstatic about it. I don't get this way very much and so I like to share things with her. I think she is colorful.

Response, KT:

Yes, I would like to have WL in my cottage because of her spirit. She wasn't very good in sports when she was new and she was so persistent I just admire her for that. She is sensitive and although the girls like her she feels hurt if they criticize her, like in games, I mean.

Response, GE, C5:

Yes, oh yes, I want WL. She is the kindest girl in our whole cottage. She is always thinking of the nicest like to take care of her. It is just too sweet for anything the way she appreciates if you do the tiniest thing for her. I always give her all the things I can't use and she makes things out of them for herself. She is clever that way. Mostly she is just a lonesome little child you just have to be fond of.

4th Choice, CN, C14:

I chose CN fourth because she isn't so necessary to me as the others. She is more a luxury. She is amusing and just naturally comical.

5th Choice, SV, C4:

I try to model myself after SV. She is highly intelligent I think, much more than I am, farther in reading books and knowing things. She is delicate and I have some influence over her in making her rest afternoons. She comes from the same part of New York state I do and sometimes we talk about how it is there.

Response, PR, C5:

No. It's only because she has a way of edging up to you and standing so close when she talks to you. There is something about her that is repulsive to me. I have a hard time to be nice to her when she comes near to me. I felt this way about her even before I found out about her having secret meetings most every day with colored girls. It seems she just can't live without them. She doesn't just go with them herself but she tries to get new girls to carry her notes so they'll get interested too. I think it's just too bad about her. If she came out in the open with it you wouldn't get so disgusted with her. But she gets the new girls on the sly. She promises them all kinds of things if they will do it for her and then she forgets all about her promises.

thing to do for someone. I didn't choose her because I chose all girls I play around with who aren't so busy as WL. She has to study more and is older than the girls I go with.

Response, CN, C14:

Yes, we are very companionable. She always understands my jokes and doesn't get angry like most girls do when I make sharp remarks.

3rd Choice, SV, C4:

WL keeps me from being homesick. She always has something to talk about and although she is moody she never acts bored; is always interesting. I think she has a beautiful way of acting, like when she greets you on the walk. You feel she is really happy to be talking to you in particular.

3rd Choice, PR, C5:

I like WL very, very much. She doesn't talk to me much, though. always says she is busy, has to read, or something. I don't know if it is true or not. She is the most attractive girl in the cottage I think; has such a nice complexion and keeps her hair all curled. She is just lovely.

7. SOCIOMETRIC CLASSIFICATION

On this basis we were able to classify each individual and each group of the given community according to its position within it. We were aware that we had to approach the classification problem from an angle which is in sharp contrast with the current methodologies. Classification methods according to type, as Jung's, Kretschmer's, and others, have in common with psychometric classification methods which measure an individual's intelligence, aptitudes, and abilities, that their attitude of classification is centered upon *one* individual singly, whereas the individuals and groups around him are only summarily considered. In contrast, we do not deal with an individual separated from the sociodynamic situation in which he lives, within which he appears continuously, attracted to and rejected by other individuals. The crucial point of our classification is to define *an individual in relation to others,* and in the case of groups, always *a group in relation to other groups.* This is sociometric classification. The approach was not a theoretical scheme but the product of empirical induction growing logically out of our initial precept to discover and control the psychological currents in a given community.

The following sample demonstrates the sociometric classification of one individual and the methods employed to develop an increasing degree of precision in the formula.

The individual WL chooses 2 inside and 3 outside her group in respect to living in proximity. She is chosen by 1 inside and 3 outside her group. " L " designates the criterion, living in proximity. The figures above the horizontal line signify choices made by the subject; those below it, the choices received by the subject. The figures to the left of the vertical line are related to choices made or received by the subject inside her group; those to the right, outside her group. Thus Formula I is as follows:

		in	L	out
WL	sent	2		3
	received	1		3

Through the process of interrogation rejections and additional attractions were revealed. (See p. 77.) The following formula gives the total number of attractions and rejections made or received by WL inside and outside her group. Formula I changes accordingly as the number of rejections are indicated by a figure immediately following the figure indicating attractions (and is separated from it by a dash). Thus Formula II is as follows:

$$\text{WL} \begin{array}{c} \text{sent} \\ \text{received} \end{array} \begin{array}{c} \text{in} \\ \underline{2 - 1} \\ 3 - 0 \end{array} \begin{array}{c|c} & \text{out} \\ \mid & \underline{3 - 1} \\ \mid & 4 - 0 \end{array} \quad \text{L}$$

Formula II becomes further differentiated into Formula III as the choices are designated by *ch* with the number of the choice, first choice, second choice, etc., designated by a number after the *ch*, and the responses designated by *R*, with a letter, a, b, c, etc., designating how many responses there are.

$$\text{WL} \begin{array}{c} \text{sent} \\ \text{received} \end{array} \begin{array}{c} \text{in} \\ \underline{\text{ch2 ch3} - 0} \\ \text{ch3 Rab} - 0 \end{array} \begin{array}{c|c} & \text{out} \\ \mid & \underline{\text{ch1 ch4 ch5} - 1} \\ \mid & \text{ch1 ch4 ch5 Ra} - 0 \end{array} \quad \text{L}$$

These formulas express left from the vertical line the position WL occupies within the group in which she actually lives; right from the vertical line, her position within the community in respect to the criterion of living in proximity. It defines thus her status in respect to the eight factors given below in the Table of Terms in Sociometric Classification.

TABLE OF TERMS OF SOCIOMETRIC CLASSIFICATION

Positive or Negative:	Positive, the subject chooses others; Negative, the subject does not choose others.
Isolated:	The subject is not chosen.
Extroverted Position:	The subject sends the majority of its choices to individuals outside its own group.
Introverted Position:	The subject sends the majority of its choices to individuals inside its own group.
Attracted:	The subject chooses 3 or more individuals.
Attractive:	The subject is chosen by 3 or more individuals. (In or Out is added to indicate if the choices are respectively only inside the subject's group or only outside. When this is not added the choices are understood to relate to both inside and outside the group.)

Rejects: The subject rejects 3 or more individuals.

Rejected: The subject is rejected by 3 or more individuals.

Indifference: The subject is indifferent to the majority of the individuals who are attracted to her or who reject her.

The classification of WL is, according to these eight factors: Positive, not Isolated, Extroverted Position, Attracted, Attractive, not Rejected or Rejecting.

In another instance, that of TL, the formulas are as follows:

TL. Formula   I.   in   L   out
        sent   4 | 1
        received   0 | 0

TL. Formula   II.   in   L   out
        sent   4 — 1 | 1 — 3
        received   0 —16 | 0 —15

TL. Formula III.   in   L   out
        sent   ch1 ch2 ch3 ch4 — 1 | ch5 —   3
        received   0   —16 | 0   — 15

In contrast to WL, TL is an individual whose classification expresses an unfavorable position: Positive, Isolated, Extroverted Position, Attracted, Not Attractive, Rejected and Rejecting.

These eleven cases illustrate how prolific sociometric classification is in being able to differentiate the position of any individual according to sociodynamic circumstances. It informs us that an individual's RU is negatively situated, that is, uninterested in anyone particularly and no one interested particularly in her. It tells us that an individual is isolated in its own group. It discloses if an individual is in an extroverted position and whether she is wanted within her own group but herself runs outside in her choices. It, again, reveals if an individual rejects or is rejected in her group or outside of it.

Without considering yet in detail the motivations behind these attractions and repulsions, if it is fear or dissatisfaction or whatever, a study of these cases, without a knowledge of

TABLE 9

ELEVEN EXAMPLES OF SOCIOMETRIC CLASSIFICATION

Name	Formula I	Formula II	Positive or Negative	Isolated	Extroverted or Introverted	Attracted	Attractive	Rejects	Rejected	Indifferent
Elsa TL	4/0 1/0	4-1/0-16 L 1-3/0-15	Pos.	X	Extro.	X		X	X	
HW	4/4 1/1	4-1/4-3 L 1-0/1-0	Pos.		Intro.	X	X		X	
UQ	3/1 2/0	3-8/0-3 L 2-1/0-1	Pos.	X	Intro.	X	X	X	X	
GL	2/5 3/12	5-2/5-0 L 12-2/12-0	Pos.		Extro.	X	X	X		
GB	3/6 2/1	6-7/6-2 L 1-2/0-1	Pos.		Intro.	X	X	X	X	
AA	3/3 2/2	3-0/3-0 L 2-0/2-0	Pos.	X	Intro.	X	X			
LS	0/0 5/2	1-0/0-9 L 5-2/1-5	Pos.	X	Extro.	X			X	
RU	0/0 0/0	0-0/0-0 L 0-0/0-0	Neg.	X						X
LS	2/1 3/2	2-4/1-0 L 5-0/4-1	Pos.		Extro.	X	X .	X		
SR	1/3 3/6	2-4/4-0 L 1-3/7-0	Pos.		Extro.	X	X	X		
AI	5/4 0/2	5-1/3-3 L 1-1/0-13	Pos.		Intro.	X	X		X	

anything about their history or conduct, intelligence or abilities, except the knowledge that these positions continued during the period of one year, indicates that five, TL, UQ, LS, RU, AI, of the eleven cases are unadjusted within their living group.

The classification of Elsa TL as isolated, rejected and rejecting, is comprehensively corroborated by an intensive study of her conduct. See p. 172. The negative and isolated situation of RU in the community is verified by her lack of sociability. In each case the classification was sustained by clinical evidence and further testing. See p. 178. Any change in conduct was found also to be traced immediately through the sociometric test. When the sociometric test showed a change in classification, a change in conduct was evidenced.

When there is identical classification of two different individuals this does not indicate that the same motivations have necessarily led to it; it indicates only the same *social setting* in the home group. Yet even in these cases of identical classification further analysis leads to further differentiation of the formulas showing that the social setting of two individuals which appeared identical at the start may look very different from a microscopic point of view. This can be illustrated in the cases of HF and GB.

A comparison of the social setting of these two individuals shows sharp contrast. AA is attracted to and attracts individuals who appear well adjusted. She received a 3rd and a 5th choice from two girls who command a great influence in the community. The I.Q.'s of the individuals in the social atom of AA are: AA, 114; BT, 116; SA, 103; TT, 75; and MT, 87. In all but one case (TT) the girls are doing high school work. On the other hand, the I.Q.'s of the individuals in the social atom of BA are: BA, 53; AE, 68; CT, 58; YA, 70. In all but one instance (YA), they are failing to progress appreciably either in school work or vocational training. Nevertheless the actual position in the respective home group of AA and BA corroborates the precision of the classification. But the contrast shows that AA is placed in an upgrade social setting which may mature her best potentialities, whereas BA is in a downgrade social setting with individuals among whom she herself has the best classification. We may state here our observation that if two individuals have the same or similar sociometric classification, the social setting around them indicates a favorable or unfavorable prognosis in their problem of social adjustment. A further differentiation between two individuals was ascertained through study of the relation to their respective housemother and their classification in their respective work group.

Such analysis of the social setting of individuals indicates that the classification status in a social atom is relative, that it changes in significance depending upon the social atoms with which it is interrelated. This also brings up the question of the relative influence of one or the other choice or attraction between two individuals (not only in respect to themselves) in respect to their home group and to the community. We have seen that the influence of one choice differs widely from the influence of another if the network of the whole community is taken into consideration. From this point of view the individual BL, who is, according to her classification, a popular individual, being chosen by 18 persons inside and 2 outside her group, compares poorly with an individual like LP, who is chosen by only 4 individuals. But LP is the first choice of these 4, however, and 3 of these 4 command directly or by indirection about 100 choices, whereas in the case of BL the choices come from individuals who are poorly adjusted in the main and are singly almost cut off from the chief currents of the community. If it comes to estimating, therefore, which individual wields more power in the community, the number of attractions and rejections an individual has does not alone figure, but who are the choosing and rejecting one and what expansion range their networks have. In other words, we arrive here to the problem of classifying leadership.

The sociograms on p. 89 illustrate the social setting of a very popular individual in the given community and that of a very powerful individual in this community.

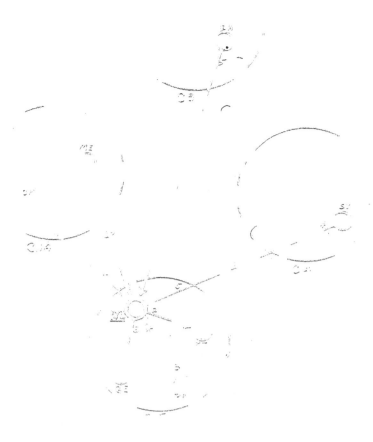

Social Atom of Individual WL
Criterion: Living in Proximity

WL attracts one and is attracted to two individuals in her house; she is attracted to three individuals outside her house and they in turn are attracted to her. She sends her 2nd and 3rd choices inside, her 1st, 4th, and 5th choices, outside. She is the 3rd choice of an individual inside, the 1st, 4th, and 5th choice of three individuals respectively outside. Two of her choices are reciprocated (WL-ME, WL-SV). Three of her choices are unreciprocated (KT, GE, and CN). She does not reciprocate two choices (PR and EH). She gravitates into three different houses (C4, C8, C14) besides the house (C5) in which she lives. The chart illustrates the method of tracing the social atom of WL in respect to the criterion of living in proximity.

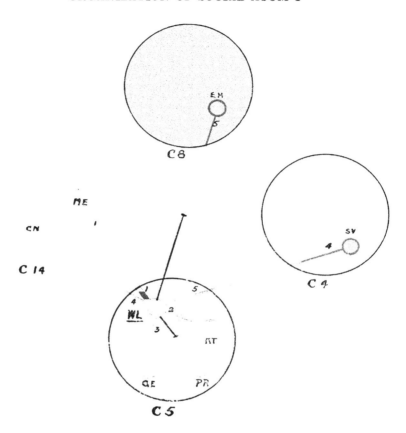

SOCIAL ATOM OF INDIVIDUAL WL
CRITERION: LIVING IN PROXIMITY

The chart illustrates the method of tracing one step further the social atom of WL in respect to the criterion of living in proximity. The responses to the choices which appeared unreciprocated are ascertained. KT, GE, and CN respond with attraction to WL. WL responds with repulsion to EH and to PR.

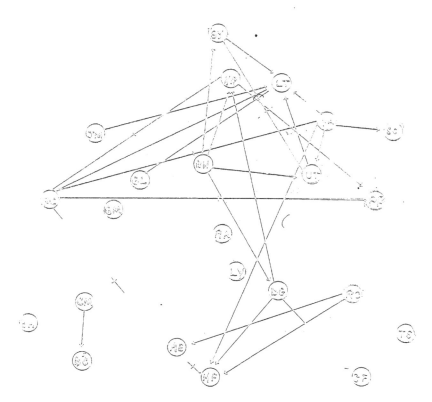

Cottage C1. Population, 23 girls. This chart illustrated a method of ascertaining the psychological organization of a home group. Criterion: living in proximity. The choices are plotted from members of this cottage to other members of this cottage. The choices as they may have come from the outside to members of this cottage or from the latter to outside persons are not here plotted. The organization resulting is: Unchosen individual, 10,—BA, CM, GM, JM, GL, RA, LY, TS, RC, BN; Mutual attractions (Pairs), 6,—AE-HF, AE-PC, PC-PP, PC-YA, UT-SY, PC-KR; Triangles: 0; Chain, 1: HF-AE-PC-KR-PP.

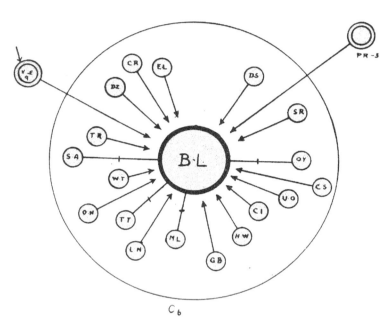

Fig. 1. A Popular Individual, BL. BL is the center of attraction from twenty individuals. Eighteen of these twenty are living with her in the same home group, the total population of which is 25 members. She is attracted to four individuals (TT, ML, OY, and SA) of her own home group. Thus she would be classified as a popular individual. But the two attractions coming to her from outside her group are from isolated and rejected individuals (VE of C9 and PR of C3) and the attractions from inside her group come from individuals who are singly almost cut off from the chief currents of the community. Therefore, notwithstanding the fact that BL commands quantitatively a great direct influence, her influence is limited to the area of her cottage, C6.

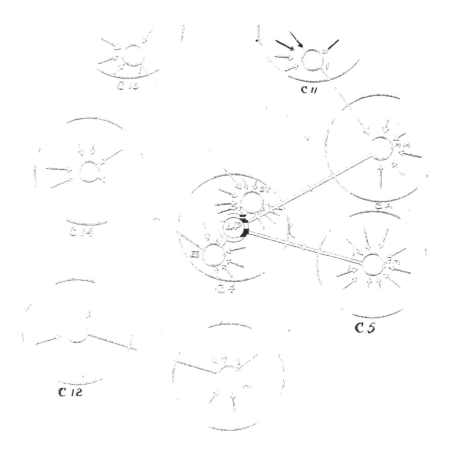

Fig. 2. A Powerful Individual, LP. LP of C4 is the center of attraction from four individuals: SV and ES both of C4, MM of C4, and KM of C5. She is the first choice of these individuals as is indicated by the numeral *1* on the side of the line extending from each of them to her. She makes use of four of her five choices and appears attracted in return to SV, MM, ES, and KM, with each of whom she forms a pair. Quantitatively she would be classified as an individual of average direct influence, but through SV, MM, KM, and ES she commands by indirection nearly one hundred individuals of whom fifty-nine are indicated in the chart. She has actually a powerful position in the community.

8. NOTE ON THE VALIDITY OF THE FINDINGS

The objective was to test a community as a whole and to reconstruct it purely on the basis of findings yielded by the test. Our guiding principle in the research has been from the start, after we had decided working in an unexplored territory, to let the direction and the expansion of the research grow out of the situation. Therefore our procedure was not fixed in advance. After the test was given each time we analyzed the findings and developed out of them the next logical move in the sense of the inquiry. The first step in the test was so simply constructed in order that we might get an immediate foothold into the spontaneous evolution of community machinery: we let every member choose his associates in respect to the criterion of living in the same home, irrespective of age, nationality, or whatever. But in the course of analyzing these choices we found the outcome so contradicting that we could not reconstruct the home groups in the community upon their basis. The foregoing chapters illustrate this. A minority only " clicked," that is, chose each other mutually, and a still smaller minority clicked by first choice. The large majority " passed by " or neglected each other for unknown reasons. At the same time the choices " broke " all the racial and religious and I.Q. lines, colored choosing white, white choosing colored, Catholics choosing Protestants, high I.Q. choosing low I.Q., and *vice versa*.

Further, we had discovered that instead of the 2,525 choices expected (on the basis of 505 persons choosing at a rate of 5 choices each), only 2,285 choices were actually made. The fact of 240 choices being missing had compelled us to make a special investigation. See chapters, Limit of Emotional Interest and Sociodynamic Effect. But the discovery of choices being missing brought about another critical speculation regarding our procedure. Besides the two factors, limit of emotional interest and sociodynamic effect, whether or not any individual has made her 5 choices in full may have a relation to the number of acquaintances she has had the opportunity to make and a relation to the period of time she has spent in the given community up to the moment of the test. As the Hudson school is a closed community, we had the possibility of tracing these factors accurately as every individual who arrived into it faced a population equally strange to her with the exception of rare instances wherein a new girl had met previously one or two of the population outside.

After having treated these two side problems we returned to the primary stage of our research. The great number of unreciprocated choices suggested to us the idea that perhaps an inquiry at the other end, from the unresponding individuals, may adjust many one-sided situations and transform them into reciprocated ones. Also, as we had found in certain cases that the mutual choice was undesirable for one or the other party, we considered more information about both ends of the relationship to be necessary. Therefore we began an investigation into the motivations underlying these choices.

It is the place, here, perhaps, to ponder upon methodical errors which we may have made up to the present point. First, the validity of subjective choice. Subjective choice to be valid requires the total absence of such factors as threat and fear and the operation of such factors as confidence in the *realization* of their choices. It is obvious that the girls in Hudson, if they wanted a desire to be carried out, would try to make their choices as sincere as they were able. Also the test was addressed to the girls by the superintendent in person, whom the girls realized had full authority and whose unlimited desire to aid each girl was often experienced by them. Furthermore, the recklessness of the choices made, as presented in our tables, is evidence that no doubt need exist as to the sincerity of the choices except in occasional cases.

Second, after the validity or invalidity of subjective choice was considered, we considered the validity of choice and response for the purpose of classification. The range of choices and responses fell between 5 and over 40. Every single statement about an individual was thus checked by 5 to 41 other statements and hence appeared well supported. Third, the fluctuating of the opinions. We considered the problem that the opinions of individuals, especially of adolescents, might be found to fluctuate rapidly. Therefore the girls were allowed a period of 90 days in which to change their choices or responses. However, they maintained their original choices and responses to the extent of 95%. Fourth, the accuracy of the girls' statements and motivations of their choices. These are, indeed, frequently inaccurate. Notwithstanding comprehensive study of each child's statements of motivations, they are sometimes, as in the cases of backward children, little more than naïve utterances. Yet in one respect the most inarticulate motivation does not differ one iota from the most articulate one. It expresses this or that individual's desire or protest regarding living in the same cottage with this or that other individual at the time of interrogation. The fact that the more intelligent person motivates her likes and dislikes more fully does not change the fact that she also only expresses a preference. Thus the real test of the situation is not how accurate statements are, but again, how spontaneous and subjectively true they are.

A further restrictive argument is that the preferring of 5 persons outside your group does not exclude your liking the persons of your own group only in lesser degree, even though to be resigned from being together with persons whom you know to be of greater inspirational value for you and your progress is hard to be reconciled to.

Our attempt to reëvaluate the accuracy of the far-reaching conclusions concerning the limit of emotional interest of individuals in respect to different criteria and the sociodynamic effect which results from the psychological pressure bearing upon each individual in large populations suggested to us to consider another source of possible error in our calculation. The members of the Hudson population, before they became a part of it, had been members of a community outside. Many of their emotional interests may reside, and certainly must have at one time resided, in the community from which they came. However, the girls have not been asked to choose for living in proximity individuals who lived at the time of the interrogation in some outside community. It is possible that if such emotional attachments to parents, siblings friends,

men or women, do not decrease in intensity even after a long
stay in the training school that this may account for the indifference some individuals have demonstrated in making use of
the five allotted choices. If the test had been carried out in
a manner not limiting the choices to the population within the
Hudson school and had allowed the girls to choose any
acquaintance anywhere, the result of the test might have been,
and we can assume it almost to a certainty, far more prolific
than the picture we have obtained. Many more communities
than Hudson would have become subject to our test. Each
of these communities may have appeared in our " Psychological Geography " map similarly as a cottage now appears. We
realize that the ideal conditions for this experimental study
should provide for unrestrained exercise of choice. However,
when we studied some groups in the community at large the
population tendencies as revealed in Hudson were found to be
similar. Further, an inclusion of individuals outside of the
school would have made the whole procedure ridiculous, as it
would have been apparent to the girls that the test was not
sincerely meant but purely academic. This may have interfered gravely with the prospect of releasing from them spontaneous and sincere expressions. Further, this fact that no
individual outside of Hudson was available for the girls made
the conditions equal for all. Still further, we have found that
with the exception of men friends, most of the purely social
acquaintances the girls have made outside are displaced by
girls whose friendship they have won in Hudson.

The question also can be raised if the sociometric test is a
necessary procedure in the determining of group and community organization. Is it not possible to determine the
organization of a group through careful observation of each
member, through interrogating one about the other, finding
the attractions and repulsions existing and the motivations
underlying them? Would classification made upon this basis
and the sociogram charted approximate classification and sociograms as arrived at by the sociometric test itself?

Such procedure is inadequate and its classification would be
false, however accurate the gathered information may be,
because it limits the investigation to the individuals of which

the group *actually* consists. But this group is not fully isolated from the rest of the community. The individuals of this group are in contact with many other persons in the community: the field of this investigation has necessarily to be expanded to every individual who may have been in contact with any member of this group. To ascertain these we should have to engage a great number of field workers watching every member of the given cottage over a sufficient period of time, and, to be accurate, every member of the community, because it is just as significant to know how many other individuals feel attracted or repulsed towards some individual of our cottage being investigated. This would mean unsurmountable labor. But even then we would get a confusing picture of the situation, little more than an acquaintance index subjectively undifferentiated,—imitating piecemeal the sociometric test.

In fact, what such a point of view fails to have is an understanding of two important items the test has brought to clarity. One is that the actual setting in which an individual lives and which is imposed upon him by whatever authority and the setting which he would like to have need not be, and we have found, seldom are, identical. It does not recognize the social atom of an individual, that configuration of emotional currents running from this individual to others in various localities of the community and which is running from each of them back to him. The second factor which this point of view fails to take into recognition is that every collective more or less successfully is organized around a definite *criterion*. This holds however inarticulate this may be in the mind of its members. It may, for instance, be the criterion of wanting to live in proximity with certain individuals which defines a configuration of emotional currents between one and a number of persons as a social atom. Without this criterion we would have a configuration of likes and dislikes between one individual and a number of others without knowing to which criterion these likes and dislikes are related. A further investigation always reveals, as we ourselves have found through experimenting with the test in this indefinite fashion, that various criteria mingle and condition this configuration,—the wanting to work in proximity, to study in proximity, sexual criteria, cultural criteria, or whatever. Therefore, the observational procedure has from a sociometric point of view the value of an auxiliary. The sociometric test, instead, is a useful *methodical guide*. It helps to draw organically and progressively information from every possible source bearing upon the social atom of individual existence.

VIII. COMMUNITY ORGANIZATION

1. TYPES OF GROUP ORGANIZATION

Electrons have the same weight and quantity of electricity when they are alone, but if they are attached together to make up an atom they begin to exhibit individuality. Similarly with men. If they are attached together to make up a group they begin to exhibit individual " differences " which did not seem to exist before.

It is one thing to ask what *causes* brought about these differences and the forming of a group. This question has been asked and many answers offered. But it is another thing to ask how is a group or a society organized. The former question is hypothetic and deals with causes; the latter is descriptive and analytical and deals with facts.

The sociometric approach of group organization is free from preconception of the contrast between individualism and collectives or corporate bodies. It takes the attitude that beyond this contrast there is a common plane, as no individual is entirely unrelated to some other individuals and no individual is entirely absorbed by a collective. The position of each individual within his kind, however apparently isolated, is one thing and coöperative acts of such individuals at certain times is another.

We have learned that groups of individuals have a tendency to develop definite organization which can be accurately ascertained and that the patterns of this organization change. (a) According to the age level of its members. See pp. 23–66. (b) According to the interest of the members for one another. See p. 99. If the group is a home group and all or an exceedingly great number of its members like to live with the ones with whom they live, this *organization is introverted* [14] (see p. 128); but if all or an exceedingly great number of its members want to live with outsiders, this *organization is extroverted* (see p. 119). An introverted group organization tends to be warm, over-filled with emotion. An extroverted group organization tends to be cold, as little emotion is spent within it. When the members are not interested with whom they live, with each other or with outsiders, the *organization is one of solitaires*. See p. 116, Fig. 12. If the introverted and extroverted tendencies reach an equilibrium, the *organization is balanced*.

(c) If the group as a whole or the majority of its members (sometimes through the influence of a key-individual) develop a hostile attitude towards one or more outside groups, its *organization* can be called *outward aggressive*. See sociogram C8, p. 123. Cottage 8 is such an instance; $52\frac{1}{2}\%$ of its outside going attitudes are aggressively rejecting. On the other hand, if this tendency is dominant *inside* the group, as in C10, the organization can be called *inward aggressive*. See sociogram C10, p. 125. (d) According to the function or the criterion of the group, as a *home* group, a *work* group, or whatever, a different organization may result in each instance and even if the members are the same in both instances. The work group may be harmonious, the home group disharmonious, in both groups the same girls function. We will come also to consider later complex organization differences due to (e) *conflicting functions within the same group*. An example is the natural family where the conflict arises between the function of the sexual grouping, the man and woman, and the function of the social grouping between father, mother, and children. Group organization changes are also found to be due to (f) *overlapping of functions*. An example is the primitive family association such as the Chinese, which includes functions which otherwise would be exercised by other units, as a school unit, a work unit, etc.

Organization and function of a group appear to be closely related. If a home group has an organization which is extremely extroverted, that is, a majority of its members would prefer to live in other groups, the functioning of this home group suffers in its different aspects proportionately and characteristically. We studied the various types of disturbances developing in home groups and ascertained to what definite form of group organization a definite aberration in function is potentially related. The same function in a cottage group, for instance, the executing of the necessary housework, is performed with differing efficiency according to the organization of the group, besides other factors. If the majority of the members attach their emotional interest mainly to individuals outside their group, this extroverted organization is a potential condition which may easily release disturbances of this function through lack of precision in work, superficiality of performance, tardiness, etc. If the organization is of the reverse type, introverted, and in addition many of the members reject each other, the same function may show a disturbance of a different nature, as friction and conflict between the members over its execution. On the other hand, an organization in which many members reject the housemother and at the same time attract one another, forming a network against the housemother, may release a different disturbance of the given function. As the accepting of directions from the housemother is essential to the work, out of this last mentioned type of organization frequently results regression in the work executed accompanied by open rebellion.

2. QUANTITATIVE ANALYSIS OF GROUP ORGANIZATION

The first problem which we faced in the quantitative analysis of home groups was to ascertain the amount of interest its members showed for their own group. This is what we call, briefly, Ratio of Interest for Home Group. We used the following technique. Cottage 8 has 26 members. To each member 5 choices are allowed. If every member of C8 used its 5 choices within its own group, 130 choices would be distributed within it, or 100%. But the members of C8 have attached only 43 choices to their own group. Computing the ratio of 43 choices to 130 possible choices, we have 33% Ratio of Interest for Home Group in C8.

TABLE 10

RANKING OF COTTAGES ACCORDING TO RATIO OF INTEREST

Cottage 13.	66%
Cottage 10	65%
Cottage 7	59%
Cottage 4	58%
Cottage 11	54%
Cottage 6	50%
Cottage 9	46%
Cottage 14	46%
Cottage 5	43%
Cottage B	37%
Cottage A	35%
Cottage 2	34%
Cottage 8	34%
Cottage 3	31%
Cottage 12	30%
Cottage 1	29%

Subsequent comparison of these ratios with the conduct of the respective cottage group revealed that with the trend of the ratios towards lower percentages, as, below 35% (C2, C8, C3, C12, and C1), the standard of conduct of the groups in this category was lower than the average standard in various respects: lack of interest of the majority of members to raise the standard of house morale, competitions with other cottages, etc., and an almost total lack of *esprit de corps* also in respect to forms of malbehavior which are related to lack of unity in the house group, as runaways, and a high number of members who apply for assignment to other cottages. With the trend of the ratios of interest towards the higher percentages, 35% and over, cottages appear on the table which have shown a better comparative standard of conduct. Nine of these eleven cottages (all except C5, C9, and C10) had no runaways for a period of nine months, while three of the five cottages with percentages below 35% had several (C2, C3, and C10). However, in all instances a high ratio of interest was not correlated to a high standard of conduct if other factors existed in the organization of the group to counter-affect this. For instance, in the case of C10 the high ratio of interest shown for its own group was a disadvantage: the members did not look for other outlets and at the same time there were numerous rejections among themselves.

The amount of interest members of a family group or of any together-living group have for it cannot go below a certain minimum if this group is to be considered a moral force in the shaping of the personalities belonging to it. What is this minimum? It seems to us axiomatic to assume that if from 2 not at least 1, from 4 not at least 2, from 6 not at least 3, if not at least 50% of a cottage group want to keep the group up and desire its continuation, then this group has to be ranked as below the minimum standard. Of course, 50% is an arbitrary estimate.

It may one day be found that the minimum is higher than 50% and not lower. But it can be speculated that the minimum of interest for the group if the group is to continue as a constructive unit can probably be the lower the larger the groups are. It is obvious that a pair relation is difficult if one of the partners is more interested in a relation to a third person. But if a group consists, for instance, of 2,000 persons, if 500 of them want to preserve the group, this group may have a better prognosis than a pair relation in which one-half is disinterested. The factor of function has in large groups greater opportunities for flexibility and specialization. For instance, in a pair relation one cannot have towards the other person but one function at the same time and exchange of function is only possible at different times. But in large groups one person may have at the same time towards a number of different persons a number of different functions. Yet another factor is significant: the influence which leader-individuals are able to exert in large groups. The distribution of power in large groups depends upon the intricate distribution of emotional currents. An individual who is in control and can steer the course of one of these currents can wield an immense potential influence out of all proportion to his immediate following.

The love and hatred members of the same home group have for each other will have an effect upon the organization and conduct of the group as a whole. We attempted to follow up this factor technically through ascertaining the distribution of attractions and rejections among the members of each cottage group separately. We followed the technique of summing up the number of attractions and repulsions respectively in the same group and calculated the respective percentages. If the members of a group expressed 75 attractions and 25 repulsions, the ratio of attractions would be 75% and the ratio of repulsions 25%. The table following presents the percentages of attractions and rejections within each cottage group:

TABLE 11

RANKING OF COTTAGES ACCORDING TO THE SUM OF ATTRACTIONS AND REPULSIONS IN PERCENTAGES

Cottages	Attractions	Repulsions
C11	85.5%	14.5%
C4	77.0%	23.0%
C5	77.5%	22.5%
C13	74.0%	26.0%
C9	69.0%	31.0%
CA	69.5%	29.5%
C14	67.0%	43.0%
CB	65.5%	34.5%
C7	65.5%	34.5%
C10	66.0%	34.0%
C6	58.5%	41.5%
C12	58.5%	41.5%
C1	58.0%	42.0%
C2	52.0%	48.0%
C8	47.5%	52.5%

The percentage of attraction among the members of C8 is 47.5 and the percentage of repulsion is 52.5. The percentage of attraction among members of C4 is 77 and the percentage of repulsion is 23. In C8 not only is the ratio of interest low but the number of repulsions exceeds the number of attractions and indicates a low standard of group organization. In C4 the ratio of interest is 58%; in C8, 34%. This illustrates how widely two home groups can differ.

Besides the summing up of the number of attractions and rejections we considered another aspect, a qualitative factor: that often a single affection of one individual for another may have in its repercussions an effect upon the group or upon the community which exceeds by far the small part it contributes in the summing up. It is a sociodynamic growth of affection.

We have tried to find for this qualitative factor a quantitative expression (see p. 152).

In estimating the popularity a. cottage group has within the community among all the other cottage groups, we considered that the greater the number of individuals in the community who desire to live in a specific cottage the greater is that cottage's ratio of attraction. To secure this we used the following technique. We divided the number of choices its members actually received by the maximum number of choices they might have received if all the girls in the various other cottage groups at the time of choosing had sent all their choices into that cottage. An example is C3. The population at the time of choosing was among all the cottage groups 435. The population of C3 was 17. Hence the number of girls in other cottages was 435 less 17, or 418. The maximum number of choices these 418 girls might have sent into C3 is 418 multiplied by 5, the number of choices allowed, or 2,090 choices. The number of choices C3 actually received from other cottage groups was 25. Dividing 25 by 2,090, C3's ratio of attraction is found to be 1.2%. The ranking of the cottage groups according to their respective ratio of attraction is presented in the accompanying table:

TABLE 12

RANKING OF THE COTTAGES ACCORDING TO RATIO OF ATTRACTION

(An Index of Relative Popularity)

Cottages	Ratio of Attraction
CB	4.0%
CA	3.8%
C5	3.3%
C4	3.0%
C2	3.0%
C11	3.0%
C12	3.0%
C8	2.9%
C9	2.6%
C14	2.5%
C13	2.5%
C6	2.0%
C1	1.7%
C10	1.6%
C3	1.2%
C7	0.9%

It appears, therefore, that the sum of all the ratios of attraction is 41%. We had found that the desire to remain in the present cottages, the ratio of interest summed up for all the cottages, is 44.81%. Hence it is evident that *the cohesive forces at work in Hudson were stronger than the forces drawing the girls away from their groupings.* The difference between these two ratios, or 3.81%, indicates that the introverted trend is still greater than the extroverted and offers an objective evidence of the balance existing in the groups of the Hudson community. (We may add here that the percentage unaccounted for when the ratio of interest, 44.81%, and the ratio of attraction, 41.0%, are added together, or 14.19%, is the percentage of unused choices among the population, 435, of the 16 cottage groups at that time.)

On the basis of the ratios of interest for their own and for outside groups, of the distribution of attraction and repulsion within a group and towards outside groups, of the ratio of attraction a group has for other groups, and other statistical calculations, a *social quotient* of a group can be developed.

3. STRUCTURAL ANALYSIS OF GROUP ORGANIZATION

In Greek mythology Eros is the god of love and Eris is the god of discord. Less well known is the interesting brother of Eros, Anteros, the god of mutual love. That is how the Greeks accounted for the forces of attraction and repulsion among men. It is most beautiful Greek poetry that when love begins an arrow flies to the chosen. The symbol of the arrow has its counterpart in our symbol for attraction, the " red line." The Greeks held that all the red lines are projected by Eros, all the blank lines by Eris, and all the mutual red one by Anteros, and that men had nothing to say about them. Instead of searching with a torch into the labyrinth of love and hatred, they had a mythical formula. We have tried to analyze this network.

The forms taken by the interrelation of individuals is a structure and the complete pattern of these structures within a group is its organization. The expression of an individual position can be better visualized through a sociogram than through a sociometric equation. In the course of reading sociograms it became evident that certain structures recur with regularity. We have lifted the most characteristic structures from the sociograms and present them on pp. 114–6.

Typical Structures in Groups, I.

1. Red Pair. Two individuals form a mutual attraction, a red pair.

2. Black Pair. Two individuals reject each other; they mutually desire to live apart.

3. Incompatible Pair. Two individuals are not compatible. One sends a red line which is answered by a black; one sends a red line which is answered to by a dotted line; two individuals send dotted lines to each other.

4. Black Chain. This structure is formed if two individuals mutually reject each other, and one of them forms a mutual rejection with a third, the third forming a mutual rejection with a fourth, the fourth with a fifth, etc. The incompatible chain mirrors the number of persons in a group who are sensitized to find fault with others; the longer the black chain the more are they so sensitized. The emotional attitude of those who enter into a black chain is in danger of becoming more and more absorbed by critical, suspicious, and hostile interests, especially if they are isolated in the group. The newcomer into a group, particularly into the groups which have a highly disintegrated organization, develops often a reputation which is unmerited and reflects the interrelation with a group which is itself maladjusted.

5. Red Chain. This structure results when two are mutually attracted and one of them forms a mutual attraction with a third, the third forming a mutual attraction with a fourth, the fourth with a fifth, etc. The compatible chain represents within the group an uninterrupted flow of emotional transference. It is the natural route for indirect imitation, suggestion, gossip, and is influential in the forming of group attitudes. It is the social telephone wire.

6. Black Triangle. Three individuals incompatible with each other form a black triangle. This structure accompanies at times widely different conduct. In one instance, the black lines each of the three sent to the other two persons were found

to be due largely to jealousy and protest against the other two, as each sought to dominate the group unrestricted and single-handed.

7. Red Triangle. Three individuals compatible with each other form through mutual attraction a red triangle.

8. Black Square. A black square (and also a black circle) are structures which are so rare that we have not encountered any in this research. This is probably due to their being reflections of such concentrated rejection that the situation in the group in which they develop has to be relieved soon after they come into formation.

9. Red Square. Four individuals who are mutually attracted to at least two of the four form a red square. Every closed structure as this has to be looked upon suspiciously as it may signify the beginning of a gang cut off from the larger group. But when the four persons are interrelated by attractions to others in the group, it is an upshoot of a superstructure well integrated into the organization of the group.

10. Red Circle. A red circle is formed similarly as a red chain except that in addition the structure is closed. In this particular circle presented in the chart eleven girls contribute to its formation.

11. Red Star. This structure is formed if 5 or more individuals are attracted to the same individual; the latter is the center of the red star. Many such structures can be noted in the sociograms.

12. Black Star. This structure is formed if 5 or more individuals are rejecting the same individual; the latter is the center of the black star. Many such structures can be noted in the sociograms.

13. Red Star rejecting the Group. This structure is formed if the center of the red star rejects the majority of those who are attracted to her.

Typical Structures in Groups. Eight Structures of Isolation.

1. Simple Isolation. This structure represents isolation of an individual not only within her own group but within the community. The individual is not rejected and does not reject. No one is anxious to live with her and she in turn does

not care with whom she lives. It is a structure of simple isolation.   .

2. In the second type of isolation represented, the individual chooses individuals outside her group but is not chosen by them or by individuals within her group.

3. In the third type of isolation represented, the individual is chosen by individuals outside her group but herself chooses individuals other than those who choose her. She neither chooses nor is she chosen within her group.

4. In the fourth type of isolation represented, the individual chooses only individuals within her group but these individuals are indifferent to her.

5. Isolated Triangle. In the fifth type of isolation represented, the three individuals form a mutually compatible triangle but each of the three individuals receive black lines from the group. It is a structure of an isolated and rejected triangle.

6. In the sixth type of isolation represented, five individuals each isolated and rejected in her group rejects one or another of these five. This structure, it was found, developed from a rejected gang which was breaking up.

7. Isolated Pair. Two individuals form a mutually compatible pair but both of them are unchosen. In this instance, one of the pair rejects the group and the other is attracted by members within it.

8. Isolated, Rejected and Rejecting. The individual is not only unchosen but rejected and she in return rejects the group.

Organization of Social Atom I.

PI, Person 1, HT. HT is the center of 16 attractions. Six girls are attracted to her from outside cottage groups and 10 are attracted to her from her own cottage. She rejects 3 of those attracted to her within her group and one other within her group. To another she is indifferent. Of those from outside groups she rejects 2 and is indifferent to 1. The clinical picture of those whom she rejects reveals that they lower the general conduct level of the community. She is selective in her friendships and definite in her rejections.

P2, Person 2, EM. EM is the center of 22 attractions, 3 from girls within her group and 19 from girls outside her group.

She has enough followers to occupy with them a whole cottage and to be treated like a queen bee, but she is indifferent to all but two (MM and CO), one of whom is her sister, and rejects 3 others. She is an artistic, self-centered child whose emotional energy is largely absorbed by creative endeavor.

P3, Person 3, LE. LE is the center of 14 rejections and 1 attraction. The 1 attraction is from a colored girl (HL) but the colored girl whom LE is attracted to (MS) rejects her, as do the three others to whom LE is drawn. The remaining two who attract LE do not respond. This structure reflects the position of a rejected individual who still endeavors to find a reciprocating attraction. Such a status did not develop at once. It is an end phase of a long process.

P4, Person 4, BU. BU is the center of 6 attractions, all of which are reciprocated, 5 from girls within her group and 1 from a girl in an outside group. BU rejects 3 individuals within the group. BU is in the position of a leader-individual within her group and in a position to reject. She can afford to be independent.

A minute research of sociograms C4 to C14, pp. 117–29, has opened the way towards a quantitative study of home (cottage) organization and their relation to behavior. One of the microscopic techniques to estimate the status of a group in regard to structure consists in calculating the number of each specific structure, as isolated structures, pair structures of mutual attraction or of mutual rejection, triangle structures of attraction, etc. See Table 13, Classification of Cottage Groups According to Structural Analysis.

Cottages 8 and 4, whose quantitative analyses are given above, showed the following contrasts in structure: Cottage 4 has no isolated structures against 13 isolated in C8; it has 28 pairs of mutual attraction against 10 in C8; it has no pairs of mutual rejection against 7 in C8; it has 5 red-black, or incompatible, pairs against 8 in C8; it has 2 chains of mutual attraction against 1 in C8; it has 4 triangles of mutual attraction against 1 triangle of mutual rejection in C8; it has 5 squares of mutual attraction against 0 in C8; it has 2 circles of mutual attraction against 0 in C8; it has 7 stars of attraction against 1 in C8; it has 1 star of rejection against 3 in C8;

it has 4 mutual red stars against 0 in C8. From the point of view of structure, C4 is better integrated than is C8.

Whether the isolated position of the 13 individuals in C8 is beneficial for them or not does not alter the fact that it is detrimental for the group as a whole if 13 in a population of 33 do not choose it as a home. Also a high standard of integration within a group does by no means imply that that group itself is well integrated within the community. The structural position of a group in the community is a different aspect and problem. It can be concluded that the larger the number of isolated structures in a group orgainzation, the lower is the standard of its integration; that the larger the number of mutual attractions, the higher is the standard of the group's integration; that a large number of mutual attractions is a soil for the finer harmonies; that these harmonies become evident as more complex structures, as chains, triangles, squares, etc.; that, on the other hand, disorganization and disharmony are indicated by a great number of mutual repulsions and of attractions which are rejected.

4. Organization of Work Groups

The research was up to this point concerned with home groups. It gave attention only to the relations between persons. But when we applied the sociometric test to the work groups in the community an additional factor had to be considered: materials, tools, machines. Therefore two aspects entered the test: (a) the relations of the workers to each other and the foreman and (b) the relation of the workers to the particular technological process. A third aspect, the economic, was not evaluated in the test as in Hudson monetary compensation is excluded. It has been an advantage to approach simpler, less differentiated work units before more highly differentiated ones. The machine devices were primitive and the factor of wages was discounted.

The sociometric test was varied to fit the new situation and given in the following manner. The tester entered the work room and tried to get into rapport with the group by explaining that sincere answering of the questions about to be put to them might lead to a better adjustment of their work situation to their wishes. Each individual was asked:

1. Did you choose the work you are doing now? If not, name the work you would prefer to do.

TABLE 13

CLASSIFICATION [15] OF COTTAGE GROUPS ACCORDING TO STRUCTURAL ANALYSIS

		Pairs					Chains		Triangles		Squares		Circles		Stars			
	No. of Persons	Isolated	Mutually Attracted Pairs (Red)	Mutually Rejecting Pairs (Black)	Attracted—Rejected (Red—Black)	Attracted—Indifferent (Red—Dotted Line)	Rejected—Indifferent (Black—Dotted Line)	Of Mutually Attracted Individuals (Red)	Of Mutually Rejecting Individuals (Black)	Of Mutually Attracted Individuals (Red)	Of Mutually Rejecting Individuals (Black)	Of Mutually Attracted Individuals (Red)	Of Mutually Rejecting Individuals (Black)	Of Mutually Attracted Individuals (Red)	Of Mutually Rejecting Individuals (Black)	Attracts 5 or More Individuals (Red)	Rejected by 5 or More Individuals (Black)	Mal Attractions to 5 or More Individuals (Red)	Mal Rejections to 5 or More Individuals (Black)
C1	24	5	15	5	3			1	1	3		1		1		1	1		
C2	26	7	10	2	2					1						1	2		
C3*	17	5	5																
C4	25		28		5	13		2		4		5		2				1	4
C5	35	9	17	4	7	2		3	1										
C6	33	7	26	2	7			1				1		1		1	1		
C7	25	5	26	3	12	2	3	1		1		2		1		2	1		
C8	33	13	10	7	8	1		1											
C9	28	3	22	1	3			2		1		1		2	1			1	
C10	33	4	31	8	12	7	3	2	1	2	1			2					6
C11	29	4	40	1	5			6		8		6		3					
C12	29	4	14	1	1	1		1								2			
C13	27	5	23	1	9		5	2		5	1	1				3			2
C14	30	12	17	2	6	1		1		2						5			
CA	20	3	15			9	2	2		2		2				1			
CB	22	3	11	4	3		2	2											

2. Choose five girls from the whole community whom you would like best of all as coworkers and name them in order of preference, first choice, second choice, third, fourth, and fifth. The individuals you choose may at present be in your home group or in this work group or in other groups. Choose without restraint whomever you think is of greatest advantage for you to work with.

* The analysis of C3 is made only in respect to the first phase, the choices.

3. Choose 3 coworkers from this group in which you are now participating whom you prefer to work with. Name them in order of preference: first choice, second choice, and third choice. Consider in choosing that some parts of the work are done by you in association with a second or third person and you may wish other associates instead of the ones you have now.

The test was given to all the work groups in the community. See p. 132, Steam Laundry. A second example is one of the handicraft groups herewith presented.

Handicraft Group. The group consisted of 9 members. Its organization was considered from two angles: the members as individuals and the members as workers.

The work process consisted in renovating household furniture. The materials used were: paint, varnish, sandpaper, cane, etc. The first process consists of removing old paint from furniture; the second, repairing and painting. The work could be carried on so that each girl could execute a process alone. But it was found by experience that to break the monotony of the work the girls conversed aloud to make themselves heard over the noise made by the scraping of the wood. Therefore they were put at the task in pairs, which had the effect that the partners talked to each other instead of to girls at a distance.

Sociometric test findings were: 6 of the 9 workers (or 66%) gave as first choice the *same* girls in the community choice as in their choice from the immediate work group. Three workers (or 33%) preferred a girl outside the work group but named one of their coworkers as second choice. One worker, May (LF), was rejected by 4 of the 9; another worker, Ella (GA), by 2 of the 9; and May and Ella rejected each other. Only 1, May, said she did not choose the work and did not like it.

Analysis. As indicated by the sociogram, p. 130, GM and RA are mutual first choices; likewise are PT and TS. GA and BI are mutual choices, first choice from GA and second choice from BI. LF is rejected by GM and also by three other workers, *i.e.*, she is a " black " star of the group. LF and GA reject each other. SI, CN, and LF are isolated. All three send their first choice outside the group. Comparison of the work choices with the home choices of the same individuals disclosed that 22 work choices are identical with the living choices, that is, 50%. (The number of possible choices in the work test and in the home test is the same, 5 choices for 9 persons, 45.) On the basis of first choices, the percentage is still higher, 66%. There is evident a trend to differentiate between the choices of the girls in respect to the collective and its function, *i.e.*, between those with whom an individual prefers to live and those with whom she prefers to work.

The importance of interaction between groups and the counter-effect the position of an individual in one group has upon his position within another group became apparent. TS, who is isolated in her home group, is chosen by 3 in her work group. Thus her position within one group is compensated for or counter-balanced by her position within another group. LF is isolated and rejected in both her work group and her home group. CN is also isolated in both groups. Their positions in both collectives are equally unsatisfactory. SI is isolated in her work group but chosen by two in her home group. BK is the center of 4 attractions in her home group and receives 2 choices in the handicraft unit. Thus the position of this individual is strengthened in each group by her adjustment within the other group.

On the other hand, we see the dynamic interplay of relationships developed in one group affecting the position of the individual within a different group. When the testing of the home groups began GM was found to be isolated, rejecting RA and the group; RA was found to be isolated, rejected and rejecting. One month later, when the test was extended to the work units, GM and RA were isolated and rejected each other in their work group. But when the sociometric test of the handicraft unit was repeated three months later, it disclosed GM in a leader-position and mutual first choice with RA, whereas they were still isolated with their home group. Five months later retesting of the cottage revealed mutual attraction between GM and RA and the favorably adjusted position of both within the group.

According to the ratings of the instructor, the two mutually attracted pairs, RA–GM and PT–TS, are the most efficient of the workers. LF received the lowest rating because of unsat-

isfactory work and wasting of materials.   It appeared that if
an operation required the working in pairs, two persons should
for the proper execution of the work be sufficiently compatible
to respect each other's work efficiency.

5. HOME AND WORK GROUPS DIFFERENTIATED

The organization of a group and the function allied with it
are closely related, as we have shown previously.   Definite
disturbance of a function within a household is accompanied
by a characteristic pattern of organization.   The functions in
a household are largely social, behaving according to a certain
standard, dining together, exchanging innumerable little
courtesies, tolerating one another in intimate group life.   But
in a work group these functions are to a large extent absent.
They are reduced to a minimum.   It is from technological
changes that new functions develop and are imposed upon the
group.   The same group of persons with a certain family
organization placed into a technological situation develop a
different type of organization.

The same structure occurring in the organization of a home
group and which may express little or no disturbance in the
functions of this group can express a very severe disturbance
in the functioning of a work group, even if the same individuals are concerned in both instances.   Such an instance is the
relationship between DR and LR.   See sociogram, p. 132.
In the home group, C10, they reject each other, but this attitude towards each other had no appreciable effect upon the
group as a whole as far as could be observed for over nine
months.   They reject each other also in the steam laundry,
their work assignment.   But in this situation their hostile
interaction towards each other had the most upsetting effect
upon the work process and the coöperation of the group as a
whole, a few times bringing the work to a standstill.   This has
a simple explanation.   DR and LR were the feeders of the
steam roller.   If they quarrelled with each other they failed
to feed the machine evenly or delayed the feeding.   A delay
or disturbance in the feeding disturbed or delayed the catchers
who temporarily had no work to do.   At other times, when
the two enemies did not want even to look at each other, one
fed the machine too hastily, the other too slowly.   One catcher

was then so overcrowded with work that she could not meet the demand fully and pieces caught in the machine to an extent necessitating the forewoman to halt the steam roller to remove them.

. Again, while an extroverted organization in a home group may predispose towards severe disturbances in function, an extroverted organization in a work group may predispose but very slightly towards disturbance. The sociogram of the rug-making group demonstrates an extroverted group organization. The efficiency of the work process was, however, not interfered with to any appreciable degree. The reason for this is apparently related to the technological process itself. Each worker works with her individual crochet hook at a speed she herself dictates. Her actions do not depend upon the actions of her associates. On the other hand, the workers, although they did not choose or like each other, had chosen the work. Interest in the work to be executed can provide compensation for lack of interest in coworkers.

The test had also been given to mentally retarded groups as well as to groups in the community outside. It appeared that the trend of differentiation between home and work choices as observed for many groups in Hudson is *decreasing* in groups of mentally retarded individuals. The same group for home and work was chosen more often. Attachment to the same persons for all social needs may have psychologically an economic advantage. Overlapping of the two functions in one group may be less demanding than their specialization into two groups for performance. It appears like a regression to forms which were prevalent in more primitive societies (Chinese family association). The trend towards differentiation seemed to *increase* for mentally superior groups in the community outside. But there were exceptions: there were a small number of groups consisting of mentally retarded individuals who favored the differentiation of groups and there were a small number of groups consisting of mentally superior individuals who favored the one group set-up. But the general trend as found is another demonstration of the *sociogenetic law* that social groups grow through a process of differentiation from simpler to more complex units.

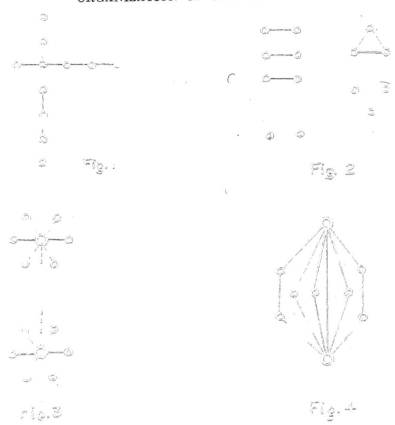

TYPICAL STRUCTURES WITHIN GROUPS

Fig. 1. Attractions between individuals take the form of a chain.

Fig. 2. Attractions take the form of isolated units, pairs and groups of three.

Fig. 3. Two sub-groups are centralized each about two dominating individuals who have no attractive forces uniting them.

Fig. 4. A group in which two dominating individuals are strongly united both directly and indirectly through other individuals.

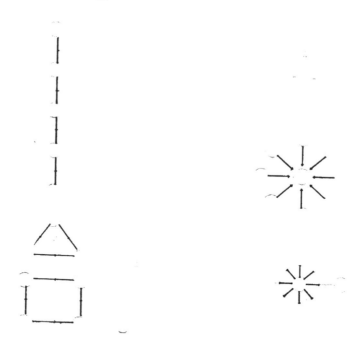

TYPICAL STRUCTURES WITHIN GROUPS

Fig. 1. Attractions and repulsions take the form of a *pair:* in *a* mutual attraction (red pair); *b,* mutual rejection (black pair); *c,* mutual indifference; *d,* attraction vs. rejection; *e,* attraction vs. indifference.

Fig. 2. Mutual attractions and mutual repulsions take the form of a *chain:* a, chain of mutual attractions; b, chain of mutual rejections.

Fig. 3. Mutual attractions and repulsions take the form of a *triangle:* a, triangle formed by attractions; b, triangle formed by rejections.

Fig. 4. Mutual attractions and repulsions take the form of a *square:* a, square formed by attractions; b, square formed by rejections.

Fig. 5. Mutual attractions take the form of a *circle.*

Fig. 6. Mutual attractions and repulsions take the form of a center (*star*): a, center of attractions; b, center of repulsions; c, center of incompatible rejections vs. attractions.

115

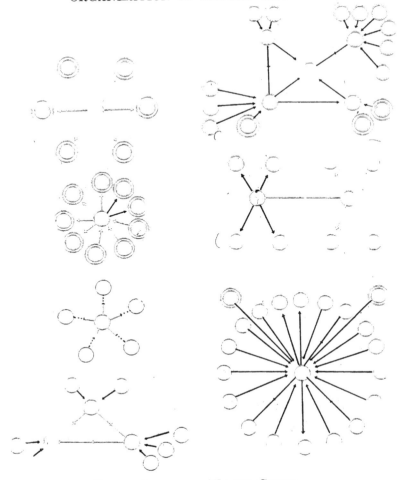

TYPICAL STRUCTURES WITHIN GROUPS

Fig. 7. Attractions and repulsions take the form of isolation.

Fig. 8. Isolation. Subject is attracted to six individuals outside of his group (outside individuals are symbolized by a double circle) who do not reciprocate.

Fig. 9. Isolation. Subject is attracted to four individuals outside of his group and rejects two more; they do not reciprocate; three others who are attracted to him he does not reciprocate.

Fig. 10. Isolation. Subject is attracted to five individuals within his group; they respond with indifference.

Fig. 11. Mutual attractions between three individuals take the form of a triangle but each of the subjects is otherwise rejected and isolated within his own group; the result is an isolated and rejected triangle of persons.

Fig. 12. Five subjects each isolated and rejected within his own group reject and isolate each other.

Fig. 13. Two subjects each otherwise isolated in his own group form a pair of mutual attraction; the result is an isolated pair.

Fig. 14. Subject rejects six and is rejected by fifteen individuals within his own group; is rejected further by two individuals outside of his own group. The result is an isolated and rejected individual.

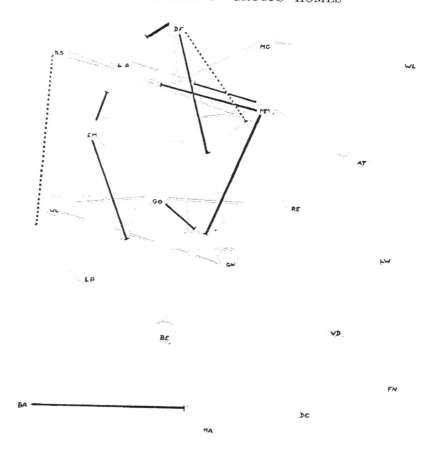

STRUCTURE OF A COTTAGE FAMILY—CA

20 girls. *Isolated,* 3, VD, LW, FN; *Isolated and Rejected,* 3, DC, BE, LA; *Pairs* (of attraction), 15; *Incompatible Pairs,* 11; *Chains,* 2; *Triangles,* 2, EM-MM-GO, EM-GO-LP; *Squares,* 2, EM-MM-GO-LP, EM-GO-WL-BS; *Circles,* 0; *Stars* (of Attraction), 1, DF. *Distribution,* 69.5% *Attractions;* 31.5% *Rejections.*

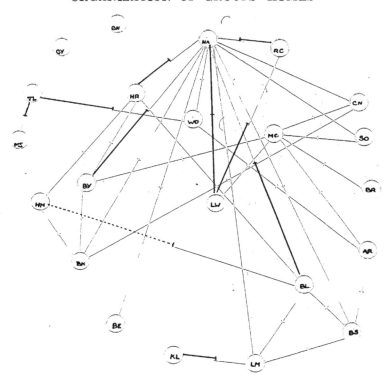

STRUCTURE OF COTTAGE FAMILY—CB

22 girls. *Isolated,* 2; *Pairs,* 23; *Mutual Rejections,* 1; *Incompatible Pairs,* 9; *Chains,* 2; *Triangles,* 2; *Squares,* 2; *Stars (Centers of Attractions),* 2; *Centers of Rejection,* 0.

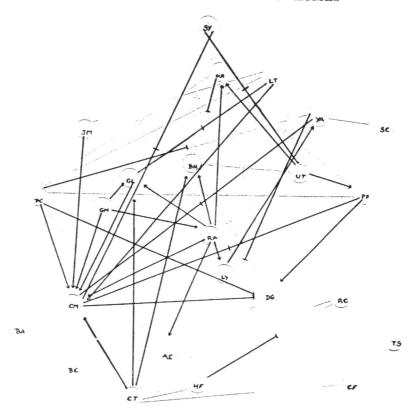

STRUCTURE OF COTTAGE FAMILY—C1

24 girls. *Isolated,* 5; *Pairs,* 5; *Mutual Rejections,* 3; *Chains,* 1; *Triangles,* 3; *Squares,* 1; *Circles,* 1; *Stars* (of *Attraction*), 1; *Centers of Rejections,* 1. *Distribution,* 58% *Attractions;* 42% *Rejections.*

Sociogram on p. 88 is here in an advanced stage of study. To the choices the responses are plotted.

Type of organization: extroverted.

119

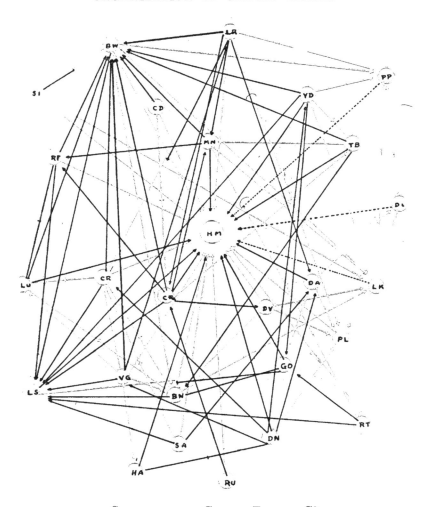

STRUCTURE OF A COTTAGE FAMILY—C2

26 girls and housemother. *Isolated,* 2, RU, DV; *Isolated and rejected,* 3, BW rejected by 11; LS rejected by 9; RF rejected by 3; *Isolated and rejecting* the group, 2, VG, DN; *Pairs,* 10, CD-CR, CR-BN, CR-SA, LU-BN, DV-LK, GO-DA, PP-LK, MN-RT, LU-CR, YD-TB; *Mutual Rejections,* 2, LU-RF, HA-DN; *Stars,* 2, LK, PP; *Chains,* 0; *Triangles,* 1, CR-LU-BN; *Housemother,* 13 attractions, 10 rejections, 3 indifferent. *Distribution,* 52% Attractions, 48% Rejections.

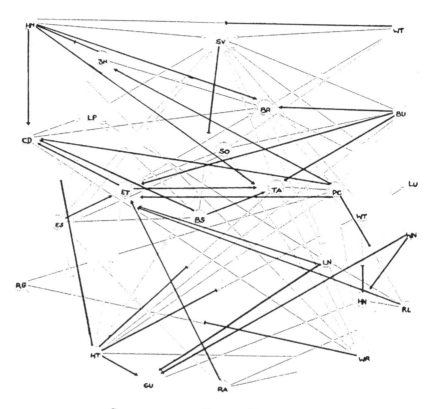

STRUCTURE OF A COTTAGE FAMILY—C4

25 individuals; isolated 0; pairs 28; mutual rejections 0; incompatible pairs 5; chains 2; triangles 4; squares 5; circles 2; stars 7.

Distribution, 77% Attractions, 23% Rejections.
Type of organization, balanced.

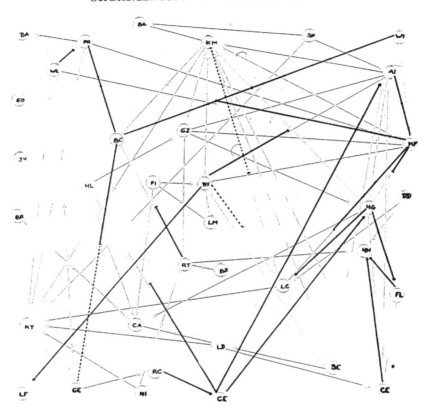

STRUCTURE OF A COTTAGE FAMILY—C5

35 girls. *Isolated*, 9; *Pairs*, 17; *Mutual Rejections*, 4; *Incompatible Pairs*, 9; *Chains*, 3; *Triangles*, 0; *Squares*, 0; *Circles*, 0; *Stars* (of Attraction), 3. *Distribution, 77.5% Attractions; 22.5% Rejections.*

Type of organization: extroverted; special feature, high number of isolated.

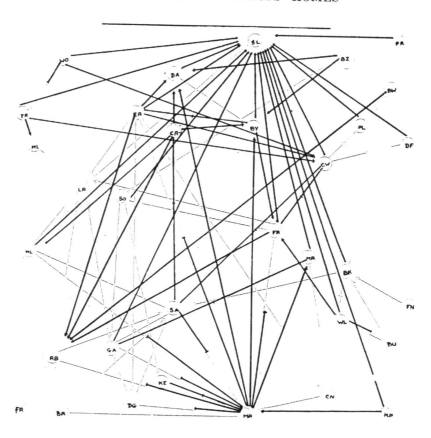

STRUCTURE OF A COTTAGE FAMILY—C8

33 girls. *Isolated*, 13; *Pairs*, 10; *Mutual Rejections*, 7; *Incompatible Pairs*, 9; *Chains*, 1; *Triangles*, 0; *Squares*, 0; *Circles*, 0; *Stars (of Attraction)*, 1; *Stars of Rejections*, 3; *Distribution*, 47.5% *Attractions*; 52.5% *Rejections*.

Type of organization: extroverted, inward aggressive and outward aggressive (see Map III).

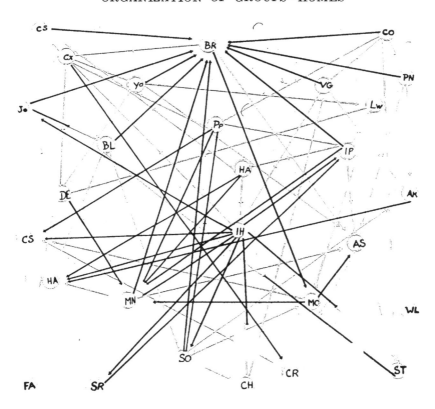

STRUCTURE OF A COTTAGE FAMILY—C9

28 individuals; isolated 3; pairs 22; mutual rejections 1; incompatible 3; chains 2; triangles 1; squares 1; circles 2; stars 3.

Type of organization, balanced.

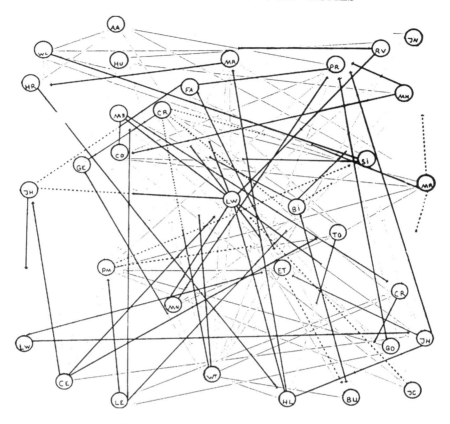

STRUCTURE OF A COTTAGE FAMILY—C10

33 individuals; isolated 4; mutual pairs 31; mutual rejections 8; incompatible 12; chains 2; triangles 2; stars 7.

Distribution, 66% Attractions, 34% Rejections.

Type of organization: introverted and inward aggressive.

125

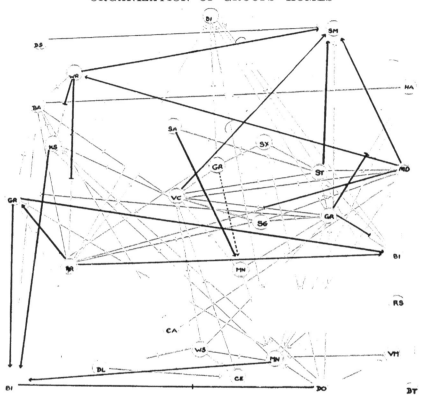

STRUCTURE OF A COTTAGE FAMILY—C11

29 girls. *Isolated,* 3, DS, RS, DO; *Isolated* and *Rejected,* 1, BI; *Pairs,* 40; *Mutual Rejection,* 1; *Chains,* 6; *Triangles,* 8; *Squares,* 6; *Circles,* 3; *Stars,* 8. The Housemother is not represented on the chart. All 29 girls are attracted to her. *Distribution,* 85½% Attractions; 14½% Rejections.

Special Feature: high degree of differentiation.

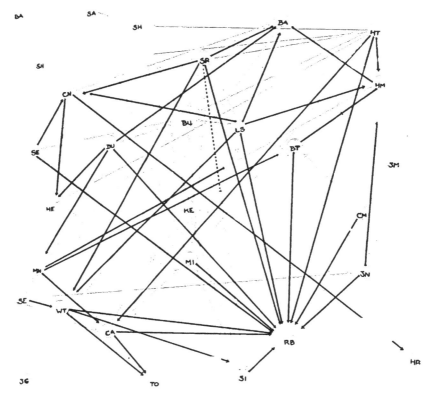

STRUCTURE OF A COTTAGE FAMILY—C12

29 individuals; isolated 4; pairs 14; mutual rejections 1; incompatible 1; chain 1; star 1.

Distribution, 58.5% Attractions, 41.5% Rejections.

Special feature, low degree of differentiation.

127

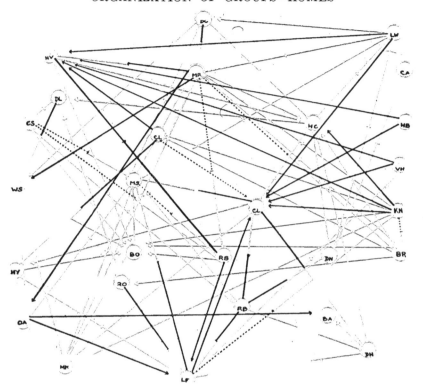

STRUCTURE OF A COTTAGE FAMILY—C13

27 individuals; isolated 5; pairs 23; mutual rejections 1; incompatible 1; chains 2; triangles 5; squares 1; stars 3.

Distribution, 74% Attractions, 26% Rejections.

Type of organization, highly introverted.

128

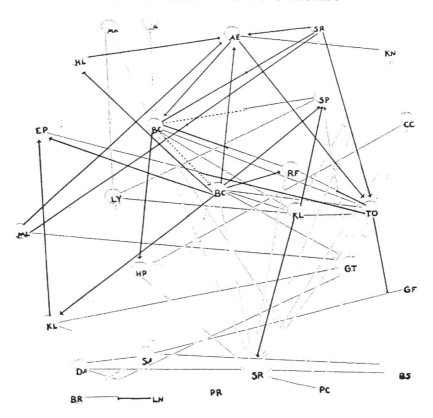

STRUCTURE OF A COTTAGE FAMILY—C14

30 girls. *Isolated*, 12; *Pairs*, 17; *Mutual Rejections*, 2; *Incompatible Pairs*, 7; *Chains*, 1; *Triangles*, 2; *Squares*, 0; *Circles*, 0; *Stars* (*of Attraction*), 5; *Centers of Rejections*, 1. *Distribution*, 67% *Attractions*; 43% *Rejections*.

Special feature, number of isolates.

129

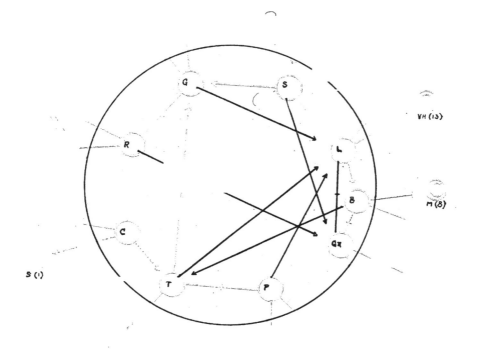

A HANDICRAFT GROUP

Fig. 1. 9 Workers. R and G attract each other (mutual first choice).
T and P attract each other (mutual first choice). B and Ga attract
each other (first choice vs. second choice). C, S, and L are isolated in
the group. But whereas C and S are simply isolated, L is rejected by
five, G, R, T, P, and Gr and four of these form the strongest pair
relations, and further L rejects Ga who is also rejected by R and S.

130

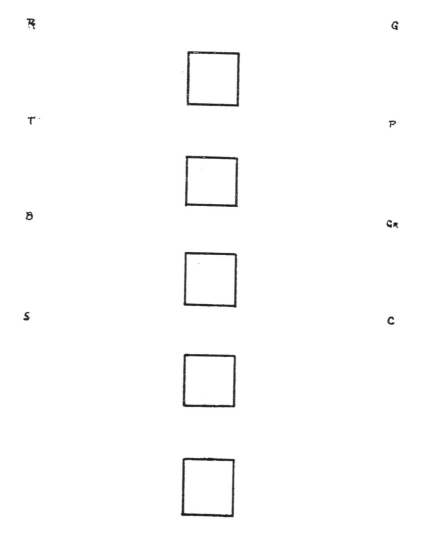

A HANDICRAFT GROUP

Fig. 2 indicates that the 9 workers from Fig. 1 work in pairs and that they have been paired in accordance with their emotional relations: G-R, T-P, B-Gr, S with C, and L alone.

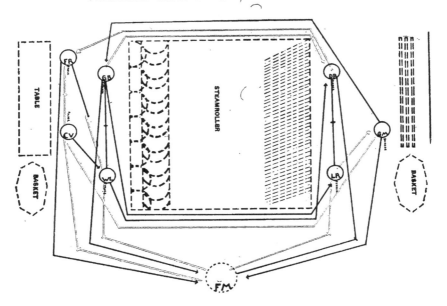

STEAM LAUNDRY

Fig. 1. 7 workers and 1 forewoman. Stella DR and Philamina LR, the feeders, reject each other. Hilda GR and Myrtle WL, the catchers, reject each other. Myrtle rejects the feeder opposite her, Philamina. Lillian FR and Rosalie CV, the two folders, attract each other. Lillian and Rosalie reject Myrtle. Esther GM, the shaker, is attracted to Lillian and rejects Hilda. Esther, Stella, Hilda, and Rosalie reject the forewoman but only Stella is rejected by her. Philamina, Myrtle, and Lillian are attracted to the forewoman. The seven workers live in C10, but all of them are not plotted on the particular sociogram of C10, p. 125, because many of them came to the community at a later date.

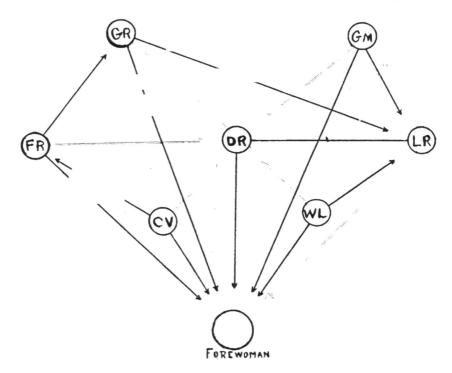

Fig. 2. Stella DR has gained a position of greater influence. In Fig. 1 she is the object of one attraction, Hilda GR; now she is the center of five attractions: Hilda GR, Myrtle WL, Lilliam FR, Rosalie CV, Esther GM, and forms with Hilda a pair. She is rejected by Philamina LR whom she rejects in return. In Fig. 1 the forewoman is rejected by four workers, now she is rejected by all but Philamina LR. The influence of Stella DR is apparent in the concentrated opposition against the forewoman. (See Chapter on Race.)

IX. SOCIAL MICROSCOPY

1. The Emotional Expansiveness of Man

The community of Hudson at the time of testing had a population [16] of 505 persons. If each person should express like or dislike towards every other of the remaining 504 persons, the community would be filled with about 250,000 (precisely, 254,016) feelings of love or hatred. The 250,000 feelings of love or hatred consist of 125,000 pair-relations. Theoretically, at least, every person in Hudson could enjoy so many contacts. Of course, the possibilities of a person in Hudson are still limited compared with those of a person in a city such as New York. A New Yorker living in a community of about seven million inhabitants would have the opportunity to produce about 49 billion different attitudes or 24½ billion pair-relations.

Fortunately, perhaps, our emotions are far more thinly spread and distributed and the quantity of their expansion, as we have proved at Hudson, can be easily measured. We say fortunately because if the expansive power of our emotional life should be so incredibly large as to enable us to produce and sustain billions of friendships or hostilities our social universe would burst from the unendurable heat of too much affection and passion.

We have given every person in Hudson the opportunity to choose 5 persons with whom she would like to live. This means that instead of expecting from each person an extent of interest up to 125,000 pairs of relations, we gave each an opportunity up to a maximum of 505 times 5 choices, that is, 2,525 relations, and if we counted the responses, many more. Incredible as it may appear, a great number of the individuals in Hudson could not make use of the 5 choices. For many girls 3 or 4 choices were fully sufficient to express their needs in respect to the home criterion. A small number did not choose at all. There were also a number who could have used more than 5 choices to express their interest.

No other social institution is more responsible for man's sociability and the shaping of his emotional expansiveness than the family. The plasticity of the newborn infant is probably far larger than that of the adult man, perhaps potentially infinite. Not only the quality but perhaps also the quantity, the expansiveness, of emotional interest has been molded by the family group. A family being a group of *few* persons forces the growing child to limit his attention to the development of few relationships, to parents and to siblings. His thirst to expand is thus early cut and channeled; he gets used to being content with a small number of relations. When growing up he feels that he cannot absorb more than a small number of relations. Indeed, the quantum of his active acquaintances will rarely rise or fall above or below the average. If he makes a number of new friends or enemies an equal number of former friends or enemies will fade out of his attention. He cannot hold beyond a certain limit, it seems, to keep a balance.

Many questions can be raised. Why is the emotional expansiveness of some persons so much larger than that of others? Is it constitutional? Maximum expansiveness going together with the spontaneous personality type? [17] Minimum expansiveness going together with the conserving personality type? Is the course of man's development towards restraint and is the restraining of man's social spontaneity desirable or will the future society develop a species of man whose social spontaneity will be infinitely larger than ours? A natural power is here given to man which is full of potentialities which may enable him to win in the race against the machine: through the expansion of his spontaneous social energy to an extent unknown heretofore.

There is one to whom we always have ascribed the power of infinite expansiveness. It is God. In our religions it is perfectly natural to think that God has a private relation to each person of the universe separately. He has no relationships *en masse*, he does not know us all together, he knows us each separately. We have figured out before that a New Yorker could have 24½ billion relationships within his commonwealth alone. For God this is not only possible but necessary and true. Will the man of the future be more similar to our image of God?

a. Tests for Emotional Expansiveness

We have tried to put this question to a test. The Parent Test (see p. 273), the Family Test (see p. 280), the Acquaintance Test (see p. 137) are, irrespective of their particular purpose, also tests for the ability of individual expansion. In the course of Parent Tests we observed, aside from the manner a housemother reacted towards the different children around her, that one housemother was able to attract the attention of more children than another, and also that some housemothers fatigued more rapidly in their interviews. After a few tests we could already rank the housemothers roughly according to their expansiveness. We followed the matter up in the respective cottage settings where we found our estimates corroborated by other facts.

A housemother can embrace with her given emotional energy only a certain number of children. If the number of girls she embraces surpasses a certain limit a process of selectivity sets in. She will develop a one-sided interest towards those to whom she is spontaneously " drawn ": the rest will fall on the sideline. This limit of expansiveness has, thus, an effect upon the organization of the group through producing a number of girls isolated from the housemother either because there are too many in the cottage or because of " faulty " assignments. One factor in " faulty " assignment is that the girl assigned to a certain cottage does not appeal to the housemother. The effort the latter has to make to reach the child is out of proportion to what she has available for her. And if two or three such individuals are assigned to the housemother, problems to her but easily reachable to others, she becomes, if she takes her duty seriously, more exhausted through dealing with them than through efforts made for a dozen other children. Eventually she becomes indifferent and she tries to mask her undoing.

Emotional expansiveness is subjectible to training. Of course, no individual can be thrown beyond what appears to be his organic limit. But in most of the cases we have studied this limitation has been due to a functional inability to make full use of its full range within the organic limit. The housemothers can be taught through an analysis of their *volume* of expansiveness, if it is shown to them that it is far larger than it appears, that it is being consumed by many other individuals and objectives outside of her actual job. Through the study of this volume and the range of its " consumers " we arrived to the problem of the volume of acquaintances an individual has in the community in which he lives.

2. ACQUAINTANCE TEST

The direct relations an individual may enter into depend, it is obvious, upon the acquaintances he actually has. We there-

TABLE 14

INDEX OF THE VOLUME OF ACQUAINTANCES OF 16 INDIVIDUALS

Name	I.Q.	Cottage	After 30 days	After 60 days	After 90 days	After 120 days	After 150 days	After 180 days
JN	100	C14	13	18	33	39	41	42
GU	121	CA	63	65	42	26	29	28
RD	62	C4	7	8	12	9	9	8
DB	85	C6	30	43	42	46	73	72
ML	80	C4	24	27	30	33	27	28
MK	86	C2	10	12	25	38	29	30
SO	112	C4	30	44	37	50	62	74
KN	87	C9	21	32	33	52	101	131
IL	116	CA	42	61	50	28	46	43
DN	85	C6	22	42	29	32	34	31
HY	102	CB	15	12	24	31	51	46
HR	65	C14	9	9	10	11	14	13
RZ	88	C14	33	14	22	25	25	26
HF	91	C8	30	44	79	84	75	82
FA	77	C8	14	16	15	32	32	33
NI	82	C9	13	25	41	42	47	49

fore tried to study the acquaintance volume of an individual, and for this purpose Hudson offered an excellent opportunity. The incoming girl arrives into a community in which she is totally unacquainted, and from the moment of entrance her new acquaintances are limited to the given population. Because of these two conditions it was possible to gauge the relative growth in volume of acquaintances of one individual to another in Hudson.

We used the following technique: (a) The test was given to unselected groups, to every incoming girl who arrived successively during a given period. (b) The conditions were the same for every individual tested. (c) The test was repeated every 30 days. (d) The instructions were as follows: "Write the names of all the girls whom you can recall at this moment to have spoken to at any time since you came to Hudson. It does not matter how long ago you made an acquaintance, if

TABLE 15

ANALYSIS OF ACQUAINTANCE INDEX OF TWO INDIVIDUAL CASES, RD AND KN

Acquaintance Volume	*After 30 days*		*After 60 days*		*After 90 days*		*After 120 days*		*After 150 days*		*After 180 Days*	
	RD	KN	RD	KN	RD	KN	RD	KN	RD	KN	RD	KN
Lost			1	3	2	10	5	6	3	11	0	12
Maintained			6	18	6	22	7	24	6	42	7	75
Acquired new	7	21	2	14	6	11	2	28	3	59	1	56
Total volume	7	21	8	32	12	33	9	52	9	101	8	131

Distribution of Volume:

After 30 days ⎰ RD: C1, C2, C5, C13, C14
⎱ KN: RC, Hosp., C2, C4, C8, C12, C14, CA, CB

After 60 days ⎰ RD: C2, C5, C13, C14
⎱ KN: RC, Hosp., C1, C2, C4, C5, C6, C8, C13, C14, CA, CB

After 90 days ⎰ RD: C1, C2, C5, C9, C13, C14
⎱ KN: Hosp., C1, C2, C3, C4, C5, C8, C12, C13, C14, CA, CB

After 120 days ⎰ RD: C2, C5, C9, C14
⎱ KN: RC, Farm, Hosp., C1, C2, C3, C4, C5, C6, C8, C11, C12, C13, C14, CA, CB

After 150 days ⎰ RD: C2, C5, C9, C13, C14
⎱ KN: RC, Farm, Hosp., C1, C2, C3, C4, C5, C6, C8, C11, C12, C13, C14, CA, CB

you spoke to her only once or many times. If you do not recall an acquaintance's full name, write her nickname or her first name or identify the person in some way. Do not include girls with whom you live in your cottage."

In Table 14 is presented an acquaintance index secured through the Acquaintance Test administered over a period of 6 months to 16 girls.

Analysis:

The acquaintance volume of the 16 girls after 30 days ranged between 7, the lowest, and 63, the highest number of acquaintances; after 60 days, between 8 and 65 acquaintances; after 90 days, 10 and 79; after 120 days, 9 and 84; after 150 days, 9 and 101; and after 180 days, 8 and 131. We recognize from a reading of Table 15 that the growth in volume of acquaintances varies from individual to individual and from time to time. In 9 instances, it can be noted, the acquaintance volume increased in general *progressively* from month to month (JN, DB, MK, SO, KN, HY, HF, FA, and NI); in 2 instances the acquaintance volume *regressed* in general from month to month (IL and GU); in 5 instances it neither increased nor decreased appreciably but remained practically *stationary* (RD, ML, DN, HR, and RZ). Analysis of the progressive cases shows that the number of new acquaintances made from month to month was in general greater than the number of acquaintances " lost "; in the stationary cases, the new acquaintances are more or less balanced by the number of acquaintances lost; and in the regressive cases the number of new acquaintances is smaller than the number of acquaintances lost; one case appeared uneven (IL) but with a regressive trend.

The acquaintance volume varies from individual to individual to such an extent that 180 days after entering the community of Hudson, living under the same conditions, and having the same opportunity to meet others, one individual, RD, had an index of 8, while another, KN, had an index over 16 times larger (131); and RD, who lives in C4, showed her acquaintances to be distributed among 5 units, whereas KN, who lives in C9, had hers distributed among 16 units of the community.

A comparison of the acquaintance indices of these 16 persons with the findings of their sociometric testing after 150 days indicated that the number of individuals any one of the 16 knows is several times larger than the social atom, the number of those who release in her a definite emotional reaction upon any criteria. For instance, RD with an acquaintance index of 9 chose only 2 individuals with whom she preferred to live and to work; KN with an acquaintance index of 101 chose 14 different individuals on several criteria.

Of the 16 individuals, after 180 days 5 are definitely stationary in their volume of acquaintances; 2 are regressive; and 3 of the 9 progressive instances show a tendency towards a halt. This may suggest that after a certain period a person in a closed community reaches his individual *average* acquaintance level.

Numerous factors have apparently a bearing upon the volume of acquaintances. GU, who has an I.Q. of 121, reaches after 150 days an acquaintance index of 29; IL, who has an I.Q. of 116, reaches after 150 days an acquaintance index of 46. GU and IL are the 2 individuals who have the highest intelligence quotients among the 16 girls. But KN, who has an I.Q. of 87 after the same period of time has elapsed, has an acquaintance volume of 101. Many similar cases have been found although our findings do not suggest any definite conclusions yet as to the relation of the I.Q. to the acquaintance index.

It can be speculated, however, that an individual whose intelligence is about on the same level as the intelligence of the major portion of the population in which he is will usually have a larger acquaintance volume than an individual whose intelligence is far superior to or far inferior to that of the major portion. RD and HR, with I.Q.'s of 62 and 65 respectively, reach after 180 days acquaintance indices of 8 and 13 respectively. The I.Q.'s of the individuals with whom RD and HR are acquainted are in the majority of instances on a similar low level. It may be that in a population the majority of which are of a similar intelligence level as RD and HR, RD and HR might reach a large acquaintance volume during the same period of time; and that in a population the majority of which are of a similar or higher intelligence level as GU and IL, GU and IL might reach a larger acquaintance volume during the same period of time.

However, the emotional and social differentiation of the group to which the individual belongs seems also to have a bearing upon the acquaintance index of any member of that group. The sociometric position GU and IL have in their respective cottages discloses that both are best adjusted to individuals who are far below their level of intelligence. On the other hand, KN, who has a far lower I.Q. than GU and IL, appears in a leader-position with followers 4 of whom are superior to her in I.Q. The superior social and emotional equipment of KN seems to be largely responsible for her large acquaintance volume and for her position within her group.

3. SOCIAL ATOM

When Democrites developed the theory of the atom he opened up the modern conception of the physical universe. To claim the atom as the smallest living particle of which the universe consists he had to close his eyes to the actual configurations of matter and claim impudently that they are composed of other infinitely small units, themselves indivisible, the atoms. Perhaps in an approach of the social universe we can learn from Democrites and close our eyes to the actual configurations social "matter" presents to us: families, factories, schools, nations, etc. Perhaps a mind not distracted by the gross facts in society will be able to discover the smallest living social unit, itself not further divisible, the *social atom.*

During the period of 1918 to 1923 we made several attempts from a philosophical angle to discover the kernel of organization within groups. One was the exposition of the Koenigsroman. The reader (I) has read numerous books. But when the reader (I) had finished the reading of a book he felt conscience stricken, guilty, and convinced that it was his duty to meet the author. And so he wrote a letter to every author he had read asking him for a meeting. The reader wanted to tell him that it would be better, instead of communicating through a book, to meet fewer men but them face to face. Most of the authors to whom he wrote accepted the meeting but seven did not answer. A psychological conflict arose between the reader and these seven authors. (See Scheme I.)

The reader continued to be conscience stricken and in the course of meditation became concerned about every reader who like himself has read all or one of these seven authors but who was not conscience stricken as he. He realized that to each of the authors another group of readers were attached who were subjected to a like fate. His anxiety about author 1, 2, 3, 4, 5, 6, and 7 was transferred now to reader-groups 1, 2,

3, 4, 5, 6, and 7. (See Scheme II.) How was he to reach the individuals of these groups? He couldn't approach them directly as he didn't know who they were. Yet he was bound to them all and to each separately,—a living psychological circle of relations in respect to the same criterion, the book they have read. This circle, changing in size and duration, may have numbered at times millions of participants. It was an organism with a certain psychological unity. All individuals outside this circle, however intimately they may have associated otherwise to the reader, were of necessity excluded from this specific participation. This nucleus of persons in respect to being in proximity with the same thing, a book, can be called a social atom. (See Scheme III.)

But in the Koenigsroman we went a step further. We tried to enter beneath the outer delineation of this circle, to discover the emotional currents, attractions and repulsions, between the seven authors and the seven reader-groups. Then we sought for the underlying structure which may have brought about the collision between the reader and the author. We demonstrated how this form of social organism in our civilization had come into being and how the technological process the book embodies and which interrupts the relation between author and reader brings this most complex and conflicting organization into existence. In a pre-book age no technological process interfered with the immediate contact between teacher and disciple. We see him the center individual forming with a number of other individuals a social atom based on the criterion of learning together. The appearance of the book has brought about a cultural situation in which the simple teacher-follower group became further differentiated into the author-book-reader group. But just as the book as a criterion forces a number of persons into an aggregation, other needs must tend to form similar aggregations.

When we look at a community fully unconcerned with its actual structure and whether good or bad, we become first aware of numerous collectives which swim on its surface: families, work groups, racial groups, religious groups, etc. And we recognize that these groupings are not wild formations but centering around a definite criterion: living in proximity, working in proximity, etc. We recognize also that the position which an individual has in these collectives is often in contradiction with his desires. If more than one person is necessary to realize and satisfy human desires a social situation develops, a social relation, a social need. The sexual desire, the desire for shelter, and the desire for aliment partaken with others, are such desires. More than one person is necessary if the aim is to bring about the realization of a home or work unit. But just as individual A, also individual B, C, D, E, and millions of others are in the same position: they need other persons than themselves to establish a home relation, a sexual relation, or a work relation. These interests are shared by millions alike but still differ in detail and degree from individual to individual. Their difference in detail and degree makes the matter very complicated. A person needs a number of other persons to accomplish his ends and a number of other persons need him to help them accomplish their ends. The problem would have a simple solution, then, if all the persons concerned mutually reciprocated. But they do not unanimously "click." One would like to live with this person but this person is attracted to ·somebody else. One wants to work with this person but this person rejects him. And so forth. Men differ in the amount of interest they have and in the amount of attention they receive. A mass of emotions, attractions and repulsions result going into every possible direction and from every possible direction, sometimes meeting each other, often crossing and running apart from each other.

But the question is how to ascertain the true position of an individual in the criss-cross of psychological currents which mold but also transgress the groups in which he lives? Just as the physical atom, also the social atom, has no visible outline on the surface of things. It must be uncovered. Through the sociometric test a method for the discovery of the social atom was won. See pp. 86–7. An illustration of a social atom is as follows: Person A is attracted to six persons: B, C, D, E, F, and G. B, C, and D reject A; F is indifferent to A; and G is attracted to A. On the other hand, the persons M, N, O, P, and Q feel attracted to A but A rejects M, N, and O, and is indifferent to P and Q. This constellation of forces, attractions and repulsions, whatever the motives of them may be, in which persons A, B, C, D, E, F, G, M, N, O, P, and Q are involved in respect to a definite criterion we call a social atom, the atom of A. Concrete samples of social atoms are presented in sociograms, Figs. 1–4, pp. 150–1. These are social atoms depicting a home complex in each of the four instances. For the sexual complex, the work complex, the racial complex, etc., a different social atom in each case can be ascertained through the sociometric test. These social atoms are not constructions: they are actual, living, energy-filled networks, revolving around every man and between men in myriads of forms, different in size, constitution, and duration.

Presented below is the classification of the complex of social atoms of an individual, Charles M. It gives an exact definition of the coteries in which he is.

Classification of Charles M.

L		W	
3 — 0	2 — 1	3 — 4	8 — 0
0 — 3	0 — 3	2 — 5	7 — 1
3 — 0	0 — 1	30 — 4	6 — 0
1 — 2	0 — 1	34 — 0	6 — 0
	S		C

These four social atoms are the living (L) (home), working (W), sexual (S), and cultural (C) atoms of Charles M., comprising in all 65 persons. His highest range of expansiveness is in the cultural (C) atom; here he mixes with 40 persons. His lowest range of expansiveness is in the sexual (S) atom; there he is attracted to 3 persons. He is isolated and rejected in his home (L) atom and he is discordant in his work relations.

We were able to determine through the sociometric test with which individuals a person wants to be in proximity and how many individuals want to be in proximity with him in respect to a given criterion, and so the *outer delineation* of a particular social atom was ascertained. (Classification Formula I, see p. 80.) Following the directions pointed out in Formula I, we were able to determine through group interview, motivations, and other procedures the attractions and repulsions going out from the center-individual to each of the individuals of his circle and from each of these individuals back to him. And so a first idea of the *inner* constitution of this social atom was ascertained. (Classification Formula II, see p. 81.) Following the directions pointed out in Formula II, we could add the intensity of these attractions and repulsions in five degrees as expressed by the subject. (Classification Formula III, see p. 81.) Following the directions pointed out in Formula II and Formula III, we attempted through the Spontaneity Test to determine the emotions of which the various attractions and repulsions actually consist, to record also which emotions are directing the currents and which are secondary.

A still deeper comprehension of the sociodynamic organization of an atom came through the acquaintance test. The acquaintance volume of a person is already a crude indicator of the expansiveness of an individual in making and retaining contacts in a given community. We secured a finer appreciation of the emotional expansiveness of an individual through the sociometric test. We found, for instance, that an individual, JN, involves in respect to the home criterion 11 individuals; in respect to the work criterion, 8 individuals; in respect to the recreational criterion, 3 individuals; and in respect to the cultural criterion, 5 individuals. Her acquaintance volume at the time of the test was 102.

Through the acquaintance test we learned if a social atom has a rhythmic growth, reaches a high point, and then sinks to more or less an average level; if it is in a phase of expansion or of shrinking; if it spreads according to the geographical location of the individual's cottage, from his cottage to the next, within his work groups on to other collectives, or if it grows inconsistently with these and erratically over the whole community; if it becomes stationary after a few weeks; if it becomes regressive after a considerable rise; and finally with which groups of the community the individual becomes acquainted and whom he can recall when the test is given.

It also further advances our knowledge of a social atom if we determine (a) in respect to the criterion of that social atom the emotional expansiveness of each individual who appears related to the center-individual of the social atom; (b) the emotional expansiveness of the center-individual in respect to *different* criteria. If the emotional expansiveness related to one criterion only is calculated for the center-individual, we receive a false picture of the total range of his interest. An individual may have a low expansiveness relative to one criterion and compensate this through a high expansiveness in respect to another criterion. Also (a), the emotional expansiveness of the individuals in his social atom indicate if their expansiveness is high that the center-individual is related to individuals who are in contact with many others; if their expansiveness is low, that the center-individual is relatively more needful to them.

The classification of the social atom illustrates in a dramatic fashion that we live in an ambiguous world, half real and half fiction; that we do not live with persons with whom frequently we would like to live; that we work with persons who are not chosen by us; and that we make love to persons whom we do not love; that we isolate and reject persons whom we need most, and that we throw our lives away for people and principles which are not worthy. The atom concept gives us an opportunity to bring the immense complexity of forms within the social universe under one common denominator. It is as if a great theater director has evolved a succession of most colorful and most attractive settings and scenes, masks of heroes, and words of eternity to distract our mind from the facts beneath. That these heroic masks are actually a bunch of ordinary people who have all kinds of human relations to each other and that the settings and scenes sprang from the fantasy of a pair of lovers. Similarly, on the stage of the social universe, millions of kinds and varieties of collectives, families, schools, factories, churches, nations, are spread before our eye in most attractive patterns and we are ourselves actors on this stage, and as if by blind necessity, we ceaselessly and indeterminately continue to bring forth ever new collectives to reign as others are faded. Perhaps because we are enmeshed ourselves in this network, it has been so hard to break the door to the actual world beneath, to recognize the human universe in all its forms as a summation, interpenetration and dynamic multiplication of social atoms.

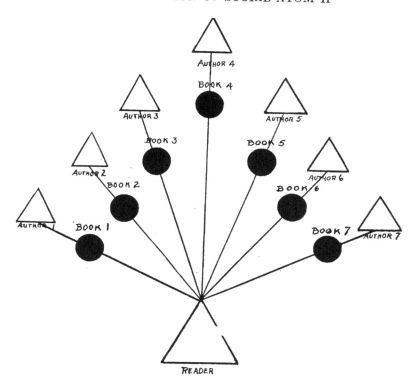

Figure 1 illustrates the initial stage in the development of a social atom whose criterion is cultural proximity. The subject is a reader. Representatives of a techno-cultural process, Books 1–7. Authors 1–7 are a part of the configuration; they are thrown into it because they have written a book; the reader is thrown into it because he has read the books.

ORGANIZATION OF SOCIAL ATOM II

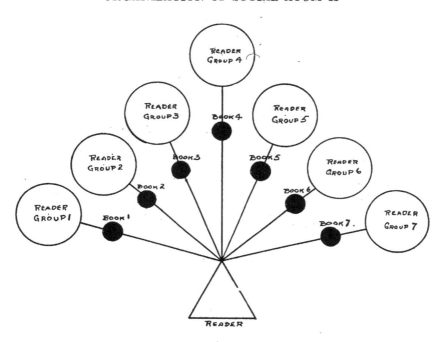

Figure 2 illustrates another phase of this cultural atom. The subject-reader appears interlocked through Books 1–7 with all other persons who have read one of these books, Reader-Groups 1–7.

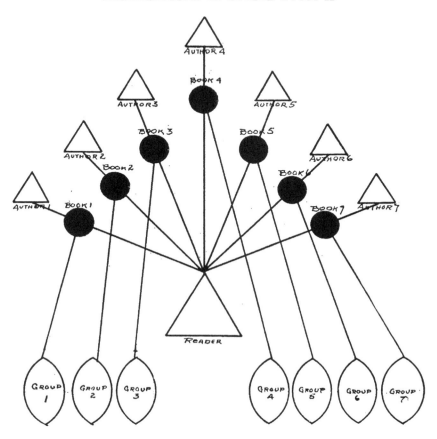

Figure 3 illustrates a final phase of this cultural atom. The subject-reader appears interlocked with Authors 1–7 through Books 1–7 and also to Reader-Groups 1–7 through Books 1–7. The cultural atom here visualized may be characteristic for this reader only and not for any of the other readers who belong to one of the Reader-Groups 1–7. No other reader may have read all seven of the books as is true of our Subject Reader.

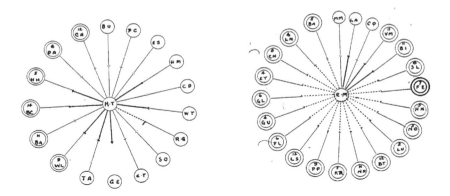

SOCIAL ATOMS: CRITERION OF LIVING IN PROXIMITY

Fig. 1. HT of C4 is a center of attraction to eleven individuals of her group, BU, PC, ES, HM, CD, WT, RG, SO, ET, GE, TA, four of whom she rejects, TA, GE, WT, and HM. One of these, RG, she is indifferent to and with the remaining six she forms mutual pairs. She is an attraction to six individuals outside of her group, WH of C9, BA of the hospital, BC of C14, HH of C5, PA of C8, and CA of C12, three of whom she rejects and three of whom she is attracted to. HT represents an individual of an all-around popularity within and without her group. The individuals whom she chooses and rejects indicate the exercise of balanced judgment.

Fig. 2. EM of CA is an attraction to three individuals of her group, MM, LA, and CO, one of whom she rejects (LA), and two of whom she is attracted to (one of the latter is her sister, MM). She is an attraction to 19 individuals, BA of C5, LN, GU, and ET, of C4, CN of CB, GL and FL of C6, LS and BT of C12, PP of C11, KR of the Farm, NR of the Hospital, LU of C2, NO of C3, HN of C5, FE of C7, SL of C8, BI and VM of C11, towards all of whom she is indifferent except to the latter two and these she rejects. Of her five choices she makes use of two only, one going to her sister. EM is an individual of immense popularity with individuals who do not have to live with her in the same cottage (psychological distance); those who have to live with her know her better. Characteristic for her is the indiscriminate indifference she demonstrates towards the wide attention she receives.

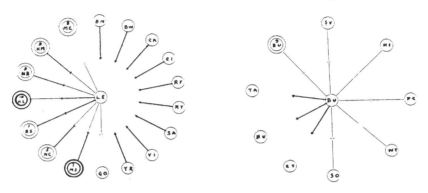

SOCIAL ATOMS: CRITERION OF LIVING IN PROXIMITY

Fig. 3. LE of C6 is a center of rejections coming from nine individuals of her own cottage and from five individuals of other cottages. She is attracted to one individual, GO, in her own cottage and to five individuals, MC, HM, NA, NC, and MS, outside her cottage, one of whom is colored (MS). These individuals reject or ignore her. LE is an individual who is isolated and rejected inside and outside her group. Her position in the group has remained almost unchanged during a period of one year. The pressure against her from the group is so persistent and general, her resentment in return so deep, that the prospect of adjustment to her own group, C6, is poor. LE is a typical case for re-assignment. But unfortunately she has made herself disliked also outside of her group.

Fig. 4. BU of C4 is attracted to five individuals, SV, HI, PC, HT, and SO, of her own group with whom she forms mutual pairs. She rejects three individuals, TA, BU, and ET, within her own group. She is attracted to one individual, BU of C9, outside her group. BU is an individual well adjusted in her own group but one who pays little attention to girls of other groups and they in turn pay little attention to her.

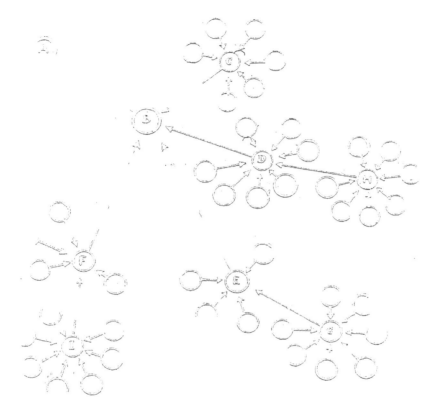

Aristo-Tele of an Isolated Individual. **A.** Individual A is the first and exclusive attraction of B and B is the first and exclusive attraction of A. (Both individuals, B and A, make use of one choice only from the five at their disposal. Except for the one tele from B, A is fully *isolated* in the community. But B is the first choice of C, D, E, and F, who in turn are the center of attractions of 6, 8, 5, and 5 other individuals respectively. Among these latter 24 individuals are three persons, G, H, and I. Each of them is the center of 7 attractions. The effect of the one tele from B to A is to connect A, like an invisible ruler, with a main psychological current and to enable him to reach 43 persons potentially predisposed towards him.

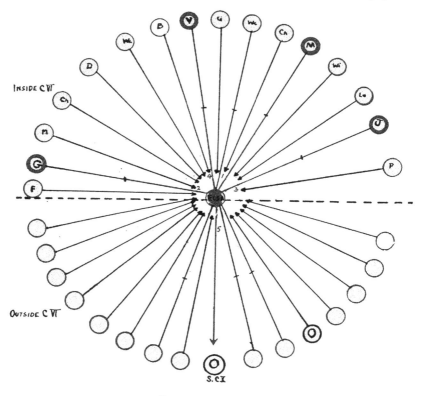

SPONTANEITY TEST

Fig. 1. Sociometric Test preceding the Spontaneity Test of Elsa. Elsa of C6 is an isolated and rejected individual in the given community. The dotted line divides the structure into two halves, the upper half indicates the position of Elsa in C6, the lower half, her position outside of it. She is rejected by 16 (from the population of 25 members) individuals within her group and by 15 individuals in other cottages. She does not reject anybody inside her group but rejects two outsiders. Four of her choices go inside the group; her first choice, to M (Maud), her second, to G (Gladys), her third to J (Joan), her fourth, to V (Virginia). The individuals chosen by Elsa are marked by a heavy red circle. Her fifth choice goes outside her cottage to a colored girl in C10 who does not respond; those whom she chooses inside the cottage reject her.

(See p. 172)

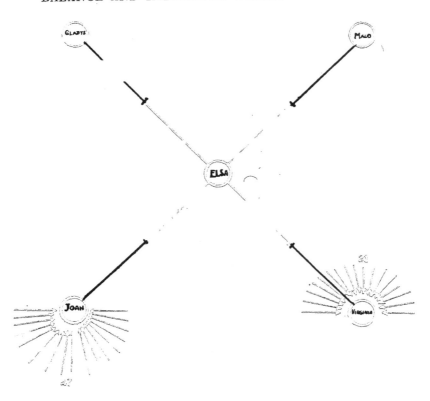

Fig. 2. An analysis of Figure 1 disclosed that from the 32 individuals who took a definite attitude towards Elsa in rejecting her 30 had an insignificant position in the networks of the given community; that therefore their attitude towards Elsa could not have harmed her beyond their immediate contact with her. Only 2, it was discovered, Virginia and Joan, commanded a widely reacting influence in the networks. It happened that these two were chosen by Elsa. Figure 2 plots Elsa in the center of the four individuals whom she chose to live with: Maud, Gladys, Joan, and Virginia. We see her attracted to each of them and rejected by each of them. But as the chart indicates, the effect of the rejection in the case of Gladys and Maud is of little significance beyond the personal fact. However, the effect of the rejection in the case of Joan who has attachment of 47 individuals in different sections of the community and of Virginia who is the leader in the cottage, with 21 attached to her, may account for the persistent and increasing dislike of Elsa.

(See pp. 173–4)

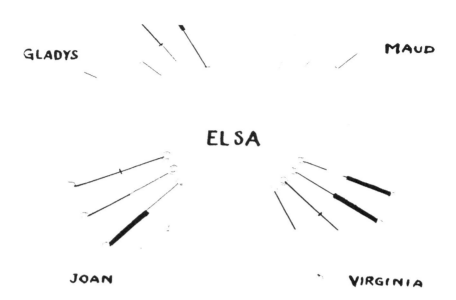

Fig. 3. Spontaneity Test. Elsa, the subject. The chart visualizes the findings of the Spontaneity Test comprising 32 situations in 16 of which Elsa took the lead four times each towards Maud, towards, Virginia, towards Joan, and towards Gladys, and in the other 16 of which each of the four girls, Maud, Virginia, Joan, Gladys, each separately took the lead towards Elsa in four different situations. For description of eight of the different situations of the present Spontaneity Test see pp. 178–82. On the chart a red line indicates that *sympathy* was produced towards the opposite partner by the individual taking the lead; a green line, that *fear* was produced; a thin black line, that *anger* was produced; a heavy black line, that *dominance* was produced. Each situation is separately plotted.

The sociometric test had revealed all four individuals to be chosen by Elsa but to be rejecting her. See Fig. 2. Spontaneity Tests of Elsa in respect to these individuals and of these individuals in respect to Elsa further clarify and differentiate the relation existing between them, as plotted in the chart above. We recognize that the rejection of Elsa by Maud, Gladys, Joan, and Virginia has a different weight in each case and that her choosing of them has also a different weight in each case. Spontaneity Tests of Elsa and Maud show each of the two girls producing sympathy towards the other, although Maud had rejected Elsa in the sociometric test on the criterion of living in proximity. Elsa persistently demonstrates displeasure towards Virginia although she had chosen her and Virginia rejects Elsa both in the sociometric test and the Spontaneity Tests. The relations existing between Elsa and Joan and between Elsa and Gladys are shown to be more complex, none of the three demonstrating unmixed feelings. The states produced by Elsa towards Gladys and by Gladys towards Elsa are shown to be split, Gladys producing sympathy in half her tests towards Elsa and displeasure in the other half, Elsa reacting similarly. Lastly, in one Spontaneity Test out of four, Joan demonstrates sympathy towards Elsa and in two out of four Elsa demonstrates displeasure towards Joan.

(See p. 183)

155

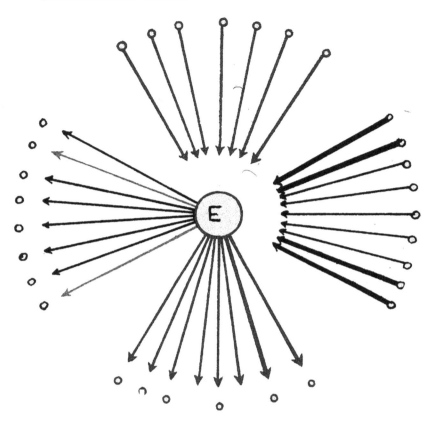

The chart illustrates that the emotions going out from individual E (towards the four characters, M, G, J, and V of her acquaintance) and coming to E (from them) in return are evenly distributed within the social atom of E. In respect to E, 16 test situations revealed the proportion between the outgoing and incoming emotions expressing sympathy to be 8 : 7; the proportion between the outgoing and incoming emotions expressing displeasure to be 8 : 9. In 64 test situations, the proportions were 34 : 28 and 30 : 36, respectively. The proportions indicate that the socially binding and the socially disintegrating emotions are in this social atom only slightly below balance. This would suggest that the attitudes aroused in E in life reality would approximately follow this proportion, whoever happen to be the chief participants in the social atom of E at various times; in other words, that these averages are probably maintained.

(See p. 191)

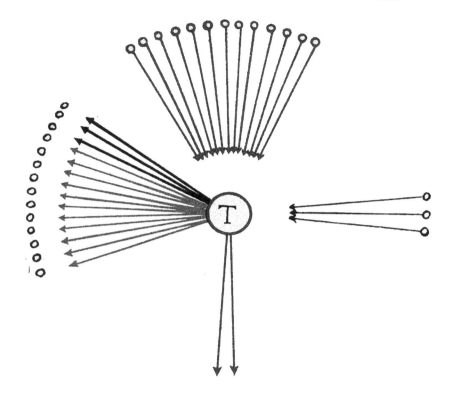

The chart illustrates that the emotions going out from individual T (towards the four characters of the group in which she lives and in respect to whom she was tested) and coming to T (from them in return) are unevenly distributed within the social atom of T. Sixteen test situations in respect to T revealed the proportion between the outgoing and incoming emotions expressing sympathy is 2 : 13; the proportion between the outgoing and incoming emotions expressing displeasure is 14 : 3. In 64 test situations, the proportions are 6 : 54 and 58 : 10, respectively. The proportions indicate that the socially binding and the socially disintegrating emotions are in this social atom fully out of balance.

Case of involutionary melancholia [19]

(See p. 192)

4. TELE

Thales of Miletus is accredited with the knowledge of the attractive power of ferrous material. He attributed to it a "soul." As soon as the physical basis of this phenomenon was recognized, Thales' interpretation was discarded. But more than two thousand years later Mesmer postulated an attractive power coming this time from "animal" bodies. He thought that in the process of hypnosis a magnetic fluid is passing from the operator to the subject, that this fluid is stored up in animal bodies and that through this medium one individual can act upon another. Braid demonstrated later that it cannot be proved that a mysterious fluid is passing from one person to the other, that the phenomena emerging in the process of hypnosis are subjective in origin. Charcot, Freud, and others developed from this point the subjective psychology of today.

Perhaps the controversy between Mesmer, Braid and Freud can be settled if we remove our attention from the relation operator-subject in the process of hypnosis or from the relation physician-patient in the process of suggestion and concentrate upon certain processes of interaction between persons which make it doubtful if these are of subjective origin only. In the Stegreif [18] experiment we could observe that some individuals have for each other a certain sensitivity as if they were chained together by a common soul. When they warm up to a state, they "click." It often was not the language symbol which stimulated them. When the analysis of each individual apart from the other failed to give up an adequate clue for this "affinity," we could not avoid considering the possibility of a "social" physiology,—*internal tensional maladjustments which corresponding organs in different individuals bring into adjustment.* At a certain point man emancipated himself from the animal not only as a species but also as a society. And it is within this society that the most important "social" organs of man develop. The degree of attraction and repulsion from one person towards others suggests a point of view from which an interpretation can be given to the evolution of social organs. One example is the functional relation between the two sexes; another example is the functioning of speech. The sexual organization of man is divided functionally between two different individuals. A correspondence of physiological tensions exists to which emotional processes are correlated. The attractions and repulsions, or the derivatives of these, between individuals, can thus be comprehended as surviving reflections, as a distant, a " tele " effect of a socio-physiological mechanism. The origin of speech also cannot be comprehended without the assumption of a socio-physiological basis. Just as we have in the case of sexuality external and internal organs corresponding, we have in the case of communication internal organs corresponding to each other, the brain centers of speech in the one person to the brain centers of hearing in the other person as well as the external organs. Speech of one person shaped the hearing and understanding of speech of the other person, and *vice versa,* which became another chief stimulant in the development of man's sociality. It seems to us a valuable working hypothesis to assume that *back of all social and psychological interactions between individuals there must once have been and still are two or more reciprocating physiological organs which interact with each other.* The principle of bisexuality is only a small part of a wider principle: bisociality. The attractions and repulsions which we find, therefore, oscillating from one individual to the other, however varying the derivatives, as fear, anger, or sympathy, it may be assumed have a socio-physiological basis.

The innumerable varieties of attractions and repulsions between individuals need a common denominator. A feeling is directed from one individual towards another. It has to be projected into distance. Just as we use the words tele-perceptor, telencephalon, tele-phone, etc., to express action at distance, so to express the simplest unit of feeling transmitted from one individual towards another we use the term *tele,* τῆλε, " distant."

The tele concept is introduced by us not for a convenience but due to the pressure of our analytical findings. The subject under investigation is not covered by any of the social and psychological sciences today. Sociology is satisfied with the mass approach of a mass. It may attempt to calculate the *trends* in population through statistical measures, the frequency of characteristic traits, etc. Mass psychology is descriptive of mass reactions, as loss of individuality in a mass, etc. Individual psychology may aim at an interpretation of mass situations through projecting to a mass the findings which relate to a single individual, for instance, hysteria, neurosis, etc. But the salient point is to investigate a mass of, for instance, five hundred individuals from the point of view of each individual contribution and of the emotional product which results in the form of mass reactions. Then it becomes evident that the frequencies of the sociologist are the surface expression of deeper structural layers in the make-up of populations, that mass psychological findings, as, for instance, the loss of individuality in mass actions, are an impressionistic description, the comprehension of mass processes from a spectator's point of view and not from that of the participants, that projections of hysteria, neurosis, Oedipus complex, etc., from an individual to a mass are undue generalization and symbolizations, that the actual processes are of a different nature. The investigations of the organization of this mass, the position each individual has within it, the psychological currents which pervade it, and the force of attraction or repulsion which it exerts upon other masses, compel us to formulate new concepts and a special terminology better adapted to the new findings. Second, up to date all findings appeared to indicate that the essential elements of existence are locked within the individual organisms and are recognizable only in respect to the individual. The social impulses also did not seem to present an exception to this rule, however great an influence in shaping them we attributed to the environment; the shape they had attained in the course of their evolution was bound within the individual organism only, nothing which mattered fundamentally existed outside of the individual organism. But there is in the field outside of the organism a special area, the area *between* organisms. Characteristic patterns of interrelation have been found to exist between individuals, definite rules control the development from stage to stage and from place to place; they are of such a regularity of form and have such a continuous effect upon groups near and distant that it appears as if social impulses have been shaped not only in respect to the individual organism but also *between individuals* and that a remainder of this process is always discoverable whenever social groups are analyzed. These relations cannot be comprehended as accidental: they are in want of an explanation as to how this order of relations developed. The simplest solution is to assume that on a more primitive level of society the individuals were physically more closely allied and that this bond weakened gradually with the development of the telencephalon and the teleperceptors.

If we imagine a monistic origin of life from a common unit it is hardly believable that the organisms which have derived from this unit and have developed to different kinds and races have broken off entirely the original bonds existent among them. Some remainder, however scant, however rudimentary, however difficult to discover, must still exist. In analogy, the social pattern in its initial stage must have consisted of such an intimate bond of interrelations that at first group reactions predominated and that in the course of evolution the emancipation of the individual from the group increased more and more. But the group bond among the individuals never broke off altogether. A remainder of it and perhaps a safeguard in emergency situations persists. Indicators of such a remainder are the persistent recurrence of various structures on various levels of differentiation from a psycho-organic level in which expression of feeling is inarticulate up to a psycho-social level in which expression of feeling is highly articulate. Concepts as reflex, conditioning reflex, instinct, mental syndrome, etc., which have grown out of the approach of the individual organism, are not explanatory of these findings and have no meaning in this area. Fifty individuals who singly are classified as suffering from hysteria may as a group reveal a pattern totally different from a mass hysteria, for instance, an extroverted group organization with a high number of incompatible pairs. Or, again, the sexual character of individual members may be male or female, heterosexual or homosexual. And from an individual point of view this is a definable condition but from the intersexual choices, attractions and repulsions among such members an organization may result which has as a totality a different meaning from that of the sexual character of its individual members alone. It may, for instance, show an organization split into two parts, a homosexual and a heterosexual gang which are in a state of warfare because some members of the homosexual gang are objects of the desires of certain members of the heterosexual gang or *vice versa*.

(a) *Concerning Tele Effect.*

Every individual man functions in a system which is confined by two boundaries: the emotional expansiveness of his own personality and the psychological pressure exerted upon him by the population. The psychological variations in population pressure affect the individual especially during his formative years. We have shown how deep its effect is even in the apparent vacuum around an isolated person, that the specific molds and boundaries we have created to shelter and shape individuals, the home unit, the school unit, and the work unit, are not actual boundaries, that the forces of attraction and repulsion pass beyond these limits, ceaselessly striving towards exchange of emotional states, that this tendency to reach out and to exchange emotions is stronger than social institutions formed apparently to protect man against the vagaries of his adventurous nature.

The relations treated up to this point may mark the beginning of a measurement of social atoms. The electro-magnetic and physio-chemical analysis of emotions is outside of the sociometric domain. Our problem is the social expansiveness of man and his transmission of emotion. Social expansion does not infer only how intensive an emotion is which is projected towards this or that person but how *many* persons a person is able to interest, to how *many* persons he can transfer an emotion, and from how *many* persons he can absorb emotion. In other words, it traces the origin of a " psychological current."

Even if one day the feeling complex, tele, should yield to quantitative measurement, from a sociometric point of view this feeling complex is separated only artificially from a larger whole: it is a part of the smallest living unit of social matter we can comprehend, the social atom. Therefore the sociometric approach of tele is closely linked with our findings in respect to the inner organization of a social atom. The first thing we meet in the social atom is that a feeling complex which goes out from a person does not run wildly into space but goes to a certain other person and that the other person does not accept this passively like a robot but responds actively with another feeling complex in return. One tele may become interlocked with another tele, a pair of relations being formed.

Tele has no social existence by itself. It is an abstraction. It has to be comprehended as a process within a social atom. But it is possible to classify it according to the equation of its social expansion, its social *effect*. This is exemplified in the following illustration:

An individual A is the first and exclusive choice of a second individual B, and B is her first and exclusive choice. Except for the one tele from B, A is fully isolated in the community. However, B is first choice of C, D, E, and F. C, D, E, and F are the choice respectively of 6, 8, 5, and 5 other individuals. Among these latter 24 individuals are three persons, G, H, and I. Each of them is the center of 7 choices. The effect of the one tele from B to A connects A with a main psychological current and enables her to reach 43 persons potentially predisposed towards her. On the other hand, another individual may be unable to exert any considerable effect upon the community as her tele relate her only to individuals who are in a relatively isolated position. Her tele are side-tracked and never reach the main currents. An individual like A, who is as a person comparatively unknown but who exerts through the medium of other individuals a far-reaching effect upon masses of people, is an invisible ruler. The form which the one tele going from the individual A to the individual B takes can be said to be aristocratic, an *aristo*-tele. Such an aristo-tele has often turned the cultural and political history of a people, as in the instance of Socrates and Plato, or Nietzsche and Wagner, or Marx and La Salle.

When we study a community in this fashion, as an interrelated whole, considering what effect one part has upon the other, we recognize that also the totality does not grow directionless or chaotically, that just as the individual organism grows towards a definite end, maturity, also groups grow with a tendency towards a definite organization which guarantees end-forms and a lasting preservation of the whole. Like the inevitability of a pre-conceived plan, the organization unfolds. At first grow out of an indefinite status a horizontal and a vertical differentiation of structure, the development of a "bottom" and of a "top." Then stage follows stage as gradually the social, sexual, and racial cleavages differentiate it further. Examining the membership of this crystallizing organization we observe again that neither is this a wild distribution of position and function. If we may be allowed to develop the analogy of a bottom and a top of the group still further, we may say that the isolated whom we find at the top of the group are relatively superior, solitaire individuals and the isolated whom we find at the bottom of the group are relatively inferior, unchosen, and unwanted individuals. The individuals forming the top of the group may become aggressive towards the members of the middle groups and the individuals forming the bottom of the group may also turn towards the members of the middle groups; and between these two groups the middle group attempts to develop a cohesive unity and coördinated strength to keep in check both the top groups and the bottom groups. And it appears that the end-forms towards which the sum total strived is one in which the representatives of the creative function (aristo-tele) come to an inter-functioning with the representatives of the social function, the leaders of the group.

X. MOTIVATION

1. MOTIVATIONS

The spontaneous and unrestrained attitudes of individuals in regard to associating themselves to persons of their choice have a significance far wider than the motivations which these individuals are able to express in explaining their attitudes. In our research the motivations the individuals themselves gave were recorded in their own words for the purpose of adjusting to and articulating in detail the desires and expectations of the individuals with the technical possibilities of the community.

When a girl was so attractive to fifteen others that they wanted to live with her in the same cottage and she had chosen but two of them to live with her, it was important in the interest of the unreciprocated thirteen to ascertain if they were unchosen by her for any particular reason and if a rapprochement was possible. And it was also necessary to know the motivations when attraction was mutual as these might reveal attractions which were harmful for one or both parties. Our method was, after the desires of each individual in the community in respect to its different objectives were disclosed, to aid them in reflecting their actions so that they might be able to attain their goals themselves. It was a theory of the subjects' own actions in development rather than a theory of our own which we sought to prove. The motivations which we collected were the reflections in their own minds concerning their wishes. The criss-crossing motivations were followed up in detail if for no other reason than to estimate further the position of every child in the community. We were able to guarantee confidence of information and no child was ever informed by whom she had been chosen or rejected or any motivations concerning her. All individuals who belonged to the same social atom in respect to any criterion were interrogated to give their motivations for being attracted to or rejecting any particular individual.

In respect to the criterion of living in proximity, 107 types of chief motivations were given, 58 of which fell under the heading of dislike, 46 under the heading of like, and 3 of indifference. They demonstrate a finer discrimination for motivations of dislike than of like. The number of varieties of motivations of dislike or rejection is far greater than the number of varieties for like or attraction. It would appear that our subjects were more articulate in giving expression to dislike than to like.

The motivations given, however inarticulate, disclose how individualistic the reactions are. Looking at any sociogram we can recognize the positions of the individuals within it only so far as their classification is charted. We can say so and so many individuals are isolated or isolated-rejected or forming mutual pairs, but we could not differentiate one isolated structure from another or one mutual pair from another, etc. But with the expressed motivations we can already begin to differentiate between these. One isolate appears as a newcomer whom the group has not yet absorbed. Another isolated individual appears as a former rejected one who is simply neglected, " because she is not intelligent and has bad habits." Similarly we see each isolated structure in a group becoming of living meaning, each different from the other. One mutual pair appears motivated from one side by " She protects me "; from the other side, " She is like a little sister to me." Another mutual pair appears motivated from one side by " Good companionship " and from the other by " I can confide in her." One structure of rejection appears motivated by " lies," " steals," " is dirty," " is mean," and " quarrels "; and another such structure is motivated by " She is always planning to run away." Each structure appears as a differently motivated dynamic expression.

The motivations give a further basis for comparison of groups. We can compare, for instance, C2, which had received a low ranking through quantitative analysis, with C4, which received a high ranking. The members of C2 produced 26 different motivations for disliking others; C4 produced 15. C2 produced 20 different motivations for liking; C4 produced 25. We can compare the highest figure any motivation of liking or disliking has in C2 with the respective figure for the same motivation in C4. In C2 the most frequently given motivation was " I want her because she is of my nationality," which was repeated 17 times. This motivation is absent in C4. There were 10 girls in C2 of nationality contrasting with that of the majority; in C4, 6. We followed up the relation to their respective housemother of the girls of contrasting nationality and found that 8 of them in C2 disliked their housemother, whereas in C4 only 3 disliked her. In C2 the housemother's relation to these girls appears as a factor conditioning the reactions. She preferred girls of native American stock and her attitude was reflected by the girls of

American extraction also within the group. A split into two factions gradually crystallized, each aspiring to dominate the other. The minority contrasting element was driven into an attitude of defense. Being fewer in numbers, they wanted to strengthen their position through getting girls of their nationality in other cottages to live with them. The most frequently given motivation for disliking in C2 was "She is a nigger-lover," which was given 16 times. This motivation was given but once in C4. The pressure of the group in C4 against friendship with colored girls was so pronounced that no girl who was placed in this group was likely to have such a friendship secretly, whereas in C2 numerous girls had friendships with colored girls and disclosure of this activity arose from jealousy of one another. Another interesting contrast is between the colored cottages, C7 and C10, and the white cottage groups. As a motivation for dislike the colored girls not once gave "She loves a white girl," but "She's a nigger-lover" was given 99 times by white girls. For discussion of the relation between colored and white, see pp. 217–24. As in these examples, in like manner further differentiation between all the groups may be traced through motivations.

The more we studied motivations given by the subjects the more we paid attention to every choice made by an individual, not in the psychoanalytic sense that it had a meaning in the development of the individual, but in the sociometric sense that it had a value in " feeling out " the associations with which persons within the realm of her acquaintances are best suited for them. But the motivations were often insufficient or inconsistent: changing of opinion, untruthful statements, statements without foundation given in respect to persons not known personally. We had to develop a method which would reflect the interrelations more intimately.

2. VALIDITY OF MOTIVATIONS

In the course of studying children groups below the pre-school age level we learned to discriminate between motivations for like or dislike which are the result of indoctrination and motivations which are the result of spontaneous attractions and repulsions. During the presocialized period children groups are on a *psycho-organic* level of development and the members are unaffected or little susceptible to indoctrination but towards the end of this period they become more susceptible. From then on the *psycho-social* level is in ascendance and also the members become sensitive to the psychological currents; gradually they become participants in the networks in the community. As we realized that the study of inter-racial and inter-nationality attractions at age levels in which individuals are opinionated or susceptible to indoctrination would be of little scientific value, we began with the study of inter-racial choices at the pre-school age level and followed these up in their development from year to year of age. We found that (a) inter-racial choices show a different pattern in the pre-school period than they do thereafter and that this is partly due to the effect indoctrination has upon the choices made (see p. 61); (b) that the sociogenetic law is applicable also to inter-racial discrimination; the pattern of inter-racial attractions and repulsions develops in the direction of higher differentiation; (c) discrimination, when indoctrination begins to show its effect upon inter-racial choice, tends in children groups instinctively to follow the psycho-organic route; the children will try to adjust their doctrines to their spontaneous likes and dislikes; (d) with the weakening of their spontaneability the older the individuals become, the more they are inclined to abandon the organic route and the more they may be swayed by indoctrination simply as it is carried to them through the networks of the community in which they live.

In the course of studying the effect psychological currents have upon individuals we discovered two other types of motivations: motivations of like or dislike about a person or a number of persons which are based upon direct acquaintance and motivations which are based upon *symbolic* acquaintance, that is, upon hearsay or mental hallucinations. An illustration of symbolic acquaintance is HU, who was regarded as a thief by 55 individuals, 10 of whom were not acquainted with her and 26 of whom reiterate a motivation from hearsay. The importance of such symbolic judgments becomes the greater the larger the networks are through which such an opinion can travel. Evidently when upon psychological networks mechanical networks are drafted, as the printing press, the radio, etc., the circulation of symbolic judgment may lose every relationship to facts. The significance of symbolic acquaintance and symbolic judgment is more far-reaching still when it is related to an individual because he is a member of a collective. For instance, LS is rejected because she is Jewish; 7 of the girls rejecting her had never made her acquaintance.

The basis for these developments are the psychological networks which pervade populations. Hence the machine and the means of mechanical transmission do not produce—they only multiply a given product.

XI. SPONTANEITY TEST

1. SPONTANEITY TEST

If we say that person A hates person B, we do not express what is actually going on if we do not indicate what this hating of B means within the whole movement. If, in turn, we say that B is jealous of A, we are failing to express what this jealousy means in the whole movement. The process is a dynamic movement with two poles, A and B. From the point of view of the movement, this hatred of A to B and this jealousy of B to A is interlocked and not static but in flux. At a certain moment it may reach a climax in A as the feeling of panic, for instance, coinciding with the mood in B of rage and desire to dominate. An analysis of the condition in A and of the condition in B separately may lead to our understanding B or A but not A and B, that is, the state arising from their interaction.

As person A did not want to live with person B and neither did person B want to live with person A, we had to analyze the emotional movement between them. The problem was to develop a method of studying states binding two or more persons together, to analyze the movements between them in order to secure a finer interpretation of these movements than their expressed motivations afforded.

Emotional states as anger, fear, or liking, and more complex states as reflection, conviction, or curiosity, are limited realities. They do not exist as they appear to the person who is filled with them. They are part of a whole, they belong to the next larger reality, the social atoms. Properly integrated into them individual subjective notions as anger or fear can be described as *group subjective* notions,—*clicking* emotions, when two individuals agree spontaneously; *crossing* emotions, when they disagree; *breaking* emotions, when a strong emotion is responded to by a neutral attitude; and *passing-by* emotions, when the object is unaware of their presence.

In the " Stegreiftheater " we said about the spontaneous state: " It is not given: we must warm up to it as climbing up a hill . . ." and " Impromptu state is not only an expression of a process within a person but also a relation to the outside through the Impromptu state of another person. It is the meeting of two different states from which the conflict arises." They are actually two poles of one movement reflecting and changing each other.

But this starting of an Impromptu state through the interaction of individuals has a great methodological significance. In the analysis of an individual we may always be inclined to relate every arising expression to former attitudes. We are always inclined to think that they may be at least in part derivatives or allied to past performances. We never seem to be able to face the *first* act, the original situation, but instead the genesis is retraced through symbols. But when we study, as in Hudson, individuals who never met before and who from their first meeting on have to live together and to be participants in the same group, we are face to face with the first act, the original situation. We see them when they enter spontaneously into interrelationships which lead to the forming of groups, sub species momenti. We study their spontaneous reactions in the initial stage of group formation and the activities developing in the course of such organization. We are present when the relationship is born, at the earliest possible stage in the social relation of the two individuals who meet, and we can develop, if necessary, the treatment *forward* instead of backward. Our procedure is *psychocreative*. We begin with the *act,* the initial attitude one person shows for the other, and follow up to what fate these interrelations lead, what kind of organization they develop. The Parent and Family Tests (see pp. 273–283) are samples of this procedure. Through the Spontaneity Tests we are able to study the more intimate relations among individuals as these develop in the course of their living together.

The subject is placed opposite the persons in the community who through the sociometric test have been found to " belong together " to the social atom of the subject. These individuals had chosen or rejected the subject in respect to a given criterion, as that of living in the same house. It is probable that the material entering into the reactions will be borrowed from experiences they have had together, which they now have, or which they wish to have in the future. To illustrate the technique of the Spontaneity Test we have selected Elsa TL, an individual from C6. We present it beginning with the classifications and motivations of her social relationships and leading through to the analysis of these relationships through Spontaneity Tests.

A. *Classification*

The central individual of the test is Elsa. Her sociometric classification (see sociogram p. 153) was expressed in the following Classification Formulas:

$$\text{Class. Formula I:} \quad \frac{4}{0} \bigg| \frac{1}{0}$$
$$L$$

$$\text{Class. Formula II:} \quad \frac{4 - 1}{0 - 16} \bigg| \frac{1 - 3}{0 - 15}$$
$$L$$

The dominant features of her classification are *isolated* and *rejected* within her group and within the community. Her classification showed that besides her housemother 31 other individuals were interlocked with her in the criterion of *living* in proximity. Data descriptive of her conduct in Hudson have been gathered from the 31 persons who expressed an attitude towards her—as far as they could articulate it—in her social nucleus. A study of the networks in which she participated showed that the position of 27 of the 31 persons were dependent in the networks upon two individuals chiefly who lived in the same house. Only two other individuals appeared unaffected by the latter. It appeared, therefore, sufficient to concentrate our attention upon this nucleus of five, assuming that information coming from analysis of this nucleus would automatically elucidate the rest. Hence only the reports of Elsa herself and of these four individuals are here presented. Although these four individuals (who were chosen by Elsa to live with: Maud, 1st choice; Gladys, 2nd choice; Joan, 3rd choice; and Virginia, 4th choice) had been living with Elsa in C6 for more than one year, they unanimously rejected her. Considering the attitudes towards Elsa within her group and within the community, it seemed that Elsa chose the four girls who appeared to her most likely to respond and to help her. The fifth choice of Elsa went to a colored girl in C10 (see p. 153).

As indicated in Classification Formula I, Elsa chose four persons within her group and one from an outside group. Formula II shows that all five persons rejected her and that, in addition, she is rejected by 12 others within her group and by 15 others outside her group, while she herself rejects one person in her group and 6 outside.

We directed our attention next to the sociometric position of the 5 individuals she had chosen. The outside choice was a colored girl whose Classification Formulas reveal her in an otherwise isolated position. The sociometric position of the four individuals she had chosen in her own group were as follows:

Maud: Class. Formula I: $\dfrac{2\ \big|\ 1}{2\ \big|\ 1}$
$$\text{L}$$

Class. Formula II: $\dfrac{3-1\ \big|\ 1-0}{3-3\ \big|\ 1-0}$
$$\text{L}$$

Maud is chosen by 3 persons whose positions are not linked to influential currents either within the group or within the larger community (see sociogram pp. 153–4). Hence her rejection of Elsa is restricted to a person to person relationship primarily. She has in common with Elsa an attraction to a colored girl, but, in contrast to Elsa, her attraction is reciprocated.

Gladys: Class. Formula I:
$$\frac{3}{1} \left| \frac{2}{0} \right. \\ L$$

Class. Formula II:
$$\frac{2-6}{0-4} \left| \frac{3-1}{0-1} \right. \\ L$$

As Gladys also is in an isolated position (see sociogram p. 154) both within and without her group, her rejection of Elsa does not appear to have any appreciable effect beyond their person to person relationship.

Joan: Class. Formula I:
$$\frac{2}{4} \left| \frac{3}{12} \right. \\ L$$

Class. Formula II:
$$\frac{4-2}{4-0} \left| \frac{3-2}{12-0} \right. \\ L$$

Joan attracts 4 inside and 12 outside her group. The follow-up of the sociometric positions of these 16 individuals reveals that Joan is the first choice of three individuals who themselves are chosen by 13, 16, and 18, respectively, in the community. As these 47 individuals each enter into 1 to 7 other relationships and their correspondents into still further relationships, the fact that Joan rejects Elsa may have a far-reaching effect: Joan is in a position to influence directly or indirectly some currents in all the networks. She was found to be a key-individual participating herself in the five main networks into which the population is divided.

$$\text{Virginia: Class. Formula I:} \quad \frac{2}{6} \Bigg| \frac{1}{1}$$
$$\text{L}$$

$$\text{Class. Formula II:} \quad \frac{6-2}{6-2} \Bigg| \frac{1-2}{1-1}$$
$$\text{L}$$

Virginia is chosen by 6 within her group and these 6 receive in all 21 choices from other members of the group. She is thus the key-individual within the group although she herself is not the most chosen. The fact that she rejects Elsa may have an effect far beyond the single relation of Elsa and Virginia. Virginia is in a position to influence directly or indirectly at least 27 persons, that is, all but four of the cottage population.

B. Motivations

Elsa towards Maud:

She is my first choice to live with. She is nicest of all to me. I don't know what I like about Maud exactly but she is likeable in spite of everything they say against her. Her biggest fault is a habit she has of saying right out how she feels about you. She thinks by doing that she will be considered frank. I don't think frankness is always just the way to act. You hurt a person's feelings sometimes more that way when you could just have said nothing or been a little nicer about it. We talk to each other a lot and we do like many of the same things and have some of the same troubles, like getting in wrong with the girls and housemother.

Maud towards Elsa:

I don't believe in trying to be friends with her any more because she talks to me about colored girls all the time and goes ahead and tells on me. But just the same I don't believe she gets a square deal in this cottage. Like she is washing dishes and the girls in the kitchen keep passing remarks. One says, " That's not the way to do it, Elsa "; or " You didn't get this dish clean "; or ". You can't even wash a glass right even if it had nothing in it but water." And they keep it up till Elsa gets nervous and stops and maybe bangs down what she has in her hands. And then the housemother says, " What's the matter with you, Elsa? " And Elsa gets sent to her room. The housemother never finds out that the kids were aggravating her because they do it under their breath, they hate her so. I am getting into trouble when I am with her. It is better if we do not live in the same house.

Elsa towards Gladys:

She is my second choice. She doesn't hold anything against you like some of the girls do. She has a forgiving nature and never says, "You are pulling the cottage down," the way Virginia does if you break a little rule. Gladys has to take a lot of blame just like myself.

Elsa towards Joan:

Joan is my third choice. I always liked Joan and wanted her for a friend but she starts to be my friend and then stops all of a sudden. She hasn't got much patience if you don't do just what she wants all the time.

Gladys towards Elsa:

I don't see that she is so terrible if the kids would leave her alone. The only time she gets my goat is when she sticks around and just stays and stays when you want to be rid of her, like a piece of molasses you can't get off your hands. She is pesty, anybody will have to say that. Expects you to let her play with you after you already get started and hanging on so you can't shake her. I do wish she was in some other cottage. We'd be happier and so would she.

Joan towards Elsa:

Kids can be sneaky once in a while but to be sneaky all the time, that's Elsa. She doesn't get happy over things you'd expect she would. Like her little sister sent her a poem she wrote and I had it put in the school paper and you'd think she would have been proud. But no, she didn't get excited a bit. One time Miss ET was scolding her and she just screamed. She usually doesn't do anything, not even answer back. So this time I felt sorry for her and I did everything for her. I loaned her a mystery story, too, and then when I asked her for it back, because mystery stories are hard to get here, she denied I ever gave it to her and then I found out she had given it to Maud. Elsa is courageous that way; she'll lie or do anything that comes into her head, doesn't seem to care what you think. Sometimes it doesn't amount to anything but it is the way she does it that makes you disgusted, always lying about not going with the colored girls when you see her dart around the corner just to get a glimpse of them, especially of her girl friend. I do not want to live with her.

Elsa towards Virginia:

She is my fourth choice. I don't care so much about her as I do about the others. All the girls try to get Virginia to be their friend but she doesn't show much partiality. She is about the same all the time. She is always criticizing me but she doesn't try to help me as much as I would like her to. If she would try to, I would get along better.

Virginia towards Elsa:

I feel that Elsa has sunk so far that it's not any use having her around. What's the reason I should bother with her? If she had any backbone she wouldn't be like she is. It just gives you shivers to have her in the same room with you at recreation. I wouldn't want to live with her.

Elsa towards the housemother:

She isn't my friend. I just feel she is against me. She listens to the girls who are against me, too. She thinks I am in wrong even when I'm not.

Housemother towards Elsa:

When Elsa's mother comes, she weeps but the next hour she has forgotten her. She thinks that she is persecuted by people. She tried once to run away with WT, a mentally retarded child. Ruth threw out of her window a pillow case full of her things and then with sheets tied to the bed she attempted to slide down. The waving sheet in front of Anna DI's window and her feet knocking against the house awoke Anna and she pounded on her door to notify me. By the time I had the lights on, Elsa was ringing the front door bell. She had sprained her ankle. She acted totally indifferent to the whole episode. On no occasion does she exhibit any temper or answering back. She is a solitaire player, never volunteers for either work or games; day-dreamer, heedless and careless in work. Bad nail biting. Her progress in school is good and she is one of the most intelligent girls in my house. She has a taste for finery which shows on every possible occasion. From some old ragged lace curtains she made a brassiere. Whatever is thrown out she will take and make underclothes and things of. One time she took cast out voile and made panties, small as for a doll, and wore them. Her room is always full of junk which she collects, anything shiny or glittering. Steals, takes things which I would give her if I knew she wanted them. At Christmas time she took about $2 worth of things from the store. The things were rings, handkerchiefs, pen and pencil sets, powder puffs, strings of beads, etc. Probably she wanted them to give to both colored girls and white girls as a short cut to friendship as she had them all done up in paper and tied with bits of ribbon when it was discovered. She didn't cry when scolded about taking them. Is persistent in running after the colored girls. My girls have lost patience with her for this. She lies about it even when they catch her in places with them. Language very dirty, and notes likewise. I believe Ruth should be given a new chance in another cottage.

C. *Testing*

The motive of the spontaneity test for the subject is the training of his emotional equipment for a more articulate expression; for the tester it is to ascertain the spontaneous reaction of the subject towards each person placed opposite him and the spontaneous reaction of each of them towards the subject.

The subject is instructed: " Throw yourself into a state of emotion towards X. The emotion may be either anger, fear, sympathy, or dominance. Develop with him any situation you.like to produce expressing this particular emotion. Throw yourself into the state with nothing on your mind but the person who is opposite you and think of this person as of the real person you know in everyday life. Also call him by his actual name. Once you have started to produce one of these states, try to maintain that emotion throughout the situation." The partner receives no instruction except to react as he would in actual life to the attitude expressed towards him by the subject. The two persons are not allowed to consult with each other before they begin to act.

The person tested is placed opposite every person who has been found to be related to him (see p. 80), and as we are interested in both ends of each relationship, we have also to make of each partner a subject towards the subject. In other words, after the subject has produced any one of the four states towards a partner, the partner is instructed to produce a state he chooses towards the subject. The person tested may choose to produce towards each partner the same state, for instance, sympathy, or he may choose to produce a different state each time, once sympathy, once dominance, etc., or any other combination of states. The reaction time, the words spoken and the mimic expression of both players are recorded as directed by the tester. The salient point of the test is that the subject is asked to exercise his full spontaneity.

This technique is illustrated in the testing of the relationship of Elsa to Maud, Gladys, Joan, and Virginia. Of the 32 situations which were recorded of the interaction of Elsa with one or another of the other four individuals, we present here the records of eight situations, that is, of Elsa towards each of the four girls and each of the four girls towards Elsa. As Elsa is rejected by the four, we have selected only the situations which appear to express anger or repulsion.

TECHNIQUE

Situation 1.* Elsa vs. Maud. Anger.

Elsa: Well, Maud, I hope you got a lot of satisfaction out of telling Miss Stanley about me walking around with my friend instead of coming right home.

Maud: Who me?

Elsa: Yes, you! You would take it to a staff member that I didn't come directly home!

Maud: Prove it!

Elsa: There is nothing to prove. You told. That is sufficient. You had some nerve accusing me!

Maud: I'm waiting for you to prove it.

Elsa: Well, my losing recreation is proof.

Maud: Well, if you dislike losing recreation so much why did you have to walk home with the girl-friend?

Elsa: Because I wanted to. And besides I notice you walk home with yours when you feel like it, don't you?

Maud: Well, why don't you go and tell on me then?

Elsa: Because I'm not like you.

Maud: I still think I didn't tell. No more talking, prove it.

Elsa: I know right well you told on me.

Maud: All right, I ask you to prove it. You can't, can you? As there is nothing more to prove.

Reaction time: 15 seconds; duration, 1 minute 12 seconds.

Mimic expression of Elsa vs. Maud: Elsa is lively toward Lena, in certain moments dominates. She moves her arms towards her, looks straight into her eye, speaks in a loud voice, rushes towards Maud, scowling and setting her jaw forward. She made Maud retreat two times. Her eyes flashed and color came and went in her cheeks.

Situation 2.* Maud vs. Elsa. Anger.

Maud: Elsa, where were you second period this morning?

Elsa: Why I was in the study hall—where I was supposed to be!

Maud: You were *supposed* to be there all right, but you didn't happen to be.

Elsa: But I was in there. Where do you suppose I was anyway?

Maud: That's what I want to know. If you were there, where did I sit anyway?

Elsa: Away up in front. I sat in the back.

Maud: You are wrong. I sat half-way back today.

Elsa: Well, I tell you I was in the study hall just as you were!

Maud: Now Elsa, I want to know where you were. I looked especially for you and you were not there. I watched for you to come in late and still you did not come. You did not come in that study hall door second period. Now before you take this any further, I want to know where you were—before I go to Miss Stanley about the matter.

Elsa: All right I'll tell you I was in the library second period. Are you satisfied?

* Elsa and Maud extemporized in all eight situations in which they acted together a friendly attitude. Situation 1 and 2 are taken from another series.

Maud: No, I'm not! You lie! You were—well, I know where you were and I'm going in and see Miss Stanley this instant.

Reaction time: 20 seconds; duration, 1 minute 30 seconds.

Mimic expression of Maud vs. Elsa: Maud is hesitant in starting. Her eyes look friendly until almost the very end. Elsa appears to reflect the same attitude of secret friendliness. Maud finally becomes encouraged by the mild reaction of Elsa to her words and in her last expression stamps her foot in front of Elsa and rushes off indignant.

Situation 3. Elsa vs. Gladys. Anger.

Elsa: Well, Gladys! You know when you polished my shoes, what was the big idea in taking all the leather off the heels?

Gladys: I never did take all the leather off the heels of your old shoes. You ought to be thankful that someone was good enough to polish your shoes for you!

Elsa: I am thankful enough that you polished my shoes but I ask you why did you ruin the heels by skinning the leather on them?

Gladys: I didn't do it.

Elsa: Humm! I suppose it got off by itself! I feel sorry for you if you can't even polish shoes without ruining them.

Gladys: Don't feel sorry for me, please! You have to feel sorry for yourself first it seems to me.

Elsa: Anyway that was a mean trick, putting my shoes marked in that condition back in my room.

Gladys: My dear, I'm sorry, but I put them back in perfect condition!

Elsa: Oh yes! Well I promise you, you won't do my shoes ever again!

Gladys: Well who wants to!

Reaction time: 18 seconds; duration, 1 minute.

Mimic expression of Elsa vs. Gladys: Elsa walks suddenly towards Gladys, looks hesitantly at her and then rushes out with her first burst of words. Gladys stands up straight with her head thrown back and smiles as she speaks words expressing anger. At this Elsa loses all aggressiveness, both in her voice and gestures, half-smiles, but eyes express sadness.

Situation 4. Gladys vs. Elsa. Anger..

Gladys: Say, Elsa Tollman, what do you mean by staying in your room last night and destroying my Junior Training note-book?

Elsa: Staying in my room to destroy your Junior Training note-book? Why, you are crazy! I was only studying it, and copying notes from it.

Gladys: Why, you have some nerve. You tore the pages out of my note-book and now you deny it. Oh, you make me furious. I could kill you!

Elsa: Well I didn't do anything of the kind!

Gladys: Well you certainly did. Now you have to buy reinforcements and fix my book. Why just think of what Miss Kinderhook will say when she sees such a book. And it's all your fault, too!

Elsa: It couldn't have been me that tore them out!

Gladys: It certainly was you. Don't stand there and contradict me. It was you!

Reaction time: 5 seconds; duration 1 minute.

Mimic expression of Gladys vs. Elsa: Gladys appears nonplussed in confronting Elsa, facial expression is angry but the tone of voice portrays no anger. Her movements are gentle and slow. Elsa stands still, taking everything she says with equanimity, looking straight at Gladys all the time but not becoming angry in return, merely defensive in posture.

Situation 5: Elsa vs. Joan. Anger.

Elsa: Well Joan, you got the recreation room to do now, haven't you?

Joan: Well—yes, why?

Elsa: Well I was just hoping that since you've got that room to do now, that you'll polish it up all nice. You know, not like you did my room!

Joan: Say, now, you look to home for those things, do you hear?

Elsa: Of course, I hear. Otherwise I wouldn't be speaking to you, would I?

Joan: A wisecrack from a dumbbell!

Elsa: Well, have you made a resolution to polish the recreation room as you should? You know, all shiny and everything?

Joan: Perhaps I could rely on you to do that.

Elsa: Me?

Joan: Yes, you! All that I have to say is, "Elsa, come polish the rec. floor!" and you come running right along.

Elsa: Oh, no! I don't!

Joan: Oh, yes, you do, and that's not all either. You come at my every beck and call and you know it.

Elsa: If you do the rec. like you did my room it will——

Joan: If you don't like the way I did your room, do it yourself hereafter. Get out of my way mighty quick!

Elsa: I happen to do my own room now since I don't room with you.

Joan: Well, dearie, where does the dirt go? Behind the door?

Elsa: No, dearie, it goes into the dustpan.

Joan: It goes into the dustpan—well, I bet.

Reaction time: 20 seconds; duration, 2 minutes.

Mimic expression of Elsa vs. Joan: Elsa leans on a chair and twists her fingers in between each other nervously. In her first verbal expression looks expectantly at Joan, eyebrows raised, anxious. Joan replies in a condescending tone, sneering. At the next remark Elsa imitates Joan's sarcastic tone and looks away from her. At this Joan aggressively confronts Elsa, causing her to retreat further and further. Joan's voice is loud and dominant. Elsa continues to resort to sarcastic tones.

Situation 6. Joan vs. Elsa. Anger.

Joan: Well may I have the book you took out of my room, Elsa?

Elsa: Were you speaking to me? I didn't take any book out of your room.

Joan: I won't argue with you but I will have you give me my book!

Elsa: But I don't know even what you are talking about.

Joan: Don't lie to me, Elsa. What's that very same book that I'm missing doing up on your corner shelf? I want the book please.

Elsa: I got that book from Miss Cranton. The book belongs to her and I borrowed it.

Joan: I happen to have been the one to borrow Miss Cranton's book and that particular book at that. Listen, you will lose your recreation indefinitely for taking things out of girls' rooms. I thought you'd realize that by this time!

Elsa: I want to use that book to do my English.

Joan: I thought you didn't take that book. And since when do you take English.

Elsa: Why, I've taken it all term!

Joan: Oh, that's a good excuse for stealing a book! By the way, what English are you taking?

Elsa: English 8½.

Joan: What period?

Elsa: Third in the morning.

JOAN: You are crazy. I take English third period in the morning and I'm sure you're not in it.

Elsa: Well I'm going to keep that book and use it.

Joan: That's what you think. Get out of my way. I'm going right into your room and get that book!

Reaction time: 5 seconds; duration, 2½ minutes.

Mimic expression of Joan vs. Elsa: Joan walks up to Elsa, stands directly before her; Elsa remains rigidly on the spot. Joan fires one remark after another at Elsa in loud, brutal voice, but Elsa retains her former sarcastic tone and mild voice throughout. Joan completely dominates Elsa's mimic expression, finally chasing her out of the room.

Situation 7. Elsa vs. Virginia. Anger.

Elsa: Well Virginia, I would like to know what happened to my dress and how you happened to tear it?

Virginia: Your dress? You are disgusting.

Elsa: Yes, my dress, and my best one at that. And since you are my room-mate and you were the last one to hang it up I think it was mean of you to tear it. You could have been more careful.

Virginia: I'm sorry! I don't know how your dress got torn. Am I responsible for the things that go on in that room just because I am your room-mate? How could I tear your old dress anyway?

Elsa: How do you know that you didn't catch it on the bed or something? My best dress too, and I tried so hard to keep it nice!

Virginia: But, I tell you, Elsa, I don't know a thing about your dress. Why don't you take it in to the housemother and don't stand there and holler at me. I don't have to take your abuse.

Elsa: You did tear it, but I won't take it to any housemother. You could at least have told me about it.

Virginia: Tell you? I don't know as I had anything to tell! I didn't tear your old dress!

Elsa: All right!

Reaction time: 22 seconds; duration, 1 minute 2 seconds.

Mimic expression of Elsa vs. Virginia: Elsa walks timorously up to Virginia, taking the longest route around a chair to get to her, and with an appealing voice speaks to her. Elsa draws a handkerchief through her fingers as if weaving a pattern throughout the whole time. Virginia consistently looks at the floor. Her color becomes higher and higher to the end. Her voice is bursting with anger but she maintains her aloof distance from Elsa, refusing to be ruffled in the slightest.

Situation 8. Virginia vs. Elsa. Anger.

Virginia: For heaven's sake, Elsa, will you stop singing? Every time you do those bathrooms you have to go and start singing. Can't you keep quiet for a change? Here I am trying to do my homework to the tune of your old singing and I'm working on a map. How can anyone concentrate with a racket like that?

Elsa: But it makes a person feel good. And people around should be happy too, when someone else is happy enough to sing.

Virginia: Well, if I can't keep you quiet, maybe Miss Stanley will. I'll simply report you to her.

Elsa: I think I sing pretty good. I enjoy it anyway!

Virginia: Well, your singing makes everybody else sick. Will you please shut up?

Elsa: Miss Stanley likes to hear singing because she said so.

Virginia: Well, I'm not Miss Stanley, and besides Miss Stanley doesn't have homework to do.

Elsa: Oh, gosh, you are the most pessimistic person I ever met. I don't see why you have to do your map in the morning anyway. Why don't you get your lessons done at night as you ought to?

Virginia: I guess I can do my lessons when it is most convenient, hear?

Elsa: Well, if singing is my only crime, I consider myself lucky!

Virginia: Well, I'd rather see you go out and kill someone than to hear you sing constantly, especially when I'm busy with my map!

Reaction time: 6 seconds; duration, 1 minute 30 seconds.

Mimic expression of Virginia vs. Elsa: Virginia swings her arms out in a gesture of disgust, looking away as if she can't stand the sight of Elsa. Her color gradually rises. She stutters twice as she attempts to express verbally what she appears to refuse to allow her mimic expression to betray. Elsa stands perfectly still, relaxed, except for her hands which grasp and ungrasp the back of a chair. She also appears to be holding back and not letting herself go fully.

D. Analysis of Attitudes

An analysis of the attitudes taken by the partners towards Elsa, the subject, and by Elsa towards the partners in the 32 situations acted disclosed that each individual differed in the frequency with which she chose a specific attitude. Maud preferred to produce four times a situation in which she could display sympathy towards Elsa, but Virginia preferred not to produce such a situation even once; that Joan chose to do so once and Glayds twice, from the allowed four occasions. Virginia, however, chose to produce four times an attitude which expressed either anger or dominance; Joan, three times; Gladys, twice; and Maud, not once. Out of the 16 possible occasions, fear was not chosen even once. The following table is a tabulation of the attitudes taken by the four individuals towards Elsa:

TABLE OF ATTITUDES 1

Towards Elsa:	Sympathy	Anger	Fear	Dominance
Maud	4	0	0	0
Gladys	2	1	0	1
Joan	1	2	0	1
Virginia	0	2	0	2

The attitudes taken by Elsa towards the four individuals is tabulated in the accompanying Table of Attitudes 2:

TABLE OF ATTITUDES 2

Elsa towards:	Sympathy	Anger	Fear	Dominance
Maud	4	0	0	0
Gladys	2	1	1	0
Joan	2	1	1	0
Virginia	0	4	0	0

Table 2 indicates that Elsa preferred to produce four times a situation in which she could display sympathy towards Maud; two times, towards Gladys; twice, towards Joan; and not once towards Virginia. But she chose to produce a situation calling for anger four times towards Virginia; twice towards Joan; once towards Gladys; not once towards Maud. Towards Gladys and towards Joan she chose to produce a situation in which she could display fear.

A comparison of the two tables with the classification of the five subjects up to this point uncovers a finer differentiation of the interrelations between Ruth and the four other individuals. We see that the rejection of Elsa by Maud, Gladys,

Joan, and Virginia has a different weight in each case. The greatest frequency of anger towards Elsa is produced by Virginia; the greatest frequency of sympathy is produced by Maud. We see, so to speak, that the repulsion from these four persons towards Elsa could be expressed in four different degrees of anger. The Table 1 also suggests that the repulsion towards Elsa is not absolute. Out of the four instances, Maud is four times sympathetic. But the fact that Maud rejected Elsa as a person to live with her and motivated this so definitely may indicate that when we took the sociometric test we caught Maud in a mood in which anger towards Elsa was dominant, due to some precipitating cause. On the other hand, Elsa had chosen Maud, Gladys, Joan and Virginia as the four girls with whom she would like to be living together. The attitude she displays towards them in the test shows sympathy dominating towards Maud only; towards Gladys and Joan, sympathy on the one hand and anger and fear on the other are appearing equally distributed; and towards Virginia, anger rises up each of the four times. This discloses that also the attitude of attraction is not an unmixed emotion. The case of Elsa shows further that if an individual has a very limited range of selection, the intensity of his being attracted to certain persons may be very slight. In the desire not to be altogether negative, he may make a choice or choices which are the best he can make under the circumstances.

In examining Elsa's performance we note that her resistance against starting is of different intensity towards each partner. Her reaction time is of shortest duration towards Maud and longest towards Virginia. We differentiate between inability to start, delayed starting, and erratic starting; but delay may be due to difficulty in finding a plot. The plot rose up most rapidly in the test Elsa-Maud and it is with the latter that Elsa held her own. Towards Virginia and Joan, Elsa's state of production appeared under-heated, weak, and hesitant; towards Maud, over-heated and verbose. Towards Maud Elsa maintains the initiative, in each situation suggesting most of the ideas, but in the situations towards her other test-associates the initiative is held by the partner. It is characteristic also that seven of the eight anger situations were finished by

the test-associate, Elsa being unable to bring about an end
without the partner directing it. For the study of attitudes
as called forth through the Spontaneity Test it is of value that
a film record is used to register the minute and subtle interactions.

Analysis of Word Material

The length of the sentences and the number of words used
in the first rush towards the other person are an indicator of
the amount of aggression the subject has towards the other
person. Elsa uses 27 words in her first expression towards
Maud; 22 words in her first outburst towards Gladys; 19
words towards Virginia; and towards Joan, 12 words. Evidently it is easier for Elsa to give expression to anger towards
Maud and least easy for her to do so towards Joan. It is of
interest to compare with this the length of sentences and the
number of words used by Elsa towards each partner during
the whole situations: towards Maud, she uses 98 words;
towards Gladys, 99 words; towards Virginia, 110 words; and
towards Joan, 112 words. The picture is then reversed. Joan,
who received the least in the first onrush of words, now gets
the most, and Maud, who got the most in the first onrush, now
gets the fewest. In the analysis of the development of the
dialogue, however, there is an indication that the greater number of words used by Elsa towards Virginia was not due to a
strength of aggression towards her but to the strong anger
reaction of Virginia towards Elsa, who was compelled to reply
and hence to accumulate a large verbal reaction.

The length of sentences and the number of words used in
the first onrush of each of the four individuals towards Elsa
were: Maud, 8; Gladys, 20; Joan, 13; Virginia, 58 words;
and the total situation, Maud 135 words; Gladys, 95 words;
Virginia, 137 words; and Joan, 161 words. The amount of
aggression that Elsa exhibits towards the various partners is
strongest towards Maud, becomes weaker towards Gladys, still
weaker towards Virginia, and reaches its weakest and softest
attitude towards Joan; considering the aggression displayed
towards her by the partners, which is strongest from Virginia
and weakest from Maud.

A summary of the anger-colored phrases used by the four girls towards Elsa in the eight tests presented follows:

Maud: You lie!

Joan: Do you hear!
A wisecrack from a dumbbell.
All I have to say is " Elsa, come. . . ." and you
    come right away.
Get out of my way!
Dirt.

Gladys: Feel sorry for yourself.
You have some nerve, Elsa.
Now you deny, Elsa.
Furious.
Kill you, Elsa.
Don't contradict.
Don't stand there.
It was you.
It's all your fault.

Virginia: Stop singing.
Keep quiet.
Hear!
I'd rather see you go out and kill someone than
    to hear you sing constantly.
Don't sing when I am busy.
A racket like that.
I'll simply report.
You are disgusting.
Your singing makes everybody sick.
Your person hanging around.
Take it in to the housemother.
Don't holler at me.
Don't have to take your abuse.
Shut up.

The anger-colored phrases used by Elsa towards her partners follow:

Towards Maud: You had some nerve accusing me.
Towards Gladys: It was a mean trick.
                      You are crazy.
Towards Joan: —— (none)——
Towards Virginia: It was mean of you to tear it.

The quantity of anger-colored expressions used by the four individuals towards Elsa also certify to the varying weights of their respective rejection of her as indicated above. Virginia produces the greatest number and variety of anger-colored phrases, Gladys is second, Joan third, and Maud produces fewest. In turn, Elsa's quantity of anger-colored expressions is towards each of the individuals almost equally weak.

The attitude of Elsa towards her partners is persistently weak and indifferent. She produces towards Joan phrases empty of content, unable to call up a motive to be angry at her. Also when the situation is reversed with Joan as the subject and angry at Elsa, she simply stands and takes her remarks passively. Joan said: "A wisecrack from a dumbbell! " without getting any reaction from Elsa. Joan also said: " I can say to you, ' Come, polish the floor,' and you would come running right along," without any reaction from Elsa. Elsa, when she accuses Virginia of tearing her dress (an act which she herself had done to another girl), was unable to carry out this motive convincingly in the situation. She practically relinquished in saying, " You did tear it, but I won't tell a housemother on you." Virginia accuses Elsa in intensive anger to stop singing and making noise, using the words, " I'd rather you'd go and kill somebody than to sing constantly." Elsa runs away from this attack, responding at the end, " If singing in my only crime, I consider myself lucky." Elsa accuses Gladys of scraping the leather from her shoes while polishing them. It appeared during the test that Elsa couldn't find any motivated reason to be angry at Gladys and in her embarrassment sought an incredible one. However, it was found that Elsa had done such an act to another girl in the cottage a few days before. The suggestion of secret activities in which Maud and Elsa participated and conflicts developing out of these is reflected in the text of their dialogue. Elsa warms up to a more natural expression in response to Maud.

Summary

It appears that quantitative analysis of spontaneous expression is a valuable aid in the interpretation of the interrelation between individuals. Elsa's position isolated and rejected is evident in each report of motivations (see p. 178). But the relation of this sociometric classification to her sexual interests and stealing was not sufficiently disclosed by the sociometric test. A further insight into her relationship to Maud was also wanting. It is at this point that analysis of her Spontaneity Tests enabled us to secure a still finer penetration of her position within the group.

The word content of the spontaneous reactions between Elsa and Maud discloses a common conflict, the relation to colored girls and the fear of being betrayed to the housemother and of being punished. This related both Elsa and Maud to a sexual current which interlocks a group of colored girls with a group of white girls. It explains the often suddenly changing feeling between Maud and Elsa as due to jealousy. The quickness with which they react towards each other and the way they " touch off " each other betrays an intimacy which is not repeated by Elsa in play with any other partner. The suddenness during one of the tests with which Maud burst into laughter when Elsa accused her of showing to the housemother a love letter she (Elsa) had written to her colored friend and which was fully out of the mood of the context, anger at each other, and the spontaneous naturalness of their acting from this point on intimated that they enacted before our eyes a scene they had done often before in actual life. Immediately afterwards both laughed at each other and we hear from their own lips the tale told how Maud initiated Elsa into the practice of carrying her love letters to a colored girl, how Elsa one day began to write to the same girl and refused to be the carrier any longer. During this last minute of their acting they seemed unconscious of the situation in which they were, absorbed in a mood of recapitulation. They embraced and kissed and petted each other. They did this making it appear as if the situation would demand it, but the tone of their warming up gestures suggested that Elsa and Maud were uncovering their private personalities. It appeared as if we were witnesses to wishes and interrelations still going on in them, not simply reconstructed from a past relationship or imagined, and that we might predict future behavior from it.

As we know from the Impromptu experiment, an emotional state once produced has the tendency to carry automatically all affect-material which is locked within it into open expression; and if, as it is in these tests, the object of this expression is not a fictitious person but the actual well-remembered counterpart in similar life situations, then this process releases, as if through a form of " medial "-understanding a similar warming up process in the other person.

Elsa and Maud did not warm up in the beginning because they both thought they had to " play." But as soon as they lost themselves they clicked. Yet this ease of production did not come because they created something but because they lived *themselves*. It was a piece of revelation on the level of instinctive spontaneity. We know that Maud is the only one in the cottage with whom Elsa likes to play or who likes to play with her. They come to each other's aid also in their various adventures. Socially they belong to the same group, although Elsa is superior in intelligence (I.Q. 115) and Maud is dull normal (I.Q. 72). Elsa's colored friend is also far inferior to Elsa in intelligence (I.Q. 65).. It appears that her attraction towards persons mentally beneath her is not due to the fact that she is not accepted by those nearer to her in mentality, but because the degree of differentiation of the social group towards which she gravitates is one which we find normally corresponding to that of individuals younger in chronological age or lower in mental development.

A study of her sociometric position before she came to Hudson indicates a simpler setting. This inability to coördinate herself to persons who might become attracted to her, remaining an *isolated* and *rejected* individual within her cottage group, unable to change her position within it through her own effort in the course of more than two years, but always running amuck, reminds us of the position of individuals in immature social groups such as the 1st and 2nd grades in public school produce. For a 17-year-old 3rd-year high school student, whose I.Q. is 115, upon the basis of such facts the socially less differentiated groups appear more natural. This may also explain why she was invariably found mixing and playing with girls far removed from her in age and mental development whenever observed on the grounds.

It can be noted that in both situations which called for anger between Elsa and Maud the motive producing anger was by each of them spontaneously initiated as related to forbidden sexuality. The sexual motive did not appear again among the motives in the situations played by either of them towards other partners. But the stealing motive was initiated three times spontaneously either by Elsa herself accusing her partners of stealing or by her partners accusing her (see pp. 178–82). Elsa warmed up well when she threw the accusation towards Gladys that she had scraped the leather off her shoes, but as soon as Gladys turned aggressor towards her she dropped her attack, became passive, and her movements depicted retreat. She found but excuses for answer, the aggressor turning excuser. The two accusations she made towards Gladys and Joan appeared so worthless and insignificant that they didn't seem to carry sufficient weight to be angry about,—both concerned simply petty tricks of one girl upon another. But as it appeared from the angry responses of those partners, these were a kind of trick she herself used continually to play upon them in actuality, and they used to hate her for this in life. Why shouldn't she get angry at them if they were treating her that way in these imagined situations?

The trend to take worthless things and to accumulate them under her bed, of which she is accused by Virginia in a test, is linked to her desire for affection which she is missing and her scheme to gain the love of those who reject her in the cottage through petty gifts as well as to win back the colored girl who had turned to Maud. It appeared that the restless, impulsive actions of Elsa are the actions of a daydreamer who is happy in her isolation but unhappy about the loss of affection she was used to receive from her mother and unable to comprehend the avalanche of rejection from others.

The strongest attitudes of anger and dislike towards Elsa came from Virginia and Joan. Joan is a key-individual and leader outside in the community; Virginia is a key-individual and leader in the cottage group. Due to their position in their respective networks it appears that the influence of their rejecting Elsa has run through the psychological currents which interlock different groups of individuals into various networks and determined or helped to encourage similar attitudes towards her on the part of others.

We are able now also to clarify the most striking characteristic in Elsa's conduct: her indifference and apathy towards censuring aggression. This is the more baffling as it stands in contrast to her lively and combative attitude demonstrated in her former environment. Neither in the early stages of her participation in Hudson did she display this indifference. The change had been brought about, it appeared, by two factors. On the one hand, her indifference was increasing in proportion to the withdrawal of her emotional interest from the group in which she lived and its transference to a hidden group in which she was allowed to express herself unrestrained. On the other hand, this appeared to be necessitated and crystallized by the continuous pressure exerted upon her by the group in which she lived. She appeared helpless, displaying a persevering apathy towards a situation she felt herself to be unequal to. She was unable to differentiate between individuals who rejected her directly and those who simply reflected indirectly the attitude of certain leaders within the group. The network which contributed to her conflict was so widely spread that a spontaneous adjustment had become almost impossible for her to attain. An attempt at cure naturally involved a whole chain of individuals with whom her position was interlocked.

B. Balance and Imbalance within the Social Atom

Quantitative studies of the emotional inter-relations of the individuals who belong to the same social atom make it possible for us to penetrate into the inter-personal environment which is the immediate setting for mental disorder. Elsa produced in the 16 tests towards her associates 8 attitudes expressing sympathy and 8 expressing antipathy (anger, dominance, or fear); the test associates produced towards Elsa 7 attitudes expressing sympathy and 9 expressing antipathy (anger, dominance, or fear).

	Sympathy	Anger	Fear	Dominance	Sympathy	Antipathy
Elsa towards her Test-Associates:	8	6	2	0	8	8
The Test-Associates towards Elsa:	7	5	0	4	7	9

About as many reactions of sympathy can be counted (7) of the test-associates towards Elsa as of Elsa towards them (8), and about as many reactions of antipathy towards Elsa (9) as of Elsa towards them (8). If the sum-total of the emotions which cross to and from Elsa, and not any one emotion or associate in particular, are taken into consideration, the complex of relations which constitutes Elsa's social atom appears to " balance." This tendency towards " balance," this tendency of the emotions going out from and returning to the center individual of a social atom to offset and to " equalize " each other, was so frequently encountered in our studies that we have come to regard it as a particular phenomenon of the social atom.

Through quantitative study we may come to a realization of the relationship of the socioatomic structure to conduct disorders. In the case of the manic-depressive or the schizophrenic, we have observed deviations of the sum-total of emotions in the social atom away from balance. This can be explained as follows: The hypoactive depressed individual whose motor behavior is retarded tends to produce a like reaction towards all of the individuals towards whom he is emotionally selective, whereas they assume towards him various and differing reactions. Whatever are the reactions of these individuals towards him, whether of love, of fear, or of pity, and in whatever frequency these occur, if his attitude towards them tends to be stereotyped into, for instance, fear towards all, the distribution of emotions within the social atom will, it is obvious, appear grossly unbalanced. See text to sociogram p. 157. The imbalances within the social atom and their reflection upon the development of psychological currents and networks give social psychiatry a nosological basis and differentiate it as a discipline from psychiatry proper. Psychiatric concepts as neurosis and psychosis are not applicable to socioatomic processes. A group of individuals may become *sociotic* and the syndrome producing this condition can be called a *sociosis*.

The therapeutic problem in the case of T [19] is to reorganize his social atom, to assign experimentally a group to him which can aid him in his attempt at cure and towards which his stereotyped attitude has not become fixed. In the formation of such an experimental group we can be guided by following the spontaneous reactions of the patient: the latter are an indicator of who should and who should not be assigned to him at any particular stage of treatment. Personality structure and the inter-personal environment are parts of one and the same organization, the social atom. Inter-personal environment is not merely a *chance* factor. There are a limited number only of inter-personal structures probable for an individual, just as there are a limited number only of probable developments of the individual organism. The individual instinctively gravitates within the united field towards relations in which he is best able to attain and to maintain balance.

2. Impromptu Function

The Spontaneity Test as it appears is able to uncover feelings in their nascent, initial state. Through it we get a better knowledge of the genuine attitudes an individual may develop in the course of conduct and clinch acts in the moment of their performance. This is the point where the various forms of testing, particularly the Binet, Free Word Association, and Gestalt have not accomplished the deed. Let us imagine that three respective representatives of these doctrines have suggested to a subject who is under their study to give free play to his ideas and emotions, either through writing or through sketching spontaneously any configurations expressing them. The Binet tester may attempt to estimate approximately the mental age indicated by the content of the writing. The psychoanalyst may attempt to give an interpretation of the conflicts referred to by the subject in the words and to find characteristic symbols which he can follow up in a further Free Association test. The Gestalt analyst may perhaps study the configurations of the material. Instead of being satisfied with the cold material the subject leaves behind after his excitement in the state of production has passed, *we* need to see him when he " warms up " to the expression. It may be argued that the subject is present during an intelligence test and also in the psychanalytic situation. But our point is that the emphasis is laid in both instances upon the material given out by the subject instead of upon the act. To act means to warm up to a state of feeling, to an " Impromptu " state.

Our experimental study of the warming-up process developing to an act led us to the observation of *warming-up indicators*. These are not mental signs only but physiological signs (altered breathing rate, gasping, crying, smiling, clenching the teeth, etc.). The bodily starters of any behavior as acting or speaking on the spur of the moment are accompanied by physiological signs. In the process of warming up these symbols unfold and release simple emotions, as fear, anger, or more complex states. It is not necessary that verbal reactions evolve in the process of warming up. They may or they may not. But the mimic symbols are always present; they are related to underlying physiological processes and to psychological states.

Warming up indicators have been determined experimentally. The experiment was so conducted that the subject had no intention to produce any specific mental state. It was suggested to him to throw himself into this or that bodily action without thinking what will come out of it. The " starting " of these actions was found to be accompanied by a process of " warming up." We could observe then that if a subject lets go with certain expressions as gasping, accelerating the breathing, etc., without a definite goal, there are nevertheless developed certain emotional trends. The latter did not seem to be related to *one* emotion exclusively but rather to a whole group of emotions with similar properties in common. For instance, the following expressions,—clenching teeth and fists, piercing eyes, frowning, energetic movements, shrill voice, hitting, scuffling of feet, holding head high, accelerated breathing, and others, tend to release emotional states as anger, will to dominate, hate, or a vague precursor of these trends of feeling. Another set, accelerated breathing, gasping, trembling, flight, twisting facial muscles, inability to talk, sudden crying out, clasping hands, etc., is developing another trend of feeling, anxiety, fear, despair, or a combination of these. Another set, smiling, laughing, chuckling, widening the eyes, kissing, hugging, etc., is stimulating a condition of happy excitation.

However undifferentiated the feelings produced may be, it is observable that one set of movements *starts* one trend of feelings and another set of movements *starts* another trend, and so on. Each of these three sets of starters appears to operate as a unit. When one set of starters was functioning and the subject was instructed to add a starter belonging exclusively to another opposing set, it was observed that the course of development was so disturbed that the state correlated to the first set was lost or diminished in intensity. For instance, if in the development initiated by the third set of starters mentioned above, the subject is instructed to clinch his teeth, the direction of the production begun is thrown off its course. Bodily movements were found to follow one another in a certain order of succession according to which is the initiating starter. If the succession is interrupted, the temporal order is spoiled and the state of feeling released is confused.

On this bases we can diagnose if an emotional state is reached or is in the making. Warming up indicators are the deciding clue as to whether an emotional state is in process of release. Verbal reactions are less reliable as signs that a state is reached or about to be reached. A subject may use apt words with little or no emotion accompanying, but it is practically impossible once an emotion is initiated, to act without being carried away by the trend of feeling produced. All verbal and other associations are *organically* related to the trend of feeling developed.

Secondly, we experimented with the *intentional* production of emotional states. In this experiment a mental starter replaces the bodily starters. The subject is told to produce a certain state. For instance, " Throw yourself into the state of anger." He knows his goal ahead. The more successful the subject is in throwing himself into the desired state the better coördinated to the state will be the verbal and mimic associations produced. If the subject initiates unfitting bodily starters, the desired Impromptu state is not attained. If the starters are slightly out of focus with the intended state, the state reached is inadequate and the organization of the production will be correspondingly undifferentiated, loose, and of short duration (inadequate states). If the starters are faultily coördinated, the production is rash, confused, and abrupt, disproportionate to the amount of effort expended (over-heated states). In the case of the well-developed state, the individual appears to approximate closely his limit of differ-entiation of the emotion.

In productions which occur on the spur of the moment these mimic signs [20] or expressions are necessary to start and accel-erate the warming up of the emotional state in question. It is different if a memorized rôle is played as on the regular stage. There, through continuous rehearsal, the actor has an oppor-tunity to modify his performance according to a certain artistic pattern. But even *he* placed into an Impromptu play falls victim to the technique of warming up the more genuine his performance. The reason for this can be explained. The motive in actual life when we warm up to an emotional state is usually another person's behavior. But in an Impromptu play this motive is missing, the fictitious partner being too weak a substitute. To start the warming up of an emotion, a special effort is needed which is the greater the simpler the emotions, an effort which has to be originated from the bodily mechanism itself. To " fake " these warming up indicators is just as difficult as to eliminate them entirely in presenting simple emotions. It is almost impossible for a person to throw himself into a state of fear, to develop its indicators and to produce simultaneously the emotion of love and a correspond-ing text.[21]

XII. CONDUCT

1. ORGANIZATION AND CONDUCT

We have often followed with our eyes birds, groups of birds in spring, and watched how they were aligned, one in front, two or three following, then a big bunch close together, then simmering down to three or four, one or two following lonely, and one or two more lonely on the sides. We often wondered by what kind of rules these groupings are governed. Probably a social instinct drives them to travel in groups. But we won-dered whether the arrangement they produce within these groupings is influenced by mechanical forces only, speed of flying, endurance, and so on, or whether attractions and repulsions among the individual birds have a part in producing the formation.

It is certainly so with people. When we observe adolescents at play on the grounds we see how three or four are anxiously trying to keep pace with one who is running ahead, one walking with another arm in arm, two or three scattered, each alone. And if we watched the same group daily, we could ascertain that this arrangement is not accidental, it is repeated at least over a certain period of time in much the same formation until, perhaps, one gets tired of the other and new attachments develop and a new leader comes to the front.

One contrasting element, a colored child, among white children produces in general an attitude of interest and sympathy. Eventually the other children may become indifferent towards her but rarely hostile. It is different if the numbers change. If into a group of twenty to thirty white individuals, three, four, five, or more colored enter, the emotional attitude tends generally to change. Each of the colored is sensitive to what happens to the other through the actions of the white group and they are inclined to form a gang spontaneously. But if the two races are about equal in numbers, hostilities are always ready to be let loose; sympathy and indifference are rarer.

The following incident illustrates such a situation developing in a cottage group. Into C11, which had 23 white girls, an Indian girl, WI, was placed. She became a pet of the housemother and of the girls. Later two half-Indian girls were assigned to the group. The attitude of the group towards the first Indian girl became critical. They were less attentive to her in play and more seldom defended her in quarrels. When the new Indian girls were scolded by the housemother, WI felt it as an affront to herself as well as to them. The three developed gradually a unity of attitude. The white girls began to feel themselves as a group apart from the Indian girls and became less intimate with them. The minority group, however, became more quickly sensitive to the changed situation. When a fourth Indian girl, SN, was placed into the group, she had to be removed from it due to the difficulties among the girls. Contrasting elements appear to have a stimulating effect up to a certain point, but become an irritating factor if this point is overstepped. A sociometric test at this date revealed the Indian girls in a gang formation, rejected by the white and rejecting them in return. The *saturation point* for Indian members seemed to be reached. Soon afterwards it absorbed readily a foreign-born Polish girl and a Russian Jewish girl. This infers that a group can be saturated for one contrasting element and still be able to adjust easily with other contrasting elements. The structural organization of the group and the degree of differentiation the group has attained indicate its status in respect to saturation for different contrasting elements.

The problem of adjusting contrasting racial and nationality elements into one group appeared to be more difficult in *home* groups than in other collectives. Since the members must live in such close proximity contrasting nationality and racial characteristics are felt more strongly and meet with greater resistance. The saturation point for negroes and Indians within the same white group was higher in work and play groups than in home groups. Members with different nationality and racial characteristics prove often to be a stimulus for competition and progress for a group. The stimulus appears of greater advantage in work and cultural groups than in home groups. We recognized the need of a balanced distribution of the different races and nationalities within each group and within the community as a whole: that is, the necessity to develop a racial quotient. It appears that one factor in the racial quotient will be found to be dependent upon the criterion of the given collective.

Just as the illustration how contrasting nationality and racial elements affect group organization and conduct, other contrasting elements, as sex, have to be considered. If within a population of 500 to 600 white girls who have lived segregated from the normally organized community, suddenly a group of men appear and reside for a time, a switching of the emotional interest of the girls from their own sex to the men takes place. It can be said that the tele is " bored " with unisexed attachments only and runs avidly into this new outlet. When a few men reside permanently in such a community they become centers of " sexual currents " and pampered due to the excessive amount of attention they receive. Another situation develops in Hudson where a group of sixty colored girls are placed in two cottages of the community. These colored girls provide a new direction for emotional interest, and under the circumstances a therapeutic advantage to the community in this respect.

In any community there are certain groupings which develop the organization of which is influenced by forces coming from within. Home and work groups as they are formed in Hudson result from forces coming exclusively from within the community. But there are also in any community certain groupings which develop, the organization of which is influenced by forces coming from without. We see an instance of this kind in existence in what we may call a " dual " organization within a state institution: on the one hand, the group of inmates, and on the other, the group of staff members. " This is an inmate," or " This is a member of the staff." Inevitably a different group attitude develops of each group towards the other, around each of these two criteria. The more the attempt is made to melt these two groupings into one, into a monistic organization, as, for instance, in Hudson, the more the community gains the character of a large, a huge family. It is then, at least for the time being, as if the children have changed their parents, as if the state has taken them into its parenthood. In this spirit, even the commitment loses its hard character as it can be said that children are " committed " to live with their own parents up to a certain age as long as they are minors.

We have already shown that groups with a population of both sexes have an organization which grows and that the developmental level of a social group can be recognized from the degree of differentiation within its structure. Just as an individual can be " socially retarded," a whole group can be " socially retarded "; it may have an organization corresponding to a developmental level lower than generally found at its age level. Again, we have observed group organizations which were broken up because one set of members within it tended towards producing structures of lower differentiation. On the

other hand, group organization can be " socially premature ";
the organization of the group is characteristic for a developmental level beyond that of the organization commonly found
at this age level. The development of differentiation demonstrates a different pattern if the population of the group is uni-
sexed. The homosexual current flowing between the members is not counteracted, as in mixed groups, by a heterosexual
current.

Through the sociometric test we were able to determine
when children begin to develop their own societies and at what
age levels these associations gained such an emotional effect
upon their members that their conduct is determined more
and more by these influences and less and less by the influences
coming from the mixed adult-children groups. It appears
that the critical age in the adult-child relation begins around
the eighth year and that about this time the *child-child relations* within children associations become more highly organized and less dependent upon the adult.

The cases of isolation which develop from the eighth year to
the period of pubescence are not simply isolated, forgotten, left
out individuals as found at the kindergarten level but result at
least partly from different causes. One set of children is
attached to and more affected by the adult group, their family
or teachers; another set of children is attached to or more
attentive to a children group. Yet there is a third set of
children. They fall *between* the two social groups which are
fundamentally related to every growing individual. They
belong to both groups but to neither fully. This sociometric
position seems to mark the beginning of many isolated characters who crystallize either apart from both groups eventually, as in schizophrenic isolation, or develop an attitude of
aggression. That these isolates prefer finally the boy-gang to
the family-gang is due to the fact that whereas their aggression towards the family ended usually with failure, the aggression towards the boy-gang met on occasion with the satisfaction
to dominate it. The isolated aggressor has here an easier
chance. It is the outcome of such developments that we could
study on a large scale in Hudson. Through the sociometric

test we ascertained that 19% of the population only was attached to and more easily influenced by adults, while 70% of the population was attached to and more easily influenced by girls. Eleven per cent remained little influenced by either group, isolated.

These facts suggested a difficult therapeutic problem within the community. The staff of adults, housemothers and teachers and others directly in contact with the girls, in all about 80 persons, appeared unable to touch emotionally the larger part of the population. It appears that this fact is the chief reason why the staff of institutions are often forced to resort to rigid discipline and particularly to inflicting punishment if they want to impress their will upon a population the majority of which escapes their spontaneous influencing. In Hudson, if the housemothers, teachers, and others wanted to impress their will upon the 70% who escapes them, they have to resort to the strategy of using the 19% as tools, intermediaries, to reach the 70%. But we have learned through our sociograms that these 19% are often not the key-individuals for the majority. They often live within their cottage group in close affiliation with the housemother, segregated and rejected by many of the others. They emulate the domineering attitude of an imitation housemother which does not stir the rest towards coöperation. And this is the case the more they gravitate in their conduct in a direction determined by emotional trends which tend towards the developing of adolescent gangs.

2. THE PSYCHOLOGICAL HOME

The family is a complex social group. It consists of two groupings each with a different criterion. The one grouping, composed of the man and the woman, is a sexual grouping. The relation between the man and woman is the dominant factor. It had been started by the two persons alone and had existed before children came into it. It had been started without intention to take additional members into it or at least without knowing whom they might be who would enter into it. The second grouping, composed of the father, the mother, and the children, is a monastic grouping, monastic because the spirit of the monastery prevails in this group. The monastery was a revolt against the first grouping. It cut it away and emulated methodically the other portion of the family. Another revolt against the family structure is the communistic attempt to divorce the nurturing of the offspring from their procreators. In this case the group two portion is cut away and the original portion remains. These revolts suggest that the two portions are of different origin and may not always have been together. Group two is probably a further differentiation after a totemistic pattern and it can be assumed that the recognition of consanguinity of father and child aided in melting the two portions into one. The psychological experience of parenthood and the distinction of being a parent derived from it must have been enormous and still is. This was somewhat shattered when man learned that his individual contribution to the child is negligible compared to the racial heritage of the kind.

The cottage groups in institutions are more simply organized than is the family. The father-mother situation is not present. Only the second, the monastic portion, is left, a uni-sexed group or a mixed group with a housemother or a housemother and a housefather, but all unrelated to one another. There is no element of blood-relation binding them one to another. It is an "experimental home."

It is difficult for girls who come to a community like Hudson to feel at home as all legitimate motives for such attitude are at first missing: the natural bond feeling as in a successful family group; the feeling of individual liberty and possession; and the feeling of permanent arrangements and objectives. But as we know from observation how important it is for children of adolescent age to produce attachment to a nucleus of persons who offer protection and a stimulus for emotional and intellectual progress, it is crucial for us to know in what this "psychological" home which some girls develop and others not consists. Is there any possibility to measure this? No girl develops this feeling if she is repulsed by the members of the group who do not produce in her any motive to stay with them. Home quality is a nucleus of attractions and repulsions and if the repulsive tendency dominates the home feeling is wanting.

Every individual gravitates towards a situation which offers him as a personality the highest degree of spontaneous expression and fulfillment and he continuously seeks for companions who are willing to share with him. The psychological home is his goal. This home idea may be identical with his actual home group or it may be related to one or more persons outside towards whom he is attracted. It may even be nothing but a vague notion within his mind. Still it may be sufficient to influence his attitude and conduct in his actual home group. The continued existence of a home depends upon the interest its members have for each other. Any home to go on successfully must have the support of some portion of the group. The only permanent feature, the only invariable in any home structure, is a configuration of relations, a psychological nucleus. The larger the membership of the home group the more important it becomes to determine, from the point of view of its continued existence and of its influence upon the conduct of its members, which members gravitate to persons outside of it.

An illustration may be taken from one of the cottage groups in Hudson. Cottage 6 has 31 members. Its housemother at the time of the first sociometric test held the affection, sufficiently to direct their conduct continuously, of Kathryn, May, Grace, Marion, Mafalda, Anna, Jane, Bertha, Felma, Kathleen, Gail, and Dorothy. Four of these girls, Marion, Anna, Jane, and Kathleen, held strong positions within the group. Marion is attracted to and holds the affection of six girls and five of these are different ones from those the housemother holds: Alice, Sylvia, Glayds, Merline, and Lucille. Anna is attracted to and holds the affection of four: Bertha, Jane, and Kathleen, whom the housemother holds, and Laura and Helen, two others, so that she strengthens the bonds of the housemother to these four. Jane holds the affection of two key-individuals, Anna and Marion. Kathleen holds Felma, Anna, Kathryn, May, and Grace, all girls whom the housemother holds, and two others, Eva and Letitia. Two girls have a direct personal bond to the housemother only, but not to other girls, Gail and Dorothy. Six girls remain isolated from both housemother and other girls: Lillian, Violet, Louise, Virginia, Marie, and Sarah. Four girls, Norma, Edith, Eileen, and Charlotte, are bound together into a gang outside the influence of other girls or of the housemother. Thus 10 girls remain outside the psychological nucleus of 21 girls in the cottage group C6. The 10 are evidently indifferent towards the group and the housemother and gravitate towards persons outside the group. The psychological nucleus of the cottage can be described as a chain leadership with the housemother in the center and 12 girls around her. It is obvious that if by circumstance, either through parole, illness, or assignment, six of these 12 should leave the cottage at one time the housemother would be faced with a dilemma, the psychological nucleus would be shattered, and the group threatened with disintegration.

In other cottage groups the home nucleus varies in its structure. In CA, with a low membership of 19, we see the nucleus limited to the housemother and 14 girls, each strongly related to her but weakly related to one another; and five remaining isolated. In CI the nucleus revolves around one girls and the housemother remains herself outside the nucleus, more like a housekeeper. Why a large number of these girls who remain unattached to either housemother or girls do not run away is that they have *nowhere to run to* or else various objectives make the school nevertheless more attractive to them than any place they have previously known.

An important factor is the amount of emotional energy each member spends or is able to spend in his home group. This becomes the more obvious the larger the home group, and especially to the member who is anxiously interested or responsible in holding the group together, the housemother. The question is how great or small the capacity of the housemother is to hold her girls; how many girls have no attachment to the housemother of the cottage or to another individual able to encourage and adjust her to the group. From this point of view, if a cottage were to have a population of ten girls and five of them remained unintegrated, the group would be worse off than if the population were 25 in which the same number were not integrated because the larger the number of girls in a cottage the greater is the opportunity for all eventually to find some agent connecting her with the group. The measure of a housemother's expansiveness is not simply the number but also the personalities of the girls she can hold. Certain girls might require but a minimum of exertion on her part, while for others a maximum of exertion may be called for. The length of time she required to build up a relation may differ greatly from one girl to another. The ideal principle would be not to assign any new child to any group which has even one member still unintegrated. It is necessary to ascertain accurately the expansiveness of the housemother as from this depends the kind of training necessary to increase this capacity and to devise techniques to supplement and substitute natural forces.

We see the natural mother, however large her family, turning her attention to the most helpless, the last-born. This suggests that a housemother should divert her attention to the new child as soon as she comes into her group. The natural mother, when she has one child more disadvantaged, crippled, or backward, transfers to this one an exceptional love and continuously suggests the same spirit to the other members of the family. This procedure leads often to the spoiling of the child and its overdependence upon the mother, but there is a sound principle in it which can be applied to many housemother-child situations.

It suggests that the housemother should not only try herself but observe one of the older girls to whom this child is singularly drawn and place upon this girl responsibility in respect to the child. She has to learn the function of inner assignment in a group, to release numerous functions to the older girls, to turn her attention always to the weakest spot in the group, to assign one girl to another, two girls to a third, a group to a leader, and never allow it to happen that one girl is privileged. Instead, she should encourage the development of new centers all the time, as in general the very limitations she has towards the girls the superior girl-leader has also towards her followers. Such a leader has, just as an adult, a limited capacity to absorb and to respond to love and demands upon her affections. It has often been reported that large families have a greater number of delinquents than small families. This can in large measure be accounted for by the limited emotional expansiveness of man and by his limited aptitude for emotional absorption. Even a natural mother becomes a " technical " mother as soon as she has to leave one or two of her children to themselves while she performs other duties which call her away from them or because she has so many children that she cannot be attentive to all. This becomes still more obvious in our cottage groups. We see our housemothers unaware of the natural limitations of their emotional expansiveness, getting restless, nervous, irritable, apparently without reason, but behind it is always the same cause, the feeling of her inferiority to play up to all the demands and calls upon her and consequently her attempt to cover up the deficiencies in her cottage through various subterfuges. She may become supersensitive to criticism, quick-tempered when she had not been so before, and use the very slang of the girls in order to impress them quickly. This kind of conduct may delay the housemother's progress in creating a relation or break down in a moment the work of months and affect by indirection her relation to the friends and followers of the severely scolded girl. Other housemothers may try to get away from their limitations through a policy of laissez-faire, watching the surface routine of the cottage only. This is another declaration of insufficiency, another example of the technical mother, leaving an emotional vacuum in so many spots of her group unchecked by bonds between herself and the girls or between the girls themselves. But if the housemother feels that her cottage is her permanent home and the girls with whom she lives her children, she will make an effort to inject all her love and abilities into the situation. If her primary interests are outside the institution, she will be less efficient as the task of a housemother demands and exhausts all her resources.

A special problem in adjustment are the new girl and the new housemother. The more introverted an organization of a group, the harder is it for an individual to break in and to find adjustment in it. The more introverted the organization of a group, the more will the group be inclined to develop a feeling of difference and distinction from other groups and correspondingly every individual of this group, a feeling of difference and distinction in respect to individuals of other groups in the given community. When a housemother leaves and a new one replaces her, we see the new housemother beginning with great enthusiasm but soon thereafter becoming hysterical, unsure of herself, anxious for approval, and before she reaches the end of this phase, showing fatigue, discouragement, depression. She sees no way out except by giving up the position as outside her aptitude or by following some form of routine. It is necessary to develop a housemother gradually by giving her during the first six months of practice a small number of girls not exceeding the size of a normal family and including not more than one or two children who are especially difficult. When this procedure is not followed and the " limit " of the housemother (or of anyone in a similar position) is surpassed by force, the performance of this person deteriorates or the person becomes simply ill.

There is another factor which determines group reaction towards the new housemother and the new girl. It is the *preserving* influence of group organization upon the conduct of its members. When due to increased influx of population a cottage had to be filled beyond its normal capacity, the number of complaints of girls about other girls increased. It reminds us of the old argument that overpopulation leads to war. It seemed natural that the greater the number of girls who have to be accommodated within the same number of rooms the greater can be the opportunity for frictions. We calculated, if overcrowding has an effect upon the conduct of the group, then we should be able to improve the conduct of the group through reducing the number of its members. We had occasion to test this when in C2 five girls were assigned to other groups or paroled within a few days. The number of disciplinary cases dropped immediately. However, when we applied a similar test to C1 and reduced the number of its members below normal capacity, the number of disciplinary cases failed to drop. An analysis of C2 showed that the five girls who had been assigned or paroled from it reduced, on one hand, the overflow to normal capacity and, on the other, removed girls who, while they did not occupy any key-positions within the group, injected a restlessness into it either because they were anxious to be paroled soon or because they wanted to be assigned to another cottage. But when we analyzed C1 we found that we had cut out girls from its structure who were well adjusted within it and hence we had not helped the remainder of the group considerably. In other words, we learned that a *mechanical* reduction of a large cottage group to a smaller one has not necessarily a therapeutic effect: it apparently depends also upon whom are cut out and what group organization remains. C2 had a more highly differentiated structure; the assigning out of the five girls was a necessary operation: the number of disciplinary cases dropped. But in C1 the structure was so undifferentiated that as it appeared no reassignment would have substantially aided immediately.

Apparently it is the preserving influence (upon the conduct of its members) of group organization which is responsible for these reactions. C1 and C2 have as groups a historical development. As the number who are paroled from or enter new during one year into a cottage group is about one-fourth of its population, it is four years before a complete population change takes place in a cottage. All individuals who have passed through the group, according to their position in it, have left their mark. At any time incoming girls meet with an established organization built not only by the members who are present but by those who have left a surviving effect upon the group organization. They are met as well by what may be called the *survival* of psychological impressions which *predispose* the attitude of the group towards them. This phenomenon preserves the group against any radical innovations the newcomer may seek to impose suddenly. It is a group's defense mechanism. Groups which last over a period of years develop a definite character. The organization of any such group will explicitly reveal it and this, in turn, will be very suggestive as to what persons should or should not be assigned to it.

It has become evident to us that perhaps the chief factor in the growth of group organization is this survival of the impress of psychological relations. We see, for instance, a housemother conducting a group whose method has been to show affection and to attach the girls to herself personally. She leaves the cottage and is replaced by a housemother whose method is impersonal and who puts each of the girls into a plan which she has designed. If the former housemother was successful, the new one cannot break the spell of her influence upon the group over night. This influence may be reflected not only in the individual girl's reactions, but more than that, in the interrelations among the girls. Structures give way only gradually to new structures.

Similarly the personality of every individual who has been a member of a particular group may leave impressions which survive long after he has departed. We see this illustrated over and over again in certain situations arising within families. Yet we pay one-sided attention to the problem in adjustment it so frequently causes. When a son marries, we pay attention to his problem of adjustment in the new relationship but little attention to the problem arising through the change in the old family organization he has left. The complaint of the mother that no one is able to fill his place now he has left is a popular suggestion of the survival effect of an individual after departure from a group. Many disturbances within the group arise due to such negative reasons. The interrelations which are cut out of the group structure by his leaving are not at once replaced.

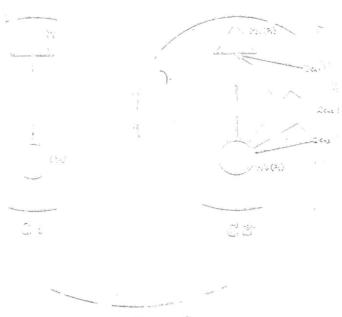

CLEAVAGE IN FAMILY GROUP

This chart illustrates the two groupings a typical family consists of. The one circle, C1, represents the sexual grouping; the other circle, C2, the monastic or totemistic grouping. The large circle indicates that C1 and C2 are two cells within the same field. Lines go from child 1, 2, and 3 (ch. 1, 2, 3), to parent 1 (P1) and parent 2 in the second cell which indicates these five individuals form a group; but no lines go from child 1, 2, or 3 to the man and woman in the first cell, which indicates that the man and woman form this group separately. The two cells represent different functions: cell 1, the sexual and reproductive; cell 2, the parental and protective. The two groupings within the family have not always been united into one pattern; they have probably had two divergent lines of evolution. As main steps in the separate evolution of the first cell can be considered group marriage, polyandry and successive polygamy; as steps in the separate evolution of the second cell, the totem group and the monastery.

CLEAVAGES IN GROUPS

Psychological Home

Cottage VI, 31 members. Outside of a nucleus of 21 are 4 individuals who form a gang and 6 individuals who are isolated.

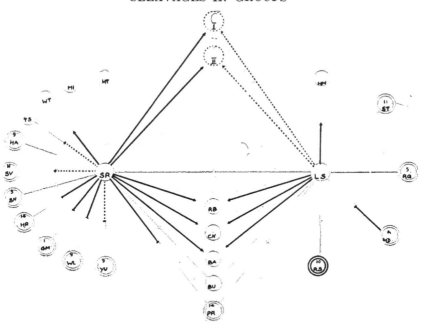

A RUNAWAY PAIR, SR AND LS

The sociogram indicates mutual attraction between SR and LS. Except for the relation of SR to BU, they form an *isolated* pair in their cottage. Both reject RB, CN, and BA, girls in the same cottage. BU, whom SR likes, is also liked by LS. SR rejects I (the housemother) and II (the kitchen supervisor) and LS is indifferent to them. LS forms mutual pairs with individuals in other cottages, RQ in C5, ST in C11, and RS, a colored girl, in C10. SR is indifferent to or rejects attractions coming from outside the home group, YU of C9, WL of C9, GM of C1, HR of C14, but is attracted to SN of C5, of whom she makes an exception. Towards members of her own group (aside from LS) she is indifferent (HT, MI, WT, and TS). Both girls, SR and LS, appear cut off from the main currents and blocked, isolated and limited to each other. SR is attracted to a man outside in the community who in turn is attracted to her (not plotted on this chart) and this persisting attraction finally precipitated the running away of both girls. It can be seen that their position within the community of Hudson predisposed to this action as they had no resistance to overcome, being not a part of the community.

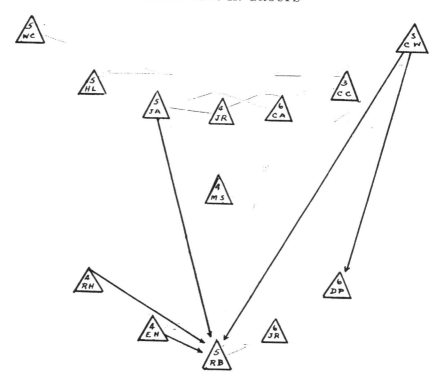

A FOOTBALL TEAM

The chart shows the football team which includes two substitute backs. Note that the quarterback 4/MS is the focus of attraction forces on team, as he should be, but that fullback 5/RB is liked by nobody on the team, and is disliked by four: 4/RH and 4/EH of the back field, and 5/JA and 5/CW of the line. It is easy to see that when 5/RB is running with the ball he is not apt to get the maximum of coöperation in interference and blocking.

(See Map of a School Community, pp. 49–50)

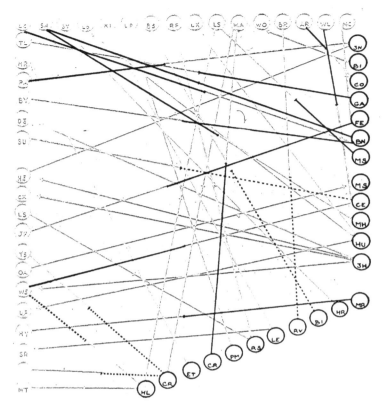

· STRUCTURE OF INTERRELATIONS BETWEEN TWO RACIAL GROUPS
Criterion: Living in Proximity

The chart indicates the interchanged attitudes in respect to living together in the same cottage of 23 colored girls and 34 white girls. Six white and six colored girls form mutual pairs, wanting to be in the same cottage together. Fourteen incompatible pairs are formed, one party wanting to live in the same house, the other not. Seven colored girls are attracted to white girls who do not respond. The population in which the sociometric test revealed these inter-relations to exist consisted of 377 white and 58 colored girls.

214

3. A RUNAWAY PAIR

In the fall of 1932 two girls from C12 ran away. Both girls, Ruth, 17, and Marie, 16, were daughters of foreign-born Italian parents and had been brought up in an Italian neighborhood of two different cities of New York state. Ruth was married at 14. Her husband was unemployed and had a long court record. He placed her into a house of prostitution. Upon her protesting, he beat her so severely that she became unconscious. After two days in the house she ran away. He was arrested and sentenced and the marriage was annulled. Thereafter Ruth did domestic work for one year. At the end of this period she contracted syphilis from another Italian, a bootlegger and robber, and applied voluntarily to be sent to Hudson. She was afraid of the two men who had brought her misfortune but retained an affection for another Italian who had lived next door to her.

Marie, on the other hand, had had no sexual experience. She came from a broken home. Her parents had been divorced, each had married again, and she had lived alternately with each of them except for a period of five years between the ages of 8 and 13 years, when she was placed in a convent school. Her commitment to Hudson resulted chiefly from the plea of her mother that she was incorrigible.

All reports of the conduct of the two girls in Hudson up to the time of their running away, which was a first attempt, had been excellent. The sociometric classification of Ruth in August, 1932, was:

$$\text{Formula 1.} \quad \frac{1}{3} \bigg| \frac{3}{6} \qquad\qquad \text{Formula 2:} \quad \frac{2-4}{4-0} \bigg| \frac{1-3}{7-0}$$
$$\quad\quad\quad\quad L \qquad\qquad\qquad\qquad\qquad\qquad L$$

Marie's classification of that date was:

$$\text{Formula 1.} \quad \frac{2}{1} \bigg| \frac{3}{2} \qquad\qquad \text{Formula 2:} \quad \frac{2-4}{1-0} \bigg| \frac{5-0}{4-1}$$
$$\quad\quad\quad\quad L \qquad\qquad\qquad\qquad\qquad\qquad L$$

The sociogram on page 212 illustrates the sociometric position they had in Hudson at that date. This was one year after they had come to the school. The test was repeated after one month and revealed no change in their respective positions. On the basis of their classifications we state that their position in the community predisposed them to run away. Their names were placed on the list of reassignments to take place as a result of our study. Before their desired transfer to another cottage was made they ran away.

The sociogram indicates the mutual attraction between the two girls, SR, Ruth, and LS, Marie, in respect to living in the same cottage. They were also mutual first choices for working together. Marie was the first girl whom Ruth became acquainted with in C12. Their attraction appears deeply intrenched as the same girls within the cottage whom one rejects the other also rejects, RB, CA, and BA. It is significant that the girls they reject are generally rejected within the group. The one girl whom Ruth likes, BU, Marie also likes. With the one exception of BU, who was paroled in September, both girls reject or are indifferent to even those girls of the group who are attracted to them. Ruth rejects the housemother (I) and the kitchen officer (II), while Marie is indifferent to them. The two girls form an isolated pair in their cottage and it appears from the motivations of this circle of persons that Ruth usually took the lead in determining what attitude they should both take towards others. The position of Marie outside of her cottage is more openly friendly than that of Ruth. She forms four mutual pairs with girls in other groups. Her friendship with the colored girl, RS, gave the only instance for friction between Ruth and Marie.

Both girls appeared cut off from the main currents and blocked, isolated, and limited to each other for BU had by this time been long ago paroled. In October Ruth heard through a new girl that some of her boy-friends were still thinking of her. The precipitating motive for running away was given. As an Hallowe'en party was in progress in the cottage, a third girl, JL, acted as " dummy," fainted, distracted the attention of the housemother and the other girls, and Ruth and Marie ran away.

The act of running away can frequently be foretold and preventive measures taken if a careful sociometric classification of each individual of the population is made at regular periods. Just as a child in the community outside may feel pressed to run away from his family or may feel pressed to run away from the whole complex of personal connections, including the town in which he lives, so the child in a closed community develops similar attitudes. We differentiate three classes of runaways: First, individuals who are unattached in their group and run away from their cottage. Frequently they ask for assignment to another group and try through various strategies to secure it. As soon as they have a more favorable adjustment their restlessness vanishes and they settle down. They are potential runaways until such adjustment has been made. However, there are isolated and rejected within cottage groups who do not run away, as they have attachments to members of other cottage groups. Second, individuals who run away from the community. They are cut off and blocked not only in their cottage group but in respect to other activities of the community as well. If classification signifies this position in an initial stage, motivations for attachment can be developed as preventive measures. The adjustment of these cases is more difficult. Third, individuals who run away by sudden impulse. Many individuals who appear to be impulsive runaways were found to have an explanation for their action in their position; their spontaneous action was found to be intimately interwoven with the setting. Often, as we have seen in the case of Ruth, the sociometric position of an individual in the town where she comes from and the emotional currents to which she had been related in the past have to be studied parallel with those of the immediate community.

4. RACE

The question may arise if it is possible through the study of the organization of a given community to foretell in advance not only behavior reactions, as running away, but greater outbreaks involving a group of persons, and which can be very harmful to one or another part of the population. We have shown that it is possible to recognize early within the group organization of the community signs which predispose to such disturbances. Up to date either the individual unrelated to the community as a whole was studied or a mass unrelated to each individual of which it consists. But the application of sociometry to the problem reveals the psychological position of *each* individual within a mass and traces through the numerous interactions of specific individuals the predisposing zones out of which spontaneous mass reactions arise and the gradual development of such reactions.

Such a zone in miniature which existed over a six months' period was studied within a section of the colored population in Hudson.

At the beginning of the research

The colored population was housed in C7 and C10. The sociometric test disclosed at the beginning of our research the organizations of C7 and C10 charted in sociograms on p. 125. In C10, in the center of 19 attractions within a population of 32 girls, were Susan and Sarah. Mutual attraction was indicated between them. Through the motivations and Spontaneity Testing, Susan was revealed to be the dominant partner in their relationship. Susan was thus the actual leader of the group. The evidence of her leadership was strengthened through the analysis of her rejections. She rejected nine in her group. The analysis of the spontaneous reactions of these nine towards her showed fear as the leading emotion. Characteristic for her position is a mutual rejection between her and Jane MS. Jane, who had the highest I.Q. (116) of the group and was the most advanced student, was isolated and rejected by the group except for one attraction from a newcomer. In C7, besides three key-individuals, Elizabeth is the center of attraction and leads the group. The map indicating the relations within the whole population (Psychological Geography of a Community, p. 242) depicts numerous rejections between C7 and C10. This appeared to be related in part to the attitudes between the two house-mothers, who reject each other. The colored groups centering around Susan and Elizabeth showed also in their work units to center around these two girls, and during the time they held such position no serious disturbances arose.

Four months later.

Routine testing of the population during the next four months did not reveal any alarming change in the colored group organizations. But at the end of this period Susan and Sarah had been paroled and a number of newcomers had entered, among them Stella. The two groups were retested again after the four months had ended. The group organization of C10 showed major changes. No individual centers the attractions of the group. The group appears decentralized into six factions. The only consistent factor is the relation of the group to Jane. Four girls are attracted to her but all four have insignificant positions within the group. She is rejected by 12, 11 of whom are former adherents of Susan or of Sarah. The motivations of the girls interpret this as the position of a rejected leader. Spontaneity tests of Jane and the 12 who reject her demonstrated that in nine cases behind the rejection was anger at her idea that she is better than they are. Stella's position is inconspicuous. She rejects and is rejected by Philamina, who is also her coworker in the steam laundry, and by Jane. Two other coworkers, Hilda and Rosalie, are attracted to live with her. C7 shows also a major change in organization. The housemother herself has taken the place of Elizabeth, who had been paroled, and is the center of numerous attractions. And in neither home group could any alarming structure be traced.

But when we tested at this time the colored work groups, we met in the steam laundry an organization of relationships which, according to our experience, indicated predisposing grounds for serious disturbance. A group of seven girls, all from C10, Stella, Philamina, Esther, Hilda, Myrtle, Rosalie, and Lillian, were occupied in this work unit. The organization of this group as revealed by the sociometric test is charted in sociogram Fig. 1 on p. 132. Stella and Philamina, the two feeders, reject each other. Hilda and Myrtle, the two catchers, reject each other. Myrtle rejects the feeder opposite her, Philamina. Lillian and Rosalie, the two folders, reject Myrtle. The two folders attract each other. Esther, the shaker, is attracted to Lillian and rejects Hilda. Hilda is attracted to her opposite feeder, Stella, and the latter is attracted to Rosalie and rejected by Myrtle. Esther, Stella, Hilda, and Rosalie reject the forewoman, but only Stella is rejected by her. Philamina, Myrtle, and Lillian are attracted to her and she likes them. Motivations, in brief, were: Philamina states she is afraid of Stella because she has hit her. Stella states, " Philamina is against us; she sides in with Miss O." Hilda is against Myrtle because she is against Stella. Myrtle opposes Hilda because " Hilda always thinks Stella is just right even when she upsets our job." Lillian says, " Stella wants Rosalie to join her in making tricks against Miss O., but she listens to me and won't do it." Rosalie says, " Stella is a good fighter; she will take the blame for you, but Lillian always helps me with the work." Esther likes Lillian because " She is decent and doesn't talk against white people like Stella does," and dislikes Hilda because " She is dumb; she listens to the craziest things Stella wants her to do." Myrtle rejects Philamina because " She is friends with Jane MS and tells everything we do in laundry to her, and then Jane tells our housemother." Lillian and Rosalie dislike Myrtle as " She is too friendly with white girls." Stella dislikes the forewoman: " If she has to stop the machine she says it's my fault. She always thinks that I'll hurt myself if I just go fast around the machine to help Rosalie." Hilda says, " She blames me and Stella that we don't listen to her and we do so listen." Esther and Rosalie dislike her but do not " know why." The forewoman said, " I like them all except that Stella is defiant, stubborn, and always stirring up others to some mischief."

Four weeks later

Retesting of the steam laundry group revealed Stella as the center of all attractions except from Philamina. She and Stella reject each other. All but Philamina reject the forewoman.

Predisposing causes:

The sociometric test of the steam laundry revealed a group formation in its initial stage centering around Stella. The situation depicted in the sociogram and the motivations given by the seven girls suggested a conflict existing between Esther and Hilda versus Philamina and Myrtle, and incompatible relations existing between both pairs and the forewoman, predisposing the ground for Stella. Esther and Hilda had often felt a passing grudge against the forewoman, who had censured them when they were careless and slow. But Myrtle and Philamina opposed Esther and Hilda; they had been in the steam laundry before the latter and were on the side of the forewoman for the most part. The forewoman, however, was able to offset this conflict. It is into this situation that Stella entered. As she had the impudence to ridicule the forewoman behind her back and to challenge the others to act similarly, she succeeded so far that Esther, Hilda, and Rosalie joined with her immediately and emulated her actions. They agreed collectively upon an attitude of insurgence. When the test was repeated four weeks later, all sided with Stella except Philamina, who was her partner in feeding the steam roller. Stella persisted in working as her mood dictated,—often too rapidly or too slowly for Philamina to coöperate with her. Then, on the other side of the machine, Hilda and Myrtle, the catchers, were rushed and confused or simply idle. Sometimes after quarrels with Philamina she stopped working altogether. At other times she fed the machine too many articles at once, ran around it, and grabbed them before they could become caught and tie up the machine. But in doing this she made such a game of the process by tossing her hands into the rolling hot machine that she endangered herself.

The testing of the cottage group C10 failed to disclose any disturbance at that time as coming from Stella and her group Also the enmity between her and Philamina had not penetrated the cottage situation. But upon the basis of the findings in the test of the steam laundry we feared a larger disturbance within the colored population of C10 if nothing were done to check its spread. With a population of 33, C10 disclosed at this time 35 disagreeing or incompatible pairs, more than any other home group in the community. Due to its introverted organization frictions involving its members were concentrated in the cottage. It had been without a leader since the parole of Susan. Both colored cottages in

Hudson had favored an organization with one leader, following her blindly whatever course she took. When Susan and Sarah were paroled, it was expected that Jane, the most intelligent girl in the house, would come into their position of leadership. While she developed the trust of the housemother, the group persistently rejected her and she in turn rejected them. The organization was loose and rapidly disintegrating.

It was in this period that Stella came to Hudson and was assigned to C10. Stella mixed with girls who disagreed with Jane and she and Jane began to quarrel from the start. The group in the steam laundry had crystallized around Stella as leader and was vaguely directed at the forewoman. It could be expected that the same individuals would bind themselves together into a similar attitude towards the white house-mother. It was a zone of chronic emotional excitation.

The organization of the cottage groups, besides the effect of the emotional differences described, was influenced by attitudes towards racial differences among its own members. The girls discriminated among themselves in favor of the darkest colored girls and in disfavor of the light colored girls, who numbered about 10% of the group in C10, whenever any occasion arose when they had an opportunity to do so. It is in this respect characteristic that the leaders in both cottages were among the darkest colored girls, and that Jane, who was among the light colored, was the more rejected the more she offered her council. Also the association with the housemother, which had made Susan and Elizabeth the more important in their eyes, made Jane an outcast. These two poles in the racial current we see reflected in the organization of the group also, the light colored girls having positions in the side currents only.

In a certain succession, the premonitory symptoms appeared, as in the course of a disease, and " called for " preventive measures. We suggested the assignment of Stella from the steam laundry to another work group. This assignment took place one week after the second test of her position. The local group in the laundry was thus broken up and the conduct became satisfactory.

A sociometric test given three weeks before the outbreak disclosed that the home organization of C10 had undergone major changes: Stella as the center of 12 attractions; Jane as the center of 15 rejections; Stella rejecting the housemother and Jane; Jane and the housemother mutually attracted to each other; the nucleus of the gang around Stella are in part her former coworkers in the laundry, and eight of them are among those who reject Jane. The motivations reveal Jane ridiculed for her friendship with a while girl in CB as well as for her particular attention to the housemother. Numerous little offenses against the colored girl's sensitiveness as to her race appeared in the motivations to have a point around which to center (racial current). The current travelled rapidly through the existing network in which C10, C7, and part of C13 participated.

Precipitating causes

1. The housemother of C10 goes on vacation. A substitute takes her place.

2. During the next few days numerous minor disturbances occur in the house.

3. Stella's mother visits her. After she leaves Jane says in the presence of other girls: " Stella's mother is all right, but she is big and black and sloppy." Stella hears of the incident through her followers and confronts Jane. Jane denies having said it.

Final phase:

The next day was critical. Twenty-six girls of the population of 35 girls sided with Stella against Jane, who may in fact have said also about their own mother that she is " black and sloppy." They felt Stella justified in defending her mother and her race. Six of them held repeated councils with Stella (four of whom were in the steam laundry group). Stella went to beat Jane up. Jane ran into her room and had another girl lock her in. Stella and her gang rushed to the house-mother and demanded the key to get into Jane's room. The housemother saw that they had scissors and other objects. She and the other officers attempted to quiet them. From this moment on the fight aimed at Jane turned towards the housemother and all who came to her aid. They started to

yell and to break chairs, desks, tables, glasses, lamps, everything that was near at hand.   ⌐

It becomes evident, first, that the excitement was in its detailed formation dependent upon the organization of the groups
and upon the organization of the community in which the
individuals who have appeared as chief actors in the incident
had participated.   Second, that it is possible to reveal the
development of these organizations from step to step in respect
to each individual concerned and that these organizations
themselves have acted as predisposing causes.   Third, that
the outburst was not a mass reaction in the mass psychological sense but the end phase in the interaction of many
individuals within the given community in which each individual had a definable position and acting under a definable psychological pressure;   that the short-cut emotions and
attitudes, as jealousy, hatred, racial inferior feelings, and so
on, developed visibly from simpler, less differentiated to more
highly differentiated forms until they consolidated into the
attitudes in the end result.   Fourth, that numerous, minute,
spontaneous attitudes in many individuals and their interactions were continuously penetrating the collectives of which
they were a part.

5. Racial Quotient

In the course of the sociometric classification of the given
community we found that the increase in its population was
chiefly of two kinds.   First, the arrival of individuals who are
of the same type as the majority, even though as individuals
they may be widely distinguished from one another;   second,
individuals who are not of the same type as the majority and
who apparently for this reason are inclined to join with others
of the same nationality and social character in the forming of
a collective.   We have seen that a homogeneous population
may be homogeneous in a certain respect without that its
members are aware of it and without that homogeneity becomes a psychological factor.   For instance, a population consisting of many nationalities of the white race, heterogeneous
in many respects, suddenly begins to distinguish itself as
belonging together as soon as a group of colored members

arrive and reside in that community. It is, therefore, important to recognize that the same group may be homogeneous in some respects and heterogeneous in others, and that no advance is made in the knowledge of a group so long as its organization is not uncovered in respect to these differences.

In chemistry we call a solution saturated which can remain under given conditions in the presence of an excess of the dissolved substance. Similarly, there is a sociometric point of saturation of a specific homogeneous group for a specific other contrasting element under given conditions. In the case of a chemical solution its point of saturation for a certain substance may change, for instance, with the fall or rise of temperature. In the case of social groups the point of saturation may change with the organization of the interrelated groups.

A sketch of a community situation may clarify this contention. A group of negroes migrates into a white community. The situation arising can be looked at from three angles: the organization of the white population, the organization of the incoming negro group, and the psychological currents developing from their interaction. Up to a certain limit the influx of negroes may not produce any apparent discord. But as soon as such a limit is passed various disturbances begin. Before the immigration of the negro the white community enjoyed a certain degree of economic prosperity. A great part of its members desired more leisure at the same time. The corresponding negro group, being in economic misery, were able to satisfy a double want of the white population, cheap labor and more leisure, with the accompanying distinction of the white men and women of being regarded and regarding themselves as superior. The desire for distinction was satisfied until then by some part of the white population being members of the domestic class and common laborers. The negro group through their arival contributed towards the compensation of these differences within the white population itself. All white men and women became then united in respect to this one thing, to feel superior to and distinct from the negro group. As long as this complex only entered into the situation, a warm social current developed between the two races. But the problem was far from being so simple. The

sexual factor was another avenue affecting the organization in
the white community. The number of men was fewer than
the number of women. Italian immigrants had migrated into
this community half a century before and had dominated the
racial mixture. On the other hand, the negro group was in
ascendance relatively unexhausted and sufficiently intermixed
with the white to become attractive at least to some parts of
the white population and to be attracted by them. This picture
of a community is certainly becoming full reality in many
other towns of the United States today, whether the immigrants are negroes, Italians, Spaniards, or whatever.

Through the sociometric test an instrument is provided to
go beyond these symbols and to ascertain the actual relations.
It informs us about the intersexual choice between members
of the two different groups, between the white men and the
colored women, the white women and the colored men. It
informs us, second, about the currents of repulsion which in
consequence develop automatically as soon as a group of white
women is aroused at the intrusion of the colored or a group of
white men is incensed by the relations of colored men to white
women. These sexual affinities and disaffinities produce an
effect upon the organization of both groups, the sexual currents
drawing them together and the interracial currents drawing
them apart. In the course of time these processes bring about
further complications. If the two groups are mixed in school
and workshops, even if their respective homes are located in
different boroughs, social and cultural currents develop among
them which may tend partially to offset the interracial
currents described.

Through sociometric classification also the rôle of leadership
within groups can be ascertained. Social groups develop
leader-individuals usually in proportion to their needs. At
every level of group development they have their own leaders.
But once a homogeneous group has reached a certain stability
it may tend towards an introverted group organization, and
with this its point of saturation for leader-individuals is comparatively low. Such a homogeneous conserving group can be
run with a minimum of leadership. If an overproduction of
leader-individuals develops within the group serious disturb-

ances in the psychological balance of the group may develop. If a surplus of leader-individuals develops a number of them remain isolated, deprived of having a part in the psychological currents which circulate throughout the community. They brood discontent, produce factions, and stir to aggression. The intrusion of a contrasting racial group into a community stimulates often such a development; for instance, if the intruder group produces more leader-individuals than they need for themselves and the surplus swamps the native population. A sociogram of such a situation visualizes the following picture: We see a native and a foreign leader group both attempting to subordinate and exploit the dependent groups of the native population. We see in a later stage interracial currents of aggression developing first between the native and the foreign leader groups, then between the native population and the foreign leader group. It is through such analysis that we are able to understand conflict situations as that between the Germans and the Jews.

It is finally possible to bring the point of saturation of groups and the expansiveness of its individual members under a common denominator. We have observed that emotional expansiveness of an individual is largest in respect to homogeneous elements. Evidently when adjustment to a few such elements has been successful, minimal further effort only is necessary in the adjustment to other similar individuals. But we have seen that the emotional expansiveness of an individual becomes the smaller, that is, the number of individuals whom he is able to understand and to adjust himself to, the more contrasting elements enter into the group and the more sharply they vary from each other. If we imagine that this low range of emotional expansiveness repeats itself with every member of the homogeneous group in respect to the contrasting elements who have entered into it we can observe that they would prefer to distribute their emotion among individuals whom they can most easily associate with and to a great number and that they will refuse to expand towards individuals with whom it is more difficult for them to associate. From the emotional interaction of the members and their emotional expansiveness a group expression results, its point of saturation for a certain contrasting racial element, its racial quotient.

6. Sex

The percentage of inter-sexual attractions in the classes of boys and girls in the 8th grade of the Public School under study was 8%; the percentage of homosexual attractions was 92%. The percentage of attractions of girls to girls in Hudson in groups at the same age level as these 8th grade pupils was found to be 96.7%. The percentage of attractions of boys to boys in a preparatory school in groups at this age level showed an almost equally high figure (94.2%). In mixed groups the possibility of inter-sexual attractions decreases the number of homosexual attractions, whereas in uni-sexed groups the absence of inter-sexual attractions increases the number of homosexual attractions. Within the first four to six weeks after arrival in Hudson the attractions of the new girls were 70–75%, the percentage of indifference being 25–30%. After this period the percentage of indifference rapidly decreased.

These currents rise and fall, depending upon the age level of the members, the length of time the members belong to the group, the volume of acquaintances each member acquires, and other factors. It became evident (see Acq. index) that the larger the volume of acquaintances of each and all members of a community, the greater is the possibility of releasing their emotional expansiveness to their limit and the greater is the number of attractions. In consequence of this a community becomes the better consolidated and the members become the better integrated within it. In turn, the more limited the number of acquaintances of each and all the members of the community, the more restrained is the exercise of their emotional interest and the smaller is the volume of attractions. In consequence of this many members are not held to the community by the currents.

The greater the suppression of individuals to prevent their meeting other individuals whom they like the greater becomes the urge to communicate with them in some way. One of the most interesting forms of communication in a closed community is the love note. Although the restrictions imposed upon the girls in Hudson is not greater than in any private boarding school for girls that we know of, the volume of love notes is still large. The text of these notes varies from insignificant, simple, and human expressions of affection or poetic and idealistic contents to stark sexual communications. The study of the period of time which passes before the newcomer receives her first note or writes her initial one, the number and kind of individuals with whom she is involved in this respect, the volume of notes she produces, have given us an insight into this most infectious psychological phenomenon. This appears to be a normal reaction to a sexually highly sensitized environment. We found true homosexuality very rare and we have not found one case in which it developed because of the conduct described.

But one form of attraction came to our attention which, as far as we know, has never been analyzed in the literature. This is the odd sexual attraction of white girls to colored girls in communities like Hudson. In the sociometric test given to the whole population of Hudson in respect to the criterion of living in proximity 8% of the white population chose colored and 36% of the colored girls chose white.

The " Crush "

Among the normal and tolerated forms attraction takes between adolescent girls there is one phase which has often allured the fantasy of poets. Soon after a first meeting they fall into feverish courtship of each other, vow that they will be friends forever, dream and plan together, confide their deepest secrets. This is the " crush."

In institutions for girls as no other outlets for the play of sexual energies are given, these " crushes " take on often a more active and exaggerated form. They are more active and exaggerated not necessarily because the individual girls are sexually more sensitive but because of two circumstantial factors. One is the homosexual current only which dominates the community; the other, the greater rivalry displayed when the same girl is the object of several girls' attention.

As long as these crushes occur within the white population their effect upon conduct is similar to that outside in the open community. But it is different and without parallel in a

normal environment when white girls have crushes on colored
girls, not only as individuals, but *en masse*. This form of
crush greatly outdoes in intensity, variability of attitudes, and
effect upon conduct the fancy of a white girl for another white
girl. It is a paradoxical phenomenon.

This bizarre form of behavior we have rarely found to be
mutual. It is a one-sided attraction of the white girl to the
colored. The white girl goes through all the gestures of
courtship, sends notes, makes dates, and tries to keep the
mysterious conduct secret. Her mind is deeply preoccupied;
she neglects school studies, work, and even the thought to run
away. As long as it lasts, she is as if in a trance. Later, after
it has faded out, she laughs when she thinks of it and cannot
understand why she acted so " foolish." Sometimes two white
girls work in pairs, one being the letter carrier for the other
and " in " on the secret. Nothing seems to deter them—
neither the housemother's criticism nor rebuffs of other girls
who despise and publicize their conduct.

The colored girl plays a different rôle in this game. She is
the subject adored and rarely the wooer. She frequently takes
a pride in the onstorm of attention and in this pride is mingled
the satisfaction of a more subdued race which make a " con-
quest." While overtly she responds with affection, she almost
invariably ridicules the courtship. She gets fun out of it
through showing the notes and gifts to her colored friends
because it satisfies not only her as the individual receiving so
much attention but the racial instinct of the whole group.
The colored group as a race exults in being for once in a
superior position towards the white race. It is a big show for
them and inflates their ego. Often the colored girl reacts like
a proud, rough fellow who accepts signs of affection but acts
as if he doesn't care for them. When there is occasion these
crushes lead to physical contact. It appears that the blacker
the negro the more she is pursued and that the blacker she is
the more she despises the courtship. Also the blonder the
white girl, the more she is apt to be successful in the courtship.
Occasionally the dark Indian girl receives similar " tributes,"
and she reacts in much the same manner as the negro towards
the white admirers. To the white girls the colored girls appear

to be more muscular and physically stronger than they themselves. However, there are instances in which a purely idealistic and fantastic "romance" develops between colored and white girls.

Interpretation

The first impression this process gives is that it is perhaps the worst form taken by adolescent sexuality. However, a close analysis of the facts suggests another interpretation. We may study first the attitude taken by the white girl in this episode. She has been taken out of the environment in which boys and men are a natural part. She has been put into an environment in which men are forbidden and even when present are not a natural part of it. At the same time she is at an age in which fantasy-playing with the other sex is a natural process in her development. From the point of view of efficiency and pragmatic value, adolescents of both sexes "waste" much time in this direction. But from the point of view of the adolescent, what he does is at the time an exceedingly important business. What they miss in a community of women and girls is boys and men as the immediate objective of their emotional interest. In such an environment, the negro girl has the relief of being something utterly different. The relation between the two sexes in their adolescent years is so interesting, due to the "distance" between the two sexes, the unapproachability of the other sex. The physical differences of the white and colored race, the "strange" appearance of the colored girl compared with the white, seem to provide the attribute of "distance" and unapproachability. Further, the negro girl has in the imagination of the white boldness and braveness, a spontaneity of conduct that she envies, as well as appearing more muscular and stronger than herself. The negro girl is taken by the white as *a substitute for a boy*. This interpretation is corroborated by what the girls write and say themselves about it. There is, however, one feature in it which does not seem to fit into this interpretation. It is the white girl who almost invariably takes the initiative and courts the colored, seldom the colored girl who initiates the crush. This can be explained if we look at it from the point of view of the colored girl.

She is a female but she is expected by the white girl to look and to act like a boy. She is needed by the white girl as a substitute for a boy but she is a young woman herself. She doesn't receive any adequate incentive to take the initiative. Instinctively she feels that she is taken for something she is not, that she is put into a false position, and she laughs about it. She takes it very good naturedly and makes a great show of it. To fit into the "play" she acts like a boy as well as she is able, behaves wildly, and writes notes back which are an odd mixture of sexual vulgarity and exhibitionism.

This phenomenon is characteristic for closed communities in which the living quarters of the colored population are separated from the quarters for the white. In communities where both races live in the same quarters the phenomenon takes a less intense form and is more readily extinguished.[22] The living together brings to realization the similarities of the same sex, and further, if the number of colored in a white cottage reaches a certain limit, antagonisms develop due to the *psychological pressure* within the group. Both factors seem to override and destroy the romantic attractiveness which the colored girl holds for the white " in distance." It can be said that this process of courtship is a *psychogeographical projection* growing out of the need and longing of the white girls in the population for the former environment. As soon as the colored girls are moved into the same quarters with the white, the psychogeographical fiction fades.

In the familiar crush situation the child warms up to a state in which she is willing to confide fully in the partner whatever fills her thoughts. But the crux of the situation is the partner. It reveals a fine instinct that the adolescent is drawn to other adolescents because to gain the highest therapeutic effect it must call upon persons who belong to a level of social differentiation close to its own. An adult may become the object of a crush but is never the sought-for partner and companion who is continuously in an active and reciprocating rôle. Instead of driving one partner from the other, it is possible to use one girl as the therapeutic agent of the other, to utilize the interrelation existing.

XIII. PSYCHOLOGICAL CURRENTS

1. PSYCHOLOGICAL GEOGRAPHY, MAPS I, II, AND III

The mapping of the whole community, the depicting of the interrelationships of its inhabitants and of its collectives in respect to (a) locality and to the (b) psychological currents between them is *psychological geography*. Two different maps are shown here, both representing the psychological geography of the Hudson institution. Maps I–II are so designed that they show the local geography, the position of roads, buildings, localities, in respect to each other. Map III is so designed that it indicates every cottage and each individual girl who lives within each, and through the symbols for attraction, rejection, and indifference, the interrelations between the individuals. Individuals and cottages of individuals are here presented in respect to the psychological position they have in the community but without respect to geographical locality.

MAP I

Map I indicates the relation of each cottage in respect to the cottages of its neighborhood. It can be noted that the community has two quadrangles that form each a kind of neighborhood by itself: Neighborhood I, formed by C1, C2, C13, C14, C3, C4, C5, and C6; the second, Neighborhood II, formed by C7, C8, C9, C10, C11, and C12; and that a third, Neighborhood III, is formed by cottages more distant, CA and CB.

The two colored cottages border on the two ends of Neighborhood II and are distinguished by heavier black contours. By dotted lines are indicated the inter-racial relations between the white and colored girls of the population in respect to the localities in which they live. C7 is related to the white cottages, C4, C9, and C5. C10 is related to the white cottages, C1, C12, C8, C2, C13, C9, and C5.

On this map is also indicated the runaway status of each cottage from June 1, 1931, to September 1, 1933. Cottages which had no runaways during this period are left blank. They are CA, CB, C4, C7, and C8. Cottages which yielded most of the runaways (six or more) are colored black. They are cottages C3, C5, and C10. Cottages which had up to five runaways are indicated by horizontal lines. They are C1, C2,

C6, C9, C11, C12, C13, and C14. Finally, a plain line indicates at what point was initiated the runaway chain which started October 31, 1932, and lasted until November 13, 1932. It reads the direction the chain took,—from C12 to C5, to ,C3, to C10, where it ended.

MAP II

In Neighborhood I, C1 shows towards C2, .C3, C5, C6, C13, and C14 either antagonism or indifference, but towards C4 a sympathetic attitude. It is attracted towards the most distant cottages, CA and CB. Similarly cottages C2, C13, CI4, and C5 are less compatible with their immediate neighbors than with cottages located more distant from them. The only exception in this neighborhood is C4, which has compatible relations to all the cottages of the neighborhood except to C14 and to C3. In Neighborhood II, C11, C12, C9, C8, and C7 show antagonism towards their immediate neighbors except C10, which is friendly with all the cottages of the quadrangle except with C7. C7 has an exceptional position as it is either disparaged by the cottages of both neighborhoods or simply isolated. In Neighborhood III, CA and CB are friendly neighbors but their attitude is more antagonistic towards the cottages of Neighborhood II (split currents) than towards those of Neighborhood I. These relations demonstrate a trend of greater friendliness towards cottages and neighborhoods which are more distantly located and a greater trend towards incompatibility in respect to adjacent groups. Being neighbors, it appears, gives more occasion for friction to arise as contacts are more frequent and intimate. It would seem that what is present and helpful is often forgotten by neighbors and that what is unpleasant turns them away to look into distance. An exception to the rule are cottages CA and CB, which are so far removed from the rest that they are more dependent upon each other. They develop more like a single family living in two houses as the attitude of the two housemothers is conciliatory.

The inter-racial relations between white and colored groups makes another exception. The trend appears to be just the opposite: the closer the white cottages are to the colored the friendlier is the attitude between them; the further the white cottages are from the colored the less interested are both sides.

This can be explained in part as follows: The inter-racial choice and attractions are here largely motivated by sexual interest. In sexual matters proximity is more desirable than distance. For this reason the sexual current between white and colored becomes strong enough in Neighborhood II to override antagonistic racial currents. The preference of white persons to live in proximity with white persons in respect to such a criterion as the home can be counteracted by the sexual current up to a certain limit. We see this in the attitude of the neighboring white cottages towards colored cottage C7. They are incompatible with it. But this antagonism is partly due, as the motivations reveal, to former sympathies which had turned to dislike to some extent due to the attitude of the housemother, whose attitude of isolation and protest is reflecting upon her group. The greater interest of nearby white cottages for the colored, as distinguished from that of the more distant white cottages, is related also to another experience we had. Many times a white girl who had a friend in one or the other colored cottage, and who wanted to be nearer to her, begged for an assignment to a cottage in that neighborhood.

A comparison of the runaway status within the community from July 1, 1931, to September 1, 1933, with the runaway chain of 1932 shows that C3, C5, and C10, which had the highest percentage of runaways within the 27-month period, produced also the bulk of escapes in the runaway chain of the following year, i.e., C3, C5, C10, and C12. C3, which showed the least interest in living with the members of their own cottage and therefore had the most extroverted group organization among the cottages described, has also the highest number of escapes in the 27-month period. The cottage which figured next highest, C5, for the period, produced the highest number of escapes in the runaway chain. At the time of the runaway chain, C5 consisted of a well organized group, deeply attracted to the housemother, but with nine members isolated and cut off from the group. The cottage which figured next highest, C10, shows in its sociogram of that date (see p. 125) the highest number of incompatible pairs, attraction responded to by rejection or indifference. It is always the organization of a group which keeps an individual within the fold or which throws him out.

MAP III

On Map III are represented 435 individuals, the whole girl population of Hudson August 20, 1932, who were living in cottages except those within C6 and C3, of which special studies were made.[23] Each individual is represented by a circle, a light circle for a white girl, a black circle for a colored girl. They are plotted into 14 large circles, each representing a cottage. Several thousand lines express the attractions, rejections, and indifference existing among the individuals. Through this map it is possible to see at once any individual within her cottage and towards which individuals in other cottages as well as in her own she is attracted or otherwise related. The relations here depicted consider only the criterion of living in proximity. The same individuals produce different maps if the criterion is different, as, for instance, if it is working in proximity.

The representation of a community in this fashion can be of value for the analysis of its inner organization. It makes structural relations visible which can be calculated only with difficulty. The inner working of society is here expanded and put under the microscope and its invisible structure made free for exploration.

Upon first view the map shows that the currents of attraction, repulsion, and indifference are not equally distributed but that some sections of the community have more of them, some less. Closer inspection shows that two of the cottages which are themselves closely interlocked are cut off from the general network except for a few lines coming in from here and there. They are the two colored cottages. They have the position of *isolated* groups in the community. Then we are struck by the big streams of light lines which come to one cottage from all centers in the community except C7 and C10, the colored groups. It is CB which has the position of the most attractive group in the community. Then we see some cottages in mutual attraction, forming pairs, as CA and CB, C5 and C14. Then we see other cottages in mutual rejection, as C1 and C14, C5 and C2. Then we see cottages which are incompatible, one attracted to another, the other rejecting or indifferent to it, as C11 and C9, C*A* and C11. Then we see cottages whose attitude towards another cottage is split, part of its members being attracted and part rejecting or indifferent, as between C1 and C9. We call this attitude *dual*. Then we see cottages which are most rejected, as C12, which is rejected by C*A*, C*B*, and C11, and receiving only indifference from C2. Then there are cottages, as C*A*, C*B*, and C5, which form a triangle. Then there are others which are forming a chain, C14, C5, C9, C13, C8, C2, C4, C1, and C11.

Analysis

As the sociogram enabled us to present a structural analysis of a group, psychological analysis enables us to make a structural analysis of the whole community. These structures within the organization of Hudson have a relation to the conduct of the inhabitants who are responsible for their formation. The isolated position of the colored groups indicates that for the overwhelming majority of white inhabitants the desire to live apart from the colored is still greater than the sexual interest for them. In other words, the racial current tending towards a separation of the races is stronger than the sexual current which tends towards elimination of such barriers. C*A* rejects or is indifferent to many of the cottages which are attracted to it. It looks as if C*A* were populated by a higher class of people or so considered itself. It has, indeed, an exclusive position as it is the most newly constructed cottage in the school; also, it is geographically in an exclusive position. And the housemother herself is a very fine lady who expects from her girls a lady-like conduct. C2 and C5 reject each other with a vehemence as if they were in a state of war.

As apparent from the attitude of each individual of one cottage towards each individual of any other cottage, a certain attitude of a whole cottage results and it is by these criss-cross currents that the reputation of a cottage is shaped. In view of this the member of a rejected or less attractive group has to make a greater fight to hold its own. It is apparent that it is also in Hudson not an indifferent matter into which group a person is placed when she arrives.

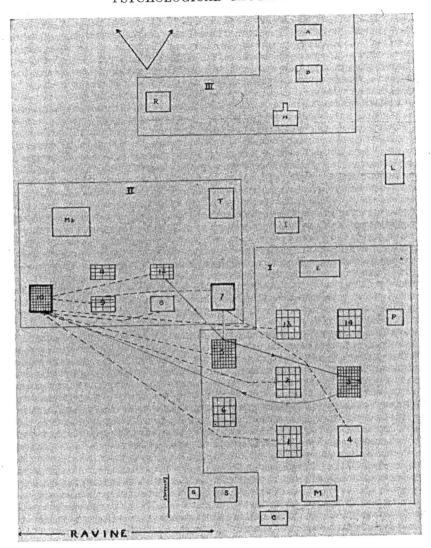

MAP I

PSYCHOLOGICAL GEOGRAPHY

MAP I

The map illustrates the topographical outlay of Hudson and the psychological status of each region in respect to runaways produced and in respect to inter-racial trends.

The community has three different sections which form each a kind of neighborhood: Neighborhood I, formed by C1, C2, C13, C14, C3, C4, C5 and C6; Neighborhood II, formed by C7, C8, C9, C10, C11, and C12; Neighborhood III, formed by CA and CB. The two colored cottages border on the ends of Neighborhood II and are distinguished by heavier black contours.

The broken lines indicate the inter-racial choice between colored members of C7 and white members of C4, C9, and C5, and between colored members of C10 and white members of C1, C12, C8, C2, C13, C9, and C5.

The runaway-status of each cottage from June 1, 1931, to September 1, 1933, is indicated as follows: Cottages which had no runaways during this period are left blank, CA, CB, C4, C7, and C8. Cottages which yielded most of the runaways (6 or more) are indicated by small black squares, C3, C5, and C10. Cottages which had up to 5 runaways are indicated by large black squares, C1, C2, C6, C9, C11, C12, C13, and C14.

A continuous line indicates at what point was initiated a runaway chain which started October 31, 1932, and lasted until November 13, 1932. An arrow indicates the direction the chain took: from C12 to C5, from C5 to C3, from C3 to C10, where it ended.

A, B, 1, 2, 3, 4, 5, 6, 7, 8, 9, 10, 11, 12, 13, 14. Cottages

I	Neighborhood I
II	Neighborhood II
III	Neighborhood III
G	Gatehouse
S	Storehouse
C	Church
M	Main Building
P	Paint Shop
E	Educational Building
I	Industrial Building
T	Teachers' Cottage
Mb	Mercantile Building
L	Laundry
H	Hospital
R	Receiving Cottage

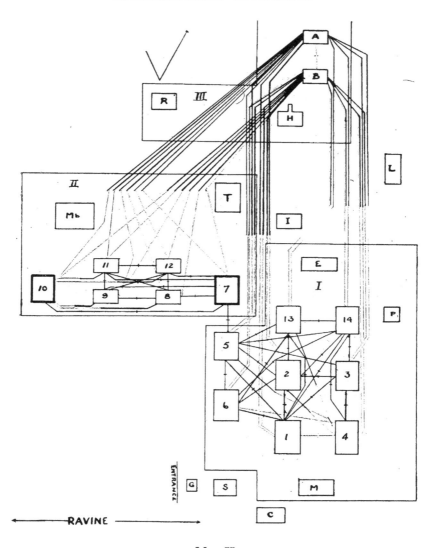

MAP II

PSYCHOLOGICAL GEOGRAPHY

Map II

The map presents the topographical outlay of Hudson and the psychological currents relating each region within it to each other region. For description of the topographical outlay see Map I. Red, black and double (red and black) lines from one cottage to the other indicate respectively cross currents of attraction, of repulsion, and of split currents, half attraction and half repulsion.

The streams of red, black and blue lines (plotted in detail on Map III) going out and coming from one cottage to the other have been classified as follows: (a) when all lines going from one cottage to another cottage were of one color, the stream was classified as a red current, a black current, a blue current, respectively; (b) when the lines of one color going out from a certain cottage to another numbered more than the lines of the other colors together, the stream was classified as a *dominantly* red current, a dominantly black, a dominantly blue current; (c) when the lines going out from one cottage to another were of two colors and almost equal in numbers, the stream was classified as a split current (red-black, blue-black, red-blue).

The plotting of these findings on the basis of such analysis would have visualized only the currents as they have developed in Hudson on the basis of the criterion of living in proximity. As indicated in other parts of this book, the criterion of working in proximity presents at least in part a different distribution; the criterion of sexual, recreational, or cultural proximity each in itself would have accounted for a different distribution also.

On the present Map II the synthetic findings coming from the combining of the different criteria studied in Hudson is plotted.

Description. In Neighborhood I, C1 shows towards C2, C3, C5, C6, C13, and C14 either antagonism or indifference, but towards C4 a sympathetic attitude. It is attracted towards the most distant cottages, CA and CB. Similarly cottages C2, C13, C14, and C5 are less compatible with their immediate neighbors than with cottages located more distant from them. The only exception in this neighborhood is C4 which has compatible relations to all the cottages of the neighborhood except to C14 and to C3. In Neighborhood II, C11, C12, C9, C8, and C7 show antagonism towards their immediate neighbors except C10 which is friendly with all the cottages of the quadrangle except with C7. C7 has an exceptional position as it is either disparaged by the cottages of both neighborhoods or simply isolated. In Neighborhood III, CA and CB are friendly neighbors but their attitude is more antagonistic towards the cottages of Neighborhood II (note their split currents) than towards those of Neighborhood I.

The *original* chart of Map III plots for attraction, rejection and indifference red, black and blue lines respectively. In the copy enclosed here light lines indicate attraction, dark lines rejection. However in describing the technique of analyzing psychological currents it appeared to us that red, black and blue are symbols easier to remember.

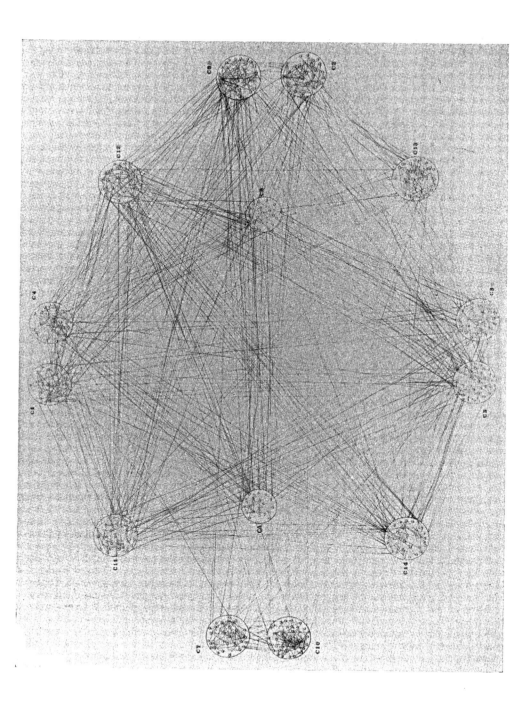

242

MAP III

435 individuals, the whole population of Hudson who were living in cottages (except in C3 and C6) at the date August 20th. The individuals (small red circles) are plotted into fourteen large circles each representing a cottage.

Technique. Each individual chose up to *five* individuals of the given community with whom she would like to live together in the same house (criterion of living in proximity). Thus from each individual up to *five outgoing red lines* were plotted. The response of each individual chosen towards each chooser was then secured. Thus lines were plotted going from the chosen individual back to the chooser (response lines). The lines numbered five or less depending upon whether or not the chooser had made use of all the choices at her disposal. The response lines are red if they represent attraction, black if they represent rejection, blue if they represent indifference. Five outgoing and five return lines make ten lines per individual for 435 individuals, 4,350 lines. But this figure needs a correction: 9½% of the choices remained unused and many a chooser was simultaneously chosen by another individual (pair) in which case choice and response fell into one, further reducing the number of lines. In addition to choices and responses, the individuals expressed freely with whom they did *not* want to live in the same house. The number of black lines plotted was thereby considerably increased and the reductions mentioned above almost compensated.

Description. It is possible to see at once any individual within her cottage and towards which individuals in other cottages as well as within her own she is attracted or otherwise related. Due to the dynamics of the situation the position of the individuals differ within a wide range. There are individuals plotted without any outgoing line and without any receiving line. Such individuals did not choose anybody, were not chosen by anybody, and were not rejected by anybody, simply isolated. There are other individuals plotted with five outgoing red lines, without receiving red lines but receiving a considerable number of black lines. These are individuals who were choosing but remained unchosen and, in addition, were refused by a great number, simply isolated and rejected individuals.· There are other individuals plotted with outgoing lines far exceeding five and receiving far more than five, individuals who command a particular interest in the community. Several thousand lines, red, black, and blue lines, express the attraction, rejection, and indifference existing among the individuals.

C7 and C10, the two colored cottages, appear almost cut off from the general network except for a few lines coming in from here and there. They have the position of the *isolated groups.* CB has the position of the *most attractive* group in the community. Except for C7 and C10, the colored cottages, all the cottages send red lines to it. We see cottages in mutual attraction forming *pairs,* as CA and CB, C5 and C14, and we see other cottages in mutual rejection, as C1 and C14, C5 and C2. Still other cottages are incompatible, one attracted to a second and the second rejecting or being indifferent to it in return, as C11 and C9, CA and C11. We see cottages whose attitude towards another cottage is split, part of its members being attracted and part rejecting or indifferent, as between C1 and C9; and also we trace cottages which are most rejected, as C12, which is rejected by CA, C13, and C11, and receives only indifference from C2. CA, CB, and C11 form a triangle. C14, C5, C9, C13, C8, C2, C4, C1 and C11 form a chain.

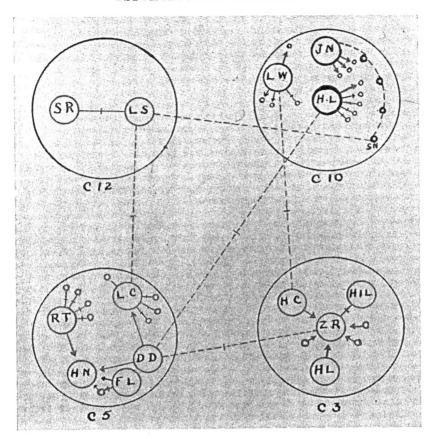

A RUNAWAY CHAIN

14 individuals comprise four sets of runaways. The positions of the sets are seen to be as follows: Set in C12, SR and LS are an isolated pair; set in C5 are interrelated and all except RT show unadjusted positions; set in C3, ZR, center of attractions of 7 individuals, a mutual pair with HIL, and attractive to HC and HL; set in C10, LW, HL, and JN, each isolated but interrelated by indirection. The interrelations between the sets are seen to be as follows: LS in C12 forms a mutual pair with LC from C5; DD in C5 is interrelated to ZR in C3; HC in C3 is interrelated to LW in C10; further, LS in C12 is interrelated with SN in C10, who, while not a participant with the set, is in a chain relation to JN in C10; also DD from C5 forms a pair with HL of C10.

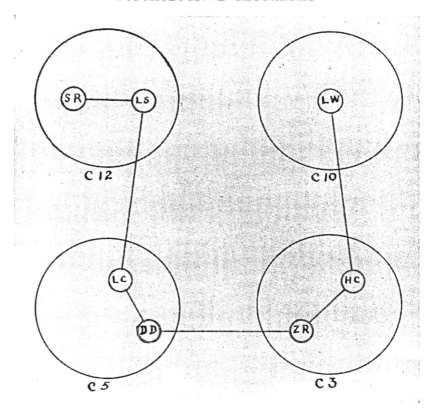

MAIN LINE OF THE RUNAWAY CHAIN

The main line of the network seems to go from SR to LS in C12 to LC and DD in C5, hence to ZR and HC in C3, and from there to LW in C10.

245

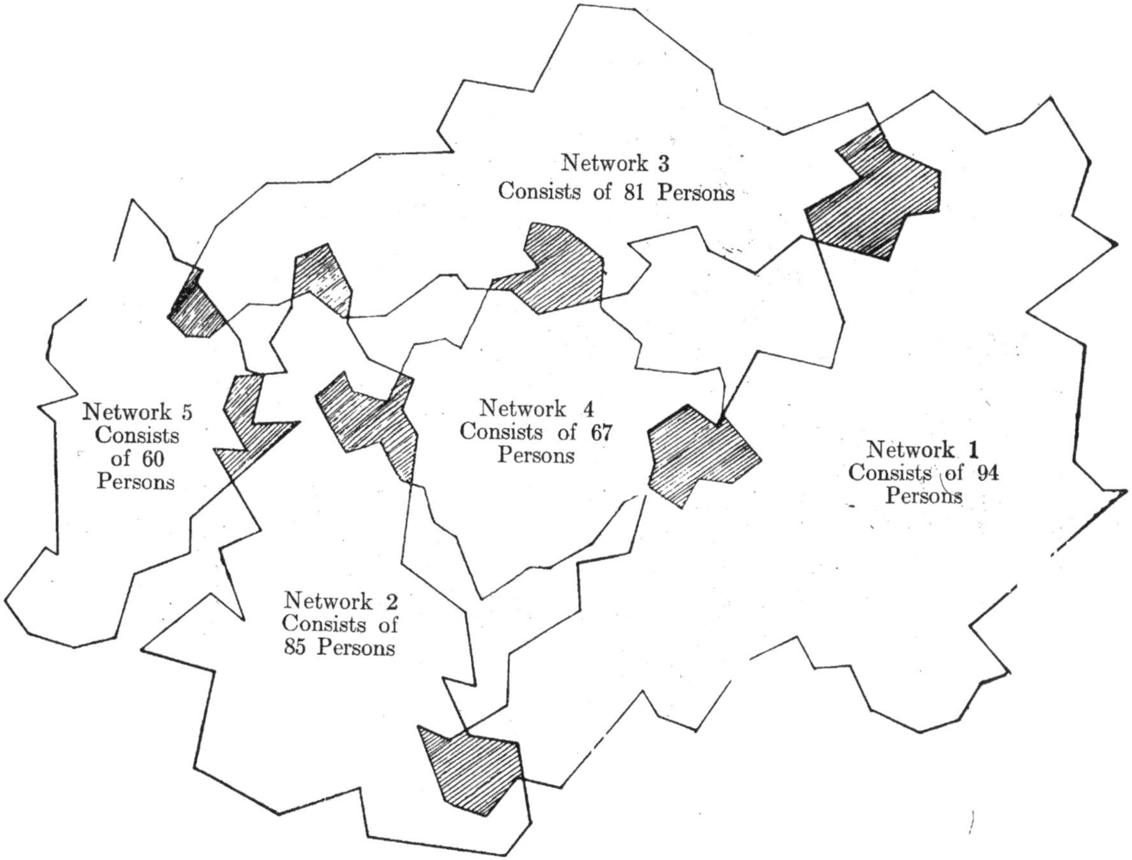

Network 1
Consists of 94
Persons

Network 3
Consists of 81 Persons

Network 4
Consists of 67
Persons

Network 2
Consists of
85 Persons

Network 5
Consists
of 60
Persons

NETWORKS IN A COMMUNITY

The chart illustrates the subdivisions of the whole community into five more or less distinct bundles, each comprising a specific number of individuals. The individuals who belong to each of these networks were found to be so interlocked directly or by indirection that emotional states could travel to the members of the respective network with the least possible delay.

These networks are invisible. They were traced through inspection of Psychological Geography Map II by means of a microscopic technique as follows: Each line (tele) which went out from a member of any group to a member of any other group and from this person on to a member of a third group and from this person on to a member of a fourth group, etc., as long as the chain continued. Only such persons are counted who are interlocked as belonging to the same network, irrespective of the cottage in which they lived. We began the counting with a certain individual in Cottage 2, following the line which went to an individual in Cottage A, and from this individual to another individual in Cottage 4, to find that this individual in Cottage 4 had a line going to another individual in Cottage 5, to find that this individual in Cottage 5 had no line going out to any individual in another cottage. At this point the network broke up. We returned to Cottage 2 and proceeded in a similar manner with every individual in the cottage who showed connections to individuals in other cottages, until again we arrived with each of them to the point where the net broke up. In this manner we were enabled to construct what we called the *main line* of the network.

Once the members of the main line of the network were ascertained, we began to trace from each of its members those individuals within her own group who were *directly* related to her. These branches formed the side lines of the network. It is understood that again each individual of a side line was followed up to determine her contacts to members of other cottages and if such new members were found in other cottages, for them also. On this basis we ascertained in Hudson a complicated net: from the same cottage, for instance, Cottage 2, a number of individuals belong to one network, Network I, another number of individuals unrelated directly to the former belong to another network, Network 2. The individuals belonging to it are in general different from the ones involved in Network I. But they are by no means fully cut off from them. As an example, in Cottage A some of the same individuals share in four different networks. But not every group is so promiscuous.

Except for small bridges crossing between these networks, which we have indicated by lines in the sections which are overlapping, we could distinguish within the community five more or less distinct bundles: Network I consisting of 94 individuals, Network 2 consisting of 85 individuals, Network 3 consisting of 81 individuals, Network 4 consisting of 67 individuals, and Network 5 consisting of 60 individuals.

2. SOCIOMETRIC SPECULATIONS

The accurate use of figures for comparative sociometric statistics is of methodological importance. The figures have to be related, first, to collectives which have the same criterion; second, to collectives whose members are of a similar chronological age level, especially if these members are in their formative years of childhood or adolescence; third, to collectives which have a similar distribution in respect to the sex or sexes of their membership. Mixed sexual groups and uni-sexed groups tend towards different structure. Likewise groups in which the sexes are equally distributed tend towards different structure from groups in which one sex is predominant in numbers. Fourth, to collectives which have a similar distribution in respect to race or nationality.

On the basis of the quantitative analysis of each class group in P. S. 181 (comprising 42 classes), we made a quantitative analysis of the whole school as a community (see pp. 46–7). Within its population of 1,853 children between the ages of 4 years to 16 years, 260 pupils or 14% remained unchosen; the number of mutual attractions between girls was 238; the number of mutual attractions between boys was 208; the number of mutual attractions between a boy and a girl was 13. As this school has a cosmopolitan composition representing many different nationalities, these figures may, through further investigation, be found to hold approximately for the whole school system of New York. Among one million grammar school children there may be 140,000 unchosen children in their respective class groups.

On the basis of the quantitative analysis of each cottage we made a quantitative analysis of the whole community of Hudson. Within the population of 505 individuals, consisting of girls between 12 years and 21 years of age, the number of isolated or of isolated and rejected is 58, or 11.5%; the number of mutual attractions is 358; the number of mutual dislike pairs is 48; the number of incompatible pairs is 139.

As the figures given for Hudson concerned home groups and the position in the home group is the most consequential one for an individual, they may suggest a similar position in the other collectives for the majority of the population. It appears possible at first sight to use them for computations on a national scale; for instance, how many isolated or isolated and rejected individuals may exist in the United States. The tentative figure for the population of 133,836,000 [24] (census of 1928) is then about 15.4 million (or 11.5% of 133,836,000) isolated or isolated and rejected individuals. Even if this figure were very close to correct, reservations must be made against generalizing in this manner. There are fundamental differences between the structure of the Hudson community and that of the nation at large. The size of a family (cottage) group in Hudson is five to six times larger than that of an average sized family outside. It may be argued correctly that in families of larger size more individuals remain unadjusted than in average sized families. But on the other hand, families of 20 or more provide the members within its own fold with a social group also and offer them more opportunity for clicking with someone, whereas members of an average sized family, especially in the large cities, if they are unhappy at home, have to search incessantly for as large a number of social contacts. It is probable, therefore, that in urban populations far more individuals fall in between than in Hudson. When the sociometric test was given to 52 individuals between the ages of 18 years and 25 years, 26 single men and 26 single women living in New York city, to ascertain their position within their respective family, the number of the isolated among the men was found to be 12.2% and among the women 13%. But as these 52 single individuals were selected for study on a purely accidental basis, no conclusion can be made from these figures.

The Hudson figures can be seen in another light. After the first phase of the sociometric test was given the analysis of the choices revealed that among a population of 435 persons,[23] 204, or 46.5%, remained unchosen after the 1st choice; 139, or 30%, after the 2d choice; 87, or 20%, after the 3rd choice; 74, or 17%, after the 4th choice; and 66, or 15%, after the 5th choice. (The further reduction of 15% to 11.5% resulted from the two following phases of the test. Then, through further inquiry, it was found that numerous individuals who had not been chosen spontaneously were still found attractive by one or the other correspondent to a choice.) These relations are illustrated in the accompanying triangle. Those who are chosen first are on the pinnacle of the triangle. Next are those who are chosen second; next, those chosen third; next, those chosen fourth, and then those chosen fifth. At the base of the triangle is the volume of those individuals who, after all five choices, have remained unchosen. This means, figuratively speaking, that there are millions of individuals among us who, when they love a woman, at least five are ahead of him who are more attractive to her. Such an individual is perhaps the tenth or the twelfth in line. If he applies for employment, five are already ahead of him who are more attractive to the employer. He is perhaps again the tenth or twelfth in line. Even in the home of his parents he has been less attractive to them perhaps than his brothers and sisters were. And these millions are not the physically or mentally defective of our population but apparently a cross-section of it. Again, it should not be forgotten that it is often in the midst of the social groups to which they *belong* that they find themselves isolated or rejected. This tragedy can befall whole groups and eventually whole nations. We have shown that these processes are intimately related to the structure of groups and of communities. But what are these people doing if they find themselves again and again in disadvantage?

There is no question but that this phenomenon repeats itself throughout the nation, however widely the number of unchosen may vary from 1st to 5th or more choices due to the incalculable influence of sexual, racial, and other psychological currents. For New York, with a population of 7,000,000,[24] the above percentages would be after the 1st choice, 3,200,000 individuals unchosen; after the 2nd choice, 2,100,000 unchosen; after the 3rd choice, 1,400,000 unchosen; after the 4th choice, 1,200,000 unchosen; and after the 5th choice, 1,050,000 unchosen. These calculations suggest that mankind is divided not only into races and nations, religions and states, but into socionomic divisions. There is produced a socionomic hierarchy due to the differences in attraction of particular individuals and groups for other particular individuals and groups. Whether or not these differences in attractibility are intrinsic, they have been the greatest deterrents and stimulants of the will to power. It is natural that less attractive individuals and less attractive groups will try to attain through the arbiter of force what spontaneous attraction and ability fail to provide them with.

3. PSYCHOLOGICAL CURRENTS

The mapping of the psychological geography of a community enables us to survey its psychological currents. Two electric currents produce mutual attraction of their conductors in the case that both have the same direction. They produce mutual repulsion in the case that the direction of one current is opposed to the direction of the other current. Similarly, a psychological current between two groups can be a current of mutual attraction or of mutual repulsion. Although far more complex than in electro-physics, there is also in psychogeography in respect to a certain criterion either a yes or a no, whatever the motivations of this yes or no may be. We call the yes attitude attraction and the no attitude repulsion without implying any specific emotional state. And as in an electric circuit the differences of potential and the density of current flow in such fashion along the conductors that a balanced state is produced, we call the attitude that is neither a yes nor a no indifference.

Psychological currents consist of feelings of one group towards another. The current is not produced in each individual apart from the others of the group; it is not ready in everyone only to be added together to result in a sum, as, for instance, anger which dominates each individual of the group to the end that the whole group becomes angry as a totality and each of its members equally angry. The contribution of each individual is unequal and the product is not necessarily identical with the single contributions. One or two individuals may contribute more towards determining what feeling is directing the current than the rest. But from the spontaneous interaction of such contrasting contributors currents result if all these contributions have the same direction, that is, if they are related to the same criterion. Through the mapping in the form of psychological geography of the emotions of the Hudson population we were able to study varieties of psychological currents.

Sexual Currents

A group of girls were studied from the day of their arrival in respect to their sexual conduct. They had been assigned to C10, C14, and C11, which are in Neighborhood II. We traced that after a period of from 50 to 110 days 9 of these 15 girls began to show an interest in the colored girls of the neighborhood, as apparent from communications between them. From the motivations given and the conduct the current appeared to be sexual. But as we have described elsewhere in this book, the current was a perversion of primary sexuality: it was a substitute current for both groups. The white girls were the active, initiating agents and the colored girls responded after a time: it was a counter current to the spontaneous current of the white group.

This group of nine girls became not at once but gradually interlocked with eight colored girls. At the start only two of the white girls, A and B, were individually attracted to two of the colored. Both had had colored boy friends outside. A third, C, was the letter carrier of A and a few days later started to imitate A by herself courting. The next "caught up" by the current was E, an isolated girl who received no attention from the other girls of her group. A sixth, F, appeared to break into the current because the housemother was against the practice and F was antagonistic to her. Within three weeks she employed three different girls, G, H, and I, as carriers of her notes, and they finally found pleasure in it themselves. From the side of the colored group, the activity began in C10 with three girls who had received attention before and two who were newcomers. The other three girls were from C7. These 17 girls, white and colored, formed their own network and broke up group lines. They formed a current that led others into its laid pathway.

Racial Currents

The development of a *racial* current has been followed from its traceable beginnings to an open and manifest stage. See p. 217. The white population, being in the overwhelming majority, produced in the colored group, which composed only 14% of the population, a potential sensitiveness in respect to being regarded as inferior. In the first phase, alternating reactions within a group of girls of C10 formed an inter-racial current of aggression between two gangs, one of dark colored girls led by Stella and another of light colored girls led by Jane; in the second phase, we saw the Stella gang turning aggressive towards the white forewoman in the work unit and gradually developing in a terminal phase to a racial current aggressively pointed at a section of the white adult population. The majority of the colored girls almost until the last stage were indifferent or undirected. But the organization of the group was ready: predisposed to the coming development. It appears that when aggressive currents arise in respect to self-preservation or racial difference that a very small minority may come to the front and direct the currents which are set for release.

Social Currents

Map III indicates all the reactions of the girls in each cottage of the Hudson community in the sociometric test on the criterion of living in proximity. It shows into which direction the population of the different cottages gravitate in their desires in respect to a home for themselves. From this map we can see that the current runs in four main directions. The one which is perhaps the strongest among them runs from Neighborhoods I and II to Neighborhood III. The second largest stream is running between C5 and C8. Streams of rejections can be traced, the largest going to C3. The mixed current towards the colored cottages leaves them in comparative isolation. These currents demonstrate that even in a community as small as Hudson there are different social strata.

We can differentiate psychological currents (1) according to their causation into (a) sexual, (b) racial, (c) social, (d) industrial, and (e) cultural currents; and (2) according to the principle of their formation into (a) positive and negative currents, (b) spontaneous and counter currents, (c) primary and secondary currents, (d) initial and terminal currents, and (e) main and side currents.

These currents can be measured according to expansion. By examining May III we see no social current can be traced in the Hudson community between members of cottages C10 and C14, C10 and C11, C10 and C4, C14 and C7, C7 and C1, C7 and C11, C7 and C12, CA and C14, and there was also none traceable between C6 and C12. Among these nine pairs of cottages between which no currents could be found, the two colored cottages (C7 and C10) figure seven times. Only the remaining two pairs consisted of white groups. On the other hand, CB was found to be the center of social currents flowing from every group in the community. This is a sample of the degree of expansion of currents related to a given criterion. And as the same group can be related also to many other criteria, it can be the crossing point of numerous other currents.

We can measure expansion of currents in relation to a particular group (whatever portion of the group is involved) by determining the number of other groups affected by their currents and figure the average emotional expansion for a group in a given community. For instance, the quantity of the current between C7 and C11 is zero tele; the current from C7 to C4 measures 1 tele; from C2 to C8, 8 tele; from C14 to C12, 20 tele; from C10 to C7, 27 tele. Such figures indicate the crude index of the potential power of a current in the community. Besides this number, the effect of each tele has to be classified and considered to gain a more accurate index of the real power of a certain current. If it is an isolated, sidetracked current, then the ablest individuals with the most influential positions within it will end with the current itself in a blind alley. But if it joins the main current of the community, the same tele as before may produce a many times more powerful effect.

Due to pressure within populations the mass of psychological currents going out from individuals is far larger than the amount of counter-currents coming in response to the individuals from the objects of their affection. In this criss-crossing a great amount of emotional energy appears wasted and a great amount of dissatisfaction seems unavoidable. But perhaps just as we have been able to correct the direction of rivers and torrents, we may be able to correct the direction in which psychological currents flow. Just as there are millions of forgotten, isolated individuals in the world, there may be millions of isolated currents within the world population.

We succeeded to estimate the bio- and psychological make-up of these currents,—whether the dominant emotion is fear, hate, jealousy, or love, etc., or whatever the combination of these, whether they are simply intellectual decisions or organic conditions from which feelings are derived secondarily,—underlying such attractions and repulsions between individuals. This was gained through a technique which attempts to introduce a sociodynamic interpretation of a tele and of a current.

These psychological currents do not rest in individuals but run into space and there they do not run entirely wildly but through channels and structures which are erected by men: families, schools, factories, communities, etc., unrestrained or lifted by boundaries which are erected by nature: climate or race. This is the reason why it was deemed insufficient to present the facts through sociometric equations only. We had to consider also their expansion in relation to the various anchorages of our social structure. If the sociograms of each individual group of a community were combined into a graph, the sociogram of each family, factory, church, etc., depicting also the psychological currents which flow from individuals in one group to the individuals in the other groups, then a picture of a community results which is geographic and psychological at the same time, its psychological geography. We need to study human nature not only in the aspect of its past, not only from the aspect of its consciousness or unconsciousness, but from the aspect of the actual presence of the powerful, psychological currents in whose production each man participates as so infinitely small an agent.

4. NETWORKS

The psychogeographic mapping of the community shows, first, the relationship of local geography to psychological processes; second, the community as a psychological whole and the interrelations of its parts, families, industrial units, etc.; third, the existence of psychological currents which break group lines, as racial, social, sexual and cultural currents. But these bonds are not the deepest level of the structure which we have tried to raise. There are still deeper layers. We had suspected that beneath the ever flowing and ever changing currents there must be a permanent structure, a container, a bed which carries and mingles its currents, however different their goals may be. Speculating in this direction, we reminded ourselves of two instances. One is the findings through structural analysis of groups. Certain forms (as pairs, chains, triangles, etc., see p. 104) recur regularly and definitely related to the degree of differentiation a group has attained. The other is the trend of individuals to break group lines as if mysteriously drawn by certain psychological currents. (See pp. 251-5.) We have found that these currents which break group lines and even community lines are not lawless. They are related to more or less permanent structures which bind individuals together into large *networks*.

Proofs That Networks Exist

In the fall of 1932 an epidemic of running away occurred in Hudson. Within 14 days 14 girls ran away. The incident was unusual for this community, as the girls are generally most anxious to stay. In the whole seven months preceding only 10 girls had run away. The rush appeared to be without motivation: the motivations, however convincing for the individual cases, failed to explain the *chain*, the fact that so many felt themselves motivated to run away just at this particular time and within so short a period. To say that it was caused by mass suggestion is not a satisfactory explanation either. Also, our classifications and sociograms indicate that far more individuals than the participants of this chain have shown a sociometric position within the community which predisposed them to run away just as well as the 14 girls who did. A better explanation is that networks existed of which these 14 girls were a part and from which the rest who were equally predisposed were left out.

Two girls, LS and SR, ran away on October 31, from C12. The next day, November 1st, 5 girls from C5 ran away: RC, GA, RT, HN, and FL. Four days later, November 5th, 4 girls from C3 followed: HC, HL, DR, and HIL. A week later, November 13th, 3 girls from the colored C10 followed: LW, HL, and JN. Thereafter no runaway incident happened until January 8, 1933. In the corresponding period of 1931 there were only 3 runaways.

That the 14 girls belonged together in a chain within a network is supported by the following: Only 2 of the 14 girls, FL and HN, both from C5, had made an attempt to run away before. Chronic centers for running away were thus only in this one set. The other three sets were free of them. HN had made her attempt about 15 months previously when she was in another group. FL had run away from C5 on August 27th, about nine weeks before her second attempt. The question arises why did the chain of 14 just described not start at this time? An analysis of the position of the four sets at that period offers an explanation. FL was then in an isolated, insignificant position within C5. It was another girl, CE, who had for weeks contemplated a runaway. She looked for a companion for the venture. On the 23rd she confided in FL, who in an impromptu fashion decided to go. FL was found and returned to C5 a few days later. CE, the source of the inspiration in August, did not belong to the network which we have described above, but to a different one, and apparently did not succeed to inspire those within it. FL herself was not an inspiring center and no current was initiated by her sufficient to sway others to emulate her action. To say it figuratively, the best road, here a network, cannot make a car run through it. The driver must contribute. The position of FL in the network was not yet crystallized or established.

We traced the positions of these 14 on the Psychological Georgraphy Map III and found that interrelations existed among the girls who belonged to the same cottage and also between individuals of each of the four runaway sets. We have lifted this network from the map and presented it in Chart I, p. 244. The positions of the sets are seen to be as follows: Set in C12, SR and LS are an isolated pair; set in C5, RC and GA, an isolated pair; FL and HN, isolated and reject each other; RT, forming mutual pairs with three members of her group; set in C3, ZR, center of attraction of 8 individuals, a mutual pair with HIL, and attractive to HC and HL; set in C10, LW, HL, and JN, each isolated but interrelated by indirection. The interrelations between the sets are seen to be as follows: LS in C12 forms a mutual pair with RC from C5; FD in C5 is interrelated to ZR in C3; HC in C3 is interrelated to LW in C10; further, LS in C12 is interrelated with SN in C10, who, while not a participant with the set, is in a chain relation to JN in C10; also FL from C5 forms a pair with HL of C10. The main line of the network seems to go from SR to LS in C12 to RC and FL in C5, hence to ZR and HC in C3, and from there to LW in C10.

These relations had been ascertained through the sociometric test in respect to the criterion of living in proximity. Only a part of these relations are for each individual conscious and intentional. For instance, SR is fully aware of her relation to LS and of all the detailed planning developed step by step to the goal of running away. But she was, as we ascertained, unaware of the processes going on within the other three sets. LS in turn was conscious of the part she played with SR, and as she was related to RC in C5, she was aware that RC was discontented and had ideas about escaping. However, she had never become intimate with RC in respect to running away. RC had also kept it secret from LS that she was entangled with FL, HN, RT, and GA. Therefore, LS was fully unaware of the processes between FL, HN, RT, and GA, with whom she was not even acquainted, and unconscious of the further entanglements of the set in C5 with the set in C3, whose intermediary agents were respectively FL and ZR, two others with whom she was not acquainted. Similarly, as the set in C12 was unaware of the set in C5 and C3, the set in C5 was unaware of the set in C12 and C10; in turn, the set in

C10 was unaware of the set in C5 and C12, and the set in C3 unaware of the set in C12 and partially also of the set in C5.

The individuals of each of the four sets, although living in different sections of the same community at the time before the episodes took place, were absorbed by a similar idea and yet unaware of the fact that the social current flowing back and forth among them had developed gradually a number of fixed contacts and produced channels through which emotions and suggestive ideas could pass uncensored from one to the other without the majority in the community having knowledge of them.

But when FL was found and returned to the cottage the situation had changed. The publicity which she had received from her first escape brought her into particular contact with four girls of her cottage who ruminated in a similar direction. Thus the set in C5 consolidated itself more and more between August 23rd and November 1st. When on October 31st SR and LS in C12 ran away, the impetus was provided and the suggestive current travelled through the minds of those who belonged to the same network and who were ready to be " touched off " by the action. If the network would not have existed the chances are that the runaway pair in C12 would have remained isolated actors: the idea would not have spread.

Another factor is in need of discussion. Rarely is it that a girl runs away alone. When this is the case, as with BN from C10 on August 28, 1932, or with CI from C3 on November 14, 1931, they are fully isolated individuals. They belong to the few who *fall between* networks, either because they are newcomers in the community or because they did not attach themselves in the community to anyone, perhaps never having the intention to stay. In the 27 months period studied only four ran away alone. The overwhelming majority went either in pairs or in groups of three or more. The companion is for the potential runaway of similar importance as the letter carrier for the " nigger lover " (see p. 229).

A further proof that networks exist is that a series of runaways which started in C2 with DV, TB, and DN on August 18, 1932, did not develop into a chain of runaways. On August 23rd CN ran away with FL from C5 and on August

28th BN escapes alone from C10. Then the episode dies out. The latter, BN, was unrelated to any network and the others did not develop a chain evidently because no roads were established through which their suggestion could travel unhindered.

The described runaway chain broke off on November 14th after 14 girls had run away. As the networks to which they belonged consisted of 94 members, 80 more girls were touched by the current and 13 of them we considered potential runaway cases if the intensity of the current had continued with equal strength and if no resistance had developed. But three instances can be considered to have contributed to stop it. One is the added watchfulness of the officers the larger the number of escapes became. Another is that the last set of runaways in the chain came from C10, which is a colored group, and it is just there where the network is thinnest. The chances that from there new impetus would come was poor, as few contacts went from C10 to other parts of the community. Just as an electric current has differences in density within a circuit, also a psychological current has differences in a network. Finally, the two girls who started the chain had been returned to the school and to their cottage, C12, on November 4th, five days after their escape. Their failure and disappointment associated with it ran now rapidly through the same network and caught the same individuals who had received an impetus before. It produced, thus, an anti-climax. It could not stop the running away of the set in C3, who escaped the next day, but it may have cautioned and delayed the set in C10 and stopped many potential developments.

Another proof that networks exist is the spreading of news or gossip into a certain direction of the community and not into others. We cite here the case of TL in C6. She had stolen a few things of little value from the school's store with the intention to give them away as gifts. But before this could happen it was discovered. As TL had a wide acquaintance in the community, we followed up how the news of her conduct spread. We followed the expansion of the spreading in three phases, after 24 hours, after one week, and after six weeks. We found that after 24 hours only such individuals knew about it as belonged to the Network II, but not all individuals of this network. With the exception of a few persons, C14, C12, C5, CA and CB were left entirely out, as they did not belong to this network. After a week the story of her action had reached the whole network, consisting of 86 individuals, and it had filtered into large parts of the second and third networks. Six weeks later no further spread could be ascertained. It had apparently given way to news of more momentary interest.

Another instance may be mentioned before we close the discussion here of proofs that networks exist. It is the spread of the news in detail of the incident in the colored group of C10 described in a previous part of this book. It was traced to have spread through large portions of Networks I, III, and IV, but Network II was left completely out. This was so much below expectation that it demands a special explanation. Besides the current of resistance from the side of the officers to keep an event of such unpleasantness as secret as possible, it may be that the fact that it happened during vacation, when the school was closed, blocked it. Certain networks were, figuratively, *temporarily disconnected*.

Causes and Organization of Networks

The network is related to the current which run through it as a glass is related to the water which fills it except that the network is molded by the currents and the glass is not shaped by the liquid it holds. The psychogeographical network is analogous to the nervous system, whose network is also molded by the currents that run through it and which is so organized also as to produce the greatest effect with the least effort. It cannot be compared, however, with a telephone system, as the latter is unrelated to the currents which run through it, is not molded by these currents.

According to the principle of the forming of social atoms, each individual is related to a certain number of individuals; the majority of individuals in his community are "left out," that is, no tele relate him to them. This is the sociodynamic cause for the development of networks. Another cause for their existence is the economic principle of producing the greatest effect with the least effort.

There are still other causes responsible for the organization of a particular network. We have found, for instance, that certain psychological currents produced by certain emotional states and attitudes are even towards the regular networks occasionally selective. In general news, gossip, ideas, all external and factual matter and all intimate matter which does not hurt its reporter pass without resistance through the networks as we have described them. But if it comes to a certain secret activity concerning sexual, racial, or political activity, this does not filter through even the regular and established parts of the networks. We followed up this phenomenon in respect to the love making between colored and white girls and in respect to the secret intention to run away, activities which were severely criticized by the housemothers and other staff members. Participants in these activities always have to be on guard against a squealer. The housemother tries at all times to find out through a trusted girl which girls of the family have the intention to run away, and her trusted girls try instinctively to get in touch with the girls who belong to the network in which such ideas are simmering. A careful housemother is always also on the watch to find evidence of sexual interests, as love notes, etc. For these reasons the girls are on guard against coming into a bad reputation. In her anxiety to hide her activities she produces an instinctive reaction against the networks as if she would sense that networks exist and that they are her greatest enemy, as if she would dread the nets which would automatically spread her ideas to individuals who may report the facts to their confidants or to the staff. She cannot eliminate these networks, as they are produced by her own emotions. But she may try in collaboration with her companions to keep information away from certain untrustworthy individuals in her network. This attempt of hers is, of course, the larger the networks, the less easily met with success. Thus the effort to keep a secret and to limit information to a selected group usually ends in failure. One day it filters into the general networks. However, these finer nets within the networks exist and are an important psychogeographical organization. They are like private roads with different labels saying into which direction they lead. One has a label, sex; another has a label, run-away; another has the label, staff versus girls; etc. Ideas in regard to these cannot be conveyed to everybody, not even to friends, or friends of friends. It is like having telephone numbers which are not listed in the telephone directory.

Technique of Determining Networks

We followed on the Psychogeographic Map III each tele which went out from a member of any group to a member of any other and from this person on to a member of a third group, and from this person on to a member of a fourth group, etc., as long as the chain continued. We counted only such persons as belonging to the same network as were interlocked, irrespective of the cottage in which they actually lived. (See Scheme of Networks, p. 246.) This can be called the main line of the network. We followed then each member of this main line of the network and counted those individuals within her own cottage who were directly related to the member of the respective network. These branches formed the side lines of the determined network. It is understood that again each individual of a side line was followed up to determine her contacts to members of other cottages, and if such new members of the network were found in other cottages, for them also.

We began the counting with certain individuals in C2 who share tele with a number of individuals in CA, who in turn share one part of their tele with individuals in C4, C5, and C14. These, in turn, send a fraction of their tele into C7 and C9, forming a network which, like a subway, connects many sections of the community. We found in Hudson several of such networks. From the same cottage, C2, where this particular network has members, a number of individuals unrelated directly to the former participate in a second network with groups of individuals in C1, C4, C7, and C12, forming Network II. The individuals belonging to it are, in general, different from the ones involved in Network I. We say " in general " because they are by no means fully cut off from them; for instance, in CA some of the same individuals share in four different networks. But not every group is so promiscuous. Except for small bridges crossing between these networks, we are able to subdivide the whole community into five more or less distinct bundles: Network I, consisting of 94 individuals; Network II, 85 individuals; Network III, 81; Network IV, 67; and Network V, 60 individuals.

Unavoidably the larger a network is the larger becomes the number of *dead links*,—that is, the number of relations which are not reciprocally effective, so to speak, emotions which run without registering in the intended other person. They can be called resistance links and their sum of resistance is caused by the intrinsic character of the network. This factor is practically negligible in small networks, but in larger ones it plays a definite rôle. The larger the network is, as in the organization of cities or political parties, the larger may become the influence of this resistance within it.

Function of Networks

A certain constancy in the organization of a community is the condition of free and independent life of its members. The mechanism which makes this constancy possible in a community is its networks and the psychological currents which flow through them. This form of free and independent life for the single individuals is the privilege of such communities as have reached the heights of complexity and differentiation. Therefore societies which are lacking in constancy and differentiation are unable to offer to its members the privileges of free life, as we have demonstrated in the organization of children societies. These are less constant and less differentiated, especially below the eight-year age level, and therefore the members are unfree and dependent, just as the groups which they form are dependent upon the more highly differentiated ones. The networks have also an architectonic function in the community. By virtue of this they are the controlling factors of its development. The older and the more mature the society is the more the whole network system becomes a controlling super-organization.

The local district or neighborhood is only physically one unit. This analysis shows that it is broken up, not, however, into small units, but into parts which have their corresponding parts in other districts and neighborhoods. The local districts are, so to speak, transversed by psychological currents which bind large groups of individuals into units together, irrespective of neighborhood, district, or borough distinctions. These networks are the kitchens of public opinion. It is through these channels that people affect, educate, or disintegrate one another. It is through these networks that suggestion is transmitted. In one part of a community a person has the reputation of honesty; in another part, of dishonesty. Whatever the actual facts may be, this reputation is due to two different networks in which two different opinions about him travel. In Hudson the suggestion may go through them to run away; in the world at large the idea of war. These networks are traceable and we may learn to control them.

5. LAW OF SOCIAL GRAVITATION

We have accumulated in this volume two series of data. One series of data has a temporal aspect. It is concerned with distinctions found in group organizations according to the developmental level. It suggests that the most differentiated forms of group organization have evolved from the simplest (sociogenetic law).

The other series of data has a spatial aspect. It is concerned with distinctions found in group organization according to the population make-up in different geographical areas. The distinctions precipitated by spatial proximity appear very early in the development of groups—horizontal and vertical differentiation.[25] The further differentiated a society becomes the more varied will become the social atoms it produces, and with them the more differentiated will become the organization of the groups formed by them and the more varied and differentiated will become the collectives contained within them. On different developmental levels (see p. 26) the differences in group organization take place as the individuals and the interactions among them mature. In psychogeography the differences in organization develop from contacts between near and distant collectives. But the wider apart one group develops from the others through certain distinctions, the more it tends to become isolated from it. In fact, we can well picture a society in which numerous groups have reached this status of isolation and self-sufficiency. It recalls to us the analogous situation of numerous isolated individuals in a group, individuals who had become isolated through a sort of self-sufficient superiority. These isolated groups then develop more and more an introverted organization; but when this type of organization is not attainable or when, after it is attained, frictions grow within it at the same time, then a part of the group (due to surplus of leaders or to whatever cause) may turn to the outside, become aggressive, and eventually carry the whole group with them, the group as a unit exhibiting all the signs of an extroverted organization.

But these processes of horizontal differentiation do not go on unbounded. After a certain point of expansion is reached we can observe the development checked by a counter process. As described, psychological currents have a spatial pattern of distribution between individuals and groups which are differently located. The greater the variety of psychological currents uniting and dividing parts of the population, the greater appears the tendency to develop roads for them through which they can travel (networks). The mechanism of psychological expansion which drives individuals, groups, and currents towards further and further differentiation produces also its own controls. One process, the process of differentiation, draws the groups apart; the other process, the process of transmission, draws the groups together. This alternating rhythm can be called the *law of social gravitation*.

PART IV:

CONSTRUCTION AND RECONSTRUC-
TION OF GROUPS

XIV. INTRODUCTION

Religion has given us a wonderful myth. Long before we are born we live on another plane in Eden and the wise father of the universe, who sees all the beings who are born and who are not born and who knows all the needs on earth and elsewhere, decides where we should be placed, on which planet, in which country, and in which family. This story can be called the "assignment myth." It wants to make us believe at least for a moment that our arrival into a special environment is not a genetico-social product but is the best and wisest choice for us, that it is our assignment place. Should we take this myth as a prophecy that men will one day turn this scheme of the creator into truth?

The most fateful moment for a man is his entrance into the world. The biological process of reproduction is over and the process of living in this world, of unfoldment, begins. But as a fatalistic consequence of reproduction his parents and guardians are identical with his procreators and with it the first social organization in which he grows up to a person. *Parents are given instead of chosen.* It is curious that this first commandment in the social domain sounds so much more provoking than that other commandment in the biological domain— procreators are given but not tested. But with whom we should live and whom we should emulate is not less pertinent than who should live or who should survive. It is perhaps more obnoxious because in the first instance a human pair is endowed with or deprived of an opportunity only, but in the second instance a reality is given or taken away from them. The born child is regarded as a possession, as a property, perhaps as a reward for the suffering and sacrifice entailed in giving it birth. This feeling has a counterpart in the relation of the creative mind to his work. Also he is inclined to regard his work, his child, as his property. But both the parents and the creators are most humanly the victims of the same lust which can be called the *parental illusion*. Predom-

269

inantly an emotional illusion in the first case, predominantly an intellectual, in the second. This may deserve a broader explanation.

A creator, as soon as his work has emanated from him, has no right to it any longer except a psychological right. He had all rights upon it as long as it was in him growing, but he has forfeited these as soon as it is gone out of him, a part of the world. It belongs to universality. An individual is rarely aware of the position he holds in the cultural currents of his community, of the vast material he continuously absorbs, material produced and oftentimes shaped by thousands of other individual minds to whom he is anonymously indebted. However central his position is within myriads of currents, the material of his work is contained and predisposed within universality. It is far more literally and more deeply true with the parent. Biogenetics is still in its infancy, but we know the units which go into the making of a child are not the product of the two individual parents. Continued genetic research may teach that their biological contribution is more pertinent than we think today, but still cannot be but small compared with the contribution of the whole kind, of mankind. Just as the creators of works, parents have no right upon their offspring except a psychological right. Literally, the children belong to universality.

We array these facts not for the advocacy of a Platonic or Communistic utopia. "All" is as good as nobody. And universality is flat. Or more precisely, universality is not the thing with whom children could live and whom they could emulate. Furthermore, during the pre-socialized period the child's need of a guardian is obvious. It is not the abdication of the individual parent but his clearer definition which we propose. Parenthood cannot but continue to be an individual parent and an individual matter. Observation of the relations between children and adults throws further light upon this subject. We know about parents who are careless of and cruel to their own children, and we know about childless people who become their most useful parents. The instinct for reproduction and the instinct for parenthood are not identical. We propose, therefore, the specialization of the notion of parenthood into two distinct and different functions,—the *biological* parent and the *social* parent. They may come together in one individual or they may not. But the problem is how to produce a procedure which is able to substitute and improve this ancient order.

The first situation which is awaiting us when we enter the world is duplicated again and again throughout life. Brothers and sisters are given instead of chosen, our colleagues in school, our comrades in factories or in business, and so on. We see our universe consisting of organizations which are either molded by mechanical and economic pressure, as the factory, or by biological pressure, as the family, but we do not see man's own world realized. Yet if we want to make a world after man's own feeling we have to have first a social society.

A community like Hudson offers to sociometry an unusual problem, as it has two deficiencies. The biological set-up that controls the community at large is absent. The economic set-up which dominates the community at large is also absent. But just these two disadvantages make it possible to concentrate on one front, the socionomic, which in the community outside is continuously crushed in its expression from the pressure of these two major issues. A community is here given free from blood relations and free from economic relations at the same time. In this community, to find the realization of and the proper treatment for the needs of the population and to find the government for it, is one and the same thing. In contrast to the principle to build the state on the biological set-up primarily or to build it on the economic set-up primarily, the principle is here attempted to build the Hudson community on the psychological and social set-up primarily.

It is on the basis of the analysis of this community that a therapy of the community as a whole has been attempted. To the tests which analyze the organization of groups correspond techniques which aid to produce and to organize the various groups necessary to the community. To the tests (Spontaneity Tests) which analyze emotional, social, and vocational abilities correspond techniques which aid to shape and to develop these abilities. To the tests which analyzed

the psychological currents of a community correspond techniques which aid to direct, to shape, to control, and to produce
such currents.   In other words, the analytical unfoldment of
the community which has been presented up to this point,
phase by phase, beginning with the home and ending with its
psychological geography, is complemented now by the positive
unfoldment, the steps which have been taken to create a
community according to socionomic principles.

XV. INITIAL ASSIGNMENT

The Family

Two persons, a man and a woman, go one day to a city hall
to be united as man and wife by a justice of peace.   Love
and reproduction takes care of the rest.   Thus people become
parents and babies become their children.   Love for the child
goes a long way in shaping that unique relationship which is
still the cornerstone of our community life, the interrelation-
ship of child and parent.   This love is already present long
before the child is born and runs up to true performance from
the moment that the child is born.

From all over the state children are sent to Hudson because
for one reason or another they have lost or forfeited their
parents and their belonging to a natural group.   Within the
scope of a few miles these children, numbering in hundreds,
are gathered together.   On the other side of the fence a number of women are appointed by the state to be mothers to these
children.   But how should we bring these people and these
children together if not by force or mechanical regulations?
Where is the mother cry here, the instinctive mother attachment a child shows to its natural mother?   Where is the call
to become a mother to a particular child among the crowd of
children?

It was meant to provide these children with a situation
which was equal to or better than the one which the children
had outside.   The process of the natural development of a
family has to be duplicated here, but as the natural means of
attachment are here cut off, we have to replace them *synthetically* with something which is equally efficient.   Thus we

have to strive after the ideal to fit a child to a mother as well as a child is fitted to its natural mother and to fit a child to the other children here as well as a child is fitted to its brothers and sisters in a natural family. The question is how do we know which parent is desirable for which child and which child is desirable for which other child?

1. PARENT TEST

Technique

The Parent Test is so designed that all girls newly arrived at the community are placed opposite all the housemothers who have a vacancy in their cottage. As the test is so delicate in nature the technique of arrangement is most important. A meeting is called at the Receiving Cottage to which only the participants are invited. First the tester addresses the new girls with these or similar words: "You will meet a number of ladies, each of whom is willing to act as your parent during your stay in Hudson. You have an opportunity to choose your housemother and to decide to whom among them you feel most attracted. They, of course, have the same opportunity to express their opinion before they take you into their house. It is a serious matter. You have to visualize that you are going to decide upon the person towards whom you are so drawn that you feel that you can confide in her as in a mother and from whom you would be glad to take advice, and also that you decide upon the person with whom you shall live together until you have finished your training in Hudson."

The tester then addresses the housemothers with these or similar words: "A number of new girls have come to Hudson for training. You have chosen to act as their parent during their stay. You know well that a discordant home is of the greatest disadvantage for a child and that a harmonious home is the greatest blessing for it. We want to know your reaction to the child before she is sent to your house. This, for two reasons: You may feel attracted to one child more than to another and you may feel better able to help one child than to help another. Then, too, you know your family. You may feel that one child is better fitted to adjust with your group of girls than another child. Talk with each of the girls freely and make your judgment as spontaneous as it arises."

The new girls act as hostesses and receive the housemothers as their guests. Each girl entertains one housemother at a time in her room. It is important that these two are left alone so that they can come into rapport. In succession one housemother after another converses with each girl until each has met every new girl.

The tester then approaches the housemother and the girl *immediately* after they have finished to get the fresh, spontaneous impression of each separately about the other. After all the meetings are over and the tester has received the impressions from each of the pairs, the tester comes back to each girl to ask: "Whom of these ladies would you like to have as your housemother?" After she names one, the tester continues: "If, for some reason, you couldn't have this housemother, to whom else would you like to go?" After the child names a second housemother, the tester continues: "Should it not be possible to place you with this housemother, is there any other woman among them whom you would choose?" After the child has named a third, she is asked to give free expression to her feelings concerning each of the women she has met and her motivations for feeling more drawn to one than to another. Each statement of the child is recorded in her words and in her presence. The children have no suspicion as they know that it is a procedure constructed with the aim to advance their own longings.

The tester then comes back also to each of the housemothers and asks: "Which girl would you like to have in your family?" After she names one, the tester continues: "If, for some reason, this child cannot come to you, whom else would you like to have?" After she names a second child, the tester continues: "If neither of these girls is available for you, is there anyone else you would choose?" After the housemother has named a third, she is asked to give her impressions about each of the girls and the motivations of her preferences. She has no suspicion towards the tester, as she knows that the greater her sincerity the more she is apt to receive her choices.

Method

The crudest form of assignment and the one overwhelmingly in use in our institutions is that based upon the fact that there is a *vacancy* in a particular cottage or dormitory. The individual has "to stay put" in this placement until he is released. This is the logical outcome of the procedure which treats the individual singly, whether through psychoanalysis, hypnosis, suggestion, or whatever, and not as a part of a group. Only when disagreeable incidents take place between two or more inmates who have been placed together does the administration become aware of the fact that they do not "get along," and if other means, as personal influence or punishment, fail, they are placed apart. The tendency is always to make as few changes as possible. It is expected of an inmate that he "stay put." This attitude towards the population can be observed in penal institutions, reformatories, training schools, hospitals for the insane, orphanages, etc., but also in our public schools, factories, and business offices. Yet there have been exceptions from this rule, especially in the training school field. Based upon a sort of "trained intuition" gained through experience, a child is placed in a cottage into which she appears to be well fitted. These placements end sometimes with success and sometimes with failure. Yet, as the proceduce is not based upon analytic principles, we are not able to learn anything in either case. And even when these intuitive assignments are recorded and an attempt is made to determine the reasons for success or failure in each case, the results are meager, due to the complexity of the factors which enter into the situations. As we have found through our own experience with this method, we run the risk to make early generalizations in theory and snap judgments in practice. In the wilderness of factors which might have an effect upon the situation we miss an archimedic point in which a methodology of assignment could be anchored.

We searched for a procedure which might substitute the trial-and-error method by an *organic* method of assignment. It was then that we paid closer attention to the choice factor in the interrelation of individuals. It appeared to us that an assignment without that the reactions of the individuals who are to live together with one another are known deprives these individuals of expressing their feeling in a, for them, fundamental matter and deprives us of an equally fundamental method of inquiry. The assignment to a cottage of a child who comes into a training school is a most important business— the more so as she must have been poorly "assigned" to a family outside or she would not have been sent to an institution. To leave, then, this "therapeutic assignment" to an individual, if it is now a psychologist, a social worker, or whomever, is to base it upon the emotional reactions of this individual towards the housemothers of the different cottages and towards the newly arrived children. It is to allow to some individual dictatorship powers over situations in which the wisest person may err. But the emotional-social reaction towards one another of the individuals who have to live together may be important and significant. Instead of putting an individual like a merchandise into a situation with other individuals who had been put there before in the same manner, they can be brought together to a test.

The notion "to stay put," that is, to stay and to be stable wherever you are and under all circumstances, has had a similar history in the field of marital relations. Until not so long ago for most of humanity, and still practiced here and there, marriages were made by parents. The emotional reactions of bride and bridegroom, towards each other were discounted. Although marriages are made in civilized countries today largely through the choice of the participants, no scientific study has been made so far of the emotional-social reactions and motivations of couples about to be married. It is probable that the application of the sociometric test to this problem would increase our insight into the causes of marital failures.

We have made the meeting of the individuals who are to live together or to work together, or in respect to any other criterion, the first step in the sociometric procedure. If the individuals had not met each other before, we called their reaction towards each other *spontaneous* (spontaneous interaction), and their placement initial assignment. If the person to be found for the newcomer was to act as parent, we called the procedure a *parent* test. If the persons to be found for the newcomer were to act as siblings, we called the procedure a *family* test. In this manner the tests have been constructed to meet the needs of the individual.

Initial assignment of an individual to a cottage upon her arrival at the given community is based upon (a) the Parent Test; (b) the Family (or Cottage) Test; (c) the organization of every home group as determined by the sociometric test; and (d) the organization of the individual's home group outside.

Procedure

The following is a sample of the test and its procedure. Eight children, Louise (age 15 years), Dora (15), Hazel (16), Lena (14), Adeline (13), Evelyn (16), Shirley (14), and Muriel (13), were newly arrived in Hudson. There were vacancies in C2, C8, C9, C11, C14, and CB. The housemothers of these six cottages came to the meeting. The test resulted for each child as illustrated in the following sociogram.

A crude analysis of this sociogram indicates a different *mother* reaction for each of the children. From the eight children, only one, Muriel, was not wanted by any of the housemothers present. The other seven were wanted by at least one of the housemothers. But a second child, Shirley, remained isolated because she did not want the only housemother who wanted her, the housemother of C8. Thus from the eight girls, six formed with five different housemothers six mutual attractions. Two of the children did not click. Among the six housemothers, only one, the housemother of C9, failed to click, although she was wanted by one child, Lena. We see, so to speak, one housemother and two children eliminated from the test. A closer analysis of these reactions between the housemothers and children indicates numerous fine distinctions made by them. There are only two children, Dora and Adeline, and only two housemothers, one of CS and the other of CB, who want each other respectively by first choice. Hazel is drawn to the housemother of C14 and the latter to her, both by second choice. Lena is drawn to the housemother of C11 by first choice, but the latter is drawn to her only by third choice. Lena also exchanges second choices with the housemother of C2. Louise exchanges second choice with the housemother of C8, who wants her second. The one whom she wants first, the housemother of CB, rejects her. Evelyn exchanges third choices with the housemother of C8.

We see further how varied the degree of attractiveness can be. Dora is chosen first by three of the housemothers and second by two others, and rejected by one. Louise is chosen first by two housemothers, second by two, rejected by one, and one is indifferent to her. Lena is wanted second by one housemother, third by two, rejected by one, and two are indifferent to her. Hazel is wanted second by one housemother, third by one, rejected by one, and three are indifferent to her. Evelyn is wanted third by two housemothers, rejected by one, and three are indifferent to her. Adeline is wanted first by one housemother and five are indifferent to her. Shirley is wanted fourth by one housemother, rejected by one, and four are indifferent to her. Muriel is wanted by none, rejected by four, and two are indifferent to her.

Another characteristic reaction is the force of clicking an individual has. Dora clicks with two of the five housemothers who want her; Louise, with two from the four; Lena, with two from the three; Evelyn, with one from the two; Hazel, with one from the two; Adeline, with one from one; Shirley, with none from one; and Muriel, with none from the none. The force of clicking the different housemothers have is likewise characteristic. The housemother of C9 is wanted by one and clicks with none; the housemother of C8 is wanted by six and clicks with three; CB's housemother is wanted by five and clicks with two; C2's housemother is wanted by one and clicks with her; the housemother of C14 is wanted by four and clicks with one; and the housemother of C11 is wanted by six and clicks with but two. This discloses that far more emotional efforts are made besides those which are successful and click. It indicates the tendency of emotion to expand further than the possibility of its satisfaction. It appears that a certain amount of emotional striving is always wasted. This is the socionomic counterpart to the observation of

Malthus that populations tend to increase faster than the means of their subsistence.

The emotional-social reaction of each housemother towards the given group of children can be classified with the following formulas, which include also the reactions of the children towards her.

Housemother of C8:

Parent Test

Sends choices to 4	Rejects 2 (Indifferent 2)
Receives choices 6	Rejected by 0 (Indifferent 2)

C11:
$$\frac{3 \mid \overset{P}{3} \ (2)}{6 \mid 0 \ (2)}$$

CB:
$$\frac{3 \mid \overset{P}{1} \ (4)}{5 \mid 1 \ (2)}$$

C14:
$$\frac{3 \mid \overset{P}{1} \ (4)}{4 \mid 1 \ (3)}$$

C2:
$$\frac{1 \mid \overset{P}{2} \ (5)}{3 \mid 3 \ (2)}$$

C9:
$$\frac{2 \mid \overset{P}{6}}{1 \mid 2 \ (5)}$$

Interpretation

Our experience up to date with the Parent Test indicates that mutual rejection between housemother and child is the poorest risk for assignment. If the housemother rejects the child, although the child may want her, such an assignment is still a poor risk. If the housemother wants the child but the child rejects her, such an assignment is a better risk than in the two previous instances. If the housemother and the child attract each other mutually, this is the best risk of all for a successful assignment, particularly if they have chosen each other by first choice. These rules are valid if all other circumstances are equal: that is, if the motivations behind the attractions do not point to disadvantages for the child, as, for instance, a housemother wanting a mentally retarded child because she thinks she would make a willing slave for her, or if other tests do not suggest other assignments to be better. If one or another individual appears as a poor risk for assignment after the Parent Test, she may still change her status through evidence in other phases considered in initial assignment.

Muriel appears unassignable to this set of housemothers as she is rejected by the one she wants and is not wanted by anyone else. Shirley also appears unassignable to these housemothers. One housemother wants her as a fourth choice, but towards just this one she is indifferent; those she wants are indifferent to or reject her. Dora appears assigned best to the housemother of C8, with whom she is a mutual first choice. She appears also to be assignable to the housemother of CB, although less well. To the housemother of C11, who wants her by first choice, she appears also assignable, although Dora is indifferent towards her. To C2, C9, and C14 she appears not to be assignable. The decision for her assignment has to be made between C8, CB, and C11. The best assignment for Adeline appears to be CB, with whose housemother she is mutual first choice. No other cottage among those in the test can be taken into consideration. Louise can be assigned to C8 or C11, with whose housemothers she forms a mutual attraction, or perhaps to C2, whose housemother wants her. To the others she cannot be assigned. Lena can be assigned to C2 or C11 on the strength of the housemother test, as she forms mutual attractions with both housemothers, but Hazel can be assigned to C14 only and Evelyn to C8.

2. Family Test

The child has to be placed in a cottage not only with the housemother but with all other girls who form the family. We have demonstrated that children from a certain age level on tend to develop social groups of their own independent of the adults who are in contact with them, and that these groups . become more and more differentiated the older the children become and deeply affect their conduct. Whatever attitude the group assumes towards the newcomer into it largely determines what adjustment the newcomer makes. The Family or Cottage Test is designed to determine what group appears to be best fitted to her.

Method

From each cottage whose housemother was a participant in the Parent Test the tester selects one girl who represents the general tone of the cottage. The better adjusted the girl herself is within her cottage, the more will she be able to react towards the new girl not only for herself but also for the other members, and the more articulate she is the better will she be able to express her reactions. Besides the analytic function to give the emotional-social reaction of the cottage family as a whole, the representative girl has also the productive function to break into her group the newcomer to whom she feels especially drawn. As the housemother is a permanent member of the group, her reaction pattern in the test situation is within a certain range more or less inflexible. To balance this it is desirable to make the Family Test as flexible as possible. A different girl from each cottage represents the group at each Family Test, and each member has at some time the opportunity to break in a new girl into her cottage. This has the added advantage that no one girl can gain an exceptional prestige through being called to be a representative. If, due to the inability of certain members to express their reactions, this desirable technique cannot be fully carried out, then at least every individual who holds a key-position in the group should at some time become a participant in the test. Through this procedure the population itself becomes active agents in the formation of its groups.

The Family Test is given in a similar manner as the Parent Test, except that instead of the housemothers the representative girls from each cottage take part. The tester addresses the representative girls in these or similar words: "A number of new girls have come to Hudson. You were once newcomers yourselves and you remember how it felt. And you remember how important it has been to start right, to feel welcome, and to get into the right cottage. Converse freely with each of them. You may be attracted to one and be able to help her. You know the other girls of your group. Try to visualize how each new girl would fit in not only with you but also with them. Talk to each girl and make up your mind to whom you feel most attracted."

Procedure

The representatives of C2, C8, C9, C11, C14, and CB were respectively Ruth, Leona, Harriet, Marion, Alberta, and Katherine. The reactions of attraction, rejection, or indifference given by them and by the new girls in respect to each other are charted in the accompanying sociogram.

As indicated in the sociogram, Dora has a mutual attraction with Leona of C8 and with Harriet of C9. She is chosen by three other girls, but she is indifferent to or rejects them. According to the rule before mentioned, the assignment of Dora to Leona is the best risk, as their mutual attraction is a first choice. The assignment to Harriet is less desirable, their choices being respectively third and second. Marion of C11, Alberta of C14, and Ruth of C2 do not click with Dora and so cannot be considered in her assignment. Katherine of CB is indifferent to Dora, who chooses her second. Therefore the decision has to be made between C8 and C9.

Adeline indicates mutual attraction, first choice and second in return to Katherine of CB. Her relation to the girls from all the other cottages are discordant. The only assignment which appears desirable on the strength of this test is CB.

Louise shows a mutual attraction, first choice, with Harriet of C9; mutual attraction with Ruth of C2; third choice from Louise and first choice in return; mutual attraction with Marion of C11, second and first choice respectively; the relation towards the three other representatives is discordant from

Louise's side.   On the basis of this test, the decision has to fall between C9, C11, and C2.

Lena shows mutual attraction with Ruth of C2, third from Lena, and fourth from Ruth.   All other relations are discordant; in respect to C9, C8, and CB, from both sides; in respect to C11 and C14, from the cottage side.   On the findings of this test the best assignment appears to be to C2.

Hazel indicates discordant response to representatives of each cottage present.   On the strength of this test no assignment appears to be more desirable than another, except, perhaps, that special consideration should be given to C8, whose representative she chooses first.

Evelyn indicates a mutual attraction with Leona of C8, second and third choices respectively.   All other relations are discordant.   On the findings of this test the best assignment of Evelyn appears to be to C8.

Shirley shows discordant relations with representatives of all the cottages present.   On the strength of this test no assignment to these cottages is indicated as desirable.

Muriel indicates mutual attraction with Ruth of C2, first choice from her and fourth from Ruth; mutual attraction with Marion of C11, third and second choice respectively; mutual attraction with Katherine of CB, fourth and third choice respectively.   The remaining relations are discordant. On the strength of this test and assignment to CB, C2, or C11 appears equally desirable.

Classification

On the basis of the Parent Test and the Family Test, the classification of the eight new girls is as follows:

Dora

$$P \frac{3 - 1\ (2) \qquad 3 - 1\ (2)}{5 - 0\ (1) \qquad 5 - 0\ (1)} F$$

Louise

$$P \frac{3 -\!\!- 3 \qquad\qquad 3 - 3}{4 - 1\ (1) \qquad 6 - 0\ (0)} F$$

Lena

$$P \frac{3 - 0\ (3) \qquad 3 - 0\ (3)}{3 - 1\ (2) \qquad 1 - 1\ (4)} F$$

Evelyn

$$3 - 0 \ (3) \qquad 2 - 0 \ (4)$$
P———————————————F
$$2 - 1 \ (3) \qquad 4 - 0 \ (2)$$

Hazel

$$3 - 0 \ (3) \qquad 3 - 2 \ (1)$$
P———————————————F
$$2 - 1 \ (3) \qquad 0 - 1 \ (5)$$

Adeline

$$3 - 0 \ (3) \qquad 1 - 0 \ (5)$$
P———————————————F
$$1 - 0 \ (5) \qquad 2 - 0 \ (4)$$

Shirley

$$3 - 0 \ (3) \qquad 3 - 0 \ (3)$$
P———————————————F
$$1 - 1 \ (4) \qquad 2 - 1 \ (3)$$

Muriel

$$3 - 3 \ (0) \qquad 4 - 0 \ (2)$$
P———————————————F
$$0 - 4 \ (2) \qquad 3 - 0 \ (3)$$

3. ORGANIZATION OF COTTAGE GROUPS

The organization of C2, C8, C9, C11, C14, and CB determined through the sociometric test was as follows:

C2. Quantitative Analysis:
Ratio of interest for own cottage, 34%.
Distribution of attractions, 52%; of repulsions, 48%.

Structural Analysis:
Isolated, 7; Pairs (mutual attraction), 10; Mutual rejections, 3; Incompatible pairs, 2; Red triangle, 1; Red stars, 4; Black stars, 2.

Position of Housemother: 13 attractions, 11 rejections and 3 indifferent to her.

C8. Quantitative Analysis:
Ratio of interest for own cottage, 34%.
Distribution of attractions, 47½%; of repulsions, 52½%.

Structural Analysis:
Isolated, 13; Pairs, 10; Mutual rejections, 7; Incompatible pairs, 9; 1 Red chain; 1 Incompatible triangle; 1 Red star; 3 Black stars.

Position of Housemother: 4 rejections and rest attractions.

C9. Quantitative Analysis:
Ratio of interest for own cottage, 46%.
Distribution of attractions, 69%; of repulsions, 31%.

Structural Analysis:
  Isolated, 3; Pairs, 22; Mutual rejections, 1; Incompatible pairs, 3; Red chains, 2; Red triangle, 1; Red square, 1; Black circle, 1; Red stars, 3; Black stars, 2.

Position of Housemother: 3 rejections and rest attractions.

C11. Quantitative Analysis:
  Ratio of interest for own cottage, 54%.
  Distribution of attractions, 85½%, or repulsions, 14½%.

Structural Analysis:
  Isolated, 4; Pairs, 40; Mutual rejections, 1; Incompatible pairs, 5; Red chains, 6; Red triangles, 8; Red circles, 3; Red stars, 8; Mutual red stars, 6.

Position of Housemother: All attractions.

C14. Quantitative Analysis:
  Ratio of interest for own cottage, 46%.
  Distribution of attractions, 67%; of repulsions, 43%.

Structural Analysis:
  Isolated, 12; Pairs, 17; Mutual rejections, 2; Incompatible pairs, 7; Red chain, 1; Red triangles, 2; Red stars, 5; Black star, 1.

Position of Housemother: Rejections, 3; Rest attractions.

CB. Quantitative Analysis:
  Ratio of interest for own cottage, 37%.
  Distribution of attractions, 65½%; of repulsions, 34½%.

Structural Analysis:
  Isolated, 3; Pairs, 11; Mutual rejections, 4; Incompatible pairs, 5; Red chains, 2; Red star, 1; Black star, 1.

Position of Housemother: All attractions.

On the basis of the quantitative and structural analysis of these cottages, C2 and C8 appeared to be poor risks for individuals who are unattractive to the housemothers and the representative girls of these two cottages. Their members show a lower interest to stay in their group and high number of isolates. C2, in addition, had a high number of runaways in the last season. Individuals, as Shirley, Muriel, Adeline, and Hazel, run a greater risk to stay isolated or to be among the number of the discontented than they should in the other cottages. If all other circumstances are equal, these two cottages should be given the opportunity to receive individuals who have appeared especially and spontaneously attracted to the housemother and the girl representative and who may aid in balancing the group. New girls, as Dora, Louise, Lena, and Evelyn, if they are drawn to these two cottages as strongly as to the other cottages represented, should preferably be assigned to them. On the strength of the quantitative and structural analysis of their organization, the cottages B and 11 should be preferred as assignments for poor risks in adjustment, as Adeline, Muriel, and Shirley.

The position of the different housemothers in their respective cottage indicates that the housemothers of C2, C8, and C9, respectively have to meet at present a great amount of dislike from the members of their own group. On the strength of this fact, none of the new girls who dislike them should be assigned to them, as Muriel in respect to C2 and C9 or Dora in respect to C2 and C9.

The position of the cottage representatives within their respective cottage indicates that all have a favorable situation among the other girls and also in respect to the housemother. Each appears, therefore, well selected by the tester to break in a new girl into her cottage. However, Marion of C11, Katherine of CB, and Leona of C8 appear for different reasons especially well fitted. Marion is the center of seven attractions, five which are mutual, and through these she dominates the network. Therefore the new girls, Louise, Muriel, and Dora, with whom she forms mutual attractions, would have a marked advantage if assigned to C11. Katherine of CB forms three mutual attractions within her group, and all three of these are interlocked into chains which include almost every member of the cottage. Her position would be thus of significance in aiding Adeline and Muriel with whom she forms mutual attractions. Leona has a mutual attraction with a star of her group and is attracted to a second star. Dora and Evelyn form with her mutual attractions. She is thus in a position to break in Dora or Evelyn.

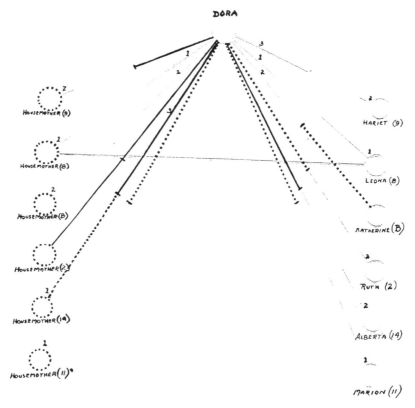

DORA

HOUSEMOTHER (9)

HOUSEMOTHER (8)

HOUSEMOTHER (B)

HOUSEMOTHER (2)

HOUSEMOTHER (14)

HOUSEMOTHER (11)

HARIET (9)

LEONA (8)

KATHERINE (B)

RUTH (2)

ALBERTA (14)

MARION (11)

The chart illustrates the findings of the Parent Test and the Family Test of Dora: the reactions of the housemothers of C9, C8, CB, C2, C14, and C11 to Dora and Dora's reactions to them; the reactions of a representative girl of C9, C8, CB, C2, C14, and C11 to Dora and Dora's reactions to them. The number on the side of the lines indicating attraction of Dora towards a particular individual relates to the degree of choice,—first, second, or third. The line drawn between the house-mother of C8 and the representative girl of this cottage indicates that C8 has been selected as the initial assignment for Dora.

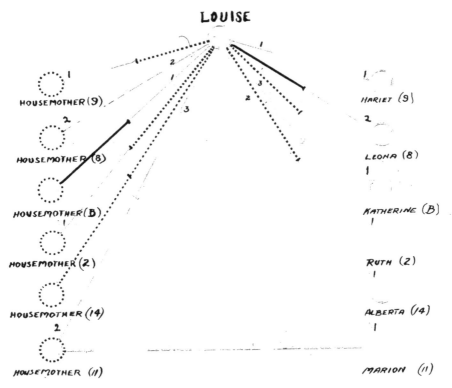

LOUISE

HOUSEMOTHER (9)

HOUSEMOTHER (8)

HOUSEMOTHER (B)

HOUSEMOTHER (2)

HOUSEMOTHER (14)

HOUSEMOTHER (11)

HARIET (9)

LEONA (8)

KATHERINE (B)

RUTH (2)

ALBERTA (14)

MARION (11)

The chart illustrates the findings of the Parent Test and the Family Test of Louise: the reactions of the housemothers of C9, CB, C2, C14, and C11 to Louise and Louise's reactions to them; the reactions of a representative girl of C9, C8, CB, C2, C14 and C11 to Louise and Louise's reactions to them. The number on the side of the lines indicating attraction of Louise towards a particular individual relates to the degree of choice,—first, second, or third. The line drawn between the housemother of C11 and the representative girl of this cottage indicates that C11 has been selected as the initial assignment for Louise.

LENA

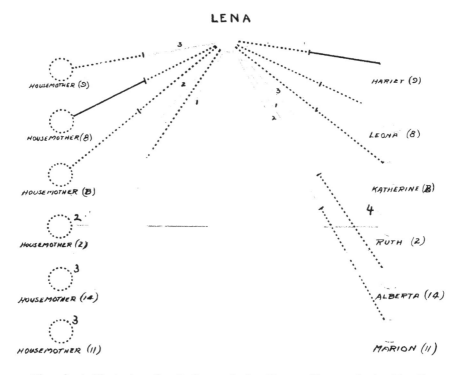

The chart illustrates the findings of the Parent Test and the Family Test of Lena: the reactions of the housemothers of C9, C8, C*B*, C2, C14, and C11 to Lena and Lena's reactions to them; the reactions of a representative girl of C9, C8, C*B*, C2, C14, and C11 to Lena and Lena's reactions to them. The number on the side of the lines indicating attraction of Lena towards a particular individual relates to the degree of choice,—first, second, or third. The line drawn between the housemother of C2 and the representative girl of this cottage indicates that C2 has been selected as the initial assignment for Lena.

INITIAL ASSIGNMENT—PARENT AND FAMILY TESTS

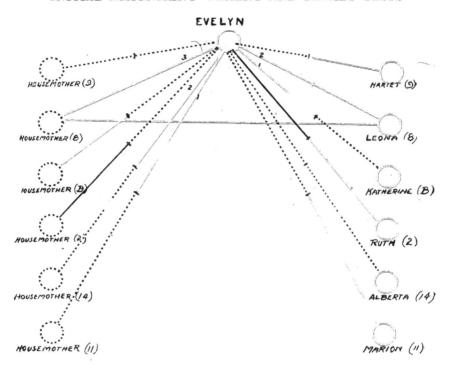

The chart illustrates the findings of the Parent Test and the Family Test of Evelyn: the reactions of the housemothers of C9, C8, CB, C2, C14, and C11 to Evelyn and Evelyn's reactions to them; the reactions of a representative girl of C9, C8, CB, C2, C14, and C11 to Evelyn and Evelyn's reactions to them. The number on the side of the lines indicating attraction of Evelyn towards a particular individual relates to the degree of choice,—first, second, or third. The line drawn between the housemother of C8 and the representative girl of this cottage indicates that C8 has been selected as the initial assignment for Evelyn.

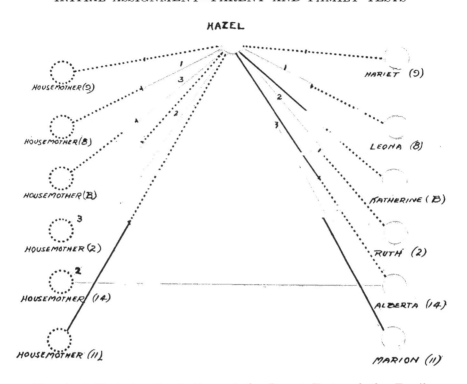

The chart illustrates the findings of the Parent Test and the Family Test of Hazel: the reactions of the housemothers of C9, C8, CB, C2, C14, and C11 to Hazel and Hazel's reactions to them; the reactions of a representative girl of C9, C8, CB, C2, C14, and C11 to Hazel and Hazel's reactions to them. The number on the side of the lines indicating attraction of Evelyn towards a particular individual relates to the degree of choice,—first, second, or third. The line drawn between the housemother of C14 and the representative girl of this cottage indicates that C14 has been selected as the initial assignment for Hazel.

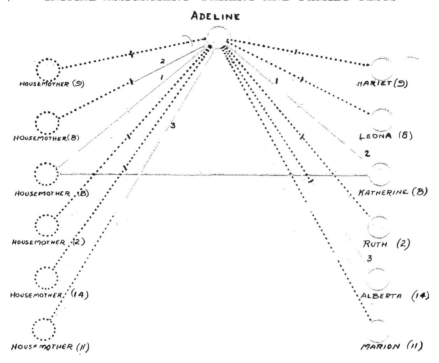

The chart illustrates the findings of the Parent Test and the Family
Test of Adeline: the reactions of the housemothers of C9, C8, CB, C2,
C14, and C11 to Adeline and Adeline's reactions to them; the reactions
of a representative girl of C9, C8, CB, C2, C14, and C11 to Adeline and
Adeline's reactions to them. The number on the side of the lines indicating attraction of Adeline towards a particular individual relates to
the degree of choice,—first, second, or third. The line drawn between
the housemother of CB and the representative girl of this cottage indicates that CB has been selected as the initial assignment for Adeline.

SHIRLEY

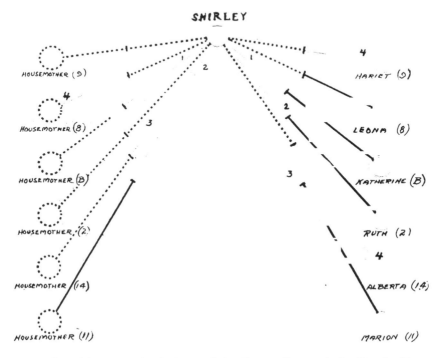

The chart illustrates the findings of the Parent Test and the Family Test of Shirley: the reactions of the housemothers of C9, C8, C*B*, C2, C14, and C11 to Shirley and Shirley's reactions to them; the reactions of a representative girl of C9, C8, C*B*, C2, C14, and C11 to Shirley and Shirley's reactions to them. The number on the side of the lines indicating attraction of Shirley towards a particular individual relates to the degree of choice,—first, second, or third. No assignment is plotted.

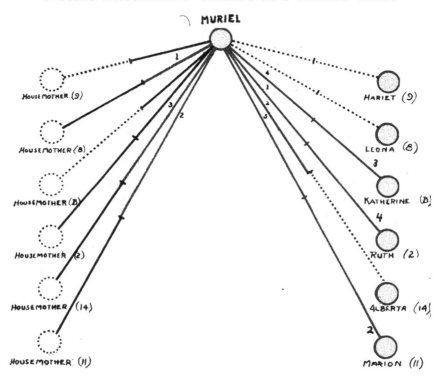

The chart illustrates the findings of the Parent Test and the Family Test of Muriel: the reactions of the housemothers of C9, C8, CB, C2, C14, and C11 to Muriel and Muriel's reactions to them; the reactions of a representative girl of C9, C8, CB, C2, C14, and C11 to Muriel and Muriel's reactions to them. The number on the side of the lines indicating attraction of Muriel towards a particular individual relates to the degree of choice,—first, second, or third. No assignment is plotted.

4. Psychological Currents

Cottages 8 and 9 appeared on the Psychogeography Map IV to be caught in sexual currents with the negro population. However, none of the new girls appear particularly suggestive to an interest in the activity. C2 appeared disturbed by a racial current. Ten of the 11 girls who reject the house-mother in C2 are of foreign nationality. None of the new girls are of foreign nationality. But this factor has played a rôle in other tests. For instance, in the initial assignments of the week before there was an Indian girl whose assignment was so difficult that C11 and C8 were excluded because of this factor. C2 and C9 appeared with a high number of escapes in runaway status. Therefore Dora, who had run away many times outside, should preferably not be assigned to this group initially.

Assignment.

		Suggests assignment to:
Adeline:	Parent Test	CB
	Family Test	CB
	Organization	CB or C11
	Position of Housemother	CB or C11
	Position of Representative	CB
	Psychological Currents	CB
	Social History	CB or C11 or C14
	Final Assignment	CB
Dora:	Parent Test	C8, C11, or CB
	Family Test	C8, or C9
	Organization	C8 or C2
	Position of Housemother	C8
	Position of Housemother	C8 or C11
	Psychological Currents	None
	Social History	Any
	Final Assignment	C8
Louise:	Parent Test	C8 or C11 or C2
	Family Test	C11 or C9 or C2
	Organization	Even
	Position of Housemother	Even
	Position of Representative	C11
	Psychological Currents	None
	Social History	Excludes C2
	Final Assignment	C11

Lena:	Parent Test	C2 or C11
	Family Test	C2
	Organization	C2 or C8
	Position of Housemother	C2
	Position of Representative	Any
	Psychological Currents	C2
	Social History	Any
	Final Assignment	C2

Evelyn:	Parent Test	C8
	Family Test	C8
	Organization	C8
	Position of Housemother	C8
	Position of Representative	Any
	Psychological Currents	Any
	Social History	Any
	Final Assignment	C8

Hazel:	Parent Test	C14
	Family Test	Any
	Organization	C14, C11 or CB; not C2 or C8
	Position of Housemother	Not C2, C8 or C9; others even
	Position of Representative	Even
	Psychological Currents	Not C2 or C9
	Social History	Any
	Final Assignment	C14

Shirley:	Parent Test	None
	Family Test	None
	Organization	C11 or CB
	Position of Housemother	C11 or CB
	Position of Representative	Even
	Psychological Currents	Not C2 or C9; even
	Social History	Any
	Assignment	No assignment made

Muriel:	Parent Test	None
	Family Test	CB or C2 or C11
	Organization	CB or C11
	Position of Housemother	Not C2, C8 or C9
	Position of Representative	CB
	Psychological Currents	Any
	Social History	Suggests hospital
	Final Assignment	Hospital

Shirley and Muriel are left over to be tried out with housemothers and representatives of another group of cottages as soon as a few more girls have arrived. An illustration that this procedure is practical and successful is the case of Lena, who is among the girls whose assignment has just been described.

She had been " left over " from the previous set of girls whom we had tested for assignment a week before. The findings for Lena suggested no assignment yet. She appeared unwanted by the cottages represented at that testing. But in this, her second test, she found a housemother for herself.

A comparative study of 102 initial assignments made through the foregoing procedure indicates that the best risks in assignment have been cases in which the majority of the factors disclosed in the test coincided. The analytic basis for each assignment is filed and the success or failure of every assignment methodically followed up. A new line of research develops from this point to determine what relative value the different factors have upon which the assignments have been made.

The natural next step in the application of the Parent and Cottage Tests and the subsequent procedure to families in the community outside is to the foster home. The foster home into which one or more children are placed by some social agency often develops frictions between the genuine members of the family and the foster members. The natural grouping versus a social grouping drafted upon it predisposes a situation potentially disadvantageous to the foster child. This is the point in which training schools have an advantage, as all their members are on an *equal* status towards each other and towards their houseparents. This difficulty is partly alleviated when the foster parents are childless or when their own children have already grown up. Placements may become more adequate and successful if instead of leaving it to the judgment of the social worker sociometric testing is employed. The Parent Test can be used in a similar manner as described. All applicants for a foster child are invited by the social agency to meet all the children who are considered for placement. Each parent, then, meets each child. The fathers and mothers are tested in separate meetings. After an exact analysis of the findings, the Family Test is given. The form of this test as used in Hudson may be somewhat modified. In families of average size or smaller, all members should be tested, especially if there are children near in age to the prospective foster child. On the basis of the findings and their evaluation, the particular family for a particular child can be decided upon.

XVI. ASSIGNMENT THERAPY

The rise of new psychological currents in a community and the decline of old ones effect a slow but continuous change in the community structure. Therefore to keep a community in a status of equilibrium corrective means are necessary.

If we look at the universe we see the life of its organisms interlocked in a state of interdependence, and if we look particularly upon the organisms which reside upon earth, we see this state of interdependence in two aspects, a geographical, *horizontal structure* of interdependence among the organisms and a *vertical structure* of interdependence among them. We see that more highly differentiated organisms rest in and depend upon the less highly differentiated. It is this heterogeneity of order which makes bacteria and algae indispensable for the more complex structures resting upon them and which gives creatures so vulnerable and dependent as man the possibility of existence.

The vertical line of structure, the tendency of binding higher with lower forms, to express one part through the other and to exploit one part through another for a common aim, can be observed in every part of nature. In the human body the head rests upon the trunk and the trunk upon the legs. In the topography of the mind the lighter and finer elements, the ideas, rest upon the heavier and rougher elements, the emotions, which in turn rest upon instinctual drives. And it appears that the mental health of the individual depends upon a happy mixture of these elements rather than from the absolute predominance of one factor at the cost of the other. There seems to be a point of saturation in respect to how much intellect a man with a given emotional equipment can stand, how much of his emotional energy should undergo sublimation, or, in turn, how much emotional energy should be spent by a particular individual with a given emotional capacity.

The two directions of structure can be observed in respect to social groups. No individual will stand long apart from the other and no group isolated from others if they live in geographic proximity. They will sooner or later come to an exchange of emotions and other social values and thus produce horizontal structures through interdependence and collectivistic differentiation. The vertical line of structure can be observed in groups which tend to endure over a period of time. We see a number of dependent elements at the "bottom" of the group and a number of leading elements at the "top" of the group, and often also a number of intermediary agents between them. The members at the top need the dependent groups as a medium to express themselves and the dependent groups need the members at the top as a medium to express themselves. The analysis of groups in earlier pages of this book has demonstrated that the actual organization of a group is far more complex than this simple division indicates, but one principle appeared always to prevail, the tendency to produce groups which are therapeutically fit for survival. And it appears further that this demand was responded to best by such groups as were provided with a well-balanced vertical mixture of individuals differing in respect to numerous factors, as, for instance, mental capacity, ability, chronological age. It indicated, however, that this heterogeneity could not go on without limit, that there existed a point of saturation for leader-individuals, for contrasting racial elements, for individuals of retarded mental development, and other factors; neither could heterogeneity be reduced to a minimum without reaching stagnation and gradual disintegration.

The condition of a group in which a certain individual member has failed to produce a successful adjustment after a period of six months or more was our first concern aside from the condition of this individual himself. The group can be in *ascendance,* that is, developing from a lower to a higher level of organization, or it can be in decline, regressing from a higher to a lower level of organization. The situation of a newcomer is influenced by the condition of the group he enters. In the process of adjusting himself to the group he passes through a phase of ascendance, the gradual acquaintance with the members of the group, the gradual developing of a position within it which gives the best possible expression to his strivings and abilities against the pressure brought forth by the other members around him. Secondly, he enters into a phase of maintenance of the position attained. The latter takes place when the process of ascendance ends in a relatively successful adjustment of the individual to the group. But sometimes it is observed that this process of ascendance is blocked, either at the very entrance of the individual into the group or in some of the later phases. Resistances against his adjustment come from the group or from himself or from both sides, and may not melt either through attempts of the individual or through attempts from outside, and if this arrest is maintained for a period of six months or more, then some therapeutic approach to the problem becomes urgent. This maladjustment may be due to particular individual difficulties which he has developed previous to entering the group. If the group to which he is assigned has besides him a number of other individuals who suffer from similar or other difficulties, then such members of the group as are aiding in their adjustment may be overburdened. He, with his difficulties, is already too much for the group, and he may become rejected by them. Or his maladjustment may not be due to particular individual difficulties but to difficulties within the collective itself. Specific social, racial, and nationality characteristics may produce disturbances among the members if the group is already saturated with individuals of his particular nationality and differentiation. Or, again, his maladjustment may be due to the fact that the group is saturated with leader-individuals of his abilities and tendencies and he is in consequence handicapped in developing and expressing them. These and similar conditions may suggest the conclusion that this individual is of disadvantage to the group and that the group is of disadvantage to him, and that he aids to throw the group out of balance and that the group aids to keep him out of balance. And this may be due not only to causes originating in the subject or in this and that member of the group or to the interaction of the subject with the members but also determined by the developmental level of the group, due to the type of organization it represents and to the point of saturation for certain elements which are important for the maintenance and survival of the group as a whole.

When the organization of a group is uncovered through the sociometric test, the contribution is revealed also which each of its members makes towards the mental or social disorder by which a particular individual is especially caught. This recognition of the community structure and of the position of each individual within it can be used for therapeutic ends through a form of individual treatment, through group therapy, or through assignment therapy.

The individual approach may consist in acquainting the individual with the sociometric findings which bear upon his situation, to bring the individual to a full awareness of every relation in which he participates, to disclose for him every psychological current by which he is touched. For individuals who have a developed analytic sense, particularly for certain adults, such a method may be useful. But by its very nature this method is not applicable to children or adolescents.

Group therapy treats not only the individual who is the focus of attention because of maladjustment but the whole group of individuals who are interrelated to him in the community, just as in medical therapy, while we concentrate our attention chiefly upon the organ affected, we pay attention also simultaneously to all other organs which are or may be co-affected. Again, this kind of " group therapy " can be analytical, that is, it can bring to the realization of every individual of the group the harmful effects their interrelations produce upon this or that particular individual or upon them all and attempt to affect these through suggestion.

On the other hand, group therapy can take an activistic form through the treatment of each individual of the group who is related to the same conflict. The rôles of the various persons in the conflict are uncovered through the Spontaneity Tests (see p. 169). Treatment consists in the interadjustment of the individuals to one another through training (see Spontaneous Therapy, p. 324).

We have found, however, that the group therapeutic approach is applicable only in mild cases of maladjustment; and secondly, in exclusive cases in which during the treatment the group is artificially cut off from the community as if the rest of the community were non-existent and as if the influence coming from it could be disregarded. But the salient point is that certain conditions may develop in a group which group therapy in this limited sense cannot affect, as, for instance, the condition arising from a surplus of leader-individuals or from a surplus of certain racial elements, and so on (see p. 224). Even if the problems of a particular individual were solved by it, if he could be brought to such a degree of sublimation that he would take the exigencies of the situation cheerfully, still the source for these adverse attacks against him would continue to exist. While the problem might be solved for him, for the community it would remain unsolved. The task would really be to sublimate the individual and the group as a whole: in other words, the sublimation of the whole group or of the whole community, an ideal which the Christian monasteries so rarely attained and which is, as it appears, for communities of children and adolescents impossible of attainment. There becomes necessary then a therapy which is not sectional but totalistic, an assignment therapy.

When such a situation is diagnosed, then the removing of this individual from one soil to another and better soil for him is another possible measure to apply. But how are we going to recognize or to produce a better soil for the development of an individual? It is accomplished through a comparative analysis of every home group with every other home group. Just as a gardener knowing the composition of the soil which thwarted the growth of a plant transfers it to a soil from which such factors are eliminated, so we, when planting individuals, see carefully that the conditions which brought failure in the first place are not repeated in the second place.

The individual who becomes delinquent outside according to the laws of the community at large is one problem and the individual who becomes delinquent towards the rules in a closed or institutional community is another problem. Therefore the information received concerning his conduct outside is of little value to the sociometrist of the closed community. It is not a sociometric study of the groups in which the individual participated. But through the sociometric test the position which an individual has acquired in the new community is accurately defined. Whatever the results of this test may indicate, actual or potential maladjustment, adjustment in some respects and poor adjustment in others, as the structure of the whole community is similarly studied, we are able to aid the individual in his adjustment within the area studied. Whereas a newcomer has a clear page for the population and staff and they are a clear page for him, the residents who have been members for any length of time develop a reputation within the closed community. The reputation is shaped by behavior of the individual and by the various psychological currents by which he is caught and by notions which are spread about him through the networks of that community.

The individuals who fail to adjust themselves to the institution, as non-social and unsocial individuals, runaways, pilferers, produce in such communities which are set up to cure them the same problem which has compelled the society at large to establish institutions. It is only natural that the same psychological forces which have compelled the state to establish jails and correctional institutions may force their administrators to resort to similar measures in fact, if not in name. Indeed, we find in many institutions special houses for the delinquent who fails to adjust to the institution. As an institution is at least in intent a therapeutic society and all factors which are referring an individual to it expect his training for cure, administrators of institutions are faced with a most perplexing problem. The conduct of the individuals under their supervision may be such that they are in want of a therapeutic measure to control them.

The high ideal towards which the monastery in the early Christian centuries was striving may aid to clarify the position and the possible future of the correctional institutions in the modern scheme of things. The monastery aimed to be not only a number of single saints but a community of saints, a therapeutic society. It wanted to put an example of a community before and against the world in which not only every member was in control of his own conduct, but also in which no warfare existed among the members. Similarly, the administrators of correctional institutions and its population, which also consists of " sinners," of incorrigibles in the world, have an opportunity to give their communities, which are the most extreme expression of human weakness, a deeper sense. They can demonstrate that an individual who appeared incorrigible outside in the world may appear corrected and adjusted within its fold, and second, that whereas the community as a whole cannot function without developing places for the degraded, jails and correctional institutions, that they can function without them.

It is in Hudson that we have made studies in assignment therapy. Before the maladjustment of an individual with a group becomes flagrant, its assignment to another group can be arranged. Such an assignment to be therapeutic has to be made at the psychological moment. If it is made too early, before the individual and the group she belongs to have made every effort for successful adjustment, the effect of the procedure may be lessened. If it is delayed an attitude of indifference and resentment towards the whole environment may develop which may destroy in the child the possibility of an enthusiastic beginning in a new family group. The assignment has to be made at the proper time and then rapidly, preferably after she herself spontaneously asks for transference. The technique for the assignment of new individuals to cottages (see p. 295) has to undergo a change when it is adapted to the assignment of individuals from one group to another.

Technique of Reassignment

Case of Anna GU, an example:

1. Case History.

2. Sociometric Testing. The sociometric test in respect to the criterion of living in proximity disclosed the position of Anna in the community. She chose no one in her own cottage (C4). All her choices (5) went to members of other cottages. She was not chosen by any member of her cottage but received choices from members of other cottages (3). Two of these choices were mutual.

$$\text{Classification Formula 1:} \quad \frac{0 \mid 5}{0 \mid 3} \; L$$

In the follow-up of these choices she appeared rejected by three members of her cottage. She herself rejected no one. From the five she liked outside, three responded with liking (in C8, C2, C2) and two with indifference (in C4, C9).   She was not rejected by anyone outside and rejected no one.

Classification Formula 2:

$$\frac{0-0 \mid 5-0}{0-3 \mid 3-0}^{L}$$

Of the staff, she rejected her housemother, who was attracted to her; she was drawn to the housemother of C8, who wanted her, and to the housemother of C4, who was indifferent to her. Hence the Formula 2 becomes:

Classification Formula 2A:

$$\frac{0-1 \mid 7-0}{1-3 \mid 4-0}^{L}$$

The sociometric test given at that date in respect to the criterion of working in proximity disclosed further her position in the community.   She chose two from her Art class and three from classes (Salesmanship and Handicraft) of which she was not a member.   These five also chose her.   Of the staff she was drawn to two teachers and rejected three.   They were respectively attracted to (Art and Handicraft teachers) or rejected her (teachers of other groups) in turn.

Classification Formula 2A:

$$\frac{3-0 \mid 4-3}{3-0 \mid 4-3}^{W}$$

Position of Anna in C4 six months later:

She and the housemother of C4 rejected each other.   She rejected 12 members of the cottage and was indifferent towards the remaining members.   Six of them rejected her.   She was attracted to two girls in other cottages (in C8, C4).

Classification Formula 2A:

$$\frac{0-13 \mid 2-0}{0-6 \mid 4-0}^{L}$$

Her work situation remained unchanged:

Classification Formula 2A:

$$\frac{3-0 \mid 4-3}{3-0 \mid 4-3}^{W}$$

Position of Anna in C4 twelve months later:

She rejected the housemother of C4 and was rejected by her. Anna was attracted to one girl of the cottage who was attracted also to her. She was indifferent towards all other members of the group, 18 among them rejecting her. She was attracted to the housemothers of C5, C8, and C4; the first two being drawn to her, the third indifferent to her. She was attracted to two girls in C8 who were drawn to her, and to two others in C4 who were indifferent to her.

$$\text{Classification Formula 2A:} \quad \overset{\text{L}}{\frac{1-1 \mid 7-0}{1-19 \mid 4-0}}$$

On the criterion of working together she was attracted to the same girls as six months before, but two of them at this date rejected her. Her relation to the staff remained the same.

$$\text{Classification Formula 2A:} \quad \overset{\text{W}}{\frac{3-0 \mid 4-3}{2-1 \mid 3-4}}$$

The sum of Anna's relations in respect to living and work groups presents the following formula:

$$\text{Total Classification Formula:} \quad \overset{\text{L and W}}{\frac{4-1 \mid 11-3}{3-20 \mid 7-4}}$$

3. Cottage Organization.

	C4 at the Outset	C4 18 Mos. Later
Population	25	25
Ratio of Interest (for own group)	54%	71%
Sum of Attractions (in per cent)	77%	70%
and of Repulsions (in per cent)	23%	30%
Index of Popularity	3%	3%
Structure:		
Isolated	0	1
Pairs	28	31
Mutual rejections	0	3
Incompatible pairs	18	10
Chains	2	3
Triangles	4	5
Squares	5	6
Circles	2	6
Stars	7	9

4. Acquaintance Testing. The acquaintance volume of Anna at the outset was 37 (distributed in C8, CA, C9, and C2); six months later, 55 (in C8, CA, C9, C1, CB, C14); 12 months later, 101 (the majority distributed in C8, CA, and C5, with every cottage included).

5. Parent Test. As all other cottage groups in the community had been tested and their structure disclosed, the tester was able to eliminate such groups from among them as appeared to present conditions for Anna similar to those which confronted her in C4 and to pick from among the cottage groups those which appeared more desirable for her. The evidence gathered indicated C4 to be undesirable for her development and suggested CA, C8, or C5 to be better possible placements. Therefore a meeting was arranged between Anna and the housemothers of these cottages. Anna chose the housemother of C8 first and was chosen first by her. The housemother of C5 was her second choice and the housemother of CA her third choice, but both of these housemothers rejected her.

6. Assignment. It can be seen that through sociometric testing at intervals we gained a knowledge of Anna's situation at the outset, a knowledge of how she developed within the group during a year, a knowledge of how the group developed during this year, and a knowledge of her situation at the end of the year. A study of her position in relation to the chief psychological currents pervading the community revealed that she remained untouched by the sexual and racial currents but that due to her relation to two girls in CA, to the Art teacher, and to three other members of the staff, she was caught by a cultural current. Whereas the position she had in C4 tended to drive her away from the community, the position she had attained in respect to the cultural currents tended to provide a counterbalance.

The mutual attraction between Anna and the housemother of C8 weighs heavily in favor of assignment to this cottage. The cottage organization of C8 was inferior to that of CA or of C5, but it might offer to Anna, in her desire for recognition and for independence, less resistance than the more highly organized and more rigidly disciplined C4, C5, or CA, in which the chief emotional positions within the group are crystallized.

Sociometric Testing   suggested   C8 or CA
Cottage Organization   suggested   C5, CA or C8
Parent Test   suggested   C8
Psychological Currents   suggested   CA or C8
Acquaintance Test   suggested   C8 or CA or C5
Assigned to C8

Development in C8.

The organization of C8 when Anna was assigned and its organization after a period of 18 months were as follows:

	C8 at the Outset	C8 18 Months Later
Population	33	32
Ratio of Interest (for own group)	34%	29%
Sum of Attractions (in per cent)	47.5%	55.5%
and of Repulsions (in per cent)	52.5%	44.5%
Index of Popularity	2.9%	1.7%
Structure:		
Isolated	13	5
Pairs	10	18
Mutual rejections	7	3
Incompatible pairs	9	3
Chains	1	1
Triangles	0	3
Squares	0	0
Circles	0	1
Stars	1	2

Position of Anna in C8 after three months:

Classification Formula 2A:

$$\begin{array}{c} \text{L} \\ \dfrac{3-0 \mid 2-0}{7-0 \mid 5-0} \end{array} \qquad \begin{array}{c} \text{W} \\ \dfrac{3-0 \mid 3-3}{2-2 \mid 4-2} \end{array}$$

Position of Anna in C8 after 12 months: Chooses in C8 five girls and two of the staff (her own housemother and assistant housemother), and is chosen by the latter as well as by 12 girls within her own cottage; is attracted to two girls and two housemothers of other groups and to two teachers; rejects one girl in another cottage; is the choice of three girls and six staff members of other groups. Her classification is therefore as follows:

Total Classification Formula 2A: $\dfrac{7-0 \mid 6-1}{14-0 \mid 9-0}$

We recognize that after an unfavorable start in C4, Anna's position in that group became more and more that of a radically unadjusted individual during a period of one year. The new individuals who had been assigned to that cottage during this period did not materially contribute to improve her position either directly or indirectly. Her choices for housemother and friends ran persistently to three other cottages (C8, C5, and C4) and the majority of her acquaintances consisted of girls belonging also to these groups. Her Total Classification Formula 2A given above expresses the degree of adjustment attained in the new group, C8, after one year. The process which happened in and around Anna can be described as a mental catharsis through assignment to a group.

Each case offers a different picture and may be in need of different assignment. For instance, in contrast to Anna, who was isolated and rejected in C4, Flora CM (in C2) formed a mutually attracted pair with another girl of the same cottage, but they were rejected and isolated as a pair. See sociograms presenting the atomic structure of Flora's position before and after assignment, pp. 314–5. Whereas Mary DA, another example, was a leader in her group, but the leader of a gang of seven who acted in concert to oppose the other members of the cottage and the housemother. See sociograms, pp. 314–5. Again, Betty PW, an Indian girl, presented simple isolation in the first group after a period of three months, and in the second group repeated the same picture after a period of eight months.

Technique of Reassignment in a Work Group, An Example.

Case of Stella DR and of Myrtle WL, both from a steam laundry group. The removal of Stella DR, who had become the leader of a gang among the workers in the steam laundry, and of her collaborator, Myrtle WL, from the laundry to another work group where a better adjustment for them was expected, and their replacement by two new girls (RS and CE), relieves the forewoman from emotional strain and the group from pressure. See Structure of Steam Laundry, pp. 132–3.

Accumulative Effect

The value of assignment can be estimated in its accumulative effect upon the community as a whole and upon the groups within it. The continuous assignment of new individuals to the different cottage groups produces changes in the social structure which can be traced later through the sociometric test. A single case of initial assignment already concerned numerous individuals. The report given above (p. 295) involved directly 20 individuals. Indirectly, however, more than 200 individuals were in some way involved when there is taken into consideration the social atoms, the volume of acquaintance, and the position in the networks of each of these 20 individuals.

Within a period of 18 months, 102 individuals, about one-fifth of the population, had been initially transferred to a cottage or assigned from one cottage to another. At the end of this period, the status of each cottage group had changed considerably compared with the status it had shown before our assignment techniques were employed.

TABLE 16

RANKING OF COTTAGES ACCORDING TO RATIO OF INTEREST

	Original Status	Status at the End of the 18 Months Period
C13.................	66%	48%
C10.................	65%	66%
C7..................	59%	62%
C4..................	58%	38%
C11.................	54%	71%
C6..................	50%	47%
C9..................	46%	62%
C14.................	46%	70%
C5..................	43%	53%
CB	37%	62%
CA	35%	70%
C2..................	34%	65%
C8..................	34%	29%
C3..................	31%	55%
C12.................	30%	45%
C1..................	29%	43%

| Average Ratio of Interest | 44.8% | Average Ratio of Interest | 55.4% |

TABLE 17

RANKING OF COTTAGES ACCORDING TO THE SUM OF ATTRACTIONS
AND REPULSIONS GIVEN IN PER CENT

Cottages	Original Status		Status at the End of the 18 Months Period	
	Attractions	Repulsions	Attractions	Repulsions
C11...........	85.5%	14.5%	84.0%	16.0%
C4............	77.0%	23.0%	70.0%	30.0%
C5............	77.5%	22.5%	77.0%	23.0%
C13...........	74.0%	26.0%	65.0%	35.0%
C9............	69.0%	31.0%	85.5%	14.5%
CA	69.5%	29.5%	75.5%	24.5%
C14...........	67.0%	43.0%	72.0%	23.0%
CB	65.5%	34.5%	69.0%	31.0%
C7............	65.5%	34.5%	67.0%	33.0%
C10...........	66.0%	34.0%	85.0%	15.0%
C6............	58.5%	41.5%	62.0%	38.0%
C12...........	58.5%	41.5%	65.0%	35.0%
C1............	58.0%	42.0%	59.5%	40.5%
C2............	52.0%	48.0%	48.5%	51.5%
C8............	47.5%	52.5%	55.5%	44.5%

TABLE 18

RANKING OF COTTAGES ACCORDING TO RATIO OF ATTRACTION

(An Index of Relative Popularity)

Cottages	Original Status Ratio of Attraction	Status at the End of the 18 Months Period Ratio of Attraction
CB	4.0%	1.5%
CA	3.8%	.8%
C5.................	3.3%	2.0%
C4.................	3.0%	3.0%
C2.................	3.0%	1.0%
C11................	3.0%	.4%
C12................	3.0%	2.4%
C8.................	2.9%	1.7%
C9.................	2.6%	1.0%
C14................	2.5%	.7%
C13................	2.5%	3.0%
C6.................	2.0%	2.3%
C1.................	1.7%	1.9%
C10................	1.6%	2.0%
C3.................	1.2%	1.0%
C7.................	0.9%	0.9%

Table 16 indicates that 12 cottages have increased and four have decreased their ratio of interest, and that the average ratio of interest has increased by 10.6%. Table 17 indicates that the sum of attractions expressed in percentage has increased in 10 cottages and has decreased in five cottages. Table 18 indicates that the index of popularity has increased for four cottages and decreased for ten.

The runaway status of a community like Hudson is an indicator to what extent the said community has become the psychological home for the members of its population. There is no other state institution known to us where the number of runaways is so low as the case in Hudson. However, a remarkable drop of runaway incidents has been noted during the last year.

The drop in the number of runaways can be appreciated fully when it is considered that *initial* assignments through sociometric techniques *began* February 22, 1933. After a period of four months an effect of assignment became evident within the community. The number of runaways gradually dropped and during the following nine months (July 1, 1933–March 1, 1934) the number of runaways was unprecedentedly low, a total of six, unusual as well for an outside population consisting of an equal number of adolescents. As no essential change in the set-up of the community had been made during this period, either in personnel or in the general character of the population received, the greater inclination of the girls to remain in Hudson can be ascribed to the procedure of assignment. A greater number had reached this minimum of adjustment, that they did not run away from it.

The problem of the runaway is closely related to the problem of migration, the psychological causes in the latter case, however, being more obscured. A sociometric study of the migrating groups would probably show the gradual isolation and rejection of such groups within the area and would indicate in what manner psychological currents develop and contribute to the readiness of such groups to resort to migration and to be swayed by economic motives.

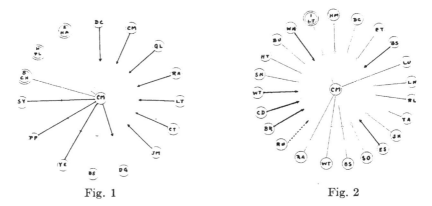

Fig. 1   Fig. 2

ASSIGNMENT THERAPY

Fig. 1. Indicates the position of Flora in her first assignment, C1. After a *two years stay* within it she had developed the position as charted. From her four choices three go outside the group and one inside to BS with whom she forms a pair. But BS herself is isolated. Flora CM is rejected by ten individuals of her group (PC, GM, GL, RA, LT, CT, JM, YE, PP, SY) and she rejects four (DG, YE, PP, SY). She rejects the housemother and is rejected by her (not plotted on this chart). Mutual rejections with three individuals or more have been in this case and in many instances a fruitful source for frictions. Isolated with BS in the cottage they had both planned to run away. Flora forms mutual attractions with individuals in different houses, HA in C4, PL in the hospital, and CH in C8. This indicates that although isolated and rejected in her present cottage she is able to produce attachment to other individuals in the community. As she is a typical Re-Assignment case, they may indicate where to find a better placement for her in the given community.

Fig. 2. Flora has been assigned from C1 to C4. The chart indicates the position which she has developed after a period of six months in C4. Of her five choices, four now go into the group, to LU, BS, WT and RA with whom she forms mutual attractions. One choice goes outside the group to LT in C1. She is attracted to the housemother who is attracted to her in return (not plotted). A study of the whole membership of group revealed that 15 of the 23 members were attracted to her and that 6 rejected her

313

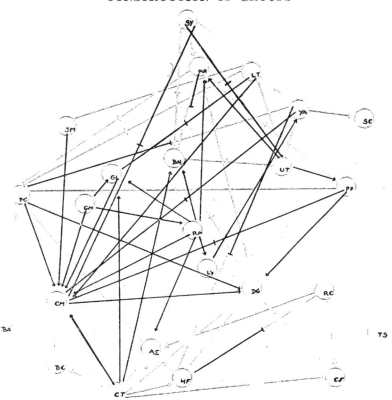

STRUCTURE OF THE COTTAGE FAMILY C1—BEFORE RE-CONSTRUCTION

Fig. 1. 24 girls. *Isolated*, 5; *Pairs*, 15; *Mutual Rejections*, 5; *Incompatible Pairs*, 3; *Chains*, 1; *Triangles*, 3; *Squares*, 1; *Circles*, 1; *Stars (of Attraction)*, 1; *Centers of Rejections*, 1; *Distribution*, 58% *Attractions*; 42% *Rejections*.

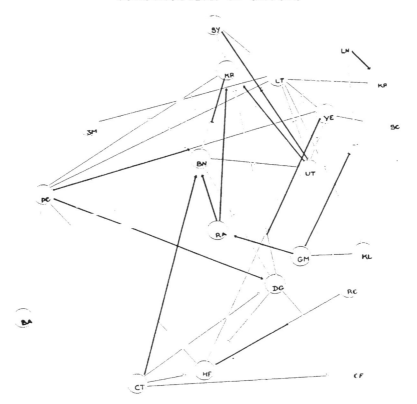

STRUCTURE OF THE COTTAGE FAMILY C1—AFTER RE-CONSTRUCTION

Fig. 2. 20 girls. C1 has been re-constructed through assigning to other groups the isolated and rejected pair, CM and BCS, the isolated, rejected and rejecting individuals, LY and GL, the isolated TS, and PP, whose position does not strengthen the group. AE was eliminated through being paroled. Compare with original structure of C1 presented in Fig. 1. One new individual has been added to the group, KR. Analysis of C1 after its re-construction: *Isolated*, 3, CT, RC, and RA; *Pairs*, 13; *Mutual Rejections*, 1; *Chains*, 1; *Triangles*, 1; VE-UT-LT; *Squares*, 0; *Circles*, 0; *Stars (of Attraction)* 1, LT. *Distribution, 74% Attractions; 26% Rejections.*

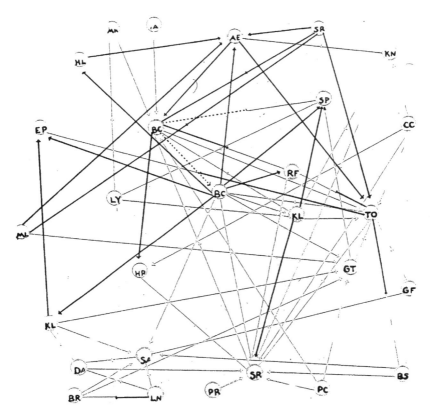

STRUCTURE OF A COTTAGE FAMILY—C14—BEFORE RE-CONSTRUCTION

30 girls. *Isolated,* 12; *Pairs,* 17; *Mutual Rejections,* 2; *Incompatible Pairs,* 7; *Chains,* 1; *Triangles,* 2; *Squares,* 0; *Circles,* 0; *Stars (of Attraction),* 5; *Centers of Rejections,* 1. *Distribution, 67% Attractions; 43% Rejections.*

Special feature, number of isolates.

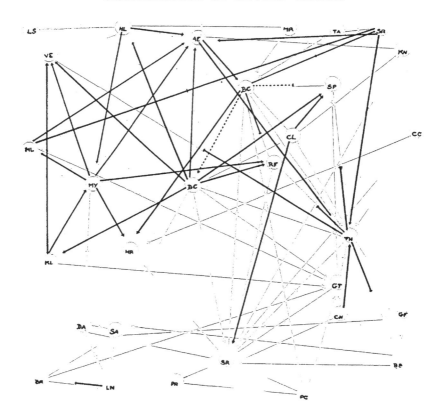

STRUCTURE OF COTTAGE FAMILY C14
AFTER NUMEROUS ASSIGNMENTS
Number of Isolates Reduced (3)

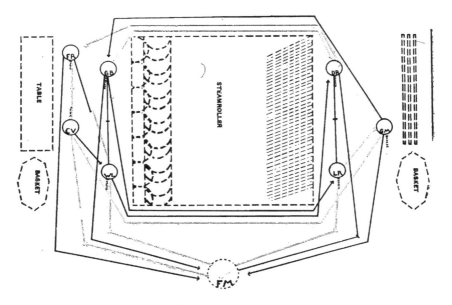

STEAM LAUNDRY
STRUCTURE BEFORE RE-CONSTRUCTION

Fig. 1. 7 workers and 1 forewoman. Stella DR and Philamina LR, the feeders, reject each other. Hilda GR and Myrtle WL, the catchers, reject each other. Myrtle rejects the feeder opposite her, Philamina. Lillian FR and Rosalie CV, the two folders, attract each other. Lillian and Rosalie reject Myrtle. Esther GM, the shaker, is attracted to Lillian and rejects Hilda. Esther, Stella, Hilda, and Rosalie reject the forewoman but only Stella is rejected by her. Philamina, Myrtle, and Lillian are attracted to the forewoman. The seven workers live in C10, but all of them are not plotted on the particular sociogram of C10, p. 125, because many of them came to the community at a later date.

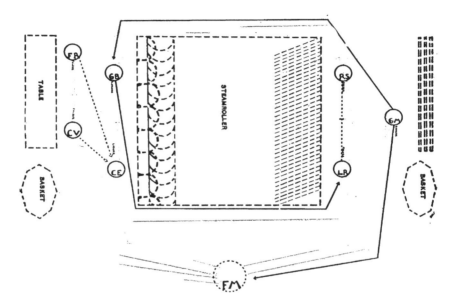

STRUCTURE OF A WORK GROUP—STEAM LAUNDRY—AFTER RE-CONSTRUCTION

Fig. 2. After assignment of DR and WL to another work group and their replacement by RS and CE the psychological structure of the group is here plotted. (Compare with Steam Laundry, Fig. 1.) The two feeders, RS (new member) and Philamina LR, attract each other. The two catchers, CE (new member) and Hilda GR, attract each other. The two folders, Lillian FR and Rosalie CV, attract each other. The two catchers are attracted to the two feeders opposite them. All the workers except Esther GM are attracted to the forewoman.

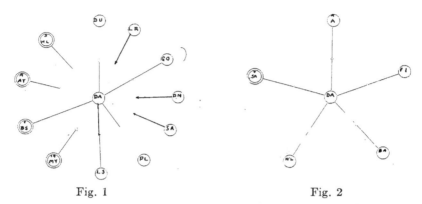

Fig. 1   Fig. 2

ASSIGNMENT THERAPY

Fig. 1. Indicates the position of Mary DA in her first assignment, C2, after a period of 14 months. From her four choices she sends three into her cottage; two remain unresponded to and one is responded to favorably by GO. She is rejected by three individuals, LR, DN, and SA, within her own group and she herself rejects one, LS, who is attracted to her. She forms a mutual attraction with BS in C1 and is chosen by HL in C3, AT in C4, and MY in C14. She rejects the housemother and is rejected by her in return (not plotted).

Fig. 2. Mary DA has been assigned from C2 to C5. The chart indicates the position which she has developed after a period of four months in C5. Four of her choices go inside her group and she forms mutual pairs with AI, FI, BA, and WL, the leader-individuals of the cottage. She is rejected by none. She is chosen by the housemother to whom she is attracted (not plotted).

These results suggest that distribution and redistribution of the population within the given community on the basis of sociometric classification are a valuable aid in the betterment of its general status. After practicing assignment therapy in many communities, our knowledge of technique will increase and perhaps we will begin to realize that no individual should be segregated from the community at large before an attempt is made to find a place for him within its fold, and that correctional institutions in the modern sense may disappear when legal and economic planning of society is supplemented by psychological planning.

We may take occasion here to discuss an argument which has often been made since these tests were inaugurated. It is, are not communities treated in this manner in danger of becoming too harmonious and too peaceful, and when these individuals return to the world at large are they not in danger to fail? These communities do not become more harmonious and peaceful because their heterogeneous elements are eliminated from them or because their contrasting elements are discouraged or replaced or because the aggressive elements are prohibited and suppressed. Just the opposite approach is true of our procedure. We bring to unfoldment and awareness all the spontaneous movements which are potential within the population and begin then, in coöperation with the whole populace, to reorganize and coördinate their currents. It is not a flat harmony but a harmony in which the harmonies and disharmonies are balanced within a larger scope. It may be said also that the danger of too happy homes and too happy communities is very small. Unmixed harmony and love are rarely evidenced. Just this study has certified the frightening truth that our social universe is overwhelmingly filled with aggressiveness, cruelties, and jealousies of all sorts, and that these are deeply imbedded not only within the individual, and this is the point, but within the complex structure of social interaction.

XVII. SPONTANEITY TRAINING

If we should have succeeded to adjust each individual to every possible group within the fold of the given institution, this would still not be a guarantee for an adjustment later in the community at large. The perplexing problem of a community like Hudson is the necessity to return its population after a period of training from a given environment to a more complex environment. Theoretically we may imagine a solution in the idea of conditioning the individual through throwing him successively into many environments to learn through trial and error. These environments, however, may not always be available, or, again, incorrigible habits may develop. Yet in want of a manifoldness of natural environments we can resort to the creating of *experimental* environments, and in want of a manifoldness of living rôles we can resort to fictitious rôles which are brought as close as possible to the living ones. To accomplish this aim we have developed techniques for training spontaneity.

The problem can be looked at also from another angle: the more similar the set-up of a closed community to that of the community outside the more it will be a reality test. Therefore the better defined the social reality, the better we will be able to define the techniques necessary to attain in Hudson potential preparation for it. But the difficulty starts right here. We have no means whereby to define with any amount of precision this reality to which the individuals return. We have been able through the sociometric test to obtain a good idea of the psychological reality, Hudson. For us who have made this sociometric study, Hudson is the known, the world the unknown. We have gained a criterion for measuring the success in adjustment of an individual here, but we have no criterion as yet to predict whether an adjustment to the community at large will or will not be successful,—more especially since the set-up of Hudson, in which the social and work situations into which the individuals may enter are limited in number and readily definable, is so relatively simple compared to that of the community at large. If the world were of such a permanent structure as we imagine society was in the Middle Ages, then we could preview the social and vocational situations, their number and character, for which the individuals have to be trained. But today these situations differ from country to country, often from state to state, and undergo transformation within a few years even within the same town. It is a reality which does not stay put, a changing reality. The technological process destroys well accredited vocations with new invention and develops new ones. While inconformity with the law is technically sufficient to define an act as antisocial, this is no criterion to decide whether or not an individual has attained successful adjustment to the persons in his community.

The trend towards greater complexity and differentiation reflects not only upon the social and vocational situations but also upon the instinctual drives of man, particularly upon the sexual and parental impulses. And it is for failure to command these impulses to the advantage of the individual and the kind that the majority of the population of women's institutions are committed. The fact that they are sent to institutions is irrelevant. The problem would be the same in any case. Irrespective whether or not they have transgressed the law, these girls and many others who remain unapprehended have in common that they develop a comparatively larger emotional expansiveness in respect to sex than in respect to other criteria without, at the same time, being able to direct their emotions. As the difficulties arise in respect to the other sex, the problem is one of emotional learning how to behave towards the other sex. But it is for just this problem in adjustment that no therapeutic approach exists either in our institutions or other schools.

Two conclusions can be made, however, concerning the psychological reality of the community outside and the equipment required for an individual who meets these demands adequately. The first conclusion is a negative one. The lack of fixed vocations and their transitory character, the impermanency of the social situations, and the constant uprising of new varieties make it unwise to take these as a criterion around which to construct a program of training. The second conclusion is based upon sociometric studies as far as they have been made up to date in the community at large. Social groups have a definite organization in respect to the age levels of their members and in respect to the criterion of the particular collective in which they participate; the position of an individual in a group which has one kind of organization is a means by which to prognosticate the position he will attain in groups of a like or closely similar organization.

But successful adjustment to a plurality of environments requires a flexible spontaneous personality make-up. The question, however, arises how can such a personality make-up be obtained and what attributes does this personality have. The objectives of our systems of education in the past have been to train man for a series of rigid social situations and for a series of rigid vocations. The roads through which the individual had to travel were given. Development or perfection could be obtained only within these dogmatic and clear-cut boundaries. Outside of these were chaos and disintegration. But within the last century a change has taken place. This change did not move from the old dogmatic situation to a new dogmatic situation, but to one of flux and uncertainty. The argument has been raised that the cause of this development is the industrial revolution and that the remedy lies in halting the progress of the machine, or, again, that the cause lies in a perversion of man's instincts and the remedy in a return to a more primitive civilization. But another point of view can be taken: that man is resourceful enough to become more highly differentiated and more flexible in accord with a more highly differentiated and more flexible form of society which, as it appears, is in the becoming.

We had observed in the case of Elsa TL that the spontaneity testing was accompanied by a by-product: the attitude of many members of her group towards her underwent a modification although no other effort had been made except the placing of the members into experimental situations to act with her. As it appeared, during these acts Elsa was stimulated to uncover aspects of her personality which she had not had an opportunity to reveal in the disciplined course of cottage life, and likewise the other members of the acting group had an opportunity to uncover towards Elsa aspects of their personalities which had remained hidden or little displayed. The suggestion arose out of these observations to supplement the routine group life through activities in experimental play situations, giving the members of the group a chance to act in a variety of functions and rôles and enabling them to release and shape their interests. The possibility was given through this medium to make each member of the group, the inter-relations among the members, and the group as a whole more flexible. The conflicts of the actual family constellation and of love and business relations, etc., were lacking in this community. We introduced just such situations as might arise in such relations in order that conduct in these situations might be improved through incorporating functions relating to them into plays. In this manner we had a means provided to offset and fulfill the lacks intrinsic to a closed community.

The individuals chose the situation and the rôles which they wanted to act and the partners whom they wanted to act opposite in a certain rôle, or they exchanged the rôles they had in life, or they were placed in selected situations. As the acting was pure improvisation, the performance was a yardstick of how they might perform in life situations. But whereas conduct in a life situation is irrevocable, here every phase of performance is open to correction through criticism made by the other participants, the instructor, and the subject himself, and a technique how to differentiate attitudes which may have been at the start insufficient can be learned by the individual. We found it advisable to construct the situations as close as possible to the position the individual expects to assume in the community outside. For instance, if the individual receives training in a specific vocation, she is placed in a variety of situations which might arise in this vocation.

Social life has the tendency to attach a definite rôle to a specific person so that this rôle becomes the prevailing one into which the individual is folded. Anxiety, fear, resentment, or feelings of difference and distinction are often increased by this condition and the accruing strains and tensions reflect into the group life. They, however, can be reduced through the release and training provided by skillful guidance of the individuals in the performance of play situations.

Many things which one girl would not tell to another or to the housemother in life she may act out in a play, and the humor of it may prevent and heal many potential grievances which might otherwise have led to actual conflict. And there is another aspect which is the more important the more rigidly differentiated social life is. Everybody is expected to live up to his official rôle in life,—a teacher is to act as a teacher, a pupil as a pupil, and so forth.' But the individual craves to embody far more rôles than those he is allowed to act out in life, and even within the same rôle one or more varieties of it. Every individual is filled with different rôles which he wants to become active in and that are present in him in different stages of development. And it is from the active pressure which these multiple individual units exert upon the manifest official rôle that a feeling of anxiety is often produced.

The method has numerous advantages compared with training in adjustment through actual life experiences, particularly for the individual in the formative age. First, in actual life situations an individual often has difficulty in learning from a mistake due to the earnestness of the situation. In his anxiety he may repeat such error when a similar occasion occurs, thus retarding his learning to overcome the error. Second, for many individuals actual life situations encourage an emotional inertia if the performance is successful in a given rôle, and more is not demanded. Third, in actual life situations, even if these develop an individual for fitting perfectly into a certain rôle, they make him single-tracked and exclude from his horizon other varieties of situations and vocations. As a *developmental* technique Spontaneity Training is thus superior to life training. Through training of individuals for conduct in possibly arising situations, in a variety of rôles and functions they may have to assume towards a variety of persons in the possible rôles they may assume, the subject learns to meet life situations more adequately. The training makes him more resourceful and versatile and the possibility can be envisioned to direct man's evolution with the aid of Stegreif techniques into avenues which enlarge and differentiate the spontaneous base of his heritage, his spontaneability. Thus the problem of learning becomes not to induce and conserve habits but to train spontaneity, to train and develop man to the habit of spontaneity.

A series of life situations calling for the embodiment of specific attitudes are constructed. This series is not arbitrary but organized upon the basis of the findings of the sociometric and Spontaneity Tests in relation to the specific individual under training. Each of the situation-patterns is constructed through several phases ranging from the simplest possible form of a given situation-pattern through the more complex forms to the most highly differentiated, all carefully graduated according to the requirements of the subject. Hence the subject is trained through acting in the simplest of rôles in any specific situation-pattern through several degrees of differentiation of the same situation-pattern until he can command the pattern adequately. As in life the individual must perform in many situation-patterns, Spontaneity Training must also include not only many varieties of any single situation-pattern but many different situation-patterns.

An example of how such training is graduated to develop and sustain a specific attitude in a given rôle in several varieties of the same situation-pattern is as follows: For instance, in the first stage the subject produces the attitude of sympathy towards another individual. In the second stage he has to produce the same attitude in a rôle in which he has to command a certain function, for instance, the rôle of a salesperson in a dress shop and in relation to certain things, dresses. In the next stage, the subject has to produce the same attitude in the same rôle as above but in a situation selected by the instructor, as selling dresses to a business-like and ready customer. In a later stage, the task is further differentiated. The subject produces the same attitude and in the same rôle but the instructor selects a customer who is to act resentful and argumentative. The task of the subject is to sustain the cheerful, sympathetic attitude in the face of such resistance. The differentiation of this pattern can be further elaborated in accord with the ability and progress of the subject.

In some phases of the training in which the situation, his own rôle and the partners are selected by the subject, the position of the instructor is that of a critical observer. But in the process of graduated training the part of the instructor becomes more active. One of the most important problems is then *how to get the subject started*. The instructor may have arrived at certain conclusions in respect to what kind of attitudes the subject is deficient in and what kind of persons he needs to adjust to. He constructs situations in which the subject is to act in a certain rôle opposite one or more other persons. In the instructor's mind the pattern of this situation, the details of arrangement, and particularly the rôle the subject should act, gain a definite, clear form. The instructor is thus himself warmed up to the state and rôle he realizes needs to be embodied by the subject. In this condition the instructor discloses to the subject the rôle to be acted by him. This procedure wherein the instructor transfers to the subject the rôle and the possible form it may take is called the *Act of Transference*. Upon the impression the act makes upon the subject and upon the clarity of the thought which formulated the rôle the value of the training in part depends. The Act of Transference itself has only the significance of providing a " starter." The rest of the procedure remains the free expression of the subject.

Another important phase of the training is an analysis of the acting *immediately* following. Such an analysis may reveal that an act was successfully embodied but too hastily, perhaps because the subject was too anxious to succeed, warming up too early, jerking while in the state, and jumping into higher levels. Such an Impromptu state can be called " overheated." Or it may reveal the inability of the subject to produce a state demanded of him. Such a state can be called " rudimentary." Or it may reveal the inability of the subject to stop, to *finish* the act, that is, to finish in accord with the demands of the situation. Or it may reveal the anxiety of the subject to be in the lead all the time, unwilling or unable to collaborate with a partner in a given situation-pattern. Or, again, it may reveal the inability of the subject to coördinate his bodily movements of arms, legs, etc., to his verbal expressions and to the bodily and verbal expressions of his partners. Or it may reveal the lack of factual information in respect to the matters which are brought to expression in the situations acted. These and other analytic findings may have a bearing upon the next situation and rôle to be selected for the subject, and are also an indication of the progress he has made in the training.

As the training of impromptu states and not the learning of

contents is the objective, the attempt is made to loosen the fixed associations between states and contents as they have become established in the course of education by traditional methods. Emphasis upon contents results in the split of the individual into an *act* personality and a *content* personality. We found it a valuable hypothesis to assume that two different memory centers develop, an *act center* and a *content center,* and continue as, in general, separate structures without connection. A content is not received at the same moment when an act arises, but the former in a dull, untoned state and the latter in a highly heated state; they trace in the nervous system different paths. In consequence they do not recur simultaneously, filling one moment, uniting the whole personality with one action, but at different times, separated from each other. The material learned does not reach the act-center of personality. A shut-in memory develops and prevents the integration of the factual knowledge into the active personality of the individual. The knowledge remains undigested, unabsorbed by the personality, and hinders its full influence upon his activity and judgment. But in actual life situations the supreme desideratum is exactly this facility of integration.

But there is another problem in the course of mental growth which has to be considered. An individual may begin any specific activity with improvisation. But the more often improvisations around that complex are produced, the more the tendency develops in the individual to pick out from past efforts the best thoughts, phrases, etc., in other words, to improvise less and less and to develop more and more a content until this individual is able to forsake improvisation entirely in respect to this specific complex and to rely upon the censured and recensured product of his improvisations, that is, upon a " content." Spontaneous expression was only a starting form of the process which in the end resulted in a product, a content which became *sacred* through repetition. The effort at spontaneity is now unnecessary; it dies out. Therefore if we want to develop and sustain a spontaneous and flexible personality make-up, a technique of Spontaneity Training as described has to come to the rescue to offset the resignation and inertia of the individual.

It has been observed that when soldiers return from a war in a foreign land they can be divided into two groups: in one group are the men who have gone far towards mastering the foreign language and in the other are the men who have remained almost in entire ignorance of it. One can always make the observation that this fact has little to do with the intelligence of the men. While often a man of superior intelligence returns ignorant of the language a less intelligent man may have attained a remarkable command of it. The freshness and originality of his speech is frequently surprising. Inquiry has often revealed that these men have gone through some intensive emotional experience, for instance, falling in love. It is, of course, not the emotional experience itself but certain processes accompanying it which largely account for the greater facility of this group over the former in acquiring the language.

It would be in point to study the learned contents of several minds with a view to ascertaining characteristics of conditions which have controlled specific learnings. Every one of us realizes the relative availability of various factors of his knowledge. But the question arises why is certain knowledge always at hand and other knowledge which we have struggled to win always slipping away when most needed? Among other factors, learning is affected also by the rising and falling of the spontaneous states in the learner.

We may refer again to our illustration of the learning of a foreign language in the case of the soldier. Some men, more or less ignorant of the new language, may have tried to learn it in the popularly accepted way, that is, by memorizing words and phrases and picking up characteristic idioms of speech occasionally. In other words, their learning took place when they were in low, untoned states. But when they were in a highly heated state and had to deliver the words, their memories did not function adequately to the sudden need of the moment. It can be assumed that experiences connected with impulses which tend to produce toned and heated states themselves establish special associations. We have found that contents which enter the mind connected with highly heated states may recur more easily with the recurrence of similar states than with untoned ones.   On the other hand, contents which enter the mind associated with untoned, unemotional states tend to recur with these and not with highly heated states.   We have to assume also that between these states close associations exist.   The man who failed to acquire the foreign language well was at the time in the behavior of learning when he tried to memorize the phrases, but he had to deliver them in the behavior of acting.   He had not the emotional experiences of the man who learned to use it more effectively.   The latter's conversation was keyed to an emotional pitch.   Love relations are as a matter of course accompanied by intensively heated states.   Every word and phrase exchanged in these states remain associated with them.   The contents entered the mind when the subject was in the behavior of acting.   Later, when he was anxious to use them in emotional situations again, they recurred, spontaneously connected with the present act.   Since he began by receiving contents in a spontaneous activity, he could finish by delivering them as a spontaneous expression.   This way of learning not only increased his knowledge but shaped and gave more unity to his personality, his learning became not apart from but essentially connected with his acts.

PART V:
SOCIOMETRIC PLANNING
OF SOCIETY

The motive which led to the first study presented in this book was constructive: to organize groups of children in a public school to the greatest advantage of the individual members and of the groups as wholes. This had logically to be preceded by a study and recognition of the evolution and organization of their groups. The motive which led to the second study presented was constructive also: to organize home and work groups in a closed community to the greatest advantage of the individual members and of the groups as wholes. This had logically to be preceded by a study and recognition of the organization of the given community, breaking it up into its parts. After psychological analysis and reconstruction of an existing community had been attempted the psychological planning and organization of a new community came within methodological possibility.

It was a propitious coincidence that the government of the United States initiated as a part of the program of National Recovery the creation of new small communities to be established in various parts of the country, the so-called "homestead" projects. Each project provided an agricultural set-up and a small community factory. The population was drawn from urban or rural problem areas,—in other words, it was a form of voluntary mass assignment. What complicated the problem was that the total population had to move in practically at once, not gradually as a natural settlement would develop, and that the intention was to *select* the population, not to populate the new communities hit-or-miss. When we were consulted on the question of principles applied to this problem, we realized that sociometry may be able to assist such an undertaking with working methods, not with solutions.

We weighed the obvious differences and similarities between a closed community as Hudson and an open community. The inhabitants of a closed community cannot leave it freely, out-

siders cannot come freely and take up residence, the natural
family unit is missing, the conflicts coming from economic
situations and conflicts coming from situations between the
two sexes are non-existent. The inhabitants of an open community must permit in principle of the coming and going of
anyone, the factors of the two sexes and family life as well as
economic competition come into display, psychological currents bind them to the surrounding communities. In consequence classification of its individuals and groups is beyond
the range we have studied in the closed community.

It is of significance also to weigh the similarities and differences of the new community projects with the early American
frontier settlements. The early American frontier was a
spontaneous movement of people. The availability of vast
unsettled territory was the condition which made this spread
of settling possible. The movement of population was comparatively unrestrained except for the barriers of nature. But
since the frontier days a society has grown up with the most
exacting social, industrial, and cultural patterns. The back-
to-the-land movement today is restrained by this social structure and the established rights of the people. In this instance, at least, the process of migration is in need of planning.

But we need to examine first the course which natural evolution takes before we consider any technique of planning. We
have to settle the question whether the process of natural
evolution is still not the best course in itself, for if this remains
the case planning is not only vain and unnecessary but possibly harmful. Furthermore, any motive for planning has to
be clearly established before a natural outgrowth of planning
can follow justifiably.[26] We may look in succession into developmental aspects of our society—social, industrial, cultural,
and governmental.

In the pioneer days of community formation, as in the days
of the American frontier, there is either rough equality or the
inequalities which develop as natural expressions of individual
differences—physical and mental. In the natural course of
social evolution, social institutions are created which enable
the pioneer not to continue in pioneering but to secure the
wealth and property amassed. In the succeeding generations

new inequalities develop within the population which cease to be a natural expression of the organic individual differences, physical or mental, and the superior individual may find himself, due to circumstances which are beyond his control, in a social situation which is in total discord with his capabilities. On the other hand, individuals who may be average or inferior may find themselves in social situations which provide them with authority and power. Class distinctions develop which are eventually the reverse of the more natural distinctions of the pioneer phase. In the sociometric sense the described situation reflects the developmental level a society in evolution has reached if it is allowed to follow its course blindly.

A critical point is found again in industrial evolution. Mechanical invention and the development of the machine which appeared at first to be for the good of society gradually developed new difficulties. The execution of machine work became necessary without regard to the adjustment of man to it. A split between the industrial and psychological development of man grew out of the situation man-machine,—in contrast to the relative unity of man's relation to his occupations in the handicraft era. This unity was due to the interlocking of his instinctive work abilities and his occupations, a condition which was favorable to his development as a creative organism. But if we should be able to bring these instinctive work abilities into accord with machine work, the interrelation man-machine, which at present is a source of potential conflict and disintegration, may be readjusted. The Spontaneity Test is a working method accomplishing this end. Aside from detecting the various work abilities, it provides a course of training to foster the individual's adjustment to a new industrial situation and opens up the possibility that man will be stimulated to develop as a creative organism with a wider range of flexibility. The drawback which the machine brought about may become, as in former crises surmounted by man, but another obstacle to be overcome and an aid to his progress as a race.

The critical point of natural growth up to a crisis appears also in cultural evolution. At the beginning of national cultures, the cultural forms, dance, music, drama, religion, custom, are improvised, created in the moment, but as the moments of inspiration pass man becomes more fascinated by the contents which have remained from the by-gone created acts, by their careful conservation and estimation of their value, than to keep on and to continue creating. It seemed to man a higher stage of culture to forsake the moment, its uncertainty and helplessness, and to struggle for contents, to select and idolize them, thus laying ground for our type of civilization, the civilization of the *conserve*. An example is the *extempore* Dionysian plays of the old Greeks. It ended in the written drama; this was its natural fate. The process beginning with inspired Dionysian acts, ended in a sacred content. This was not accidental. It was an intentional evolution. As soon as its goal, an organized expression, the drama of Aeschylus, Sophocles, Euripides, was gained, the creative process was conserved forever, and so then the unnecessary attempt at spontaneity could die out. It seems we experience today a similar case in Russia. Since the revolution Russian workers have enjoyed acting the revolution *extempore*. Their goal, however, is not the moment and with it in consequence the flexible spontaneous personality, but the mass man, the functional man, the man who can be *exchanged,* and with it the repetition of a sacred political rite, a conserve, the revolution.

The vicious cycle between the creative act and the conserve in which the creative instinct of man is caught was brought to test in our experiments of play improvisation. We studied groups from day to day and found that if the players were left to themselves, although they might have the intention to improvise each time again, repartees which had been most brilliant and gestures which had been most effective were repeated, and after a few months of work, if every phase of the process had been recorded, they ended in stereotypes. It was this phenomenon which led us to invent techniques to protect the individual against the enfeebling of his instinctive spontaneity, Spontaneity Training.

The critical point is found again in the forms taken by government. An illustration is self-government if it were literally executed. In its ideal form it is meant to allow every individual to have an equal share in the government. In its realization it produces the opposite effect. Only a minority of the population have a chance of self-expression. A minority not necessarily superior to the rest secures power, assuming authority also to know in what the happiness and welfare of the majority consists. In the sociometric test studies we found that the leaders in the community were not necessarily the ones who received most of the choices, that the key positions are often held by individuals whose quantitative influence is small. We came to realize that when the forces within the population are let loose, sociodynamic mechanisms hinder the majority of the individuals from actually fulfilling their strivings. We found that the spontaneous choice factor may come into collision with the spontaneous choice factor of many other individuals and that this possibility of collision is the greater the more unrestrained the individuals are allowed to become in their expression. The study of networks disclosed that every individual is almost fully unaware of his position within the community. It may be that no intelligence is supreme enough to be aware all the time of all the psychological currents by which he is affected.

An emotional continuum of relations lies below all the patterns of community life, families, clubs, labor, political, or religious units. This is the true vehicle of power. Yet at no time in history has an attempt been made to base the government upon this continuum itself instead of upon its upper structures. There is no doubt that in certain critical moments in the history of man, however, these parts of our social structure rose up and flooded the barriers. Indeed, if we study the principles from which our forms of government and public representation emerge we see that they are often constructed in utter disregard or ignorance of this underlying continuum of human relations. We stave it off and accept and use techniques unrelated to the basic forces, artificial substitutes for the factors which are actually creating the world. Through socionomic government the true and factual organization of a community would be brought to expression and the expression would change on the surface only if it changes also beneath. And if there is an hierarchy inherent in its make-up, the true hierarchy would come to lead the rest in accord with sociometric findings.

XIX. POPULATION TEST

The first phase in the sociometric planning of a community is the classification of its population. It may aid in selecting individuals and groups most easily adjustable to each other, best fitted for the occupations made available within the environment of the new community and most easily adjustable to the populations in the adjacent towns or areas.

In the pursuit of this problem we began to inquire into what evidence had been ascertained from study of the population at large and how such information could relate to it. The current sociological studies were unable to give us an insight into the psychological structure of large populations—neither through data nor through a methodological approach. In the studies of interracial attitudes towards negroes, Chinese, Germans, Jews, Italians, etc., the differential attitude of the subjects towards each individual negro, Chinese, Jew, German, Italian, etc., is not considered. In the study of group behavior the collective as a whole is considered, the individual being neglected; in consequence the structural characteristics described do not reach beyond outer appearances. The classifications arising were an intermingling of facts with symbols; either the individual was made a symbol, that is to say, *left out,* the ratios being calculated for classes of people, or the group was made a symbol, *left out,* the classification being made of individuals. Studies in respect to the marriage rate, the delinquency rate for different areas of the country, the suicide rate, quantitative analysis of public opinion, reading habits of different communities, business cycles and other cyclical phenomena, etc., however significant they may be as such, do not carry any weight if it comes to the concrete questions what position the individual X has in Kansas City, what position the family unit B has in Forest Hills, or a certain group of negroes, in Miami, Florida.

But the sociometric test—as we have learned in other parts of this book—is able to provide a basic element in classification which no other methodology has worked out. It appeared able to uncover the position of each concrete individual and each concrete group in the given sample of population on one hand and, through the accumulative effect, through inter-individual and inter-group reactions, the trends in the population on the other hand, with the added advantage that the trends were not presented like the frequency curve of a histogram but were further broken up into a configuration of individual detail (see p. 242). Similarly, the sociometric test can be of aid in the classification of the population for a prospective community. The number of criteria ought to be enlarged to include more than the three criteria, living, working, and studying in proximity; it ought to include as many criteria as appear to operate in the groups of an average community in a problem area. The more criteria the test is executed in respect to, the more accurate will become the classification picture. However, experience may suggest that the testing in respect to living and working in proximity is sufficient for practical purposes. It is our experience that it is easy to gain the coöperation of the people tested as soon as they come to think of the test as an instrument to bring their wills to a wider realization, that it is not only an instrument for exploring the status of a population but primarily an instrument to bring the population to a *collective self-expression* in respect to the fundamental activities in which it is or is about to be involved.

It is obvious that whether an economic or other kind of distress suggests the shifting of a part of the population, *mechanical* assignment may carry with it the germ of disrupting tendencies into the new area affecting its population and the newcomers. The selection of the new area and the selection of the population cannot be made on the basis of either physical and economic evidence or ordinary social investigation only. A *Population Test* needs to be given which will at the same time aid in recommending through its evidence the most desirable composition of area, geographical and ethnical, and the kind of persons best fitted to live within it.

But another factor is involved in the classification. Each new community, in whatever part of the country it may be established, will be exposed in the course of its development not only to the forces within it but to the population pressure coming from outside and expressed in the rising and falling of psychological currents. Thus before we occupy our minds with a technique of procedure adapted to a particular community it is necessary to gain an insight into the distribution and character of the population in the immediate neighborhood and the character of the main psychological currents which cross the population at large. This may be accomplished through giving of the sociometric test to a score or more typical communities in crucial sections of the country. In the course of the analysis of numerous new communities the sociometric evidence needed may become available.

XX. SPONTANEOUS AND GUIDED MIGRATION

One of the most significant features the analysis of this evidence should clarify is the psychological aspect of inter-state migration. The recent closure of the borders to immi-gration eliminated one difficulty in the way of classification, the continuous flux in the ethnical composition of the Amer-ican nation. It gives the peoples who are already living within this geographical area a more constant character, end-ing perhaps the first period in the evolution of the American nation, the phase of expansion and development and begin-ning a new period, the phase of organization and concentration.

But there is another aspect of impermanency: the spon-taneous migration of people throughout the territory of the United States from the country to the city, from one state to the other, from East to West, from the South to the North. A few figures [26] in this respect are significant. In 1920, 19.2% of the native-born population were living in states other than those in which they were born. Before 1910 the migration of the native population was largely westward. But from 1910 to 1920 this movement stopped, and instead an increased migration developed of whites from the northern states to Florida, Texas, and California. And this north to south movement was balanced by the northward negro migration. Whereas some large parts of the population are at one time in movement, other parts are stationary. The most stationary part lives in the south Atlantic and southeast central states, showing over 90% of the population born in the state of residence. On the other hand, in Oklahoma, Colorado, and Montana more than 50% of the population was born outside of the state. What is of interest to us is the psychological currents behind these facts, instigating these movements of population. Sociometric evidence may disclose the attractions and repulsions between individuals and between groups and the motives behind these attractions and repulsions. It may indicate that the desire for migration is many times larger than the migration which becomes manifest and towards which parts of the country these potential migrations tend, that only the recognition of the restlessness prevailing in the depths of the population opens the way to a full understanding of migratory movements, and that the economic situation is often only the precipitating factor. (See Psychological Geography of a Community, p. 242. The actual number of inter-cottage assignments made in Hudson, compared with the number who desired to move from one group to another, is exceedingly small. The unsatisfied feelings and tendencies of the individuals desiring such assignment produce powerful currents which express this far better than the actual figures of reassignment.) Whether these migrations are always desirable for the persons themselves, for the places which they forsake, for the places to which they move, and finally for the national organization as a whole, is a large question.

When these migrations occurred in the pioneer stage of the country there was plenty of free land and no crystallized social or economic structure to restrain, divert, or prohibit these movements and the spontaneous instinct of the migrating population was a rough but in general reliable guide for the advancement of the projects they had in mind. However, today the dependence of the individual upon the social and economic structure is far greater than his dependence upon nature, and the problem of migration is far more complex. The administration of the sociometric test to populations in problem areas, thus revealing the spontaneous trends and potential movements, may lay the ground for a procedure of *guided* migration. Such a procedure could not only unburden urban centers of a surplus of industrial population but also relieve areas from the accumulative effect of emotional tensions.

Another factor which has a bearing upon the depopulation of one part of the community and the repopulation of another part is the social shock which the establishment of a new community produces upon the surrounding populations, especially if the population coming into the new community is from a different part of the country and is of a relatively contrasting ethnical composition. The psychological motivation of this shock can be given through a description how out of a social pattern as simple as the family large and unified groups develop.

Through the study of historical lineage the common ancestors of two or more individuals can be determined. Down to a certain historical point it is demonstrated that they belong to the same family tree. This does not imply that they are of the same blood in a racial sense but relatives in a family sense. It is the family idea seen not only in its present but in its retrospective composition. In a certain geographical area a great number of these family trees will be more or less interlocked. But these family trees may continuously break up and new ones may start greatly affected by population movements as immigration and emigration. As individuals who are members of the same family live in the same house, individuals who are of the same family tree have often the tendency to stay in the neighborhood of each other or to live in proximity. This living in proximity in groups has, as we have described, numerous effects. First, it ties up these groups to the same geographical area, and the more this proximity expands from the family and social collectives into the agricultural, industrial, and cultural collectives the greater is the probability that *protective* currents will develop among all these groups which live together in the same area, just as they are expressed within one family or within one family tree. These protective currents may bind these individuals together even after they have moved away from the area. There is developed a *social* unity. Hence, whenever new groups immigrate into this area the degree of proximity necessary for them to become integral parts of the already existing organization cannot be defined by deduction.

We could divide the members of a cottage in Hudson into two groups: those who stay put and those who want to change their cottage for another. The proportion between these two groups decided whether or not a cottage group had an introverted or an extroverted organization. We saw then that groups with an introverted organization disclosed a stronger craving for difference and distinction than those with an extroverted organization, and that this feeling of difference and distinction could easily turn into a current of aggression against intruders from neighboring groups who wanted to join them. Although the motivations for it are largely subjective, this feeling of distinction appeared to further social differentiation within the community and finally to implant this feeling of difference and distinction within one community towards another. An intimate study of the population structure in a local geographical area will probably demonstrate that the consanguine groups, the family trees, are the strongest centers of introverted organization and that the craving for difference and distinction is strongest tied up to them. In just this sense national groups are psychogeographical units, and what we call a " nation " is a closed psychogeographical organization.

XXI. MANAGEMENT OF PSYCHOLOGICAL CURRENTS

The procedure of guided migration will be the more accurate the more complex our knowledge is of the development of psychological currents. We have learned that psychological currents are in general not produced at will but that certain conditions within a population predispose to their development. Specific groups racially can become saturated in the attempt to adjust incoming elements which are racially or in other ways contrasting. Up to the saturation point a wave of sympathy may prevail. As soon as this point is surpassed, states of anxiety, fear, jealousy, anger, or whatever, rise up in individuals and in groups, building up gradually the predisposing constellation for aggressive currents.

1. AFFINITIES AND DISAFFINITIES BETWEEN GERMANS AND JEWS

But it is not quite so simple a matter in dealing with the development of, for instance, racial currents, as to say: here we have a homogeneous population, for instance, of 60,000,000 Germans with certain cultural and social constellations, and there we have a contrasting population, for instance, of 600,000 Jews with certain cultural and social constellations; let us determine within this mixed racial group the point of saturation of the nationality group which is in the majority for the minority group and organize the population within the critical geographical area accordingly. The problem is far more complex. We have to consider the numerous factors which affect group organization as they have been brought forth in this volume if we want to get even a dim understanding of how racial conflicts arise. There is, for instance, the emotional expansiveness of the individual Jew and of the individual German and whether the emotional expansiveness of the individual Jew exceeds on the average that of the German. If this is the case, then we have to consider the rise in acquaintance volume with the rise in emotional expansiveness. Then the factor of sexual proximity gains in significance far beyond the factor of the numerical proportions of the German and the Jewish populations. It is said that the Jews comprise 1% of the German population, but it would be significant to know how many German women have been attracted to Jewish men, and *vice versa* how many Jewish women have been attracted to German men than would be proportionate to their numbers within the population as a whole. Evidently the amount of sexual attraction members of a minority group, the Jews, exert upon members of the opposite sex in the majority group, the Germans, and *vice versa*, has a definite bearing upon the point of saturation of the nationality group which is in the majority for the minority group. Such disproportions are able to give rise to psychological currents due to jealousy or other emotions expressing displeasure. Another factor is the social positions held by the members of the minority group. The Jews in Germany held more positions in the professions and arts and industry than would have been proportionate to their numbers. This added to their possible influence upon German women. Had the 600,000 Jews been farmers and manual workers, the reach of their acquaintance volume and consequent influence would have been drastically less, as the life of the farmer and the manual worker is socially limited in scope compared with that of the tradesman or person of the professions. We have seen in our sociograms that a boy receiving attraction from a girl who is wanted by a great number of other boys is bound to be the center of jealousies and distrust, whereas the boy who receives attention from a girl who is isolated passes unnoticed. The attention a man of the Jewish minority received from a German woman who is the center of admiration of numerous German men may produce within the psychological networks a " tele " effect, that is, an effect far beyond the two persons and the immediate group of persons involved in the matter. The frictions increase if the individuals rejected or overlooked belong to the " top " of the group. If the German woman sought after by a Jewish man belongs to a higher social or intellectual class, jealousies and distrust aroused may come largely from Germans who belong also to the crucial top groups within the population. If the sexual attraction members of the minority group exert upon the majority group is great, even a comparatively small percentage of the majority group who are non-participants, males and females, may develop powerful psychological countercurrents which consequently will reduce the point of saturation for the minority nationality group considerably below what it would be otherwise. It is therefore not sufficient to say that there is a sexual conflict naturally arising between two distinct nationality groups. But it is necessary to weigh the significance and force of the conflict, all the ramifications which are entailed in the intersexual choice have to be studied in detail through psychogeographical charting. Another element prominent in our inter-racial charts is the factor of leadership. Applied to the German-Jewish conflict, the question is whether the Jewish population in Germany produced more leader individuals than their numeric proportion, either because the Jews suffer from a surplus of leader individuals or because the Germans suffer from such an insufficiency. The surplus of leader individuals among the Jews may, however, be apparent only, a false effect due to the crowding of the Jewish intelligentsia into certain professions and industries which give to their members considerable prestige. But whatever the causes of the surplus of leader individuals of Jewish origin among the German population may be, we see here a conflict arising between the two leader groups both driven by the desire to claim and command for themselves the following of the dependent groups. As the majority of the dependent groups are German, we can imagine feelings of resentment arising among the German leader groups, together with the conviction that they have a more natural right than the Jewish leaders to direct the German masses of workers and farmers.[27] Also, from a sociometric aspect, events more microscopic are equally significant. A German population labelled " homogeneous " may disclose a multitude of contrasting elements within such population, as may likewise a Jewish population labelled in like manner. If this picture approximates the conditions which have existed in Germany, then the point of saturation of Germans for Jews evidently cannot be based upon the simple numeric proportions of the two nationalities, that is, how many Germans can live with how many Jews within a certain territory in peace without either side resorting to oppressive measures. There is need also to ascertain for the United States the point of saturation for its different nationality groups.

2. SELF-REGULATING MECHANISMS

The sociometric test, if given to the whole population of the United States, would disclose a picture similar to that found by us in the small community. We would find a structure of national organization entirely different from the outward composition which appears to prevail in the villages, cities, and states. The population may be found to be broken up into sharply divided nationality and social groups, more or less homogeneous, or we may find certain groups within one nationality crossing over well into another nationality group, the remainder being relatively cut off from this process. We may find, for instance, large parts of the negro population separated from the rest *en bloc,* an isolated psychological state. We may gain an insight into the psychological nearness or distance among the numerous nationality and religious groups comprising the population of the United States. It can be expected such data regarding psychological nearness and distance would give a truer picture of the emotional trends in the population, as it would be based on the reactions of one concrete individual to another concrete individual and not upon the reaction of one individual towards a class of people, as in the so-called social distance tests. The findings would become a tangible basis for a redistribution of the population within any part of the given area.

Psychological currents appear to have a self-regulating and curative mechanism. When a racial current, for instance, of a white group against a colored and a counter-current of negroes against whites develop in any predisposed region, we commonly observe the current rushing and climbing up to an intensity and expansion on a certain level. After the initial excitation is over the current gradually finds its natural level. This process can be well compared with the warming up of an individual to an Impromptu state, as this state also tends to fall to its natural level. This trend of a psychological current towards maintaining its natural level is an important self-regulating mechanism.

We have differentiated between the spontaneous, organic determinants of a psychological current (see pp. 168–9), such as the feelings which arise from the individuals themselves, and the artificial or mechanical determinants, such as means which succeed to initiate or influence from without such feelings. The spontaneous determinants may produce a movement of a certain intensity, duration, and direction. The artificial or mechanical determinants may either accelerate or retard the intensity, duration, and direction, that is, accelerate or retard the development of a current. They may also excite a current to rise beyond its natural level to an unnatural intensity and prolong it beyond its natural duration. The groups in power in a community may be interested to, and often do, exert such influence.

The tendency to interfere with the self-regulating mechanism of a current is a phenomenon which may be daily observed in a community. After a conflict between two gangs in a neighborhood has subsided, another group may be interested that this warfare continue and may devise methods to' spread stories which materially contribute to extend it beyond its natural limit. Our knowledge of the networks by which a large population in a given geographical area is inter-connected suggests to how far an extent a group in power may be able *to degenerate* the development of psychological currents through the use of the modern technological methods for the dissemination of propaganda. We may not be able to command psychological currents but we may be able to extend, to accelerate, or to retard them,—in other words, *to denaturalize* their spontaneous unfoldment. A group in power may even attempt to produce psychological currents *at will*, synthetically. Such management of the networks and currents in a population is a most dangerous play and may produce greater disturbances in the depths than the momentary effects upon the surface at first may indicate.

XX. EXPERIMENTAL PLANNING OF A NEW COMMUNITY

It is a good practical rule to look at the project of a new community strictly from the point of view of the population which is going to fill it. The point of view of the population is perhaps most drastically expressed in the conduct of people who migrate to a new land upon their own initiative, groups of pioneers. It is instructive to study their actions. The conduct of such a group of pioneers can be divided into two phases: (a) when they get the idea to move from their present place of residence to a new place of residence, to the land of " milk and honey "—this can be called the preparatory phase; (b) when the group arrives at the new place and begins to act upon it, to struggle with the unexpected in a mood of on to victory—this can be called the pioneer phase. The initiative, the vision, the emotional and intellectual qualities of the pioneers are in operation. One or another leader of a group of settlers chose a locality upon which eventually a community developed. It was one or another's ingenuity which developed the type of house, the groupings within it, and the government itself. These two phases can always be distinguished in the evolution of pioneering. The feeling experiences as they arise in the initial stages are in conjunction with the project of the pioneers the most characteristic feature. No community project can be seriously considered which does not attempt in some form to make it similarly an expression of the population of which it is to consist and which does not call through some technique these people themselves into coöperation and prepare them in all questions which are related to the community to be.

1. PREPARATORY PHASE

The technique to be used naturally depends upon the type of population and upon the conditions in which they are. It will be for a population of predominantly old American stock from Virginia whose homestead, let us say, is projected far from their original residence, for instance, to Arizona, very different for a population comprised predominantly of American Indians whose homestead is projected close by their original seat of residence. But in whatever setting a certain population is found, one necessity is common to all. The population itself has to be made interested in the task before them and prepared to take an active part in it. They have to become attached to the cause and this cause has to appear among them embodied by the leader or leaders. The goal is, by necessity, to produce in them and with them that pioneer spirit and pioneer phase which alone may provide the substance through which a valuable community can be worked out. But to bring them into this phase they have to be prepared for it, worked up to a state of mind through an emotional process into which the goal, the new community, is well integrated. The production of this emotional process, this attachment between leader and population, one to another, and the whole population to the common objective brings us to consider what is usually called the problem of transference.

The form of transference arising in the psychoanalytic situation physician-patient is a by-product of the course of treatment. It is an emotional experience in the patient in the production of which the physician does not assume a direct and active rôle. But the situation in which a group of pioneers find themselves is of a different nature. They are driven forwards. They are in the midst of producing a series of successive acts; they are in need of throwing themselves into purposive action. If any form of guidance should reach them constructively, a new form, a more active and direct form of transference, has to be used. Their minds have to be directed not towards an emotional experience and conflict in the past but towards a task in the *present* and the emotional attachment to be developed in respect to it. It is this present which is in need of analytical reflection. The helper towards this has to approach the subject or subjects directly; he has to produce an act, an *act of transference.*

At first it may look as if we would regress to the more primitive concept of suggestion as developed about fifty years ago by the Nancy school. They also expected the hypnotist and the suggester to assume an active and direct rôle during the respective procedure of hypnosis or suggestion. We did return to this older approach but from a *different* point of view. As in suggestion, the act of transference is likewise direct communication of one person to another. But, in contrast, the act is not based upon the absence of logical reasoning for acceptance of the contents transferred. It is not blind. The immediate aim of the hypnotist-suggester is to make the subject do what he wants him to do. In the act of transference it is to make the subject create, to stimulate his spontaneability. Redirected through analytical reflection, the old method of suggestion becomes a more highly organized procedure.

An illustration of the technique of the act of transference is its use in Spontaneity Training of dramatic groups, which was the occasion for its first development. In this experiment the hypnotist-suggester is substituted by the *poet.* In spontaneous play-acting no written play is given. The poet-creator becomes bodily the initial source of information concerning the play to be. Instead of throwing the plot, the characters, and dialogue upon paper, he transfers some expression of these to the players. He becomes to an extent a hypnotist and suggester towards them. But in the inner motive of the procedure he is more than a hypnotist or a suggester. In the poet's mind, moods and visions of the rôles have been continuously in the process of becoming. After having passed through various stages of development they have reached a certain maturity of expression within him. The clearer they are within him, the more he is warmed up by them in the moment of transference, the more effective will be his attempt to throw the players themselves into creative action.[28]

In need of a technique for the guidance of groups we used the act of transference as a method of inspiration. In the pioneer situation the *leader* substituted the rôle of the poet in the play-producing situation and the rôle of physician in the physician-patient situation. The leader assumes consciously a direct and active rôle, but he is not the leader of traditional type. He has undergone a change. It is not more or less blind enthusiasm with which he infects his followers and in which he develops the project, but it is an enthusiasm articulated into the group. It is based upon the spontaneous motives each individual has in respect to each other member of the group and in respect to their common aim; second, upon the organization of the group, as the guidance of groups ought to be based upon the knowledge of their organization. The leader thus gains in objective strength through considering the spontaneous forces within the group and does not impair the subjective strength of his own spontaneity. In his attempt to initiate and reconstruct the state of mind of the pioneer, that naturally flowing enthusiasm and unity of attention the latter devotes to his objective, he is during the preparatory phase directed by the emotional status of the population to be led. To prepare his group for the pioneer phase is his immediate aim. This preparedness of the population for the pioneer phase may be in various degrees of development. One sample of a population may be lethargic, another may be stirred up by economic considerations chiefly, and other groups within it, which, although not having reached through their own initiative the pioneer state of mind, may be potential material for this state through rapid transference from the leader.

The pioneer phase of such an undertaking begins when the concrete population becomes actively related to the project (a) in choosing the locality of the new community and (b) in organizing its set-up. An essential first phase is the selection of the population for the new community.

2. Process of Selection of Population

The problem is to select a population for any given community in a manner that is not arbitrary but an outgrowth of the spontaneous forces operating within this population. In order that each settlement can be expected to develop into a community it is necessary that the selected population shall be a harmoniously interrelated whole. Any selection which neglects to take into account the spontaneous attractions and repulsions existing within the population may lead to the including of families which, however worthy they may be as individual units, together make up group formations which may later have a disrupting effect upon the progressive development of the whole population.

The sociometric technique secures the interrelation of each family unit to all other family units to which it has an interrelation, and out of this evidence we are able to construct the kernel group around which to relate the rest of the population. Thus the project can contain from the start a socially interrelated organization: it can be a "community." The principles gained from the study of the psychological organization of communities can be followed in order to secure a composition of population which can be expected to progress and survive as a community, and there can be avoided other factors which have been found to cause disintegration and decline. Whether the geographical location of a community is in an urban or a rural section, whether the size of the population is large or small from which the selection has to be made, whether the population is of one nationality or another, etc., has a practical bearing upon the selection. Certain relations which have been found to affect the harmonious functioning between the abilities and strivings of the workers with the available work situations have also to be considered in the selection of the population. It is calculated within certain limits what proportions among the different nationality, racial, and religious elements the community may be able to absorb; the most appropriate distribution of the sexes, of leaders and followers, of individuals who are able to develop the industrial, social, and cultural activities to the greatest satisfaction of the demands of the population. It may be disclosed that certain units gravitate towards each other and produce cohesive groups drawn together by a " natural selection," whereas great numbers remain isolated and disconnected. The motivations ascertained why a certain family unit wants one family included and another excluded will aid to interpret the causes behind the position of each family in the structure of the selected population. It may be that a certain homogeneous element is small in numbers but that it forms a closed group. This small group of a given nationality, for instance, may be more disadvantageous for the community in producing frictions than a larger number of the same nationality who are less united among themselves and better integrated into the fabric of the whole population.

The selection has to supplement the natural course of development also for other reasons. Communities do not crop up today in a comparative wilderness as in the pioneer settlement period, but are planted in the midst of a highly differentiated and well organized group of villages and towns with definite traditions and cultural trends. The structure of the selected population must be of such texture that adjustment to the neighboring towns will follow as an outgrowth of their functioning in proximity.

The population from which the selections have to be made may fall into the following three classes: Class 1: the family units are acquainted with a number of other family units within the population. Class 2: the family units are totally unacquainted with each other. Class 3: the family units are in part acquainted with other family units and in part acquainted with none. In the first instance the technique uncovers the social relationships already existing among them. In the second, it discloses the spontaneous attractions and repulsions arising through initial meeting. In the third, the two techniques just mentioned are combined to secure the essential information.

In a typical case, from a population of about 250 families applying, 125 families have to be selected, as this is the maximum number that can be accommodated in the particular community project. The total population applying is invited to a meeting and addressed in respect to the question of how the population can be selected for the new community. The need, it is explained, is to make the selection approximate as closely as possible that of a community spontaneously formed; that is, it should consist of a nucleus of family units naturally interlocked through interest and activity in common undertakings. The authority to select the population can come from outside or inside the population. If it comes from outside it can be purely dictatorial, based on fictitious assumptions, as, for instance, that only " Greeks and Italians should be selected for an agricultural community," or it can be based on the empirical knowledge of how populations in other communities are comprised. But we have found that findings in respect to one population do not hold true for another and hence cannot be mechanically transposed upon another population without regard to many factors. The authority to select the population can come also from inside the population, from an individual who appoints himself to make the selection or from a particular group which feels especially informed to know what is the best for all. But our studies show that, due chiefly to psychological pressure and the limits of emotional expansiveness, any *part* of the population is prohibited from arriving at an awareness of the total process. The only comprehensive method of approach remaining is to bring the total process to a differentiated expression through a *population test*. Whatever additional knowledge may be used in reaching a final selection, this population test has to be so constructed that its findings disclose the psychological structure of the whole collective and every detail individual-to-individual relation at the same time.

The test is given as outlined on page 357 and the findings analyzed. This procedure is taken as the first step in selecting the population from Class 1. The situation is different in the case of Class 2, the group of families who are strangers to each other.   In this case a personal meeting of representatives, one from each such family, is necessary so that they may be able to feel each other out and to express to whom they are drawn.   If the number who are totally unacquainted is large, several meetings have to be held.   (See Initial Assignment, p. 269.)   In the instance of Class 1, such a meeting is unnecessary;   it is not even necessary that the people are called to a gathering to make their choices. . The field worker may visit one family after the other and collect the choices and the motivations.   The procedure in the case of Class 2 appears more time consuming, but it has to be realized that in practice only a small portion of the population will be totally strange to the rest.   As to Class 3, for that part of the population in which the families are acquainted with each other to some extent, the procedure is as described for Class 1;   for the remainder, the procedure is as described for Class 2.

POPULATION-TEST

Family X *

FORM   A

1. Whom do you select to live in the new town with you?

Choices	Name of the Person	Motivations
1st Choice		
2nd Choice		
3rd Choice		

2. Which families do you select *to live in the new town with you?*
From each family two representatives (one of the parents and one of the children) express their choices separately.

	Parent		Child	
Choices		Motivations	Choices	Motivations
Name of Family				
1st Choice			1st Choice	
2nd Choice			2nd Choice	
3rd Choice			3rd Choice	

3. Whom do you select *as a co-worker in any occupation in the new town?*

Choice	Name of the Person	Name of the Occupation	Motivations
1st Choice			
2nd Choice			
3rd Choice			

* or homegroup.

4. Name three occupations you would like to be employed in in the new town, giving them in order of preference. Also state your former occupations and in which occupations you have been most successful.

Choice of Occupations	Former Occupations	Most Successful in Which Occupations
1.		
2.		
3.		

5. Which families do you select *as your neighbors* in the new town?

From each family two representatives (one of the parents and one of the children) express their choices separately.

Parent		Child	
Choices	Motivations	Choices	Motivations
Name of Family			
1st Choice		1st Choice	
2nd Choice		2nd Choice	
3rd Choice		3rd Choice	

Population Test Form A can be an aid in the process of selecting the population for a new community in the event that the individuals or families are *acquainted* with each other. If phase 1 of the test is not practicable, phase 2 can be used as an alternate. Population Test Form A can also be given to a community which is already established; its aim is then to determine the existing psychological organization and eventually to disclose the spots in which disrupting tendencies prevail.

POPULATION-TEST
FORM B

Family X		Initial Meeting
	Name of the Person	
Choices	(or Family)	Motivations
1st Choice		
2nd Choice		
3rd Choice		

Population Test Form B can be of aid in the process of selecting the population for a new community when the individuals are *unacquainted* with each other. In the ideal application of the test every individual should meet every other individual of the group from which the selection has to be made. Practically it will often suffice if representatives of the different families meet with one another. However, even this may be impracticable when these families are not only unacquainted with each other but for one reason or another cannot be brought to an initial meeting. Then Population Test Form A can be used (a) to determine the position of the family unit in the *old* community and (b) when the family knows at least one or two of the other families who wish to move into the new community, the position of the family within this small group may disclose important evidence.

Analysis of the material is made according to organization, according to interracial and intersexual attraction, and in respect to industrial, social, or cultural criteria around which groups may develop in the new town.

The evidence may indicate that 125 families, the number for which the project is planned, group themselves as a coördinated unit, leaving out about half of the population, or it may be that the whole population breaks up into a number of small groups. Then the question would arise, in the latter case, which of these groups should be combined to make up the community. The evidence is a clearing process to this end, clarifying the position each group has in respect to other groups. It may reveal also that the composition of the population contrasts in respect to social and cultural traditions so considerably from the surrounding towns that the new community may appear, so to speak, as a " sociological island " and the possibility of its gradual adjustment to them be hindered from the start.

The data gathered is a basis for the classification and selection of the population. As the existing organization within the sample population has been ascertained, it is then necessary to take the second step: to analyze and carefully weigh all the factors. The selection made should include those family units which together produce as balanced a psychological organization as possible. This does not at all mean that there should be included only those families which have been most chosen; in fact, to do so may put the organization out of balance, forcing the inclusion of too many leader-families for the size of population, making the community a potential center of conflicts through too keen competition among the leaders. Also the fact that certain families have not been chosen at all should not, on that ground alone, exclude them. They may be of such composition that they add an element of stability both to the economic and to the social set-up, and they may be a check on the psychological currents dominant in the community. On the other hand, a sufficient number of mutually attracted families should be selected or there will not be produced that feeling within the

population that they are a community, mutually inter-
dependent, with a unity just as that of any town in the nearby
areas. As practically all the population have to move into
the new community at once, mutually rejecting families
should, as far as possible, be separated and considered for
different localities. The inclusion of, for instance, two leader-
families which mutually reject each other may prove to be a
dangerous experimentation, since there are sufficient other
sources of conflict in the building of a new community.

4. Distribution of the Selected Population within a Community

The geographical distribution within the community area
provides an avenue which can be directly utilized to provide
the most auspicious distribution of the population which has
been selected. The problem of neighbor selection cannot be
solved by a purely arbitrary distribution of the population, as
the family units must reside permanently in relatively close
proximity and each family will have certain other families as
neighbors with their land adjoining. Through the evidence
gathered through the sociometric technique the families can
be assigned as immediate neighbors who are mutually attracted *and* mutually beneficial. The family units can be so
located geographically that harmonious social relations already
existing are stimulated and other less advantageous relations
discouraged.

The question arises whether the houses should be arranged
in the form of long chains or if they should be grouped in several neighborhoods. Commonly this problem is decided by
accident or according to architectural or industrial planning.
There is another possibility opened up through the population
test to reflect into the physical organization of the town the
psychological structure of the initial population. In this
manner, perhaps, the forces of social gravitation which draw
the groups together or apart may suggest the grouping of the
houses and the distribution of the population within the
town.[29]

PART VI:
WHO SHALL SURVIVE?

XXIII. WHO SHALL SURVIVE?

The weakest point in our present day universe is the incapacity of man to meet the machine, the cultural conserve, or the robot, otherwise than through submission, actual destruction, and social revolution. The problem of remaking man himself and not alone his environment has become the outstanding problem the more successfully technical forces prosper in the realization of the machine, the cultural conserve and the robot; and although the development of these is far from having reached its peak, the final situation of man and his survival can be clearly visualized, at least theoretically.

First, one may ask how it is possible that a machine-like device can become dangerous to man as a creator. Following the course of man throughout the various stages of our civilization, we find him using the same methods in the making of cultural products which are used later and with less friction by the products of his mind, his technical devices. These methods have always amounted simply to this—to neglect and abandon the genuine and outstanding creative process in him, to extinguish all the active, living moments, and to strive towards one unchangeable goal: the illusion of the finished, perfected product whose assumed perfectibility was an excuse par excellence for forsaking its past, for preferring one partial phenomenon to the whole reality. There is a shrewd motive in this procedure of man because if only one stage of a creative process is a really good one, and all the others are bad, then this chosen stage substituting for the entire process can be memorized, conserved, eternalized, and can give comfort to the soul of the creator and order to the civilization of which he is a part.

We can observe this strategy in all the cultural attempts of man and this strategy could deceive man and be regarded as worthy and beneficial as long as the process of industrial revolution did not produce an unprecedented world situation. As long as the mechanical device did not enter *en masse* into the economic situation in the form of the book, the gramophone, and the talking film, man had no competition in the execution of his conserves. Once an ensemble of actors had rehearsed and acquired a play to perfection, this ensemble was the only owner of their particular bit of merchandise which they offered for sale. Their only competition could come from another group of persons. Once a group of musicians had rehearsed and perfected a certain number of musical compositions, they were the only owners and executors of this product. Through the process of repetition they earned money. The introduction of cultural devices changed the situation completely. Man was not needed any more for the repetition of his finished products. Machines did the work just as well and perhaps even better, and at a much smaller expense.

In the beginning of this industrial process man tried to meet it with aggressive action. But the nearer the avalanche of ghosts rolled towards him the more he tried other means of defense. He invented socialism and hoped that through changing the present state of production and distribution the mechanical device would become of even greater help and comfort to him than it had been.

One angle of the problem, however, has been overlooked. There is a way in which man, not through destructiveness nor through economic planning, but as a biological being and a creator, or as an association of creators, can fight back. It is through a strategy of creation which escapes the treachery of conservation and the competition of the robot. This strategy is the practice of the creative act, man, as a medium of creation, changing his products continuously. Spontaneity as a method of transition is as old as mankind, but as a focus in itself it is a problem of today and of tomorrow. If a fraction of one-thousandth of the energy which mankind has exerted in the conception and development of mechanical devices were to be used for the improvement of our cultural capacity during the moment of creation itself, mankind would enter into a new age of culture, a type of culture which would not have to dread any possible increase of machinery nor robot races of the future. The escape would be made without giving up anything that machine civilization has produced.

The eugenic doctrine, similarly to the technological process, is another promiser of extreme happiness to man. The eugenic dreamer sees in the distant future the human race so changed through breeding that all men will be born well, the world populated with heroes, saints, and Greek gods, and all that accomplished by certain techniques through the elimination and combination of genes. If this should really come to pass the world would be at once glorious, beautiful, and God-like. But it may be reached at the cost of man as a creator from within himself; it would have, like Siegfried in the myth, a vulnerable spot into which the thorn of death could enter,—a tragic world, a world in which beauty, heroism, and wisdom are gained without effort, in which the hero is in want of the highest reward, the opportunity to rise from the humblest origin to a supreme level. It sums up to the question whether creation in its essence is finished with conception or whether creation does not continue or cannot be continued by the individual after he is born.

The eugenic dreamer and the technological dreamer have one idea in common: to substitute and hasten the slow process of nature. Once the creative process is encapsuled in a book it is *given;* it can be recapitulated eternally by everybody without the effort of creating anew. Once a machine for a certain pattern of performance is invented a certain product can be turned out in infinite numbers practically without the effort of man. Once that miraculous eugenic formula will be found a human society will be given at birth perfect and smooth, like a book off the press.

In the face of the two vehicles of thought and power, eugenic rule and machine rule, man ought to call to mind their meaning: that they both aim to remove the center and the rule from within him, the one into a process before he is conceived, the other into a process which is conserved, both aiming to make him uncreative. Technology may be able to improve the comfort of mankind and eugenics may be able to improve the health of mankind, but neither is able to decide what type of man can and should survive.

It is from the actual embodiment and performance of man within the psychological cross-currents which turn upon him from birth to death—that is, how he stands up in the psycho-geographical test,—that a decision, if any, can be made; and the conclusion we can draw from a survey of the position of man as a biological being in the world of today is that thrown into an industrial environment he does not stand up well in the conflict with the machine and that the solution of this conflict lies in an heroic measure, not to surrender to the machine, not to halt its development, but to meet it on even terms and to resort in this battle to resources which are inherent within his organism. Beyond the controversy, destruction of the unfit or survival of the fit, is a new goal, the survival of a flexible, spontaneous personality make-up, the survival of the creator.

Another tragic insufficiency of man is his failure to produce a well integrated society. The difference between the social structure in which he functions and the psychological structure which is an expression of his organic choice and the tension arising between the two constantly threaten to disrupt the social machinery so painfully built up by him. It was from a study of the integrating and disrupting forces in the development of society, by which means they operate and by what techniques they can be controlled, that these inner disturbances were disclosed as a permanent feature of social organization. We found it characteristic for the most undifferentiated as well as for the least differentiated groups. It must have been an attribute of human society since its early days. The weakness of human society appears to have the same cause as the weakness of the individual organism. The question is therefore not only the survival or passing of the present form of human society but the destiny of man. As all races suffer in this respect from a common insufficiency they are going to live or perish together. An alternative and a solution may come from the conclusion that man has a resource which is inherent in his own organism and in the organization of human society which he has never used beyond the rudimentary stage—his spontaneability. To bring this

to full development requires the concentration of all agencies—
technological, psychological, and eugenic.

It has helped us in the beginning of the investigation to
think of mankind as a social and organic unity. Once we had
chosen this principle as our guide, another idea developed of
necessity. If this whole of mankind is a unity, then tendencies must emerge between the different parts of this unity,
drawing them at one time apart and drawing them at another
time together; these tendencies may be sometimes advantageous for the parts and disadvantageous for the whole or
advantageous for some parts and disadvantageous for other
parts; these tendencies may become apparent on the surface
in the relation of individuals or of groups of individuals as
affinities or disaffinities, as attractions and repulsions; these
attractions and repulsions must be related to an index of biological, social, and psychological facts, and this index must be
detectable; these attractions and repulsions or their derivatives may have a near or distant effect not only upon the
immediate participants in the relation but also upon all other
parts of that unity which we call mankind, the relations which
exist between the different parts may disclose an order of relationships as highly differentiated as any order found in the rest
of the universe.

Whether in the end this guide will be proved to be a universal axiom or a fiction, it has aided us in the discovery and
demonstration of the social atom, the psychological current
and the network. It may be permissible to let the fantasy run
ahead of demonstrable proof and derive another necessity
which seems to follow logically from the conception of mankind as a correlated unity. Just as we have seen the individual in the socionomic domain as the crossing point of numerous
attractions and repulsions which at various times shrink and
expand and which are not necessarily identical with the relations within the groups in which he actually lives but breaking
through group-life lines, it may be that also in the eugenic
domain an individual cannot be classified but as a crossing
point of numerous morphological affinities and disaffinities
which are not necessarily related to the individuals with whom

he actually propagates the race, but that they break through racial lines and the different levels of mental organization. It may be that certain individuals belong to the same *eugenic group,* due to selective affinities for which an index of eugenic facts must exist, and that they do not belong to all other groups, at least not with the same degree of selectivity. It may be also that the balances and imbalances we have found within the social atom exist in some fashion also in the eugenic groups and that once such an evidence is secured a basis for eugenic classification similar to our sociometric classification is won.

Since Linnaeus (1744) advanced the theory of the origin of the species by hybridization and Mendel's discovery of the laws of inheritance,[30] it is assumed that the bringing together of many diverse genes by hybridization and their various interactions are largely responsible for the increase of complexity found in the evolution of organisms. But the causes for successful and unsuccessful hybridization are in doubt. The beneficial and the dysgenic result of the meeting of differently constituted germ plasms may be due to morphological affinities and disaffinities operating among the genes themselves or among complexes of them. And upon these affinities and disaffinities may depend the pooling of appropriate or disappropriate hereditary factors contributed to the offspring by the two parents. As long as the nature of eugenic affinities is not established by biogenetic research, we shall assume two practical rules: that psychological nearness or distance is indicative of eugenic nearness or distance [31] and that clinical studies of crossings lead to a preliminary classification of eugenic affinity.

The scant clinical evidence as far as available today appears to give support to the hypothesis. We have the one extreme, a point of view held by many eugenic writers, that the physically and mentally abler members elevate the race through propagation and that the physically and mentally inferior through their propagation cause the race to regress, and the other extreme, that members of the superior class produce with members of the inferior class (and members of one race with members of another race) better offspring in general than when they remain within their own sphere; both extremes appear to find a point of coincidence in the hypothesis of eugenic groups, inter-biological relations which are not identical with the biological groups as they appear on the surface.

From the point of view of such a biometric or eugenic classification the constructive approach of biological planning comes into a new light. Similarly to therapeutic assignment in social groups looms the possibility of *eugenic assignment* to eugenic groups. Then the notion of the unfit, at least for a large number of those who are now considered in this category, becomes relative, as there are uncovered numerous groups of varying eugenic value. Some groups among those today classified as unfit for propagation may be found unfit when in relation to certain groups, but fit in relation to other groups, just as we have found in respect to populations that some groups which foster disintegration and decline in certain communities aid in the fruitful development of others. It is a foregone conclusion that then our present palliative measures such as sterilization will be discarded or undergo modification. We may have gone too far with our disrespect for nature's wisdom just as in times past too far in respect for it. It may be demonstrated in the end that the slow and "blind" methods of nature's planning, however wise they have appeared at one stage of our knowledge and however deficient in parts at another stage of our knowledge, are true, taken as a totality. A new appreciation may then arise of the sense of the old myth which all great religions have brought forth in remarkable unison, the myth of the father who has created the universe for all, who has made its spaces so immense that all may be born and so that all may live.

SUPPLEMENTS

SOCIOMETRIC STUDIES

A sociometric case study endeavors to give an accurate account of how an individual or a group grows and changes, not as an individual or a group singled out but as a part of the community in which it is, and not in metric relations only but through the widely ramified actual expressions of the inter-related subjects. This task,—since it has been found that the specific relationships in which an individual lives can be disclosed through a simple test,—opens a novel procedure to the caseworker: the follow-up of the social atoms towards which a certain individual gravitates at different age levels with different persons, the various criteria which initiate them, the psychological organization of the atoms, and the meaning which the balances and imbalances within them have for the status of the individuals in question.

SURVEY OF CHILDREN GROUPS

It is well known that the human infant is born with only a few and weak unlearned reactions but with a plasticity for learning, a high degree of spontaneability. Our study of group organization indicated that humans long beyond the first years of life are unable to develop permanent associations, that they compare unfavorably with certain highly developed animal societies, that very few organization trends are inherent. The greater amount is produced through the interplay of their spontaneability. But the older the individual the more the growing differentiation of organs and functions within his organism breaks and regulates spontaneous activity. Also the older an association of humans, the more differentiated society, the more the original spontaneability tends to become restrained and resigned to function like a rudimentary organ.

We arrived at this conclusion through the study of the relation of infants and children at different developmental levels towards other infants and children. Observation of infants

373

has, to our knowledge of the literature, been confined to what responses a certain infant is able to release when *occasionally* placed with other infants or adults. Studies of the emotional and social development of infants have left untouched the evolution of group organization among infants, perhaps because babies do not group themselves spontaneously and an artificial experimental situation is needed to uncover the underlying possibilities of organization on the different developmental levels. To meet the problem we placed a group of nine babies in proximity in the same room from the day of birth. They were studied over a period of 18 months. The inquiry focussed on what developmental level the babies reached *as an association,* not what developmental level this or that infant reached. (The lengthy report of this survey cannot be presented, due to limitations of space.)

We present herewith children groups from the fourth year to the fourteenth year age level. As in the baby groups, we noted also here how much more directionless and lacking in integration children are in groups than singly. Through a sociometric survey of the motivations given by children spontaneously, we were able to record verbatim the expressions as they were given by them. Using the means of selecting a number of typical instances from the first test of a public school, we here attempt to give in miniature a survey of the whole material. Each motivation has been broken up into the phrases of which it consists. The frequency of motivations occurring at different age levels in respect to the criterion around which the children groups were intended can be calculated. Each of these motivations has been evaluated in respect to its meaning in group organization and in respect to the developmental level at which it was found.

KINDERGARTEN
(Ages 4–6 Yrs.)

Neil chooses Loretta:	"She looks nice all the time. She has a nice hankie and a nice dress."
Neil chooses June:	"She takes me to her house and gives me cocoanut."
Joyce chooses Robert:	"Because he wears so much nice clothes and he always comes around to play with me."

Joyce chooses Howard:	"Because he lives on my block; because all the time when I tell him to come down and play with me 'cause I can't come up, he always does."
Howard chooses Helen:	"Because she's my friend. She's nice."
Lucy chooses Mary:	"She's nice to me. She lets me hold her flowers."
Lucy chooses Rose	"She's nice to me. She lets me hold her flowers too. Sometimes she lets me play rope with her."
Howard chooses Joyce:	"She lives around my block and she plays with me every day. She's my friend and she never fights with me."
Robert chooses Howard:	"He always comes around my way and he always skates with me and he always calls for me when I come home from school."
Frank chooses Joyce:	"She's my friend. I like her because I want to go over to her house some time. I never went to her house yet."
Frank chooses John:	"Because I like to play with him."
John chooses Joyce:	"She's nice. She says so nice, ' Miss Harlow, may I go to the bathroom? ' "
Eugene chooses Daniel:	"Once he came around my house and gave me peppermint candy. Then he came around my way and he gave me some candy to give to my brother."
Eugene chooses Frank:	"Because he eats with me."
Lucy rejects Frank:	"He's bad."

BREAKING UP OF THE EXPRESSIONS

In Regard to Sex	In Regard to Level of Motivation	In Regard to Race
. . . when I tell him to come down and play with me 'cause I can't come up he always does. (?)	looks nice has a nice dress wears so much nice clothes	
She says so nice, " Miss Harlow, may I go to the bathroom? " (?)	gives me cocoanut lets me hold her flowers plays with me never fights with me skates with me calls for me want to go over to her house gave me peppermint candy eats with me	*None.*

Conclusions, Kindergarten

Compared with the motivations given in later grades, the utterances of the kindergarten children are extremely naïve images which are hardly separable from the accompanying gesture and movement. The mimic-verbal expressions projected as a talking film would present the motivations more adequately. But it is evident that the attractions are definite, however inarticulate the motivations for them may be. Whether or not the phrases given are picked from somewhere and reiterated by the child does not alter the fact that they are used *in relation to a particular other child who is chosen.* Indeed, it appeared that the decisiveness of choosing and the excitement accompanying the act were greater at this age level than in later years when the children tend to become more circumspect in their choosing and more inclined to think the matter over before making their choices. The kindergarten child bubbles out with his choice instantaneously and with a particular delight as if he were in a hurry to release a pleasant secret. Whether or not the " thinking it over " of the older child makes the choices more sensible, it certainly diminishes the fresh spontaneous impression as found in the response of the pre-school child.

About a fourth of the choices of the kindergarten population are for the opposite sex. But the motivations given are still so undifferentiated that the motivations for heterosexual choices cannot be distinguished from those for homosexual choices. This does not infer that the sexual feeling is not inherent in the attraction but rather that this feeling does not become articulated except in rare instances. On the other hand, whereas in respect to sex articulation is present although weak, in respect to race and nationality no motivations whatsoever are detectable at this age level. Individuals of different nationality and race attract each other and the distribution of these attractions is as even as if nationality and race were not yet attributes of the individual.

The wild, unreciprocated choosing reflects the rôle of physical proximity in the making of association and accounts for the predominance of the horizontal structuure of differentiation over the vertical structure. The only pronounced vertical differentiation present is the primitive leader structure. The organization of the group is rudimentary. The character of the weakly articulated motivations is esthetic and pre-social.

Whether such expressions as given by children of the kindergarten and 1st grade can be classified as predominantly egocentric (Piaget), or better said, if the notion egocentric is a true duplicate of the actual process, is questionable. They often indicate inarticulate symbolic thinking. In the interpretation of Piaget they appear to be above the so-called autistic and below the so-called logical level of expression, that is, egocentric. We paid in our experimental situations particular attention not to what the subjects think for themselves irrespective of a definite other subject, but to what one child thinks of *another,* how it reflects about another in respect to an immediate purpose. We did not consider the verbal expression alone but as well the non-verbal, mimic expressions, how a child warms up towards another subject whom it chooses or how it overlooks other children as if they were not present. In fact, we considered the two phases of expression as inseparable. A very inarticulate, indefinite verbal expression was often accompanied by a definite, decisive gesture. It appeared that we overrate language as a social index if we do not take into consideration the physical and mimical relations for which the language tool is less needed. The younger the children the more they emphasize with gestures rather than with words. They project their intelligence through a pantomimic language. The older the children the more they shift their emphasis from the gesture to the spoken word. Formerly the language was a part of their body. Now it is used as a tool. However, also in the higher grades we found a percentage of children who persist in the primacy of bodily action with words but an appendage to it.

It is our opinion that sociometric classification is able to differentiate the various levels in the pre-socialized period better than individualistic classifications as autistic or egocentric. The basis of sociometric classification is not a psyche which is bound up within an individual organism but *an individual organism moving around in space in relation to things or other subjects also moving around him in space.* The tele, however inexpansive or rudimentary, is an expression of the degree of attraction among them. Our sociometric classification formula does not have else but to express the position of an individual within a group of subjects and things. Below a certain age level, when it has not yet developed the ability to express its affections clearly, no sociometric classification can be drawn from the child. The objective material itself remains, a living picture of moving subjects.

1ST GRADE
(Ages 6-7 Yrs.)

Claire chooses Marion:
" She's my best friend. She comes over to my house lots of times but she goes home very early. She tells me her mother is going to buy a nice toy for me and you. If we meet another girl and I say 'Let's walk with the other girl,' Marion says, ' No, let's walk with me and you.' I say, ' All right, let's go together.' "

Marion chooses Claire:
" I like her because she always gives me candy when I eat with her. She lends me crayons when I have lost mine. One time she gave me her Dixie cup."

Edwin chooses Lily:
" Because she's smart. She's not a chatterbox. She comes to school dressed up nice. She doesn't scream. She folds her hands nice."

Lily chooses Edwin:
" Because he's a boy. He's a nice boy. He likes me and I like him. Because he gives me things. He goes home with me. He gives me everything what he's got. He has nice eyes."

Morris chooses Tony:
" Because he gives me lots of big yellow pencils. He says he likes me. He says he likes me the best of all."

Tony chooses Morris:
" He eats with me. He helps me build with blocks."

Morris rejects Francis:
" He takes my candy."

Claire rejects Warren:
" Because he hits me."

BREAKING UP OF THE EXPRESSIONS

In Regard to Sex	In Regard to Level of Motivation	In Regard to Race
He has nice eyes. Because he's a boy. He likes me and I like him.	She tells me her mother is going to buy a nice toy for me and you. If we meet another girl	

gives me candy when I
eat with her
lends me crayons when I
have lost mine
gives me everything what   *None.*
he's got
gives me lots of big yel-
low pencils
goes home with me

dressed up nice
folds her hands nice
he has nice. eyes

helps me build with
blocks

Conclusions, 1st Grade

The motivations at this age level show an increased variety and are clearer than formerly. Besides having often an esthetic character, they include references to third persons and to work relations. Heterosexual and interracial attractions appear in approximately the same proportions and with similar characteristics as in the kindergarten. Sexual motivations are slightly indicated and interracial motivations are again missing.

2ND GRADE
(Ages 7–8 Yrs.)

Audrey chooses Muriel:
"I like her 'cause she is good, she reads so good. She always says 'Yes' when I ask her to play house with me. She doesn't leave me if another girl comes along."

Audrey chooses Herbert:
"I like Herbert very much. I think he likes me too. I like him 'cause he's fair in everything."

Herbert chooses Benny:
"I met Benny in the class I was in first, long ago. I didn't like him very much and then I got to like him more and more. He used to be bad but now he's getting good. He

Muriel chooses Audrey:
"I met Audrey in 1A. Teacher put her seat by me. She never laughed at me if I didn't do my numbers right. I want to always sit by her."

Muriel chooses Herbert:
"He likes me too, 'cause he's always lagging around me and wants me to play with him. He never hit me yet."

Herbert chooses John:
"I like John 'cause he makes all the kids laugh."

used to beat up other kids and everything. Now he acts good, like me
and some other kids."

Benny chooses Herbert:
"He's nice. He plays nice. Most
all the boys like him, he can play
ball so good. He can run fast too.
He's my best friend."

John rejects Herbert:
"I don't like Herbert. When he
reads he makes me almost deaf he
reads so loud."

Breaking Up of the Expressions

In Regard to Sex	In Regard to Level of Motivation	In Regard to Race
	'cause she is so good, she reads so good.	
	'cause he's fair in everything.	
I like Herbert very much. I think he likes me too.	now he's getting good. now he acts good. 'cause he makes the kids laugh.	
He likes me too, 'cause he's always lagging around me . . .	She doesn't leave me if another girl comes along. She never laughed at me if I didn't do my numbers right.	None
	He's nice. I want to always sit by her.	

Conclusions, 2nd Grade

The occasional development of a triangle at this age level
signifies that the children's organization in process of formation is becoming more complex and more finely integrated
than formerly. More often the relationships extend beyond
those of person-to-person character. The more such structures develop the more the children can begin to liberate themselves from the intimate home group and in particular from
the adults of their acquaintance. The child starts to function
in a double rôle, one in his home group, the second in groups
of his own choice.

Motivations given in the kindergartens and 1st grades continue and hang over into the 2nd grade. In addition, the children stress the sense of time in relation to the person liked, evaluate his dependability, and give verdicts of moral judgment. Rejections are more sharply defined.

3RD GRADE

(Ages 8–9 Yrs.)

Harold chooses Arnold:
(English)   (colored)

" He's my best friend. I knew him before I went to school. He lived acrossed the street from my house. When I first moved there I didn t have any friends, so I saw him and I called him into my backyard. And I said, ' Do you want to be friends? ' and he said, ' Yes,' and we started to play ball. Then I was little. I've never been mad at him for three years. We still live near but I moved up the block further. He doesn't get mad right away or rough, like some other boys do. He jokes and fools around a lot. I went to his house about four times. The first time we was in the 2nd grade and he said, ' Do you want to come over to my house to play games? ' so we went. Now we always play in the street."

Arnold chooses Harold:

" When I first met him he wasn't quite friends with me, but now he is. When I went to play with him he used to push me down. Then I didn't use to play with him any more for a few days; then he was nice to me. He said to me one day that he'd never fight with me and I said, ' I will never fight with you, too.' One day he lost his lunch and I shared my lunch with him. He likes the sandwiches my mother makes. I like him because he lives near me. He helps me with my homework and he tells me if I make a mistake. Sometimes he tells me the right answer. He rides me on his bicycle sometimes."

Harold chooses Anna:
(Italian)

" She lives about a block from me. I met her in 2A. She was talking to Arnold and so I went over to him and we all started to talk to each other. I thought she was a nice girl. Then we asked her to play punch-ball with us after school in the yard and she did. She was good right off. Even if she couldn't play good we would have played with her till she learned to play good 'cause we liked her. She doesn't play so much with us now outside of school. She does her work good. She's one of the smart girls. She never did anything wrong to us."

Anna chooses Harold:

" He's a nice friend of mine. He used to give me plants when he worked for the florist fixing up the cemetery. He was in my class in 2A. We were playing a game and I picked him and then we became friends. He used to like me. I play with him in play-times and I always pick him when its my turn. Only if he isn't there I pick some other boy. He never chooses other girls either. He's the monitor."

Arnold chooses Anna:

" I showed Anna where everybody lives when she didn't know nothing about anybody here. She had just come here. I used to tell her to do things and she used to tell me to do things and that's how we became friends. I help her in number stories. That is hard for her. She shows me spelling."

Anna chooses Arnold:

" He's nice. He doesn't hit girls either. Sometimes he lets me water the plants when it's really his turn. I only moved here about two years ago and I knew Arnold the next day after I was here. He was walking around the street and he had a little baby with him wheeling it, and I said, ' Hello,' and he said, ' Hello.' Then I told him my name and he told me his name and then we kept going with each other. He used to play with me mostly all the time but now he plays more with Joseph. I don't know why that is. I feel sad when he goes away from me sometimes. It hurts me. I would like to play with both of them but now mostly girls come after me. Margaret wants me to be her best friend. She says I am pretty. I like her too and she's pretty, too."

Harold rejects John:	" I don't like him . He talks bad in front of the girls and everybody. He hits the girls."
Harold rejects Rose:	" I don't like her very much. She sits down all the time, doesn't run or anything."
Anna rejects Geraldine:	" When we play ball she gives me such a rotten ball (throw) that I miss; she wants me to miss so she can go up. I'd like her if she didn't do that."
Anna rejects Carl:	" He's fresh and he's rough and he doesn't like girls either."
Anna rejects her classroom neighbors:	" I don't like any of them because they're all boys." (However, she chooses two boys to replace them.)
Arnold rejects Henry:	" He makes all kinds of noises and motions."

BREAKING UP OF THE EXPRESSIONS

In Regard to Sex	In Regard to Level of Motivation	In Regard to Race
We kept going with each other. He used to play with me mostly all the time but now he plays more with Joseph. . . . I would like to play with both of t h e m	I used to tell her to do things and she used to tell me to do things.	When I went to play with him he used to push me down. (?)
	He helps me with my homework and he tells me if I make a mistake.	

(boys) but now mostly girls come after me.

I don't like him. He talks bad in front of the girls and everybody. He hits the girls.

I don't like her very much. She sits down all the time, doesn't run or anything.

I don't like any of them because they're all boys.

I always pick him when it's my turn. . . . He never chooses o t h e r girls either.

I help her in number stories. . . . She shows me spelling.

He used to give me plants. Sometimes he lets me water the plants when it's really his turn. He rides me on his bicycle.

She does her work good. She never did anything wrong to us.
He doesn't get mad right away or rough.

Conclusions, 3rd Grade

With the decrease of heterosexual attractions and the increase of homosexual attractions, the motivations given at this age level reveal a more critical attitude towards the other sex. But a warmer feeling towards the same sex is not yet evident. No restraint is yet apparent in the exercise of choice towards individuals of other nationalities and interracial motivations for these choices are also not evident. Choices are still made for purely *individual* reasons.

The children appear to choose associates according to attributes necessary for the joint pursuit of common aims with definite goals. Their estimates are more pragmatic than before. The motivations are given largely in narrative form. With earnestness the children relate how much their friendships mean to them and how badly they feel when the other party seems not to be attentive to them. Here and there it appears in the motivations that a critical point is reached in group development. With the awareness for friendly feelings which are not reciprocated the desire to overcome this dissatisfaction looks for some compensation. We have observed children who are unchosen in the groups previous to the 3rd grade, but little Anna, who expresses the feelings of loneliness, is something new. With the feeling of loneliness the sense for distance increases and a greater awe and fear in respect to individuals who are bigger, stronger, or mentally superior, as adults, or who are different in their physical make-up, as the other sex, begin to dawn in the child. The disappointment about unreciprocated love, for instance, for a parent, does not result in subjective reactions only, as fear, running away, crying, but the child looks for more expression in associations with individuals of his own age than he naturally would otherwise. It can be said that the first total impression of the social group around him may have been for the child from early infancy the same in its general contours. But as the child grows he develops more differences within himself and becomes aware of more differences in the total picture around him. As long as these differences are experienced in a rudimentary stage they do not affect his emotional reactions and the emotional reactions of his associates, nor, in consequence, his position within the group. The feeling of these differences has to reach a certain saturation point in him and in his associates before it results in repercussions within the group.

4TH GRADE
(Ages 9–10 Yrs.)

Donald chooses Nicholas:
    (English)   (Italian)
" He's the best one in the class. He's such a nice fellow. Always he's jolly. He likes to tell jokes. He's on the football team and is a good tackler. "

Nicholas chooses Donald:
" He's always protecting me. There are some older boys who like to make passes at me 'cause I answer them back kind of tough when they call me ' Wop.' My father is always putting his pushcart by the school and when he calls out ' Bananas ' or something these kids like to kid me. Donald always sticks up for me. He says he thinks I'd make a good professional football player. I might be that."

Nicholas chooses Ruth:
                (Jewish)
" She's nice. She doesn't talk much. She is quite pretty and she says ' Hello ' to most of the boys."

Richard chooses Donald:
    (Russian)
" He's my pal. He knows a lot about sports. He's interesting to listen to. If you get him mad he has a bad disposition and tries to do nearly every-

thing in his power to get even—starting fights. Then to get over it, he says, 'Let's choose up a game of punchball," or something. He goes around nice and friendly except when he gets his disposition up. We hang out together practically all the time. He's sort of comical sometimes and other times he's very serious, gets talking about himself. I'd like to sit next to him because of just friendliness."

Richards rejects Leonard:
(German)

" Most of the time he's mad. If you go near him he starts flinging around. He says, 'What's the idea?' He likes sports but he doesn't get the ideas of sports into his head. For a minute he catches on but he gets right off it again. All he's good for is school work."

Richard rejects Harry:
(Jewish)

" He talks a lot. He's comical. Once he was my pal but now I don't seem to like him. He goes with a dumb boy, Louis, who runs with a gang. They never do anything right if they can do it wrong. Outside of school or inside either, they can't be still a minute, always shouting, not nervous exactly but always jumping."

Richard rejects Tony:
(Italian)

" For the least thing he gets mad at you. He's not interesting and he hangs out with bad boys too, mostly Italians. Sort of sneaky. If he can play a trick on you that you won't like, he does it. He and Harry and Bruno and Joseph used to form gangs and get after children that get A's and B's. They only get C's and D's. If we were playing punchball and didn't let one of them in, they'd start something. The gang was started by these boys' older brothers. The older brothers would tell the younger ones all about it and the younger ones as they got older would follow the same footsteps. This gang is still meeting and my cousin (age 12 yrs.) says that gang was here ever since he's been here and he's been here five years. His brother says they were here when he was six years old. When we play handball with the younger ones of the gang around our age they get to like us and follow us around and get reformed,—some of them, about a quarter of them. But most of them are fifteen and seventeen years old now because about twenty of the little ones left the gang for good. Some of those who left call themselves still the ' 35th Street Gang.' They're so ignorant they're not ashamed. They're proud about saying it because their older brothers are in it. We try to explain to them that it's wrong but they keep doing it anyway. The gang uses the younger boys to run errands for them. Some of the older ones work once in a while. But they get fired after a week for doing nothing and coming late. Only one of them had a steady job and he lost it too. Their fathers and mothers give them money to go out and get a job and they spend it any old way. They try to encourage them but they don't care what they do. I know they stole a car once. Some girls who live on that block go out with them. They are older than the boys, I think, and they make themselves look tough by smearing a lot of lipstick and rouge on their faces."

Richard rejects William:

(Irish)

" He can't talk clearly, sort of mumbles, so you can't understand him and it gets on your nerves. He's very clever though, but I don't want to be near him."

BREAKING UP OF THE EXPRESSIONS

In Regard to Sex	In Regard to Level of Motivation	In Regard to Race
She is quite pretty and she says " Hello " to most of the boys.	is a good tackler knows a lot about sports. interesting to listen to	when they call me " Wop."
	He's always protecting me.	
	just friendliness likes to tell jokes	

Conclusions, 4th Grade

The cleavage between the sexes is almost entirely complete at this age level. The boys choose boys very nearly to the total exclusion of girls, and girls choose girls very nearly to the total exclusion of boys. The reflection of this development in their motivations appears more characteristic and decisive in the 5th grade, where it is discussed. The motivations indicate also the forming of groups in respect to various coöperative aims, open or secret. The children work out schemes to fit reality and often also with the risks involved in life situations. This period marks the first appearance of formations working on a large scale during a long period of time towards more or less definitely constructed goals which are invented independent of adult groups and which function also independently of them.

Interracial choices appear less frequently but the reason for this is hardly detectable in the motivations. Very seldom is a term employed expressing racial feelings. Individual cases may disclose at this age level or even earlier distinct attitudes towards individuals of other nationality and social class, but here we emphasize the general trend. Elsewhere in this book the importance of indoctrination, the influence of parents' opinions upon children, is discussed. If, in some individual cases, hostile opinions emotionally most violent are expressed by parents this may stir up the child's fantasy towards such factors. But the probable reason even exciting suggestions do not seriously affect the organizations of the groups formed by children up to and including this age level is that the impressions made upon the children by these suggestions are offset in general by their spontaneous attraction to children of other nationalities, especially when the nationalities of the different class members are not disclosed and remain unknown to them. The difference between the sexes is early discovered by the children, but to the child's mind the differences between individuals who belong to this or that nationality is so overlapped by individual and social factors that he is unable to comprehend the adult's suggestion.

Then another element is important. As long as group organization is little developed, the nets binding individuals together are either entirely absent or discontinuous,—discontinuous at so many points that they cannot be made to function as avenues for shaping opinion. These networks are still rudimentary before the 4th grade and even when the sexual cleavage sets in so decidedly during this period the differentiation of the networks within the two homosexual sets is still in want of the further differentiation found in the later grades. The adults are able to throw the burning match into the fantasy of the children, but to become a permanently burning flame, to develop to a collective feeling, it has to be passed from one child to the other throughout the network.

5TH GRADE
(Ages 10–11 Yrs.)

Gertrude chooses Adele:

"Because she is *so* nice, I think. Almost everything is nice about her. She lends me books when I haven't got any. She keeps in friendship with me a great deal. She'd always help me if I didn't know a thing. She's kind to everybody, mostly everybody likes her. She makes a joke sometimes but she isn't foolish like some other girls are. She's hardly ever selfish. We may have a quarrel sometimes but the next day we meet we can't help to say 'Hello' and then, of course, we're friends again. I knew her for one and a half years. She's hardly ever sulky."

Gertrude chooses Lillian:

"I have almost the exact feeling I have about Adele. I'm sure I love these girls. They're so nice, so good. They're my real, true friends. I could always depend on them and they could always depend on me. I'm very glad she would depend on me because I'd do anything I could for her as long as I could. I met Lillian first and then Adele in the other school and I introduced them and they became very intimate friends. These friends are just somebody else you put close to you instead of a relative, that's what friendship means."

Ralph chooses Robert:

" I always play with him because he lives around my way and we have a baseball team. He's a good sport and doesn't get mad at the least little thing you do. Like you say something to him he doesn't like, he doesn't get mad right away. He can play very good and pitches on our team. When boys get into a fight he stops it and makes boys who are enemies friends. He goes over, makes them stop and shake hands. He's not stingy; he always helps the other boys and gives them anything he has. Whenever he has anything he always shares it. He acts like he knew a lot, does everything the way he should do it. He's sort of in-between, not noisy and not quiet. He's kind to animals and he has a dog and he takes care of it just like he would of a brother. On our team we have twelve fellows, nine regular and three substitutes. Robert and I started it and that kept us close friends."

Ralph chooses Augustus:

" He has lots of pigeons and he cares for them all by himself. What I like about him is, he shares. He lets me fly his pigeons. He's good-natured. I have a moving picture machine and we have some tricks. We are trying to organize a club. We have three members already. We charge 5¢ a week and I like the way Augustus is good at collecting the fees. Sometimes he brags about himself and I tell him so. We get along good."

Sidney chooses Theodore:
    (Russian)   (Russian) .

" He's one of my best friends and I seem to like him most. He's a real fellow and yet he's kind. He found a bird with a broken wing and cared for it till it could fly away. Some boys take advantage of him because he can't fight so well but I stop them. He has an arm that's paralyzed but his other arm has a lot of strength on account of that so he can play handball. I have been with him all the way in school except one term since 2A."

Theodore chooses Sidney:

" When I get into a crowd of boys and they start to fight and I can't on account of my arm, he always takes my part. I've known him since 2A. When they need an extra player and there isn't anybody to play in a game, he always asks them to take me. We ask each other riddles and all that. I ask him what he learned and I tell him what I learned and we ask each other questions. He has a lot of comical ways about him and can keep everyone laughing. He was told to make jokes for a play, it is so easy for him. He seems to be as good a friend as you can find."

James chooses Gordon:
    (Scotch)   (Scotch)

" He speaks Scotch and so do I. I think he was brave to come over alone on a boat and leave his mother there. . . ."

George chooses Chris:
    (Greek)   (Greek)

" He speaks my language. We're Greek. We play ' Cops and Robbers ' together. Chris made a golf course and charged a penny. He has a nice disposition but is sort of lazy. He's so fat that he can only do things like that well. . . . "

Adeline rejects Anna:
               (Italian)

" I don't like her so much. Sometimes she dresses so filthy I don't like to look at her. Her hair hangs all over, like most Italians."

Michael rejects Morris:
    (Italian)   (Jewish)

" He wants to play with us but we won't let him. We also beat Norman up because he was on Morris' side. They're both Jewish. We beat him up six or seven times. He takes things that don't belong to him."

Morris rejects Michael:

" He always brings his friends around who jump on me. I can't fight him anyway; he wears glasses."

Helen rejects August:

" He's colored and very funny acting. I don't have anything to do with him. I speak to him once in a blue moon. I want to say he never got fresh to me, though."

Mildred rejects Lydia:

" She is nice sometimes and sometimes I fight with her. She is Jewish and I don't bother with Jewish people. She is nice sometimes though."

Jane rejects William:

" Always digging under the ground to make tunnels and all kinds of houses. Maybe that's not silly but it seems silly to me. He makes up stuff he calls minstrels but I don't see it makes any sense. The teacher laughs with him sometimes and that makes me mad. He's colored."

John rejects George

" A girl brought flowers to school and they were very nice. But George jumped up and said, ' I'll bring some better than those; that's nothing to what I'm going to bring.' He thinks he's better than everyone else. He's a show-off and he's wild. He comes around and thinks he can hit the boys in the class. He can hit punchball best so he thinks he's best of all."

Russell rejects Vivian:

" If you step on her foot and say ' Excuse me,' she'll stamp right back on your foot. She's always humming in class. If you lend her something she isn't careful of it. Also she talks too slow. I can't stand it how she talks. And she says foolish things instead of nothing."

Edith rejects Antonette:

" She's not honest but I play with her because she's a customer of my father's. She's smart but she thinks she can tell everybody everything."

Adeline rejects Edgar:

" I don't talk to him. When I say something to him, he doesn't know what I'm saying and I don't understand him, so I don't want to sit by him. Other boys call him 'Dummy.' But I don't think it's true. I think he's smart. When he doesn't understand teacher he makes a face and pushes his head forward and the kids laugh and he starts to cry. I don't do that. It isn't right."

Jane rejects Bernice:

" She gets terribly nervous. Then she can't find her pencil box when it's right on the desk. She makes herself think things are hard. She isn't as smart as the rest of us. I'd get to fussing if I were seated by her."

Helen rejects Gloria:

" She is too quiet and she is the teacher's pet. When I'm tired I go around with her and I know she won't jump around. She star-gazes. We all tease her and she won't get angry. She likes to play with dolls. She thinks adventure is sitting on the grass and talking. And that seems like just talk to me."

Ruth chooses Gloria:

" I like the way she talks. She comes from Buffalo and has an accent. She talks very fancy like. I try to get it. She is pretty and chubby-like and quite much fun to listen to. She is always thinking up things with her imagination."

Roberta rejects Bertram:

" He talks to himself and mumbles when he is working. He has firey red hair that doesn't look nice and he cracks jokes when he is not supposed to. He is funny and no one will sit next to him."

Roberta rejects Clifford:

" I don't bother with him at all. He is always sleeping. The teacher claps her hands and then he jumps up. Maybe he is not sleeping but he looks that way.

Miriam rejects Matthew:

" He is fat and funny. We call him the fat fellow in Our Gang comedy. Even the teacher has to laugh at him. He sits in back as the seats in front are too small for him. His belly goes out too far. I don't want to be near him."

Miriam rejects Peggy:

" I keep up a smile so I won't show I don't care for her. I used to like her but when I see how she is always slapping her little sister I don't like her any more. She is fat and talks too much. She won't play, she is afraid she will reduce. When she does anything she tells you about it."

BREAKING UP OF THE EXPRESSIONS

In Regard to Sex	In Regard to Level of Motivation	In Regard to Race
	She'd help me if I didn't know a thing. She is kind to everybody . . . hardly ever selfish.	He speaks Scotch and so do I.
		He speaks my language. We're Greek.
	I could always depend on them and they could always depend on me.	Her hair hangs all over like most Italians'.
	He's a good sport . . . can play good . . . not stingy . . . always helps . . . always shares . . . kind to animals.	They're both Jewish. (?)
		He's colored and funny acting.
	He acts like he knew a lot, does everything the way he should do it.	She is Jewish and I don't bother with Jewish people.
		He's colored. (?)
	he always takes my part.	
	We are trying to organize a club.	
	I like the way she talks . . . . fancy-like.	
	I don't understand him. I'd get to fussing if I were seated by her.	
	She's too quiet . . . star-gazes.	
	He talks to himself and mumbles when he is working . . . He is funny and no one will set next to him.	
	He is always sleeping.	
	He is fat. . . . His belly goes out too far.	
	she talks too slow. I can't stand it how she talks.	
	she is always slapping her little sister . . . is fat and talks too much . . . won't play . . .	

Conclusions, 5th Grade

In the 5th grade the intersexual choices are almost totally missing. The group is now split up into two homosexual units. The motivations are often based on similarities of traits, physical and mental, of social standing, and of interests in common pursuits. In the boy groups is found warm attachment tending toward hero worship; in the girl groups, attachment tending towards devoted emotional friendship. The rejections are specifically motivated, well articulated, and based largely on differences, physical and mental. Prejudices in respect to the nationality and the social affiliation of the particular rejected individuals are frequently reflected. The number of interracial choices declines considerably in favor of *intra*-racial choices and of *intra*-nationality choices. The trend is towards a still greater cleavage within the two homosexual groups into divisions along the lines of nationality and social class (poor or rich, neighborhood of residence, etc.).

6TH GRADE
(Ages 11–12 Yrs.)

Stephan chooses Max:

" I play with boys all older than me and I criticize them and he stops them from hitting me. . . . When I first came to the school he was the one who helped me with everything. I always play with him. He's good to play with 'cause he doesn't ever try to cheat you. He's the same nationality as me, too. He's not selfish and whenever he has anything he gives you half."

Gertrude chooses Mae:

" She's Polish and Jewish like me and she's a very nice girl. Her mother and my mother cook the same way and we wear clothes almost just alike. We go to the movies together and her aunt lives in the same house as I do."

Gertrude chooses Eleanor:

" I like her for the same things almost. Only her nationality isn't the same as mine. . . ."

Betty chooses Barbara:

"I'm fat and when I try to be nice to anybody they don't seem to like me. Barbara is fat too and I like her because she has a lot of sense. She doesn't get a temper up like I do if she is teased. She's patient. I'm not and I guess that's why I like her. She always tells me not to get mad so easy."

Madeline chooses Marietta:

" She is about my size and my age. I like to walk with her 'cause I think we look nice together. She isn't noisy or rude, only once in a while she is rude unconsciously, which means she doesn't know she is rude herself. She is willing to play games that are gay and with a lot of action. We like to help each other. She is truthful. Also if you ask her to bring you something she will bring it even if she has a lot of other things to carry just the same."

Joel chooses Gunther:

" I keep tropical fish and I collect stamps and Gunther likes to see my things. He seems to be interested in them and that's what I like about him. He isn't only always wanting to play baseball. I don't see very well so I like to do other things than play sports."

Samuel chooses Daniel

" He is comical. Once he is your friend he is very loyal to you. He doesn't brag about the pictures he makes although he is about the best artist in the school. Especially airplanes, he can draw wonderful. I don't speak very good English yet and he helps me with it. Then he makes a joke about it when he is correcting me and I don't mind because of the way he does it."

Lucille chooses Anita:

" She's more companionable to you. She's different, has more personality than most people. And she's refined. She doesn't think she's better than other girls, either. Some, if they were like her, would start bragging but she isn't that kind. She minds her own business. When she says something you know it's the truth and you don't when some girls talk. Mostly too, she isn't bossy."

Anita chooses Doris:

" Everyone says she's nice and I think she is too. She has a nice family and a room by herself. We play actresses together. When you play with her, she is ready to take her turn. Like at games she will give up the ball right away. She doesn't say things to hurt you, saying ' You're no good,' like her cousin does."

Victor rejects Philip:

" He has big ears and laughs like Joey Brown. He has a big mouth like him too and all the kids make fun of him because he walks flat-footed. He's smart in school but I don't care for him."

Myrtle rejects Josephine:

" She is forever mad but not saying what kind of people get her mad. She considers herself higher than anyone else and she bosses everything."

Stephen rejects Felix:

" He always plays with one fellow and then another. He doesn't keep up a friendship right. He's a sissy. He always plays with the girls and gips them too."

BREAKING UP OF THE EXPRESSIONS

In Regard to Sex	In Regard to Level of Motivation	In Regard to Race
	plays fair. He is very loyal to you. He's not selfish.	She's Polish and Jewish like me and she's a very nice girl.
He's a sissy. He always plays with the girls.	She is about my size, and my age. I like to walk with her 'cause I think we look nice together. I'm fat . ⌐ . Barbara is fat too and I like her.	He's the same nationality as me, too.
	I keep tropical fish . . . and he seems to be interested. I don't speak very good English yet and he helps me with it. We like to help each other. We play actresses together.	
	He doesn't brag about the pictures he makes. She doesn't say things to hurt you.	
	He has big ears and . . . a big mouth . . . He is smart . . . but I don't care for him. S h e considers herself higher than anyone else . . .	
	He always plays with one fellow and then another. He doesn't keep up a friendship right.	

Conclusions, 6th Grade

The predominance of homosexual choice and a trend towards intra-racial choice continues to be evident in the 6th grade. Motivations for the choices are expressed with greater sureness and distinction on the similarity of traits and common interests in the same activities. Motivations for rejecting members of different nationality and racial groups are present (omitted in this text).

7TH GRADE
(Ages 12–13 Yrs.)

Jean chooses Henrietta:

"I think I like her because she has the same ideas I have. We both love to write. And she isn't silly about boys like Pauline and Eileen and Winifred are. We like boys all right but we don't like to be silly about them. Everybody used to snub me because I was from Sight Observation class but since Henrietta goes with me they stopped. She helps me read small print and is the only one who comes over and does it of her own free will before the teacher asks them to. We are both quite serious."

Jean rejects Lillian:

"She always moves away from me when she's supposed to sit beside me. I think it's because she's prejudiced against me on account of my nationality."

William chooses John:

"We play handball together. He's a fair dealer, not like some wise guys, picking fights and cursing. He's something like me. We're Irish and his mother is dead and my father is dead. He's a good guy. If we could sit together in class I think we could get along and wouldn't quarrel. He ain't sneaky, don't say he likes you one minute and don't the next. You can tell him a secret and he won't go around and tell everybody. He'd give you anything, even his last cent. Most of the time he's jolly."

William chooses Eileen:

"She suits my taste. She's got more sense than other girls. She's not bashful, though she is a year younger than me. She dresses nicely. A kid in class knew her and we started jumping rope with her for fun. She just says 'Hello' when she sees you on the street and doesn't make you feel funny in front of other boys by making fun the way they talk when they know a boy likes them. Now it's basketball time so I don't have time to see her. She is about my size and she has blonde hair and blue eyes. That's my taste, it's what I like."

Eileen chooses William:

"Most of the girls in the class like his eyes. I think he's the best boy in our class. He's smart. I think he is handsome. I'm the only girl he speaks to because most of the girls are babyish and he doesn't like that. I'm allowed to go to the movies with him and once I had him to my house for supper."

Sadie rejects Eileen:

"She puts on her red beret and pulls her curly hair out and makes up to some boys and says she just wanted to look nice for herself and we don't believe it. She acts dippy sometimes. One minute she will like you and the next she is sore. She has certain moods."

William rejects Viola:

"I don't like her. She's colored. I haven't got anything against her but I don't want you to put her next to me."

Eileen rejects Viola:

"If anything should happen to a kid, like he is put back, she is right there to radio it with her big mouth."

Breaking Up of the Expressions

In Regard to Sex	In Regard to Level of Motivation	In Regard to Race
Most of the girls in the class like his eyes.	She has the same ideas I have. We both love to write . . . We are both quite serious.	We're Irish.
		I think . . . she's prejudiced . . . my nationality.
She is about my size and she has blonde hair and blue eyes. That's my taste, it's what I like.	He's something like me . . . his mother is dead and my father's dead.	I don't like her. She's colored. I ain't got anything against her.

Conclusions, 7th Grade

The motivations at this age level have become more penetrating and occasionally choices are made motivated by complementary attributes. Intersexual choices begin to reappear. The motivations for them have near-adult characteristics of sophistication. Intra-racial motivations are again present (in general omitted from this text).

8TH GRADE
(Ages 13–14 Yrs.)

Evelyn chooses Ruth:

"At first I thought she was fresh and was trying to snub me. But gradually I found that she is neither fresh nor high-hatted but sweet and not stubborn. She has a nice personality, just draws you to her. None of us three (Evelyn, Ruth, Elinor) have boy friends but we talk with boys. I prefer a girl to a boy as a friend and so do Ruth and Elinor. I'll try to be her friend all my life, even when I'm grown up."

Evelyn chooses Elinor:

"I like her less than I do Ruth. She is very stubborn and fresh. If she wants to go to a certain show she won't give in. We have to follow her. But I like her very much though. She is also Jewish as I am and my mother wants me to go with Jewish girls. She is very sympathetic, too. She has funny ways about her. She thinks sometimes she is not wanted. I have a pity for her a little bit. She is so tall and thin and she is not so smart as Ruth is in school. She's bashful and it takes long for her to get chummy with people. She will express her opinion about people to us but not to their face. If she doesn't get what she wants she will insist on it and she is willing to spoil us from having a good time if she gets annoyed. But she is very fair and I am very fond of her. She bites her nails and Ruth doesn't do that. She is more shy with the boys than I am because she thinks they don't like her as she is too tall and not pretty."

David chooses Marie:

"About the 3A I noticed her and she seemed to be the highest of the girls. We talked to each other then. In the 4B she got skipped and left the school and just came back the beginning of 8B. I hardly ever see her as she's not in my room. She's better looking than the majority. Curly brown hair at the ends, blue eyes, same height as I am. I'm interested to become friends with her. I don't know her well yet. I used to in the lower grade but she seems to have forgotten. She's my idea of what a girl should be like."

Stanley chooses David:

"I was in 7B4 with him; I was new and he treated me better than all the other fellows did. I like the things he does. So do the teacher and the other pupils. Now he is my best friend. He has a very nice nature about him. Sociable. He is sort of like me. He wants to know everything and to talk out enthusiastic. He has a handsome face for a boy of his age. Only thing is he walks with his head bent down to the left as he can't see very much out of the right eye."

Dorothy chooses Peter:

"I met him while he was head monitor. At first I didn't like him at all and all the other girls liked him. I thought he had too many friends. I was taken out of line one day for talking and brought up to him. He walked me home that day and from then on I began to like him. I see him a lot in school. He has asked to take me out. I like him a great deal. It's mostly his looks that I like. He has a nice disposition and he's not fresh to girls."

Richard chooses Roger:

"I admired him at first because he played for the best team. In some ways he isn't so good a sport. Like if you hit him he gets mad. I just took a sudden liking to him. Every time you see him he has a smile on his face and if you see him often you just get to like him. I like his gameness. Like when the circus was in town he suggested we sneak in."

Albert chooses Rose:

"She once sat next to me in class. She just appeals to me. For these last two weeks I don't walk home with her because we had kind of an argument. I dropped my baseball glove and she kicked it and the boys kidded me. She doesn't pay very much attention to me."

Shirley chooses Florence:

"I like her company. She's a little more intelligent than I am. She's most agreeable. I've never disputed with her yet. She seems to me a little more mature than I am because she worries about what her friends will say about her and I couldn't be bothered about that. She is a leader. I am a leader, too, and we never try to boss each other and that's why we agree. We both like dramatics very much. We both want to be at the head in studies too. She's much better looking than I am and she's not conceited about it. She's interested in Olga who lives with all grown-ups and that's why she acts so grown-up. She's good in dramatics but I think I'm still a little bit better, though, in that."

Albert rejects Alexander:
(Irish)

"Most people don't like him. He is more Irish in his ways and our class don't like that. He talks a lot, argues, and fights, and is awful loud in gym when something happens."

Richard rejects Clara:
(colored)

"She's one of the worst, sloppy, and when she gets mad you know it."

Stanley rejects Erma:
(Jewish)

"I disliked her from the first time I saw her. It was just her manner; she thinks a lot of herself. She's Jewish. She isn't very clean either."

Patricia rejects Carmela:
(Italian)

"I'd get Hail Columbia if my mother saw me going with any of them Italians."

Norman rejects Anna:
(Jewish)

"I think it's her face. Her nose is the most prominent part of her face. I felt a little disgusted the first day I saw her, the beginning of this term. Her face is typically Jewish and my family doesn't like Jews. I was brought up that way. I was sort of conscious of it for the last three or four years. Her hair is long and stringy. She talks with a Jewish accent. She's a pain in the neck. I think boys don't like her at all. I have never spoken to her. She never did anything to me and I never heard anything about her from anyone but that's how I feel about her."

Blossom rejects Eva:
(colored)

"She doesn't make friends with white girls. She has a horrid body odor."

Ira rejects Tony:
(Jewish) (Italian)

"I don't want to be his friend. I don't take to Italians. I get antagonistic. I'm usually on the outs with him."

Ruth says of Waldo:
(colored)

" He's good. He's so polite and humorous, willing to do anything. Doesn't get sore if he is scolded. He knows if he's wrong he's wrong. Also he is brilliant. Everybody likes him. The girls like him too, even if he is colored. I wouldn't mind to sit by him but I chose my best girl friends first."

Ruth rejects Eva:
(colored)

" Nobody cares for her. She's not clean. Even other negroes ignore her. She is conceited too. Thinks she has a beautiful voice. She sings loud as she can. I asked Waldo why they didn't like her and he said she was a Western negro. I know she works after school. She has no father or mother."

Edward says of Kate:
(colored)

" She hangs out with two other colored girls and if she didn't do that I'd think she was better, but still I can't say I'd like her because she'd still be colored. The other two girls like to fist-fight. You'd think they were boys to watch them. And Kate tries to get them to stop so they are always trying to get rid of her but she hangs on to them. She's neat as any white girl but dumb to go with people nobody likes."

Harriet rejects Marie:

" I would like her but her manner of speech annoys me. She lisps. She also has funny little habits which annoy,—shaking her head and snapping her fingers."

Paul rejects Charles:

" I guess he'll be flunked. He hands in dirty, sloppy papers. He's not low or rowdy but just dumb. He isn't right in the brain. Plays with pencils and makes believe they represent something."

David rejects Arlene:

" She calls me ' Steeplechase ' and that gets me sore. I run a lot."

Stanley rejects Augusta:

" She always comes up and says ' Hello, Blondie,' and makes me feel funny."

Stanley rejects Andrew:

" I like to make things, machinery and wagons and little furniture and he is so clumsy he breaks them when you're showing him how to do something. Only think I like about him is his way to talk. He's a Southerner."

Augusta rejects Arlene:

" I can't tell what it is about her but it gives me the shivers. She walks as if she hadn't any backbone."

Ruth rejects Sally:

"Nobody likes her in our class. She's a nosey-body. Not smart at all, not good for athletics even. Doesn't like to read or sew or do anything. Really, she's useless. There's no life in her. She looks at newspaper comics and she bounces her ball and she's sixteen."

Ruth rejects Susan:

"She is a little evil-minded. She curses and has the boys chasing after her. Her mind is never off the boys. She is always talking about them."

Ruth is indifferent to Constance:

"She can't do much because she's crippled. She's so quiet you wouldn't know she was in the class but she is sociable sometimes. She reads serious books and is always planting her garden with flowers. But when she talks she isn't interesting. It is always an awkward silence if you are talking to her."

Conclusions, 8th Grade

The rise in the number of intersexual attractions in the 8th grade results from the fact that a number of boys and a number of girls transfer the dominant part of their affection from their respective homosexual group to which they had been previously attached. More or less loosely knit chain relations break in between the large homosexual units towards which the majority of the members continue to gravitate. However loosely knit these chain relations between boys and girls may be at this age, they present the potential organic basis for sexual or non-sexual boy-girl gangs. The group organization discloses that at this developmental level the group is organically predisposed to develop mixed gangs of boys and girls without the need of older individuals to initiate and direct them.

Compared with earlier age levels (except for the incipient signs found in the 7th grade), this is a novelty. These intersexual structures appear from a static point of view to be similar to the intersexual structures in the 1st and 2nd grades. But from a dynamic development point of view, they have a different meaning because they appear *after* the homosexual cleavage from the 3rd to the 8th grade has affected and shaped group organization. The new heterosexual attractions had to overcome the resistances coming from the homosexual bondage individually and collectively developed. The coöperative gangs in the 4th-5th grade age levels are uni-sexed, and hetero-sexual attachment or collaboration in earlier grades is usually a person-to-person relation predominantly and not a group relation. The recurrence of heterosexual gravitation in the 8th grade is prophetic of a renewed and more persistent attack of the heterosexual tendencies against the homosexual tenden-cies in group organization which throughout adolescence marks the group life of the individual up to maturation.

The motivations of the children at this age level appear exceedingly mature. They can well compare with motiva-tions we have secured from high school children.

To the summary given after each grade, we may here espe-cially emphasize the technique through which the interracial attractions have been ascertained. The sociometric test had been given to all individuals of a community or school in re-spect to such criteria as are of practical significance to these individuals, to live in proximity, to work in proximity, or to study in proximity. In respect to each of these three criteria, three different structures of the given community result. The evidence thus gained through the sociometric test can now be used for the uncovering and interpreting of affinities and dis-affinities which may underlie these spontaneous choices.

The evidence has been used to uncover, for instance, whether any intersexual frequencies dominate the interrelations. These frequencies were then studied in respect to the three different criteria to reveal what modifications sexual attraction under-goes when the function of the group and the position of the member in the group have changed. Throughout the testing the subjects are unaware that their intersexual choices may undergo analysis. The findings have been used also to un-cover and interpret whether any frequencies in respect to nationality or race dominate the interrelations. Again, the subjects are throughout the testing unaware that their inter-racial or intraracial choices may be used to study racial ten-sions in groups. This fact of the populations tested being taken by surprise gives the findings a great spontaneity value. There was never such a question asked as, "Do you like negroes?" or "Do you like this colored boy or that Italian girl?" Nothing of this kind entered or needs to enter into the sociometric test. *All expressions indicating racial feeling were given by the children spontaneously; not the slightest provocation by the tester was allowed. The only criterion of the interview was: Why do you want to sit beside the pupils you have chosen?* In the course of the interview it is also disclosed what reasons they have for not having chosen their present neighbors and what reasons they have for not having chosen certain other individuals about whom we know that they have chosen them. The tester simply charts the relations between the individuals as members of two sexes or as members of particular nationalities, just as he charts their relations as members of a home group, a classroom group, or a work group. The sociograms and the analysis of the motivations given by the members of contrasting nationalities offer then a growing insight into the mechanisms which underlie the development of racial cleavages.

SELECTIONS FROM A COMMUNITY SURVEY

A. INITIAL ASSIGNMENT

The initial and most important event for a newcomer in a community is what start is his, his assignment to the group of persons with whom he is going to live. When a person comes into a city, he picks the house in which he may live and the persons with whom he is going to live by circumstance, by recommendation, or hit or miss. The groups and situations into which he breaks are his social fate. The start in the new group may turn to his advantage or disadvantage in its subsequent development, but the early stages of his career in the strange community are almost entirely beyond his control. This is due to a small and often one-sided acquaintance volume which permits him to select his associates only within the boundaries dictated by circumstances. This fact has fateful consequences for the residents as well as for the newcomer.

The technique of the Parent Test and the Family Test is an attempt to coördinate the spontaneous tendencies and aims of newcomers with the spontaneous tendencies and aims of the residents of the given community. It makes the start for the newcomer more articulate. It opens the opportunity for him to break into social avenues which promise him a better development and the group a greater contribution from him. Otherwise he may eventually wander long in this community or remain blocked in a side line. The process is a technique of freedom (see pp. 10–12): it expands individual power, it brings the individual to wider social release.

The following report is a verbatim record of a Parent Test and a Family Test given in respect to eight newcomers, six housemothers, and six residents who choose and reject each other. See pp. 269–297 and sociograms pp. 287–294.

Dora B.

Chooses Among the Housemothers

1st Choice: Mrs. Reid (C8): "She looks like my grandmother and she was nice to me."

2nd Choice: Mrs. Dickey (CB): "She acted as though she could get along with any of the girls and not have a special pet among them. I like a lady who will sit down and talk to you like she does and make things plain to you."
No additional choices.

Rejects: Mrs. Brett (C9): "I didn't like her at all. She isn't cheerful."

Reactions of the Housemothers

Mrs. Reid: 1st Choice: "Her personality appeals to me: so frank and straight-forward. Talks like a grown-up person, very definite and poised. Everything would be in the open in your contact with her. I tend to be frank myself and we would get along just excellently. She would make a real contribution to my group at present when it needs such a girl, so many dependable ones having been paroled."

Mrs. Dickey: 2nd Choice: "Very attractive to me. Acts natural and unpretentious, yet confident of herself. Responds intelligently and is really delightful."

Mrs. Brett: 2nd Choice: "I need a big girl with a forceful personality like Dora to aid with so many little girls in the cottage at present. A good talker about her plans and seems to mind her own business."

Rejects: Mrs. Dorsey (C14): "She wouldn't understand me. I couldn't get along with her, not even a little. She seems cross."

Mrs. Dorsey: 1st Choice: "Ambitious high school girl, interested in music. Happy spirit and intelligent. I liked her best."

Rejects: Mrs. Bradley (C2): "I think she'd take an interest in just certain girls and not in all. Once she smiled but mostly she was stern when she talked to me. I don't want to be in her house."

Mrs. Bradley: Indifferent.

Indifferent to: Miss Nellis (C11).

Miss Nellis: 1st Choice: "It was the way she met me that won me. She wasn't too forward and not too bashful. Appeals to me most among this group. She isn't spoiled and she doesn't attempt to bluff. I'd be glad to work with her."

Chooses Among the Representatives

Reactions of the Representatives

1st Choice: Leona (C8): "Most everything about her I like. I just can't say it is any particular thing."

Leona: 1st Choice: "It's hard to decide. I never judge a person until I watch her a long time. And although I am most fond of Dora and would choose her first, I wouldn't be sure I was right in choosing her because you never can tell till you live with a person."

2nd Choice: Katherine (CB): "I choose her second because she is so much like Leona."

Katherine: Indifferent. "I like her but I feel that she can get along with most any group. She would coöperate with us in our cottage but I don't especially see her as belonging really to our cottage more than to other ones. You know what I mean. Sometimes you see a girl and just feel right off that she'd be right at home with your cottage and other times you see a girl and you think, 'She's very nice,' but it doesn't enter your head to think of her in connection with your group. I don't feel anxious about her because she will get along wherever she is. The girls I choose I think wouldn't get along so very good except in my cottage."

3rd Choice: Harriet (C9): "She has a beautiful expression and she makes you feel you can make good here."

Harriet: 2nd Choice: "Level-headed with a good attitude and wouldn't be misled by other girls."

Indifferent to: Ruth (C2).

Ruth: 2nd Choice: "A strong character. I wish we could have her. We really need her and she would get an opportunity to be a leader in our cottage because we haven't any real strong leader right now."

Indifferent to: Marion (C11).

Marion: 2nd Choice: "A real good girl. Anybody would be glad to have her in their cottage."

Rejects: Alberta (C14): "Too giggly."

Alberta: 2nd Choice: "She is full of the dickens and it would be great fun to have her."

LOUISE D.

Chooses Among the Housemothers

Reactions of the Housemothers

1st Choice: Mrs. Dickey (CB): "She has a sense of humor and I like the way she talks."

Mrs. Dickey: Rejects. "To tell the truth, I just don't care to have her; can't put my finger on what it is about her but I feel I shouldn't take her.'

2nd Choice: Mrs. Reid (C8): "Her talk is nice too."

Mrs. Reid: 2nd Choice: "She says she's in fourth year high school and that means she would be some help among the others. I like her very much."

3rd Choice: Miss Nellis (C11): "Friendly and homelike."

Miss Nellis: 2nd Choice: "She didn't appeal to me in the beginning but when talking to her her fine mentality struck me. She doesn't feel sorry for herself."

Indifferent to: Mrs. Brett (C9).

Mrs. Brett: 1st Choice: "A good girl and would fit in well."

Indifferent to: Mrs. Bradley (C2).

Mrs. Bradley: 1st Choice: "Sensible ideas, would adjust; although only fifteen years old she has suffered a lot from her marriage."

Indifferent to: Mrs. Dorsey (C14).

Mrs. Dorsey: Indifferent.

Chooses Among the Representatives

Reactions of the Representatives

1st Choice: Harriet (C9): "Very dignified and attractive."

Harriet: 1st Choice: "You can tell by the way she acts that she's sincere about everything. You can count on her."

2nd Choice: Marion (C11): "Very refined and lovely."

Marion: 1st Choice: "I think she is a good influence because of her high hopes and ambitions."

3rd Choice: Ruth (C2): "Good-looking and not vain."

Ruth: 1st Choice: "She has the aim to go ahead, same as I do, and is very friendly. She's what we need in our cottage: more girls like her who can't be swayed by every little thing that makes them mad."

Indifferent to: Alberta (C14).

Alberta: 1st Choice: "She's in high school and she's smart. She attracts me by her speech, so interesting. More my type than any of the others."

Indifferent to: Leona (C8).

Leona: 2nd Choice: "She wants to learn and she appreciates advice."

Indifferent to: Katherine (CB).

Katherine: 1st Choice: "Intelligent and knows how to talk and I think our house would be a good place for her; we have such a fine atmosphere. You know a girl like her needs the proper environment to bring out her best qualities."

LENA R. --

Chooses Among the Housemothers

Reactions of the Housemothers

1st Choice: Miss Nellis (C11): "Has hopes for you and lots of fun in her."

Miss Nellis: 3rd Choice: "She is a little rough but she could be tamed down. I think I can get under her skin. I found her very responsive."

2nd Choice: Mrs. Bradley (C2): "I talked to her a lot. She made me feel I can succeed here."

Mrs. Bradley: 2nd Choice: "Wouldn't fly off the handle or get upset easily; a healthful, outdoor kind of a girl. Is just the one for my group. Stable and steady."

3rd Choice: Mrs. Brett (C9): "Very nice. I like her next best to the other ones I said I would like to live with."

Mrs. Brett: Indifferent.

Indifferent to: Mrs. Reid (C8).

Mrs. Reid: Rejects. "She just doesn't appeal to me, doesn't leave a good impression. Think she is dull mentally."

Indifferent to: Mrs. Dickey (CB).

Mrs. Dickey: Indifferent.

Indifferent to: Mrs. Dorsey (C14).

Mrs. Dorsey: 3rd Choice: "She goes in for sports, like many of my girls do, and I feel my group would take to her quickly—she is so unassuming and direct."

Chooses Among the Representatives

1st Choice: Alberta (C14): "A wonderful, interesting girl."

Reactions of the Representatives

Alberta: Indifferent.

2nd Choice: Marion (C11): "Lovely."

Marion: Indifferent.

3rd Choice: Ruth (C2): "Would be a good friend, you can tell."

Ruth: 4th Choice: "I felt a lot of sympathy for her. She is such a simple thing and she doesn't have any high ideas like the others; only wants to be a cook. If I can have a fourth choice, I want her."

Indifferent to: Leona (C8).

Leona: Indifferent.

Indifferent to: Katherine (CB).

Katherine: Indifferent.

Indifferent to: Harriet (C9).

Harriet: Rejects. "Uninteresting. Very easily impressed by what you say to her. If anybody smiled at her she would do just what they wanted her to,—good or not, just to please. An easy-mark."

EVELYN M.

Chooses Among the Housemothers	Reactions of the Housemothers
1st Choice: Miss Nellis (C11): "I think you can treat her like a friend."	Miss Nellis: Indifferent.
2nd Choice: Mrs. Dorsey (C14): "Good to live with."	Mrs. Dorsey: Indifferent.
3rd Choice: Mrs. Reid (C8): "Very darling. I like old people and she reminds me of an old neighbor we had once."	Mrs. Reid: 3rd Choice: "Strikes me as a good girl. I can just see the group in my house that would take to her. She has a fineness of manner that attracts you although she is very unexpressive when it comes to talking."
Indifferent to: Miss Nellis (C11):	Miss Nellis: Indifferent.
Indifferent to: Mrs. Dickey (CB).	Mrs. Dickey: 3rd Choice: "A wholesome, sincere sort of girl. She is very appealing to me. I know I'd get coöperation from her. I could get right at her. I'd really take pleasure in helping her to develop."
Indifferent to: Mrs. Bradley (C2).	Mrs. Bradley: Rejects. "She is too melancholy, especially for a child of her age, and I know my group wouldn't understand her. She is no doubt a promising girl but I can't imagine her fitting into my group."

Chooses Among the Representatives	Reactions of the Representatives
1st Choice: Katherine (CB): "She understands me."	Katherine: Indifferent.
2nd Choice: Leona (C8) "She is very much like Katherine."	Leona: 3rd Choice: "Very prejudiced and doesn't want to be in our school. Says she has to have a cottage that is home-like. But there is something about her that attracts me a lot. She'd fit in with most of our girls: you know you can't fit in with all of them. There's times you fit in with one set and then for some reason they

change their tactics and you can't get along with them and you go with the group you neglected for a while. The cottage is always divided up. The girls form sets; I don't know if you've observed that. We have about five sets right now. The bunch is too large for you to fit to the whole of them at one time. I can see Evelyn fitting in with the group I'm with now. I'd do my best for her if she could come to our house. I'd show her what is what and how to get over being prejudiced. I'd make her like us."

No additional choice: " I can't choose anybody but Katherine and Leona to live with; the others are all right but these are the only ones I want to be with in a cottage."

Indifferent to: Alberta (C14).

Alberta: Indifferent.

Indifferent to: Ruth (C2).

Ruth: 3rd Choice: "You have to like her. She takes such a brave attitude and doesn't sympathize with herself even if she had a lot of trouble, like some girls do."

Indifferent to: Marion (C11).

Marion: 3rd Choice: " I would call her awfully sensitive and very sympathetic towards people. You can touch her feelings very easy. I think she needs to be in our house because our girls would know just how to treat her. In our cottage the girls respect each other's feelings."

Indifferent to: Harriet (C9).

Harriet: 3rd Choice: " Another high school girl; would help our cottage a lot, just like the first two would that I chose. Talked quite a lot to me about what is opportunity. I think she is intellectual. And we have some very intelligent girls in our house who would appreciate Evelyn. She's very likeable and I hope she can come to our house. You could say she is serious-minded and you can tell by her face that she wasn't very happy ever."

HAZEL W.

Chooses Among the Housemothers	*Reactions of the Housemothers*
1st Choice: Mrs. Reid (C8): "Seemed so happy to be talking with you. She talked as if she would like to have me in her cottage. She says she is very fond of girls."	Mrs. Reid: Indifferent.
2nd Choice: Mrs. Dorsey (C14): "She caught my attention as soon as I saw her. Before I talked with her even I knew I was going to like her. It's the way she has about her that I like so much."	Mrs. Dorsey: 2nd Choice: "She's a sixth grade girl but seems to feel that she will succeed, not afraid of the future and I like that about her. I could help such a girl."
3rd Choice: Mrs. Dickey (CB): "More like a mother. She isn't one who'd be mean to you or quarrel. If you got into trouble you could go to her and explain. After you get talking to her you feel as if you had known her a long time. Only these three interest me."	Mrs. Dickey: Indifferent.
Indifferent to: Mrs. Brett (C9).	Mrs. Brett: Indifferent.
Indifferent to: Mrs. Bradley (C2).	Mrs. Bradley: 3rd Choice: "Slow-minded but has a good character and that's what counts. I'd like to have her."
Indifferent to: Miss Nellis (C11).	Miss Nellis: Rejects. "Couldn't even talk to her. We just didn't click."

Chooses Among the Representatives	*Reactions of the Representatives*
1st Choice: Leona (C8): "I liked her from first seeing her when she was talking to another girl in the corridor. She has the nicest smile.	Leona: Indifferent.

I think she must be very good-hearted."

2nd Choice: Ruth (C2): "I'd like to know her better. She made good suggestions to me and yet she wasn't bossy."

Ruth: Indifferent.

3rd Choice: Marion (C11): "I'd like to be like her, so confident and sure she is going to succeed."

Marion: Rejects. "She is altogether different from the girls in our house and she couldn't put her ideas over with us. We are fond of sports and she isn't; she just thinks of being a missionary and says she reads the Bible all the time. At the same time she wants to be a waitress and a missionary at one time. She asked me if there was much call for missionary jobs and I said I hadn't heard that there was."

Indifferent to: Harriet (C9).

Harriet: Indifferent.

Rejects: Alberta (C14): "Too silly."

Alberta. Indifferent.

Rejects: Katherine (CB): "I couldn't feel free with her."

Katherine: Indifferent.

ADELINE K.

Chooses Among the Housemothers

1st Choice: Mrs. Dickey (CB): "Talked so kind, I love her and I can't say why it is. She's good and she's nice and she's everything like that. She likes little girls and she has a little girl in her house."

Reactions of the Housemothers

Mrs. Dickey: 1st Choice: "I would simply love to have her. At first as I spoke to her I began to love her right off. I felt my group might be too old for her but she would be an influence to uplift the other girls, I feel. You know a young child can have that effect and my girls do love little ones. Of course, she wouldn't be a bit of help with the work but just the presence of a child like her would raise the others to greater effort. She'd be just the proper playmate for my Irene and if I take such small children it's better if I have two. Otherwise Irene will get spoiled. She is on the way to becoming so now, being so petted by the group. Both children would develop better if they had each other."

2nd Choice: Mrs. Reid (C8): "She looks so nice but not so nice as Mrs. Dickey to me."

Mrs. Reid: Indifferent.

3rd Choice: Miss Nellis (C11): "Not so much as Mrs. Dickey though. They have smiles and things but they aren't so good to you when they talk as Mrs. Dickey. I really only want to go to Mrs. Dickey's to live."

Miss Nellis: Indifferent.

Indifferent to: Mrs. Brett (C9).

Mrs. Brett: Indifferent.

Indifferent to: Mrs. Bradley (C2).

Mrs. Bradley: Indifferent.

Indifferent to: Mrs. Dorsey (C14).

Mrs. Dorsey: Indifferent.

Chooses Among the Representatives
1st Choice: Katherine (CB): "She knows about little girls and talks nice. Told me I would like their little girl Irene, that we would be girl friends and do our lessons and play together and she would help us. You can just talk and talk to her and she'll listen to you and yet she is a big girl, not small like me."

Reactions of the Representatives
Katherine: 2nd Choice: "We have a tiny girl Irene and she would be an ideal playmate for Adeline and at the same time the two together would be less trouble for us older girls than Irene is alone. Besides Adeline is so smart and winning she would help Irene a lot."

No additional choices: "I don't want to live with any of the girls besides Katherine very much. The rest are all the same to me."

Indifferent to: Leona (C8).

Leona: Indifferent.

Indifferent to: Ruth (C2).

Ruth: Indifferent.

Indifferent to: Marion (C11).

Marion: Indifferent.

Indifferent to: Harriet (C9).
Indifferent to: Alberta (C14).

Harriet: Indifferent.
Alberta: 3rd Choice: "A charming doll of a kid and she would be a novelty in our house as we haven't any small girls."

SHIRLEY A.

Chooses Among the Housemothers	*Reactions of the Housemothers*
1st Choice: Mrs. Dickey (CB): "I felt she took confidence in me and that would make me not disappoint her."	Mrs Dickey: Indifferent.
2nd Choice: Miss Nellis (C11): "Nice to me and I think she likes me."	Miss Nellis: Rejects. "She seems 'flat' to me, nothing to appeal about her. I didn't take to her at all and it would be a mistake for me to ask for her."
3rd Choice: Mrs. Dorsey (C14): "Talked nice to me, is a nice woman."	Mrs. Dorsey: Indifferent.
Indifferent to: Mrs. Brett (C9).	Mrs. Brett: Indifferent.
Indifferent to: Mrs. Bradley (C2).	Mrs. Bradley: Indifferent.
Indifferent to: Mrs. Reid (C8).	Mrs. Reid: 4th Choice: "I choose Shirley as my fourth choice. I feel she is teachable and I respond to her awkward strivings."

Chooses Among the Representatives	*Reactions of the Representatives*
1st Choice: Katherine (CB): "I want to live with her most of all. Has a way about her as if she would be your best friend when she has only just met you."	Katherine: Rejects. "Pretty fresh. Interrupts you while you're talking to her. First she wants you to know she's discontented and then she starts joking. Shirley would be fun to have around all right but not worth the trouble she'd cause us."
2nd Choice: Ruth (C2): "I admire her manner and her lovely way to talk to you; makes you feel welcome to the school and that you should be glad to be here. I want to see her often even if I don't go to her cottage."	Ruth: Rejects. "Shirley's certainly not very keen on the school. She has a way of shrugging her shoulders at what you say to her. She's not so smart as she thinks she is either. I don't want to have her in my cottage. I think she'd be stubborn and bossy and take her walking papers at her first opportunity."

3rd Choice: Marion (C11): "She's quick at understanding me. I think we'd get along good together."

Marion: Rejects. "To much a 'know-it-all.' Wouldn't want to agree with the other girls. I don't like her. She's got a sneaky atmosphere about her. I think she is watching for a chance to run away. Shirley is the boldest new girl I ever saw. Just her attitude shows she's apt to get in with the wrong set. Says she wants to get ahead but her manner doesn't go together with what she says. She really wants to raise Cain."

Indifferent to: Alberta (C14).

Alberta: 4th Choice: "She's nervous and kind of uneasy about being here but sometimes she's jolly too and I'd like to have her in our cottage."

Indifferent to: Harriet (C9).

Harriet: 4th Choice: "She has ideas about not letting other people run her but I could get around her all right. Mostly it's just that she likes to show off. I think Shirley is likeable any way and our house is about the best for her in my opinion."

Indifferent to: Leona (C8).

Leona: Rejects. "Too loud and kind of conceited. Our cottage wouldn't like her at all. She's altogether too bold. Makes sarcastic remarks about everything."

MURIEL F.

Chooses Among the Housemothers

Reactions of the Housemothers

1st Choice: Mrs. Reid (C8): "She's a lot of fun and likes to hear you talk."

Mrs. Reid: Rejects. "Too nervous for my group; talks too much; can't stand or sit still a minute.'

2nd Choice: Miss Nellis (C11): "She makes you feel happy because she's so happy."

Miss Nellis: Rejects. "She is ever so cute. She said, 'I like you,' in the fashion of a very young child. But I think she is sick; when she is in better health I should like to have her, but not at present. She would be too much for my patience right now."

3rd Choice: Mrs. Dorsey (C14): " Mrs. Dorsey tells you interesting things. She knows a lot."

Mrs. Dorsey: Rejects. " Highly irritable, nervous and jerky. Said she had been ill; really doesn't look well. I don't feel she is ready for cottage life yet."

Rejects: Mrs. Dickey (CB): " I just couldn't live with her."

Mrs. Dickey: Indifferent.

Rejects: Mrs. Bradley (C2): " I just couldn't live with her either."

Mrs. Bradley: Rejects. " She complains of headaches; very nervous; difficult for any group. Should be in the hospital for a while before going into any cottage."

Rejects: Mrs. Brett (C9): " I just can't stand to live with her."

Mrs. Brett: Indifferent.

Chooses Among the Representatives

Reactions of the Representatives

1st Choice: Ruth (C2): " The best sort of girl to talk to. You feel happy with her."

Ruth: 4th Choice: " I feel I'd like to help to make her happy. She's got the best heart and she is so pitiful."

2nd Choice: Alberta (C14): " Friendly."

Alberta: Indifferent.

3rd Choice: Marion (C11): " Very nice to you in what she says."

Marion: 2nd Choice: " I'm awfully sorry for Muriel. She fidgets all the time you talk. She tries to talk but she can't be interesting; answers in monosyllables. Needs a lot of help, I think. A case for sympathy. Perhaps if someone would be motherly to her she'd be all right. She's just sort of lost. As if she'd always stood alone with none to help her. Kicked around I suppose. I'd like to help her."

4th Choice: Katherine (CB): " Cheerful and cheers me up."

Katherine: 3rd Choice: " I feel sorry for her. She seems to try hard to be nice to you. I think she needs plenty of good treatment from the girls too, besides a housemother. I could get the girls in our house to be kind to her. Our housemother is real gentle too."

Indifferent to: Leona (C8).

Leona: Indifferent.

Indifferent to: Harriet (C9).

Harriet: Indifferent.

The conduct of assigned individuals was followed up and it appeared that when a large number of newcomers who had been assigned through the test were compared with an equal number of individuals who were placed into a home without a test, the success in adjustment and conduct was more favorable for the tested than for the untested group.

B. Case Study

Mixed boys and girls groups in a class of the 8th grade of a public school. The study centers around two girls, Olga and Julia, whose choices and motivations are presented (see sociogram p. 45).

Olga. First choice: Shirley; Second Choice: Sylvia. Motivations:

Shirley seems to be different from most girls. If she thinks a thing is right she will go ahead and do it. I wasn't very much like that and I like someone who is. I admire her character. She and I agree very much on literature, poetry especially. She is loyal, true and frank, even after you've known her a long time.

Sylvia is a comfortable sort of friend to have. She seems to be able to understand your thoughts and feelings and most other people can't. She doesn't try to get your confidence but you seem to want to confide in her. She is different from most of my friends, she acts older than her age. She's good at drawing. I don't believe she is a high-minded type of girl. In herself she doesn't seem to have much intelligence. She seems to be on a standard by herself. The majority of our girls have been simply brought up. I don't believe she has. When she is with girls in our class she seems to know by instinct what to talk about and says the right thing. But when she's with Gloria and Helen they all talk in a much more grown-up manner, like they were 17 or 18, speaking of clothes and boys and going out at night. I've only been with them a few times as generally they don't bother with me. It's a sort of clique of a set type. I like her but in a different way than I like most other girls, like her more like I'd like an older girl, while the other girls I like more as companions.

Florence I sometimes like and other times when I don't I guess it's jealousy. She's been brought up differently, too; she's been given a lot more freedom than I have, freedom with money and other things. There's something very likeable about her and she's a good standby at any time, but still you wouldn't want her to be your friend at all if she had to be your second best friend, and she's naturally a leader and very close, either you like her or you don't. You can't be moderate, it's either strong or weak. She *is* my best friend. We live one-half a block away and that may be the best reason as there's almost always some little topic of discussion or argument between us. She's an attractive girl, popular and has brains. I used to trust her implicitly but now I don't with my inmost secrets. But she seems to be a representative of friendship, you might say, and it's hard to be angry with her. We once were writing a book together about two girls, ourselves.

Doris, it's hard to describe her. She's totally different. She can express more with nothing than any other girl I ever knew. If you're feeling badly, she can give your hand a squeeze and you feel better than if another girl who is always gushing tries hard to help you. She means twice as much as she's doing. In school there's a quality in her that's hard to find in anyone else I know. She seems to know more than the other girls know, she seems to have had more sorrow in her life. Her quality is rather hidden, she acts shy. She seems to be able to understand everything. She seems to know what you're feeling sometimes when you can hardly tell it yourself.

George is the nicest boy. I wouldn't want to sit near Bill. He's a coarse type. Russell, either, he's simple and unintelligent. I don't like Buster either. He's easily influenced, weak. If he had had a different bringing up he'd be altogether different for the better. And Leonard is just the same as Buster. Not Benito, he seems to me to be bluffing about everything. Outwardly appears to consider himself a man of the world, but inwardly I think he isn't that way at all. He seems to be of the same type as Sylvia only in a boyish way. Charles is another bluffer but he has more feelings than he cares to show. He hasn't a mother and pretends to be happy-go-lucky. Beatrice is sort of "half-done." Anything could turn her either way but she hasn't been turned yet. Julia doesn't seem to have a serious thought. Thinks only of boys.

Julia. First choice: Patrina; Second choice: Shirley. Motivations:

Patrina seems attaching. I like her personality: she's refined, neat, good company, jolly, always happy. You can have fun with her. We both like painting. I never really went around with her.

Shirley, something like Patrina. She likes to do the things I do. She's clean in every respect. If I take a liking to a person I go around with them because I know it's a pleasure for both of us.

Alfonso is my choice among the boys. If I could have my choice I'd choose him. He's by far the nicest of all. The only girl I really don't like and don't want to sit beside is Olga. She's too "smart" for me. Always knows everything.

RESPONSES OF BOYS TOWARDS OLGA AND TOWARDS JULIA.

Towards Olga:
Leonard: She is all stuck up.

Russell: She knows a lot and I guess she knows she knows it.

George:

Howard: She is teacher's pet. She always snitches.

Benito: Don't like the way she acts. Acts like a baby. She thinks she is too much. Thinks she runs the school.

Towards Julia:
All boys are after her. She is very attractive.

Very nice girl.

She is very amusing. All the fellows are after her.

Best-looking girl in the class.

Alfonso: Funny looking, stuckup.

All right. She wants me to go over to her house but I am afraid of her. She is good-looking.

Michael: She thinks she is it. Is always putting on the Ritz. Her actions are that way. If we are discussing poetry she always chooses just the highest class stuff and I think she does it just to be obstinate and to be proud. Even if she likes it she shouldn't act so putting on.

She is very kind to me. She always helps one out.

Buster:

I like to talk to her.

Herman:

She has a talent for drawing.

RESPONSES OF GIRLS TOWARDS OLGA AND TOWARDS JULIA.

Towards Olga:

Shirley: I don't care about her. She was too intimate when we first met. She showed me her diary the first day. Haven't gone with her much since. She doesn't seem to be my type. She is sort of fantastic and very much conceited.

Towards Julia:

I like her in spite of all her ways and she likes me. It seems to me she puts on some airs and she dresses very much like a young lady and I just have on a middy and shirt or a plain dress. She has sort of associated with boys and I don't care for any of them so sometimes I feel out of place when she is talking to them and I am standing there.

Sylvia: She is kind of babyish but studious.

Show-off. Acts too old for her age. Wants to get all the boys around her. She brags. She likes to be grown up.

Maria: Wouldn't object to sitting beside her.

Acts too much as if she owned everything. Doesn't seem to care for anything but herself. When she was new, I helped her and when she had what she wanted she turned to other girls.

Helen: Nice, very nice.

Very conceited. Not particularly good. Always trying to get boys' attention, especially Alfonso's, who fools around with her. Thinks she is hot stuff, especially when she walks. Don't like her.

Beatrice:

Conceited. She always thinks she is right. She hurts your feelings. She never sticks.

Patsy: I don't know her well.

No one likes her. She is always bragging about everything, home and things like that. Tells you a lot of bologna.

Florence: When she first came into class she looked like a showoff. If you don't know her good you don't like her much. Not many of the girls like her. You have to know her intimately. She is nice and chummy and brilliant. I would like to sit beside her most of all.

I think she is a good-looking girl but we girls don't like her much because she is rather showoffy. Conceited. She sings well and is very pretty. She is new, came this term.

Patrina: Good at writing. Likes reading. Smart, sincere. Used to be very awkward.

I don't like her. She likes Alfonso. She doesn't go in for sports, more for clothes.

Gertrude:

Entirely stuck up. Thinks she is too high to be associated with you. Sometimes hears you but pretends she doesn't. So I don't bother with her any more. She does this all the time. When you talk to her it seems to go in one ear and out the other. Snubs you and tries to boss other people around. I used to stand for it but don't any more. Most of people I know don't like her. Girls in St. Mary's where she used to go didn't either.

Conclusions.

Both girls, Olga and Julia, have an exceptional position in their group. Olga is rejected by and rejects the majority of the boys and the girls are in the main indifferent to or reject her. She appears in the position of the independent individual with leader qualifications who, as she does not appeal to the majority, rejects them in turn. Julia is in a different position. She is rejected by the majority of the girls but chosen by the majority of the boys. She is indifferent to the girls' reactions but reciprocates in part the attention given her by the boys. She is rejected by the girls because she is emotionally advanced and in a superior position in respect to the boys, whereas the exclusive position of Olga results from her being in a superior position in respect to learning and recognition for her scholarship. We recognize Julia's superior position in respect to advance in emotional development. It is significant that they both antagonize each other. They are both exclusive in their conduct but in a different direction, each representing interests in the group above the level of differentiation of the majority of the members.

It is not easy to predict the position of Julia if she were placed in a class of girls only. On the basis of the present test, if boys had not been present she would appear as an isolated rejected individual. But it is probable that a new situation of all girls might stimulate her to try harder to win the attention of girls. Her position might appear different depending upon whether the group is mixed or not. It is different with Olga. It is probable that her position in a group of girls only would be unchanged.

C. The Spontaneity Test as an Aid in Assignment.

Elsa took part in one of the Impromptu play groups and she was often given occasion to act out different rôles—the rôle of a daughter or a mother, of a girl friend or of a sweetheart, of a housemaid or of a wealthy lady, of a pickpocket or a judge. She acted these parts in a great variety of standard life situations as they impress themselves upon an adolescent who grows up in the slums of a great industrial city. In these situations she is faced with a *home conflict*—mother and father in a heated argument which leads finally to their separation, with a *work conflict* in which she gets fired from a job because she stays out late, with a *love conflict* in which she loves a boy who is as poor and rejected as she is. An analysis of the text and gestures produced in these Impromptu situations gave us clues to understand better her early family life and the emotional tensions which gradually brought about her present status. (See Elsa, 171-92.)

When our attempt to adjust Elsa to the group with which she was living—treatment by suggestion, analysis of her conduct, change of her function within the house and of her associates within the group—had not succeeded in effecting a change in her behavior we considered creating an entirely new setting for her. But the question was where to place her and with whom. The sociometric test * was at this point a useful methodical guide which indicated to us the individuals in the community to whom her affection travelled, housemothers, teachers, or other girls. When we found that her interest revolved more or less persistently around certain persons in three different cottages, we began to pay attention to these individuals, especially to the motives Elsa had in seeking association with them and how the latter responded to her affection. As her acquaintance volume in the community was small, we thought that there may be many other individuals besides these who might have a beneficial effect upon her and we tried to enlarge the number of her acquaintances by having her meet others in the play groups. Through this technique we had the opportunity to see her acting opposite the individuals chosen by her in the sociometric test and also opposite other girls whom she had not known before and in rôles self-chosen or chosen by us. When the sociometric test was repeated after four weeks, she added three others to the number of girls with whom she wanted to live and she was in turn wanted by four. The girls for whom she dis-

---

* 2d test.

played attraction we divided into those who showed attraction in return, those who rejected her, and those who were indifferent to her. To gain an insight into which associations gave promise to be more enduring and beneficial, we placed her to act with the various other persons, whether these rejected or were attracted to her, in standard life situations in order that we might surmise what their conduct towards her would be in actual life. It was our principle to let the girls work out by themselves any situation which may turn up in life and which they may one day have to meet. A comparison of a series of 82 situational records indicated that only two of the seven girls Elsa had chosen released from her spontaneous expressions which contrasted favorably in articulation of emotion and judgment with her daily behavior or and which overcame certain petty habitual trends which she had demonstrated in speech and action when acting with the other girls. It seemed that she wanted to win the sympathy of Jeanette and Florence when acting with them. After a gradual elimination of the cottages unfit for Elsa and a close scrutiny of her relation to these two girls and to the housemother of C11, cottage 11 appeared as the most auspicious assignment for Elsa.

STATISTICS

The community survey and the study of children groups which this volume presents in sociometric relations and here in their motivation and verbal reflection are now subjected to statistical treatment.

In order to ascertain if a reliable difference exists between the group per cents of intersexual attractions we have used the method of dividing the difference between the two respective group per cents by the P.E.$_{Diff}$. As the table below indicates, there is an unreliable difference between the percentages of intersexual attractions in the two different groups of kindergarten children, the two groups of 1st Grades, of 5th Grades, of 6th Grades, and of 7th Grades. In these five instances much the same factors have evidently entered into the reactions of the children. In the other four instances, the two sets of 2nd Grades, of 3rd Grades, of 4th Grades, and of 8th Grades, on the other hand, a reliable difference is found to exist. Factors which made for a wider difference in reaction must have been present. Tracing what these may be, we find several which have a very direct bearing upon the test results. The turnover of population in this Public School is not a uniform one. This means that the children who transfer out of this school are not replaced by children of like age level. The average age level of the children in the 3rd grade, for instance, may be higher or lower one year than it was the year before, and the intersexual attractions of children are directly dependent upon their age level. Also the number of children in any class of the 3rd Grade, for instance, varies from one year to another. There may be 34 children in one class, 45 in another, and 49 in still another. The proportions of boys to girls within each class as well as the respective class populations affect the results very considerably. In order to have two populations

DIFFERENCE BETWEEN THE 2 GROUP-PER CENT'S OF INTERSEXUAL ATTRACTIONS EXPRESSED IN TERMS OF THE PROBABLE ERROR.

Grade	Number (or Population)*		1st Test Per Cent of Intersexual Attractions	2nd Test Per Cent of Intersexual Attractions	Differ- ence %	PE$_{diff.}$ %	Diff. — P.E.$_{diff.}$
	1st Test	2nd Test					
Kindergarten	55	66	25.	27.	2.	4.	.5
1st Grade	102	167	·27·	21.6	5.4	4.	1.4
2nd Grade	177	177	16.5	25.8	9.3	2.5	3.7
3rd Grade	131	153	8.5	19.8	11.3	2.6	4.3
4th Grade	159	183	2.5	8.9	6.4	1.4	4.6
5th Grade	103	198	5.5	3.9	1.6	2.	.8
6th Grade	174	187	4.1	1.1	3.	1.1	.3
7th Grade	198	255	3.0	3.4	.4	.8	.5
8th Grade	203	226	8.0	1.6	6.4	.1	6.4

* The actual number of children tested in the 1st and 2nd tests made of the Public School grades was far larger than the figures presented above indicate. For quantitative and statistical analysis of the findings all choices of children who were not present at the first giving of the test in each instance were excluded. This was done in order that all participants' choices should, as nearly as possible, have been made under the same conditions.

under like conditions we should have to have the same proportions of boys to girls in the different classroom groups of each grade, the same size of population within each of the classroom groups comprising each grade respectively, and the age levels of the two populations not differing to any appreciable degree within any of the classroom groups comprising each respective grade. Another factor affecting the findings is the length of time the children have had the opportunity to associate with one another. If, for instance, at the time one test is made there are more children in the 2nd Grade who have gone to school together or lived near each other than there are in the same grade at the time another sociometric test is taken, all other factors being equal, this would make for a difference in reaction between the two populations. Also the time at which two tests are made of different populations ought to be the same: if the test is given in one case the first week of the third month the school is in session in the second half of the school year, it should be given at the same time in any second case where we wish to compare the respective findings. In our two tests of Public School populations the first test was made one month later in the school year than it was in the second test. While this is not a very wide discrepancy, it may be wide enough to affect the findings to some degree.

It is, however, highly interesting that, despite all these factors which may enter and cause an amount of difference between the respective findings at any grade level, the coefficient of correlation (product-moment method) between the two series (Kindergarten to 8th Grade) of group per cents of intersexual attractions is .80. This high correlation makes it clear that essentially the same tendencies in respect to intersexual attractions must be present in the two different populations. This finding is of importance as it is an objective evidence that frequencies in respect to intersexual attraction among children from 4 to 14 years of age do not fluctuate widely from one population to another, but follow closely the same general rules. Further, it is proof that we have in the sociometric test a device which is reliable as an instrument for measuring such social phenomena. This consistency with which the sociometric test measures what it purports to measure can also be noted from an examination of Table 2 and Table 4 (see pp. 26 and 27). The group per cents of Isolated and the group per cents of Mutual Pairs in the two series found in the two respective populations of school children parallel each other in general very closely.

We may now turn to other findings presented in this book. The attempt to measure the sociometric relations within a group compared with those found within other groups whose population is of a similar composition (see p. 101, Ratio of Attractions), the attempt to measure the relations between such groups (see p. 102, Index of Relative Popularity), and the attempt to measure the relations within a group compared with the relative attraction the group has for itself in contrast to what it has for outside groups (see p. 99, Ratio of Interest), make up three criteria by which the position of a group within the community and the structure of the group itself have been " ranked." In order to ascertain if any relation exists between these three rankings, we have calculated the coefficient of correlation (by product-moment method) between each of them. They are found to be as follows:

Between Ratio of Interest and Ratio of
    Attractions. . . . .   r   .20 $\mp$ .17
Between Ratio of Interest and Index of
    Relative Popularity. . . . .   r —.375 $\mp$ .13
Between Ratio of Attractions and Index of
    Relative Popularity. . . . .   r   .07 $\mp$ .17

Each Probable Error is, of course, very large, due to the smallness of the series, 15. (There are about 30 members in each cottage, but here we are interested only in the relations of the 15* groups of individuals.)

The correlation between the two series expressing the Ratio of Interest each group has for itself and the Ratio of Attractions within the group is so small (.20) as to be unreliable. It may be concluded that the factors which enter into these two ratios are different and have practically no relation to each other. A group which receives a high ranking in one of these two ratios may or may not receive a high ranking in the other. We note an even greater absence of correlation between the two series expressing the Ratio of Attractions within each group and the Index of Relative Popularity (.07). The same conclusions may be drawn in respect to these two ratios as just mentioned above. However, between the two series expressing Ratio of Interest and Index of Relative Popularity we find the very rare negative correlation. This inverse relation is appreciable and indicates a considerable probability that any group which has a high Ratio of Interest for itself will have a comparatively low Index of Relative Popularity.

---

* There are 16 cottages but we omit C3 from our calculations as C3 does not appear in Table 11, p. 101. See footnote 15.

In view of the mechanisms of emotional expansiveness and emotional shrinkage, and in view of the tendency of the social atom towards maintaining an equilibrium, the negative relation between Index of Relative Popularity and Ratio of Interest gains a special significance as it is a quantitative proof of the ambivalent character of emotional expansiveness. The more emotional energy a number of individuals spend within their own group, the less appears to be available to be spent outside of it, the less attention is paid by them to other groups of individuals in the community, the less attention is paid to them in return, and the less becomes their popularity.

As the development of a Social Quotient of a group is dependent, among other things, upon our knowing first whether the different criteria selected as indicative of the group's social relations are indeed different or whether they overlap each other so that a group which ranks high in one is bound of necessity to rank high in another, the indications of the co-efficients of correlation are significant. It appears that the three ratios used for ranking a group are three *different* things, each measuring another aspect of social relations.

NOTES

1. " Rede über die Begegnung " (Speech about the Meeting), J. L. Moreno (ed), 1924. See bibliography. The therapeutic conflict of the physician who goes out to treat one man in a certain village but is held up from reaching him because he meets so many others on the way whose malady is interlocked with his and because he finds that no man can be treated singly but all men together, is presented in the following words: " But how is it that I didn't reach yet the place in which he lives? That is why: between the place from which I parted and the place where he lives are many countries and each country through which I pass has several counties. And every county has so many villages. And every village has more than hundred or more than thousand souls. And every soul which I meet needs my attention."

2. The founder of scientific socialism missed in estimating religion for the same reason which made him miss in estimating the psychological factor and perhaps for the same reason which made him distinguish between the first phase of communistic society and the highest phase of it. It was a theoretical obsession with strategic procedure and for splitting a unity into two apparently different issues. The deep analyst of the relation of merchandise to man was a poor psychologist of human interrelations. Marx thought that the economic and the psychological problem of man can not be attacked at one time; that the psychological problem can wait; that, so to speak, two different revolutions are necessary and that the economic-social revolution has to precede what we have called the psychological or creative revolution of human society.

3–4. Nietzsche and Freud are essentially historians. Nietzsche, the philologist, circled around analysis and interpretation of past events; Freud, the physician, circled around anamnesis, the traumatic origins of mental disturbances. They are both psychoanalysts in that they considered mental catharsis as arising from the reflection of the past and this the more accurate the latter was reflected and the further back they succeeded in penetrating it. They recommended this returning, remembering, and analyzing as a therapy in itself. To them the "now and here" seemed superficial. They did not know what to do with the *moment*. They did not take the moment in earnest. It seemed to them that the only thing to do with the moment and its conflicts is to explain them, that is, to discover the associations back to their causes. The other alternative would have appeared an absurdity to them: to live, to act in the moment, to act unanalyzed. It would have seemed to be the end of psychology and of the psychologist. Spontaneous acting would have been refused by them because it appears to be an affirmation of immaturity, of childhood, of unconscious living,—a dangerous respect for just that which the psychologist tried to illumine. But there is an alternative: to develop a technique from the moment upward in the direction of spontaneous evolution, in the direction of life and time. " Rede über den Augenblick " (Speech about the moment), J. L. Moreno (ed), 1923. See bibliography.

5. It may be that what can survive is not worthy of survival and that what is worthy of survival cannot survive. If the future of mankind can be " planned," then conscious evolution through training of spontaneability opens a new vista for the development of the human race.

6. It consisted in assigning one person to others and all the persons to a common objective. Many interesting observations were made. We could note the conflicting tendencies resulting from the wish of the different persons to drive the situation into the direction each prefers and in consequence each individual being forced to correct his intended expression continuously as other persons within the group drive him into a different direction from the one he wants. It was evidenced how poorly men are able to adjust themselves to unexpected situations. Since an analysis of each of the persons as such did not evolve the desired effect, a psychology of

426

coördination of persons with persons had to be developed. In search of techniques of coordination it was found that two very well organized individuals can make a very unhappy team. Two erratic individuals matched with a steady third may make an auspicious triangle. The knowledge of psychological states and their mechanisms is not sufficient to determine techniques of coördination. The problem is not what kind of reactions they have individually or socially, but what attributes enable them to fit together with other persons in a course of action. We then reduced the task to its simplest form and suggested to them to let loose, unconcerned, faithfully relying upon the spontaneous aptitudes to act and react on the spur of the moment. Through such experiments we recognized that spontaneity when crude, however beautiful and disarming looked at from the point of view of the persons engaged in the acting, led in most of the cases to the gravest deficiencies of coöperation. We saw disclosed then in the plainest form the workings of our society, each individual following his longings, willing the best, but the whole thing, all together, going wrong. *Abstracted* from " Application of the Group Method to Classification." See bibliography.

7. See page 6 in " Einladung zu einer Begegnung " (Invitation to a Meeting), J. L. Moreno (ed). See bibliography.

8. Marx tried to prove that in the long run at least psychological changes are produced by economic changes; that from the division between capital and labor derives the psychology of two different classes, capitalists and proletariat, and with this all other major differences among men. The change of economic structure in Russia since the Revolution of 1918 does not appear to be accompanied by the expected change in the psychology of interrelations. Looking at the Russia of today he might say that the psychological changes lag for behind the economic changes because the communistic society is still in its first phase; that the state has not yet " withered away." But may not the communistic society in its highest state be a myth to be set aside afterwards as Utopian and unattainable as soon as the economic program of the first phase is achieved?

9. In the process of evolution natural selection has been up to date the final arbiter of survival. But man has arrived at crossroads. He can live and survive in two different environments, the one is the natural environment in which his freedom as a biological being, the function of the creator, is the most supreme criterion, and the other an industrial or, better said, a conserved and conserving environment in which his freedom and his creative function are restrained and have to flow between the bedrock of mechanical evolution. Obviously, races of men fit for the one may be unfit for the other. The criteria of unfitness are different in both environments. One line of evolution may lead inescapably to societies of men similar to societies of insects, harmonious and one hundred per cent efficient but unindividualistic. The other line of evolution may lead inescapably to a new race of men which tacitly will follow the direction of his ascendance up to date, partly will be modified by the triumph over the robot. There will be then two possibilities of survival for man: one, as a zoötechnical animal, the other, as a creator. The notion of Darwin of the survival of the fittest gains herewith a modification. Both environments may guarantee survival to man but independently, survival of such individuals as appear to be in respect to one particular environment the fittest. And in an environment in which the machine and the technical conserve is thrown not out of existence but out of rule, the fittest will be the creator man, not the servant of the machine, the machine-addict, but its master. And the type of man who is supreme in a conserving environment will be doomed to perish in the other. The future may well see two different environments flourishing side by side and breeding two different races of men and leading consequently to the most important division since man arose from certain genera of the Pliocene ape man to our own genus Homo.

10. We presented the rhythm of growth and decline in " Homo Juvenis." 1914. See bibliography. The following is abstracted from that study. The closer an individual is to the germplasm the fresher is his experience of life as a totality, however inarticulate his expression of this experience may be and however unaware he may be of the innumerable details in the universe.

The more distant an individual is from the germplasm, the weaker is his experience of life as a totality, however articulate his expression of this experience may be and however unaware he may have become of the innumerable details of the universe. The most intensive period of life is childhood and adolescence (homo juvenis), the less intensive, manhood and senescence (homo sapiens). In consequence we recognized that just as "the individual operates in space with two functions, body and mind, the individual operates in the dimension of time in two phases, homo juvenis and homo sapiens."

11. For the term "sociogram" we are indebted to *Dr. Frederick L. Patry,* Neuropsychiatrist, State Education Department, University of the State of New York. It is an interesting coincidence that the term had also been suggested by *Helen Jennings.—*The three sociograms presenting baby groups suggest horizontal differentiation of structure from about 20 weeks on and vertical differentiation of structure from about 40 weeks on. This appears to be in contradiction to some of the interpretations of investigators of individual child development. The reason for this is probably that the development of an association of infants compared with the development of individual infants is "retarded." Occasional relation of one infant to another cannot be counted as producing organization. Attention of a baby to a neighbor's voice or movements has to appear with a certain frequency and constancy before the reaction can be called a *relation.*

12. It locates for us the time points in the child's group development at which preventive measures are offered the possibility of successful application. The sociometric testing of the population of so-called delinquency areas (home, school and neighborhood groups are among its various components) in cities may furnish the psychogeographical evidence upon which constructive measures can be based.

13. Piaget in his studies of the child considers the 7–8 year level as the point at which verbal expression of the individual child becomes socialized.

14. "Extroverted" and "introverted" are psychological concepts which are used to connote specific individual reaction patterns. "Extroverted" and "introverted" group organization are sociometric concepts and have no relation to *introverted* and *extroverted* as used in the psychological sense. For instance, many members of an introverted group organization may be extroverts and many members of an extroverted group organization may be introverts. And then they are not subjective notions but exactly measurable expressions. The sociometric notions which correspond to *introvert* and *extrovert* in the psychological sense are *emotional expansiveness* and *emotional shrinkage.* But also they have been developed in regard to the functioning of the individual within a group and can be presented in a metric fashion.

A similar problem arises when we consider the theory of instincts. The dichotomy of instinct in the form of the sexual and the aggressive components may satisfy the psychoanalyst and the needs of individualistically oriented psychiatry. From their point of view it may appear that we should identify all emotions expressing attraction with the sexual component and all emotions expressing repulsion with the aggressive component. But this division, even if considered true for the individual organism, meets with methodological difficulties when applied to groups. The origin of a certain emotion, love or hate, rising from an individual, whatever the analytic definition of the end-product may be, is in its psychogeographical unfoldment interlocked with emotions rising from other individuals. Often we can see how they grow together, in symbiosis, dependent upon one another. When we say *attraction,* we indicate that a certain emotion spreads through a certain geographical area in respect to a certain criterion *to join* with a certain individual. When we say *repulsion,* we indicate that a certain emotion spreads through a geographical area in respect to a certain criterion *to separate* from a certain individual. A sexual current is not necessarily the accumulation of sexual impulses; it is often the product of many contrasting and even contradicting factors. If we should say, instead of attraction, *love* or *libido,* we would say more than we can say; we would confuse the sexual component which has an individual origin with the sexual current which has a socionomic origin. It appears, therefore, more useful to consider the socionomic area of investigation as having laws of its own and not to mix its interpretations with those coming from other fields.

15. In order to rank the groups given in this table on the basis of their structural analysis, we should have to calculate the various numbers of each structure each group would have produced if the population had been the same size in each instance; for example, if each cottage had had exactly 25 members.

The population of Hudson at the time of the first giving of the sociometric test was 505. It will be noted that the total population of the 16 cottages was 435. The 70 individuals unaccounted for were at that time residing chiefly in the hospital or on the farm attached to the school. As both these groups were formed on other criteria than living in proximity as in the case of the cottage groups (in the one instance, the criterion to be treated for illness, in the other, a vocational criterion), we excluded the findings in respect to these groups from the findings in respect to the 16 cottage groups. The second phase of the test left out C3 and so it does not appear in all the tables.

For the classification of groups, aside from the procedure discussed, a special test has been devised for determining the organization of a group when we wish to ascertain this without regard to the groups around it. One variety of it consists in letting the members of the group choose their neighbors at the dining tables. The choices and motivations given are then compared with the actual seating order the members have at the time.

16. United States Census Reports for 1920.

17. See "Application of the Group Method to Classification," pp. 13–14. See bibliography.

18. Stegreif experiment (Impromptu or Spontaneity experiment), "Stegreiftheater," pp. 26–64. See bibliography.

19. The following example (see "Application of the Group Method to Classification," pp. 95–97, also chapter on "group psychotherapy" on page 56-7) illustrates how one can apply assignment therapy to the treatment of mental disorders.

Three women were assigned as a group. Each was afflicted with a different mental disorder. S. was suffering from a severe form of involutional melancholia; R. was mildly presenile; and M., unstable and below average in intelligence. The assignment was not made, and ought not to have been made, on the basis of individual diagnosis, their assumed reaction types, or other generalizations, but *on the basis of the sum of all symptoms and all the anamnestic facts known about each and the weighting of every factor and symptom against every factor and symptom of the other two persons.*

Mrs. S. History: Age, 58. Jewish immigrant. Married early and lost her husband at 30. Didn't desire to remarry. Never became interested in learning to read or write English, and spoke it poorly. Worked to support her four small children. Had always been extremely reticent. Was the obedient servant of her children. She manifested deep attachment to her son-in-law and her daughter-in-law, but worried because there were no grandchildren and over the fact that her two younger daughters were unmarried. During her menopause she underwent an operation on the womb. Insidious onset of present disorder.

Symptoms: Incessantly proclaims somebody wants to kill her and her children and that her children-in-law are the cause of all trouble. Declares they should be punished and killed to save her and her children from further persecution. Solitaire attitude. Hostile, suspicious. Never talks to anyone. Seldom answers a question. Fears to go outside the house. Stuporous. Hears voices. Persistently un-coöperative. Reiterates: "I didn't do anything to anybody. I and my children will be killed."

Mrs. R. History: Age, 62, Jewish immigrant. Reads and writes English. Husband died when she was 40. Did not remarry. Spoiled by her two sons whom she dominated. Always highly sociable and looking for amusements. Very verbose. Spontaneous. Sympathetic. Her daughter-in-law became antagonistic towards her, claiming she is unbearable to them as she always wanted to be the center of the stage and to be served by them. They insisted she be placed in a home.

Symptoms: Incessantly talking and joking. Feeble memory for recent events. Constantly complaining and never satisfied. Sleeplessness.

Mrs. M. Age, 45. Irish-American. Opera singer. Widow of two husbands, both Italians. Periodical moods of joy and depression. Threatened to commit suicide. Uncritical in judgment about people who have taken advantage of her. Impractical in handling her own situations. Enthusiastic. Coöperative. Dysfunction of the thyroid gland.

The assignment phase presented here considers first the spontaneous choice factor, as the first reactions indicate the possible development of advantageous relationship. The more hostile to coöperation a patient is, the more important is the finding of a person towards whom he reacts favorably. The choice factor is disregarded only if all other factors and symptoms indicate that the choice is disadvantageous for either one or both persons or if the cases are so grave that the assignment has to be done fully by the attending psychiatrist, but the slightest signs of spontaneous desire for other persons should receive attention.

In this case, the following reactions were noted. S. smiled at R. when they met the first time as she was greeted by her in a Jewish-American slang with which she was familiar, and in turn R. seemed pleased with S. as she found in her someone who listened patiently and without stopping her. S. ignored M. who received her with a cheerful laughter, but M. expressed pity for S. when she saw her break into tears and began at once to mother her. R. appeared refined and clever to M. while R. took an attitude of satisfaction as though she had found someone she could command.

Further, comparison of the respective factors of the three indicated that association would be of therapeutic value:

Similar attributes: All three were widows. All were mothers of adult children. All feared men and liked the house because there were no men in it.

Contrasting attributes: S. and R. preferred to use Jewish-German slang; M. talked only English. S. and R. expected to be served by M. and M. was willing to serve only S. and not R. R. had dominated her children; S. had been dominated by them; and M. and her daughter had been like sisters to each other.

Complementary attributes: R. wanted a companion to whom she could talk, etc., and S. had always felt it her part to comply and listen to others. (R. wanted badly to have a partner on her walks and already the first day she began to nag S. to accompany her.) S. had always been unsociable and occupied only with household interests and the serving of others. M. was an indefatigable worker in the house so an additional, constructive point of coördination was present between M. and S.

Herewith some of the factors which suggested the assignment of S., R., and M. to one group are stated. S. is after eighteen months on the way to full recovery. M. and R. have improved.

The method of assignment we have described elsewhere for the prisoner consists in relating to him the nearest and closest persons, the other prisoners. Similarly it consists for the insane in an institution in relating to him the nearest and closest persons, the other patients and the personnel.

Group assignment and spontaneous therapy will be advantageous for persons who do not recover by themselves or through some form of psychological analysis or medication, but only through the interaction of one or more persons who are so coördinated to the patient that the curative tendencies within are strengthened and the disparaging tendencies within checked and so that he may influence the members of his group to their therapeutic advantage.

To make this method useful for a mental hospital, complete charts for assignment and interrelation data have to be worked out, rating the prepsychotic factors and the complex of symptoms and interpreting their interconnections. One or two trial groups may lead to various practical rules as to how the treatment can be applied to the whole population of the hospital.

20. Observers often disagree as to what emotion underlies certain mimic expressions. But whether or not there is any measurable relationship between mimic expression and emotion does not de-evaluate the significance of warming-up indicators and of starters for the subject in training.

21. The suggestion which comes from the research into spontaneous behavior is that the reflex may be secondary to the " creative act." Spontaneous functioning in the beginning of organic life may have appeared in a direct, deliberate form. Reflexive spontaneity may have superseded this primary function and become the more complex as the organisms became the more complex.

22. Major disturbances which arise from the segregation en masse of a certain nationality group within a population can be largely reduced if this mass is broken up and its units distributed throughout the community. When the same living quarters are provided for contrasting groups other disturbances develop if the saturation point within the small living-group units is surpassed.

23. See note 15.

24. United States Census Reports for 1928.

25. See sociograms, pp. 31–3.

26. In the history of community experimentation Charles Fourier and Robert Owen have earned a place of honor. Over a century ago these two indefatigable pioneers evolved ingenious schemes for social organization. It was their Utòpian concept of human nature and of human society which accounts for their not having conceived of psychological planning in their projects and to this may be partly attributed the failure of their respective efforts.

27. Also other factors which we have indicated in the developmental levels of group organization are significant. For instance, the rôle of homosexual attraction in the production of cleavages within groups (see pp. 60–64). Only a Population Test could disclose to any adequate degree the tremendous implications of psychological pressure within groups.

28. See " Impromptu," April, 1931, p. 3.

29. Preceding the physical setting up of a community should be initiated its psychological set-up. The more criteria the Population Test is determined in respect to, the more can the physical structure of the community be organized to reflect it: the location of public centers, the grouping of the houses, and so on.

30. See T. Hunt Morgan, " Biology and Physics," Science, LXV, p. 213; C. C. Hurst, " The Mechanism of Creative Evolution," pp. 172, 179, 184, 185. We may have to consider not only changes in the genes, as suggested by Morgan and others, but changes *between* the genes,—whatever mutation may have taken place in a gene and for whatever reason, mechanical, chemical, or whatever. If this mutation should be favorable, the genes must be attractive to one another, that is, must correspond to changes in some other genes. In other words, the genes must be able to produce a functional relation; morphological affinities and disaffinities between them must exist. It may be doubted whether the attraction of one individual towards another and pairing inclinations are a fair index of morphological affinity and conversely whether repulsion of one individual for another and disinclination to mate are an index of sterility or reflecting a dysgenic factor. Our opinion is that as long as no better knowledge is available, affinities of individuals for one another should be considered a practical index. It is not known to us if ever a thorough investigation of the relationships existing between psychological affinities and disaffinities and the eugenic reflections of them has been made. The more one considers psychological processes as a fair index for bodily changes and the more one considers them as an index not only for the needs of the individual but also for the needs of the kind, the more will one be inclined to expect that the factor of spontaneous choice and spontaneous clicking is not a random experience but an inherent expression of the whole organism. A definite relation may exist between gene effect (if we call " gene effect " the reflection of one gene upon another and upon the individual characters) and tele effect.

Cultural Conserve. The technical conservation of cultural values, as the book or the film, which substitutes and preserves man's creative expressions. It differs from the machine which accomplishes his labor and from the robot which is an imitation of man.

Emotional Expansiveness. The specific function of emotion to spread from one individual to others and to shrink or expand within certain limits.

Homosexual Attraction. This term does not imply true homosexuality. It simply indicates attraction between individuals of the same sex.

Heterosexual Attraction indicates attraction between individuals of opposite sex.

Network. A psychological structure which consists largely of a chain formation in which individuals comprising certain links in it are unacquainted with those in more distant links but can exert an influence upon one another by indirection. Through such chains opinion and suggestion can

Population Test. A sociometric test applied to large populations.

Psychological Currents. Feelings which spread from one group to other groups.

Psychological Distance. In distinction from *social distance,* which considers the undifferentiated attitude of an individual (or group) towards a class of people, psychological distance considers the degree of distance or nearness an individual (or group) has towards another individual (or another group) on the basis of the accumulative effect of the individual affinities and disaffinities between them (the evidence being secured by sociometric testing).

Psychological Geography. The expansion of psychological currents in relation to the various anchorages of our social structure (families, factories, churches, etc.) produce a picture of a community which is geographic and psychological at the same time. It is determined by the specific relations between the specific individuals comprising these various anchorages.

Social Atom. The smallest constellation of psychological relations which can be said to make up the individual cells in the social universe. It consists of the psychological relations of one individual to those other individuals to whom he is attracted or repelled and their relation to him all in respect to a specific criterion (as living in proximity).

Sociogram. A graph which visualizes the underlying structure of a group and the position each individual has within it. (See note 11, p. 428.)

Sociometry. The mathematical study of psychological properties of populations, the experimental technique of and the results obtained by application of quantitative methods.

Sociometric Test. An instrument to measure the amount of organization shown by social groups.

Socionomy. A science which is concerned with the psychological properties of populations and with the communal problems which these properties produce.

Tele. A feeling which is projected into distance; the simplest unit of feeling transmitted from one individual towards another.

Glossary to Charts. The charts of the home groups (pp. 117–29) and the Tabulation of page 109 do not indicate always the same number of structures as some of the charts relate to a different developmental level of these groups. On p. 74 seventy-five individuals are presented as unchosen. On p. 75, Table 8, sixty-six individuals. In Table 8, Cottage III with five and the Hospital with four unchosen are not included. This accounts for the difference. Cottage V is classified, on p. 76, on the basis of its choice structure as balanced. On p. 122, Cottage V is described as extroverted because when the responses were added to the choices coming from individuals of outside groups this trend appeared to be the more dominant one.

When a community has been put under the microscope through sociometric study, as the Hudson school has been, it is difficult to present the findings so that all aspects of the community's psychological organization can be viewed as a totality. Of necessity we have been compelled to focus our attention, now on this aspect and now on that, so as to point out what may be of especial importance not alone for an understanding of Hudson but as well for other communities. It was our aim to treat more extensively those aspects of human interrelations which are everywhere productive of conflict and tension within groups. This was done in order that our study might contribute to the understanding of these problems in the world at large. In consequence our emphasis upon any particular problem in Hudson, as racial tension, sex, or runaways, needs to be understood as arising from a penetration into the underlying factors which are uncovered when we examine beneath the surface of a community's psychological structure of organization, whether this community be now Hudson or any other. There is no structure found in Hudson which may not and does not develop in other communities outside.

The remarkable effort on the part of the superintendent of Hudson to offset these disruptive forces with an ingeniously devised educational set-up is a subject which would deserve a special writing. Further, a variety of social projects are continuously invented and new ideas and people from the outside are brought into the school to arouse interests in the girls and to rob them of the feeling that the community is closed in the rigid sense of the word. Thus creative forces are at work to produce a psychological home for the several hundred children who have been under-privileged outside.

The incidents in regard to a runaway chain of 14 individuals within 14 days (see pp. 256–60) and the incident within one part of the colored population (see pp. 217–224) were so exceptional in this institution in which nothing similar had happened during the last ten years, that it provoked our attention and stimulated our study of the underlying causes.

ACKNOWLEDGMENTS

I and my collaborator, Helen Jennings, found in the Elizabeth Fry Foundation and in the National Committee on Prisons and Prison Labor the centers from which opportunities for experimentation arose. The National Committee on Prisons and Prison Labor and the Chairman of its Executive Council, Dr. E. Stagg Whitin, have promoted this endeavor, and Dr. Whitin's early comprehension of the possibilities of this study contributed largely to its actual realization. Miss Julia K. Jaffray, Secretary of the National Committee on Prisons and Prison Labor and Chairman of the Department of Public Welfare of the General Federation of Women's Clubs, has been our continual adviser. It was due to her initiative that the way was paved for a study in the New York State Training School for Girls.

To Mrs. Fannie French Morse, Superintendent of the New York State Training School for Girls; to Dr. Nathan D. Peyser, Principal of Public School 181, Brooklyn, and to Mr. Frank Hackett, Headmaster of the Riverdale Country School, go our gratitude for their unswerving support and encouragement.

We are indebted to Miss Beatrice B. Beecher, who directed the work at the Plymouth Institute in Brooklyn; Mrs. Myrtle P. Bridge, for her work at the Grosvenor Neighborhood House in New York; Dr. Henry E. Garrett of Columbia University, for helpful suggestions for the statistical treatment of data, and to both Mrs. John Rogers, Jr., Executive Secretary of the United Parents Association, and Mr. Alexander Williams, Public Relations Director of the latter organization.

The search for new and appropriate techniques by the staff of the Subsistence Homestead Division of the U. S. Department of the Interior led to their request for our advice and the adaptation of our techniques to the vitally interesting problems of the Subsistence Homestead.

The research material has been gathered under circumstances of rare sacrifice and idealism. We wish to acknowledge particularly the contributions rendered by Mr. Richard Stockton, our associate in the work from its early beginnings, who conducted during a period of one year the study of the Riverdale Country School. Mr. Claudius B. Webster directed the second test of Public School 181. Miss Miriam Reed assisted in the initial phases both in Brooklyn and in Hudson. Miss Nellie Stevens aided in the study of initial assignments at Hudson. We extend our thanks also to: Misses Sarah Ames, Ellen Andrews, Eleanor Burns, Ruth Canis, Augusta Dockery, Esther Eckstein, Gloria Fernandez, Jane Jaffray, Catherine Jones, Isabella Lyon, Ellen MacDermott, Joan Mac-Dermott, Elizabeth McCune, Ruth Mary Mitchell, Charlotte Moller, Mary Morganstern, Olga Osi, Elizabeth Stackpool, and Gertrude Turner.

It gives us a special pleasure to thank the staff of the Hudson school for the unusual spirit in which they aided us. The application of therapeutic procedures would not have been possible except for the sympathetic coöperation of Miss Jeannette Farrell, Assistant Superintendent, Miss Florence McDermid, Director of After or Community Care, and Mrs. Ruth Esselstyn, Social Case Worker, and except for the eager interest and broad-minded attitude of the housemothers: Mrs. Ann Darby, Mrs. Maude Bothwell, Miss Rose Carter, Mrs. Fannie Daggett, Mrs. Mammie Ellis, Mrs. Bertha Fosbury, Miss Mary Green, Mrs. Dorothy Higgins, Mrs. Loretta Loughlin, Mrs. Margherita Murnane, Miss Helen Pitcher, Mrs. Mary Ploss, Mrs. Nellie Robbins, Mrs. Florence Sebastian, Mrs. Lureen Simmons, Mrs. Harriet Tanner, Mrs. Nina Tuxbury, Mrs. Alice Van Slyke, Miss Nelly Wallace, and Mrs. Eva Warner.

It is in the nature of the work that the people to whom the project is applied play a rôle that is well nigh incalculable. To the girls of the Hudson school we wish to pay here our tribute for their continuous faith and enthusiasm.

BIBLIOGRAPHY

BECHTEREW, E., and LANGE, A. *Die Ergebnisse des Experiments auf dem Gebiete der Kollectiven Reflexologie.* Zsch. d. angew. Psychol., 1924, Vol. 24, 224–254.

BERGSON, HENRI. *L'Évolution Créatrice.* Paris, 1907.

BERNHEIM, H. *De la suggestion dans l'éat hypnotique et dans l'état de veille.* 1884.

BÜHLER, C. *The First Year of Life.* 1930.

BOGARDUS, E. S. *Social Distance and Its Origins.* J. Appl. Sociol., 1925, Vol. 9, 216–226.

CHEVALEVA-JANOVSKAJA, E. *Les groupements spontanés d'enfants à l'age prescolaire.* Arch. de Psychol., 1927, Vol. 20.

COMTE, AUGUSTE. *Positive Philosophy.* Paris, 1830.

DARWIN, C. *Origin of Species.* London, 1859.

FREUD, SIGMUND. *Three Contributions to Sexual Theory.* Monograph Series No. 7.

FOURIER, FRANÇOIS CHARLES. *Théorie des quatre mouvements.* 1808.

FEOFANOV, M. P. *Psikhologia.* 1928, Vol. 1, 107–120.

GALTON, SIR FRANCES. *Hereditary Genius.* London, 1869.

GESELL, A. *Infancy and Human Growth.* 1928.

HURST, C. C. *Experiments in Genetics.* 1925.

KRETSCHMER, E. *Physique and Character.* 1925.

LAPIÈRE, R. T. *Race Prejudice: France and England.* Social Forces, 1928, Vol. 7, 102.

LE PLAY, FRÉDÉRIC. *Les Ouvriers Européens.* Paris, 1855.

LOEB, J. *Forced Movements, Tropisms, and Animal Conduct.* 1918.

MARX, K. H. *The Civil War in France.* 1872.

MEYER, A. *Fundamental Concept of Dementia Praecox.* Brit. M. J., 1906, 757–760.

MORENO, J. L. *Explanatory,* to the Psychological Planning of Institutions and Communities, 32 charts, presented at the Scientific Exhibit of the Medical Society of the State of New York, April 3–5, 1933.

—— *Psychological Organization of Groups in the Community.* Proceedings of the American Association on Mental Deficiency, Boston, 1933.

—— *Application of the Group Method to Classification,* in collaboration with E. Stagg Whitin. 1932. Published by the National Committee on Prisons and Prison Labor.

—— *Impromptu Play vs. Standardization.* New York, 1929. (Supplementing a public presentation of the Spontaneity Test, under the auspices of the United Parents Association, Grand Central Palace, 1929.)

—— *Das Stegreiftheater.* Gustav Kiepenheuer, publisher. Berlin, 1923.

—— *Über den Augenblick.* Gustav Kiepenheuer, publisher. Berlin, 1923.

—— *Rede über de Begegnung.* Gustav Kiepenheuer, publisher. Berlin, 1923.

—— *Homo Juvenis,* p. 19, in *Einladung zu einer Begegnung.* Gustav Kiepenheuer, publisher. Berlin, 1914.

MORGAN, T. H. *Theory of the Gene.* 1926.

MÜNSTERBERG, H. *Grundzuge der Psychotechnik.* 1914.

NIETZSCHE, FREDERIC. *Ecce Homo.* 1889.

OWEN, ROBERT. *A New View of Society.* 1813.

PAVLOV, J. P. *Conditioned Reflexes, an Investigation of the Physiological Activity of the Cerebral Cortex.* 1927.

PIAGET, J. *The Language and Thought of the Child.* 1926.

SHAW, C. R. *Delinquency Areas.* 1929.

SPENCER, H. *Principles of Sociology.* 1880–96.

THOMAS, D. S. *Social Aspects of the Business Cycle.* 1925.

WATSON, J. B., and RAYNOR, R. *Conditioned Emotional Reactions.* J. Exper. Psychol., 1920.

WHITE, WILLIAM A. *Outline of Psychiatry.* Nerv. and Mental Dis. Mon. Series No. 1.

—— *Foundations of Psychiatry.* Nerv. and Mental Dis. Mon. Series No. 32.

—— *Essays in Psychopathology.* Nerv. and Mental Disease Mon. Series No. 43.

NERVOUS AND MENTAL DISEASE MONOGRAPH SERIES

Edited by

SMITH ELY JELLIFFE, M.D., and WILLIAM A. WHITE, M.D.

No. 1. Outlines of Psychiatry. (Thirteenth Edition, 1932.) By WM. A. WHITE, M.D., Price, $4.00. A clearly written and concise presentation of psychiatry especially adapted for use in teaching and in public institutions for mental diseases. ILLUSTRATED.

No. 7. Three Contributions to Theory of Sex (Third Edition, 1930.) By PROF. SIGMUND FREUD, Price $2.50. A most important contribution to the psychology of psychosexual development.

No. 14. General Paresis. By PROF. E. KRAEPELIN, Price $3.00. (Illustrated.) A masterly presentation of the subject of general paresis by the renowned Munich professor.

No. 28. The Autonomic Functions of the Personality. By DR. EDW. J. KEMPF, Price $3.00.

No. 31. Sleep-Walking and Moon-Walking. By J. SADGER, Price $2.00.

No. 33. A Psychoanalytic Study of Psychoses with Endocrinoses. By DUDLEY WARD FAY, Ph.D., Price $2.50.

No. 34. Psychoanalysis and the Drama. By SMITH ELY JELLIFFEE, M.D., and LOUISE BRINK, A.B., Price $3.00.

No. 35. Constitutional Factors in Dementia Praecox. By N. D. C. LEWIS, M.D. Illustrated, Price $3.00.

No. 36. The Primitive Archaic Forms of Inner Experiences and Thought in Schizophrenia. By DR. A. STORCH, Price $2.00.

No. 37. Women Characters in Richard Wagner. By LOUISE BRINK, Ph.D., Price $2.00.

No. 38. An Introduction to the Study of Mind. By WM. A. WHITE, M.D., Price $2.00.

No. 39. The Emotions, Morality and the Brain. By C. v. MONAKOW, Price $2.00.

No. 40. The Development of Psycho-Analysis. By S. FERENCZI and O. RANK, Price $2.00.

No. 41. Studies in Psychiatry. Vol. II. New York Psychiatric Society, Price $3.00.

No. 42. Psychoanalysis and the Psychic Disorders of General Paresis. By S. HOLLOS and S. FERENCZI, Price $1.50.

No. 43. Essays in Psychopathology. By WILLIAM A. WHITE, Price $2.50.

No. 44. Hysteria. By E. KRETSCHMER, Price $2.50.

No. 45. Postencephalitic Respiratory Disorders. By SMITH ELY JELLIFFE, M.D., Price $2.50.

No. 46. Hypnosis. By PROF. P. SCHILDER, M.D., and DR. O. KAUDERS, Price $2.50.

No. 47. Stammering. By DR. ISADOR H. CORIAT, Price $2.00.

No. 48. Introduction to the Technic of Child Analysis. By ANNA FREUD, Price $1.50.

No. 50. Introduction to a Psychoanalytic Psychiatry. By PAUL SCHILDER, Price $3.50.

No. 51. Lectures in Psychiatry. By WILLIAM A. WHITE, Price $3.00.

No. 52. The Psychoanalysis of the Total Personality. By FRANZ ALEXANDER, Price $3.50.

No. 53. Brain and Personality. By PAUL SCHILDER, Price $3.50.

No. 54. Medical Psychology. By WILLIAM A. WHITE, M.D., Price $3.00.

No. 55. Psychopathology and Lethargic Encephalitis. By S. E. JELLIFFE, Price $4.00.

No. 56. The Psychological Effects of Menstruation. By MARY CHADWICK, Price $2.00.

No. 57. Forty Years of Psychiatry. By WM. A. WHITE, M.D., Price $3.00.

No. 58. Who Shall Survive? A New Approach to the Problem of Human Interrelations. By J. L. MORENO, M.D., Price $4.00.

Orders should be ACCOMPANIED BY CHECK, MONEY ORDER OR CASH and sent to

Nervous and Mental Disease Publishing Co.

3617 Tenth Street, N. W.   Washington, D. C.

ERRATA

Page 84, end of third paragraph, read AA and BA instead of HF and GB.

Page 98 (bottom) read 44 choices instead of 43, read 34% instead of 33%.

C1 on page 119 (caption) read pairs *15,* instead of *5;* triangles *2,* instead of *3.*

C4 on page 121 (caption) incompatible pairs *8,* instead of *5.*

Page 247, second line of second paragraph should read Map III instead of Map II.

ND - #0084 - 240123 - C0 - 229/152/25 - PB - 9780282985653 - Gloss Lamination